SQUEEZING
THE
LEMON
SLOWLY

SQUEEZING THE LEMON SLOWLY

KENNETH A. DAIGLER

LEVEL
TRU

First published by Level Tru 2025

Copyright © 2025 by Kenneth A. Daigler

All rights reserved. No part of this publication may be reproduced, stored or transmitted in any form or by any means, electronic, mechanical, photocopying, recording, scanning, or otherwise without written permission from the publisher. It is illegal to copy this book, post it to a website, or distribute it by any other means without permission.

Kenneth A. Daigler asserts the moral right to be identified as the author of this work.

Author Photo Credit: Pepper M. Daigler

First edition

ISBN: 978-1-68512-866-1

Cover art by Level Best Designs

This book was professionally typeset on Reedsy. Find out more at reedsy.com

To those who did, without public recognition

Disclaimer

Central Intelligence Agency Disclaimer:

All statements of fact, opinion, or analysis expressed are those of the author and do not reflect the official positions or views of the Central Intelligence Agency (CIA), the Federal Bureau of Investigation (FBI), or any other U.S. Government agency. Nothing in the contents should be construed as asserting or implying U.S. Government authentication of information or CIA endorsement of the author's views. This material has been reviewed by the CIA, the National Security Agency (NSA), and the FBI to prevent the disclosure of classified information. This does not constitute an official release of CIA information.

SQUEEZING THE LEMON, SLOWLY: A Case History
  By Kenneth A. Daigler

Introduction

To quote Gertrude Stein, in her poem "Sacred Emily," "A rose is a rose is a rose is a rose." And, an agent is an agent is an agent is an agent. But it is how you get there that matters. That seems a truism in my line of work. My given name is Kevin O'Neal, not that it matters, since my professional colleagues and all my agents have known me by different names. Even within Agency files, my operational work is officially listed under yet another name. It is all part of the trade, and not really that important. Although it certainly was a problem on one occasion when I was at a cocktail party and ran into two different targets, both of whom knew me byin different names and identities. But, those things happen in my business.

I say "profession" and "business" to describe my activities, but in reality, I tend to think of my responsibilities as those of a priest or minister: an avocation. I was a CIA Case Officer (CO) for some thirty years, focused on recruiting spies for the United States of America.

A more significant personal issue for people in my vocation is that of self-doubt—living with a constant fear of failure. That is because we face rejection, i.e. a decision by a target not to cooperate, on a regular basis. And, when we fail the effects can go well beyond our personal lives.

So, many years ago, upon assuming my first command as a Chief of Station (COS), I had a lot to worry about.

The Station did not have a good operational record, and unless it got better under my direction, this might be my last COS position. So, I had to not only motivate the officers working for me, but also develop a reliable relationship with other USG entities in the city—especially the FBI. Oh, and also keep Headquarters happy.

As a manager, dealing with employees is usually a challenging daily task. But dealing with the unique personalities of other COs, let alone other cultures such as the FBI, adds some additional pressures. Yet, I wanted a Station, and they gave it to me. Now, I have to do something with it.

Chapter One: First the Plumbing, then the Operation

The operational objective of my Station is to recruit individuals with access to the plans and intentions of foreign countries, and in my area of responsibility, over a dozen foreign countries had an intelligence presence. While the Soviets were not in the mix, their Warsaw Pact allies were, and some of them are damn good. Then, of course, we have some friendly countries represented here who nevertheless spy on us as, indeed, we do on them.

Where to start—My staff? Good people, but with varying degrees of professional capabilities. No matter how elite a group, their skills and attitudes vary. The fact they are not assigned overseas could mean they are somewhat below par, but many have personal reasons for staying in the U.S. Some others, including several newly graduated officers from training, are there to sharpen their tradecraft skills before being sent to more demanding operational environments overseas. Me? I'm here because, after so many years of working outside the official community, my path back into the mainstream of the Agency is through the domestic operating scene.

It's my job to see that my officers have every chance to succeed in their careers as COs. But, I need some leverage to get some real operations started. When I took over the Station things were somewhat sloppy, and in the process of cleaning this up most of the ongoing operations were lost. How can I get some leverage to quick start some operations? Well, it would seem my best bet is information known to the local FBI Field

Office.

Ah, my colleagues in the FBI. Relations are not always good between the Bureau and the Agency. There is a history. But, there is a large FBI Field Office here, with a sizable Foreign Counterintelligence section (FCI). The previous COS was not exactly appreciated by the ASAC (Assistant Special Agent in Charge) for FCI, and from what the staff tells me, it was a two-way street. OK, I'm new here and only have past prejudices to overcome rather than any personal dislike of me. Luckily, my past career never put me in a situation where the FBI would have any reason to suspect that I would not be honest with them—outside that is, of the usual Bureau—Agency mutual distrust.

To be fair, the relations between the two organizations have slowly improved over the years as the Cold War matured. Also, relations in the field, where senior officials' alpha dog career aspirations in the fierce and competitive Washington bureaucratic scene are distant, are usually better if some personal rapport and respect can be established. In this case, the ASAC is a nice guy and a very professional SA (Special Agent). However, I have to keep in mind that the Bureau's FCI functions have a different primary objective, as an internal security service, than does the Agency as a foreign intelligence service. The Bureau wants to identify and neutralize, through legal recourse, if possible, foreign intelligence activities. Us, we want to recruit these foreign folks and send them back to spy inside their government institutions. Sure, some FCI SAs do understand the value of recruitment, but the bureaucratic realities of the FBI management structure, and its internal security focus, place most of the emphasis on neutralization versus recruitment.

Ralph, the ASAC for FCI, however, seemed quite flexible. Our first meeting was cordial, pleasant and professionally conducted. His, and indeed that of his boss, the Special Agent in Charge (SAC) of the Field Office, dissatisfaction with my predecessor was obvious and clearly expressed with specific examples. So, there is a need for some confidence-building between us. And, since Ralph seems a pretty smart guy, at least in my opinion based upon our first encounter, as well as what Headquarters had told me about his previous interaction with the Agency, I'd better come up with something real, because he will be watching what I do closely. As indeed I would do were it the other way around.

So, the first thing I have to do is lay in the plumbing. This is a tradecraft term, and has a meaning similar to the military's concept of "prepping the battlefield." It means creating operational support mechanisms that enable the clandestine spotting, assessing, and developing of potential assets. I have a pretty good idea regarding how I want to do this. But, I'll have to explain my plan to Ralph in detail. He should be familiar with undercover operations by an SA, but our approach is a bit more complex. I propose to set up one of my officers in a commercial alias to penetrate the local international business and diplomatic scene. I think this will provide a seemingly innocent way to meet potential targets in the city, at least for initial spotting and assessment activities.

Why bother briefing Ralph? Because one way or another, he will learn about it anyway. My officer will be seeking contact with many of the very same foreign personalities that Ralph's SAs will be watching and reporting on. And, if you really want to piss off the Bureau, make them run a counterintelligence investigation on an individual in contact with a suspected foreign national only to find it is actually an Agency officer in alias. So, discussing the setup of the alias identity should accomplish a couple of things at once: demonstrate my openness with the local Field Office and establish my understanding of their role and responsibility regarding potential counterintelligence concerns in the area.

Who to select for the commercial role? I want somebody who can stay in character 24/7, living in an alias in the city. So, it is preferable for the officer to be single so as to keep the false documentation issues and living arrangements as simple as possible. I also need an officer with role-playing talents, good operational smarts, and an engaging personality. These traits seem to best fit a young female officer, assigned to me because of an illness of a parent that requires her presence in the U.S. She is socially poised and intelligent enough to carry off the role of an entrepreneurial female executive seeking business contacts in the international community.

Getting Headquarters on board for the rental of a status apartment downtown, and creation of the appropriate employment and educational history with supporting documents, is not that hard since I had been a senior manager at Headquarters prior to this tour. I knew what buttons to press and from whom to get some favors. So, within a few months, Brenda was living in a commercial alias in a penthouse apartment downtown and starting to attend social and business functions of operational interest. As she became well-known in local business and diplomatic circles, we added more clandestine tradecraft to meetings with her to protect her cover while handling her operational and administrative matters.

While not requesting any assistance from the ASAC in creating this cover, Ralph was kept well informed of its progress. I did this at more formal meetings with the Bureau and over some lunches. These lunches allowed both of us to further assess each other's motives and professional objectives, as well as develop some personal rapport. I was actually starting to like Ralph. But, in addition to Ralph, I had to ensure that his FCI SAs also realized that we were not making their job harder or trying to trick them.

Within days of our commercially covered operation going active, I arranged with Ralph to brief all his FCI Squad supervisory agents on the details of Brenda's commercial cover and its objectives. Brenda and I conducted the briefing at the FBI Field Office. We explained in detail how she would use her cover to gain acceptance as an international businesswoman in the city. Her alias apartment location was identified, and the backstopped personal and professional history created for her was provided to the Squad Chiefs. And, it was made clear that any meaningful contacts she had with individuals under FBI surveillance, or anyone of identified FBI interest, would be reported to them.

These conditions met their requirements, but there was little doubt from their responses that promises are nice, but they wanted to see actual results. Ralph, however, was supportive at the briefing. Of course, just overlooking one detail in a report or delaying notification of a contact could easily destroy any trust and rapport with the Bureau. We still had quite a long way to go before the Bureau was ready to actually help us with our operations in their playground.

Brenda quickly demonstrated her talents and professional aggressiveness within the city's international community. Using her engaging personality, she easily developed contacts in the business sections of the various Consulates, and became an accepted participant at social as well as diplomatic functions. She also used her city apartment for small parties, which further established her as a well-financed businesswoman. She was disciplined in her advisement, through clandestine contact with the Station, to the Bureau of her meeting plans and the passing of comprehensive reports on the personalities she met and the atmospherics of their meetings.

Within a few months, Brenda had succeeded in producing some decent reporting on a couple of foreign diplomats of interest to the Bureau. Some of the information made clear that a certain individual was actively looking for bribes to direct business ventures to his country's governmental Ministries. This was of particular interest to the Bureau, and it was hinted that action would be taken based upon it. We were not offered any role in their plans, and as I recall, never learned what, if anything, had transpired. We weren't yet at the point where the FBI considered us a partner.

Two of the key traits necessary to be a successful CO are patience and a constant objective analysis of the behavior of your adversary, or in his case developing ally. Confidence building is a long term effort, and requires discipline and commitment.

Chapter Two: The Bureau Offers up a Target

Patience is the key to any spotting and developing operation. Yet, Brenda had rather quickly made several contacts of operational interest. One in particular, an Asian diplomat, was identified to us by Headquarters as the regional intelligence chief for his country. However, upon discussion with the Field Office, it was made clear that he was their Target and anything we did would be in support of their efforts. Following these guidelines, Brenda was able to develop a friendly relationship with the individual and was able to provide useful personality information on the Target to the FBI. But, he was their Target, not ours, and they made this plain to us on more than a few occasions.

From my perspective, the start of the Lemon Operation, as it eventually became known, occurred about four months after Brenda started operating. At one of the diplomatic parties she attended she happened to meet an Eastern European diplomat, rather low ranking in title, but very outgoing and especially interested in business activities. Brenda wrote up her brief contact with him, and the report was passed to the Bureau as usual.

A few days later, Ralph suggested we have lunch. Nothing unusual here as our professional and personal relationship was growing. We met at one of the small, neighborhood taverns that dotted the working-class sections of the city, populated by second and third generation Eastern European—American families. Many of these people retained ties to relatives in their home countries, and therefore might be of interest to the local FCI SAs.

CHAPTER TWO: THE BUREAU OFFERS UP A TARGET

As Ralph was warmly greeted by the middle-aged man behind the bar, I naturally assumed the place was owned by a Bureau asset. It was a bit of a dump, somewhat dark, and with a bar packed with older folks who looked like they knew hard work.

We sat down, ordered beers, and after the usual pleasantries, he said, "We have to talk about one of Brenda's contacts." OK, I knew of nothing I had done, or had Brenda for that matter, that could have offended the Field Office. But, I quickly thought hard and began to prepare some general defense to explain what could only have been an innocent mistake on our part.

Ralph is a big guy, built sort of in the public image mold of an FBI SA, and when he stares you straight in the eyes, there can be some intimidation. While I had been trained and actually had some experience in how to handle police interrogations, it is not something you ever get used to. And, for a brief moment the thought crossed my mind that I had indeed done something wrong—So much for professional training in the face of solid Irish Catholic guilt.

I guess it is about time to say a bit more about Ralph and the different cultures of the FBI and CIA. The Bureau has a culture every bit as strong and inculcated as the Agency. However, the personalities attracted to each organization are usually quite different. FBI SAs enforce the law and work hard in the collection of evidence to enable a legal conviction of those guilty of crimes. They tend to follow meticulous procedures, with careful attention to details and reporting requirements, which must justify allocation of resources. A high percentage of the FBI SAs retire as GS-13s, at that grade's highest step, and with the Law Enforcement twenty-five percent addition for anticipated overtime, they have a good annual salary and a comfortable retirement pension. And, most do not seem to be frustrated by the lack of upward grade mobility or management opportunities.

Agency Case Officers, the "fighter pilots" of the Clandestine Service, are much more aggressive in wanting upward mobility in terms of grade and management responsibilities. They are trained, and reside, within a culture that values quick actions, flexible responses to unanticipated situations, and the capability to apply learned and practiced tradecraft principles in a manner suited to a unique situation without supervision. Also, they are trained and tasked to break the laws of other countries, without getting caught. In a sense, abroad, they often act like criminals, although in a nonviolent sense. So, joint planning between these two organizations often becomes a clash of cultures, with the appropriate friction and miscommunications inherent in such activities.

Once I met Ralph, I started my assessment of his personality and motivations. At our first meeting, we exchanged assignment backgrounds, as any two professionals would do. Thus, based upon his previous assignments, I was able to communicate with other Agency people with whom he had been in contact. While the Agency certainly does not keep formal records on FBI personnel, any more than the FBI does on Agency employees, there are "hall files," a collection of stories of interaction or joint endeavors, on most of the FCI SAs and certainly those in senior management positions such as Ralph's.

It turned out that Ralph had a solid background in criminal investigations, and having been involved in some major cases, he was promoted to a Squad Chief position somewhat early in his career. He did well in several major Field offices, and had also had his "ticket punched" with rotational assignments in Washington for inspection duties of Field Offices and Headquarters units. He had also served as a Special Assistant to a senior FBI Headquarters department supervisor. After several years, he was made the supervisor of the FCI squads operating in New York City. He managed them well and had successes there. Two years later, he was transferred here as the ASAC for FCI.

He was both well-liked and professionally respected by his SAs, and most of the Agency personnel who had worked with him in New York City described him as an honest colleague, but one careful to protect FBI equalities in the operational area. He was quick to identify a mistake by the Agency and insist on its correction and non-repetition. Also, and this was a very important characteristic, Ralph was neither personally nor professionally anti-Agency. He judged each of his relationships with Agency folks on the merits, progress, and results of their interaction. His lack of appreciation for my predecessor's behavior, and possibly spotty coordination of operational activities in the city, did not automatically carry over to me. My actions would dictate how he acted towards me.

Both being Irish, and liking a beer or two, helped smooth the initial phase of our getting to know each other. After almost a decade in FCI, Ralph understood it from the Bureau's perspective. He had an interest in identifying foreign intelligence officers and their collection networks, and even in manipulating them rather than just shutting them down. Several of our meetings, both in his office and over some beers and food, involved telling each other "war stories," which both amused the other, but also demonstrated our experience and expertise in our respective professions. And I developed the impression that I had an FBI colleague who would listen openly to my proposals and give me an honest chance to operate in the city.

Anyway, back to the lunch. Looking me straight in the eye, Ralph said," Dusko Bazna, the low-ranking Romanian diplomat recently reported on by Brenda, is of priority interest to the Bureau, and there were things you needed to know about him." That was it—Ralph did not want to say more in the restaurant. Considering the environment, that seemed a pretty responsible decision. Rather, he suggested we meet with his Eastern European FCI Squad Chief two days hence at their office. He also suggested that Brenda be there.

As we ate lunch and talked about the local football team and other benign subjects, my thought pattern quickly moved from guilt to excitement, and then to concern. The good news was that we apparently had a target of interest, and even better, one that the Bureau may want to work in partnership with us. However, the immediate concern involved a real clash of cultures in terms of how to proceed. The first issue that came to mind was that of the cover being employed by Brenda. Her appearance, should it be seen, at the FBI Field Office would be difficult to explain in most circumstances and in any event would draw unnecessary suspicion on her. Sure, she had been there once in a light disguise just prior to the start of her alias operation, and we could try the same approach again. But that was before she became a well-known figure in the local international community. In the Agency's rule book, you don't take chances like that.

However, FBI culture is quite different. While they have responsibilities for internal security and counterintelligence within the U.S., they are primarily trained and tend to think like cops. They are taught to control the environment in which they work, and thus have the belief that they do so. But, a CO is taught that s/he can never assume such a thing. And, indeed, must assume the adversarial security service controls the environment and plans all their activities from that perspective. Thus, taking an officer known in the community under an alias and commercial cover into an official U. S. Government office involves a serious risk to that officer's ability to operate in that environment. While Ralph would say, and believe, that he could ensure Brenda could enter the building unseen, I could not feel comfortable with that approach. Without going into details, although it would not necessarily enhance our working relationship, I could advise Ralph that I knew of several instances in past years when Soviet Bloc intelligence assets in major U.S. cities had followed FBI assets to meetings with their SA handlers and thus exposed them as double agents. But, that approach would not be helpful.

Instead, as we drank our beer and ate our sausages, I decided on a course of action which I hoped would both demonstrate our willingness to partner with the Bureau and also eliminate the need for any risk to Brenda's cover. OK, maybe my thinking pattern was more along the lines of how to manipulate the situation than enhance partnership, but often in my business these objectives are not exclusive.

So, as we were about to leave, with the look of profound innocence that is so carefully mastered by people in my profession, I asked Ralph, "Could you provide me with any information you might have on Mr. Bazna?" I explained that the Agency often has information on individuals from overseas sources that might be unavailable to the FBI. I could try to get all the information in our Headquarters' files to pass to him and his Squad

Chief when we met. This had a logical ring to it, and certainly represented a fair trading of information. He agreed—So far, so good.

That afternoon, the Bureau sent over what information it had on Bazna. Meanwhile, we sent a standard name trace request to Headquarters asking for all available information on a new contact. The response was normal, listing two previous diplomatic postings, one in Europe and one in Africa. Based upon a diplomatic status request to the local government, the European Station knew that he had been born on 23 March 1955 in Brasov, Romania. At the African post, a local Station officer had briefly met Bazna and learned he was married, enjoyed drinking scotch, and had a reputation in that country as always looking for money-making opportunities. As most Eastern European diplomats looked for ways to make some extra money, that motivation did not particularly stand out. No follow-up contact was made with him.

But, at least I had a few things to pass to the Bureau, and so advised Ralph and the Squad Chief, Matt, suggesting that since I wanted to show them the results of my query to our Headquarters, could they come to the Station for the meeting?

I had met Matt briefly before, when Ralph introduced me to his Squad Chiefs. Our brief initial conversation was formal and not particularly friendly. He, apparently, had several bad encounters with my predecessor over the targeting of various Eastern European immigrants who maintained relationships with Warsaw Pact Consulates in the city. I later learned from Agency sources that Matt had also had a poor relationship with our Station in San Francisco as a younger SA working FCI there. He apparently had built up a distrust of Agency officers. This might well become a problem, but one that had to be solved.

Regardless of the wishes of management, if the individuals at the working level of an operation did not want to cooperate, it didn't happen. This tends to be true of most bureaucracies. Sure, I could constantly ensure that Ralph was getting honest feedback on the operation, but Matt could also make other comments indicating that we were not respecting FBI prerogatives or authorities. Or, he could simply close down cooperation in administrative ways. Matt had to become a believer, or at least a cooperator.

As the Station was located outside of the city in a typical suburban office building of no particular character, its public footprint was considerably less than that of the FBI's Field Office. Still, Brenda did a counter surveillance exercise on the route between her city apartment and the Station, to ensure that she was not being followed. I doubt the FBI SAs took any such precautions, and at this point in the relationship, was not going to ask them to do so.

Ralph and Matt arrived, and I introduced them to a couple of other Station officers, including my deputy Winston, a dual American—Irish passport holder with a British accent and demeanor worthy of an upper-class British gentleman. I specifically did this to demonstrate my openness to them, knowing that Agency personnel would be working in the city. One of the historic issues the FBI has with the Agency is their concern that Agency officers are running around unidentified to them, mucking up their well-planned operations. I actually sympathized with them in this regard, as I had been involved in the past in situations where Agency Case Officers in alias had been in contact with FBI counterintelligence targets without proper coordination. When discovered, and it was since the FBI is quite good at identifying people when it wants to, the issue was raised to a senior level within the Agency to the detriment of the lower-ranking folks actually involved. This was bad bureaucratic politics and certainly not helpful at the local, operating level.

Once in my office, Brenda joined Ralph, Matt, Winston, and me to review and discuss the information we had received from Headquarters. I passed it to Ralph in the form of a memo from Station to the FBI Field Office FCI ASAC. Both SAs looked at the memo, and responded, typically, "not much information from your people." I explained that Bazna just had not seemed a priority target at either of his overseas postings. Ralph responded that Bazna certainly was a person of interest to the U.S. Government. And, he proceeded to explain why—and, he was right.

Ralph said, "We have been watching Bazna since he arrived in the city. The Department of State in Washington routinely notifies us when any new diplomat is assigned here, and advised that he was being assigned to the Consulate to replace an individual known to be the code clerk for the office." He continued, "The code clerk handles all electronic and often paper communications between the Consulate and other elements of the foreign government, and with such responsibilities is considered to be a most valuable Target to recruit."

Ralph explained "we can monitor the telephones of the Consulate, look at its mail, photograph who entered and exited its office, and put surveillance on its personnel, but we have no access to the official communications in the Consulate. That communicationconnects the Consulate to the Romanian Government as well as other Romanian diplomatic sites worldwide. Also, as a member of the Warsaw Pact, its communications may include information on Soviet and other Eastern European nations' activities in the area."

Trying not to look or act too excited, I noticed that Brenda was having an equally hard time maintaining a casual demeanor. Only Winston, with that British sense of polite indifferent seemed totally at ease. Luckily Ralph and Matt were so involved in providing the information on Bazna that they did not seem to notice our intensified interest.

Matt noted that "since his arrival, Bazna had been under a "full court press" and couldn't take a piss without us knowing how much. All our investigative capabilities are being utilized against him. A court-approved telephone tap on his residence telephone is in effect, and any conversations are analyzed daily. A Romanian-speaking FBI employee had been assigned to our office specifically for this operation. Bazna's car, the one he used when on Consulate business and officially registered to the Consulate, had been tagged with a location device that allows us to follow its travels. His office telephone in the Consulate is being monitored. And, specially trained FBI surveillance employees are assigned to follow him periodically, and always whenever he is going to meet someone or attend a social event. Also, after he had settled in, we attempted, but with only limited success, to have friends of other members of the Romanian Consulate introduced to Bazna as individuals who could assist his integration into the city. These "friends" were, of course, local FBI confidential informants with close ties to the Consulate. While Bazna was polite and friendly, and used whatever assistance these individuals could provide during his first several weeks, none of them were able to establish any kind of personal relationship with him. Apparently, he wanted to choose his own friends."

Here, I should note that while some FBI standard counterintelligence practices often frustrated Agency Case Officers, their investigative capabilities are usually highly professional. Of particular note was their surveillance capability at their larger Field Offices. The Field Office personnel assigned to surveillance responsibilities did that work daily, and thus were well aware of all the intricacies of the areas they worked. They knew the multiple exits of the hotels, restaurants, and shops in the business areas, as well as the alleys and parks where discreet meetings and exchanges could be made unnoticed. They knew how to be almost invisible in public, while trailing and observing the actions of their various Targets. This is a unique skill gained primarily through practice and time doing it. Agency Case Officers are given some training in surveillance, but usually more from the perspective of how it is structured in order to plan how to detect and defeat it. So, this was one FBI skill that I truly respected and would want to use in support of our operations whenever possible.

Matt advised us that the Bureau had been able to learn some interesting facts about Bazna. The Consul General had met Bazna while he was in a Foreign Ministry training course, and they had become drinking buddies at that time. When he was assigned to the city, he ensured Bazna was selected to replace the departing communications clerk. Because of his close friendship with the Consular General, he also enjoyed an unusual freedom to move about the city and mix in public with other diplomats and business people. This was unusual for lower-ranking Eastern European diplomats, and thus made him more vulnerable to monitoring and meetings. It seemed that the Romanian Consul General was much less rigid regarding Bazna's activities than is standard procedure with Warsaw Pact code clerks.

The Bureau had also learned a bit about his background, his interests, and family life. Banza's family was what we would describe as upper-middle class. His father was educated at a trade school in the 1930s. The wife was educated at the equivalent of a high school level. He had a sister, who died from some illness in her teens. His father had joined the Romanian Communist Party while in the trade union, and rose to the rank of a minor Party official. He apparently had, as the British would say, "a good war" and was rewarded with additional responsibilities in the trade union's Communist Party structure. This enabled him to get Bazna into the career path for the Ministry of Foreign Affairs. In his country, this meant the opportunity to travel and live outside of Romania, and thus experience a much better lifestyle and have the opportunity to obtain prized possessions not available at home. Bazna used his opportunities abroad to send back various items to his parents, which made their lives more comfortable. Also, as was the tradition in that bureaucratic culture, he was careful to provide "gifts" purchased while abroad for Ministry colleagues and senior officials. Obviously, this benefited his career as well.

While benefiting from the Communist Party connections of his father, apparently, Bazna had a very pragmatic political outlook. He had little ideological commitment to Communist political philosophy, but clearly understood that to stay comfortable in his country, he had to appear appropriately loyal to the system. This attitude was quite normal among many officials living under the Warsaw Pact brand of Soviet Communism, and often referred to in private among these people as "proletariat pragmatism." While on the surface this might seem to mean such individuals could easily be convinced to cheat on their country, this was hardly the case. Why: Because their lives, careers, family, and personal status all depended upon loyalty to the Communist Party. It was never easy to convince one of these individuals to take the risk of losing everything for themselves and their extended families.

Ralph also noted that "The Bureau also knew Bazna was engaging, apparently with the acquiescence of the Consular General, in some petty corruption, such as selling Consulate tax-free alcohol to local contacts of the Consulate. He was also talking with local friends of the Consulate, usually Romanian natives now U.S. citizens in the city, about other possible business ventures wherein diplomatic privileges could be used to his financial advantage. "

As to his family life, Ralph said, "his wife Constanta was a less socially polished person and tended to stay within the Consulate family. Also, their three-year-old son took up a great deal of her time. Her telephone conversations centered on family matters, the son's well-being, and gossip about activities among the families of the Consular staff. This gossip was of interest to the Bureau for their files on the various people at the Consulate. Whether it was a lack of babysitting options or just her personality, Constanta did not accompany her husband on his social outings. And, there were no indications that he was using these occasions to seek relationships with other women or, for that matter, men. The Bureau felt that all in all, he seemed a pretty good family man."

After the detailed briefing on him, Matt mentioned that while Bazna was a subject of interest, from a resource perspective, the Field Officer had other, more important, activities to pursue.

I knew enough about the Bureau's management system to understand that their primary mission was to protect U.S. National Security interests and that Bazna hardly seemed in this category. However, his position was one of extreme interest from an intelligence perspective. Also, Bureau resources are limited, like any other organization, and their reporting requirements demand objective demonstration of investigative progress during each reporting period. They had little that could be used to support the claim that he was a threat to U.S. National Security. Finally, the FCI group in the local Field Office, while large compared to most of the Field offices, also had a huge target base in the city. Over a dozen foreign intelligence services were present, and aggressively working to penetrate military contractors, locally located National Laboratories, regional military installations, including sensitive test facilities, and, of course, local high-tech businesses.

Upon completion of the FBI briefing, I asked Ralph how we could be of assistance. Of course, I knew exactly where this was going. Ralph recognized that Bazna offered a unique opportunity: the fact that he was

CHAPTER TWO: THE BUREAU OFFERS UP A TARGET

a known code clerk and had a great deal of freedom to roam outside the Consulate community. But, without more evidence worthy of FBI resource allocation, he could not get his headquarters to authorize additional resources against Bazna. He needed our help, since this is what we did for a living: we recruit foreign spies.

I encourage Winston and Brenda to ask a few questions, and my deputy took the opportunity to ask Ralph his views on what should be the next step. This gave me a few moments to consider how we should react, and under what terms we could work with the Bureau on this operation. After all, this was U.S. turf and the Bureau was in charge. I knew that for the Bureau, an undercover operation was a resource and administrative-heavy load, and of course, there was no guarantee that a sustainable contact could be maintained. However, these constraints were certainly of less concern to the Agency. Alias operations are a staple tradecraft tool in our business, and thus we had institutional procedures which made the establishment of covers, backstopping, and funding a part of everyday practice. And, while our ultimate chances of success might seem only a little higher than for the Bureau based on the current amount of information on the target, this was the type of risk versus gain that we did for a living. Also, quite frankly, we did it better than the Bureau because it was a core business skill of the Agency's Clandestine Service.

I quickly decided that this was a "win-win" situation for us on a couple of levels. First, a joint operation with the FCI folks was a smart move in developing better cooperation and sharing of information. Secondly, to some small degree, and I would try very hard not to let it be too small, Ralph and Matt would appreciate us employing our resources based on their interest. Thirdly, a code clerk is one of the best recruitments an intelligence service can make, and the access obtained represents a strategic intelligence success for the U.S. Government. From our perspective, this was a clear beneficial risk versus gain equation.

After about half an hour or so of further discussion, it was agreed that attempting to assess and develop Bazna would be a joint operation between the Station and the Field Office, with the Station taking the lead in placing an officer in contact with the Target. Coordination would be conducted at the field level, with all information on the target, from either FBI or Agency sources, shared in a timely manner. Also, the substance of all information on this operation reported to or from the respective headquarters would be shared in memo format between the two local offices. It was also agreed, but only after very careful parsing of phraseology, that due to the use of Agency personnel, security procedures for the operation would follow Agency guidelines. This was an area I had serious concerns about, both from an operational perspective and also from the perspective of the future careers of my officers who would be involved with the target.

We were all smiles as we shook hands with the two SAs as they departed the Station. Then, I assigned Winston the task of writing the initial message to Headquarters advising them of our decision regarding a joint operation with the FBI, and detailing all the information we now had on Bazna. We also asked for an operational crypt for the target, a file number to start an operational file, and for a more comprehensive name trace from all sources in the U.S. Intelligence Community, including the NSA. Brenda, Winston, and I then spent some additional time discussing how she could get a closer look at Bazna. We now had a high value target for her to work.

Chapter Three: Duran

Bureaucracies always seem to move slowly, especially when you are in the field trying to build an operation. But, within a few days, Headquarters did provide approval for the operation. Normally, such an approval is "pro forma" as the field station has the responsibility of selecting its targets and planning how to run its operations. This tends to be the strength of the Agency, particularly compared to military intelligence services, where their Headquarters exercise much more authority over how and when operations should be run. Another major and significant difference is that at the Agency, COs assigned to Headquarters tours function as the Desk Officers that support the Field Stations, and thus they have a better understanding of operations than purely Headquarters-bound personnel.

Anyway, Bazna was given the crypt DURAN, and as is Agency practice, that was how he would now be referred to in correspondence and all operational discussions in the field and at Headquarters. The Bureau also established its own code name and file number system—for the FBI the target was known as Briarpatch. However, since we had control of the operational activity, DURAN was commonly used in the field by both organizations when referring to the operation.

It took a while longer for complete U.S. Government trace results on DURAN to arrive at Station, and these bits of information were not of any real interest to us at this stage of the operation. NSA confirmed that he was a code clerk and had been first a junior and then senior code clerk on previous overseas assignments. He had also been employed as a Watch

Officer in the Communications Department at the Ministry of Foreign Affairs in Bucharest.

In the meantime, Brenda had been out working the social scene. However, she had failed to see DURAN. We carefully reviewed her one meeting with him, and tried to figure out how another "casual" contact could be made. The Field Office noted that he continued to meet regularly with some of their contacts in the American-Romanian community in the city.

In creating a "casual meeting" with a target, it is vital that the circumstances really do appear casual and not structured. As a Soviet Bloc diplomat and a code clerk, DURAN would have had numerous security briefings regarding approaches by American intelligence organizations. The fact that he had met Brenda for a few minutes several weeks ago did not mean that he wouldn't be suspicious if she just happened to show up again. So, we had two issues to address: how to identify an occasion for the next contact and how to structure a story to explain this second encounter that appeared innocent and logical. It had to seem just normal and natural.

The first problem was actually easier to solve since the Field Office had good electronic coverage on his telephones, and could advise when he accepted a social invitation. Also, their informants could advise if he accepted or discussed a planned event with them. As to the cover story for a contact, we eventually decided to go with a conversation that played to an interest already identified, and then let Brenda's skills keep the conversation going to discover some other item that could be used for this second and substantial contact. In the spotting and assessment phase, the first objective of a personal contact with a target is always to get the next contact.

Information from Headquarters initial traces and from the Bureau's CIs indicated that DURAN was a scotch drinker. The CIs also stated that he was proud of his "taste" for scotch, a taste which could only be developed and enjoyed on a regular basis by those in his country with overseas travel or special privileges. So, we decided to use this as the focus of our contact planning: once we knew DURAN was attending a social event, Brenda would also attend and, about a third of the way through the event, approach DURAN with a glass of scotch in her hand. She would glance at him, raise her eyebrows in interest, and approach him. As she was an attractive and poised young lady, there was good reason to believe DURAN would accept this initial approach. She would then re-introduce herself and explain, after taking a sip of her drink and making a slightly bad taste face, that she was trying to learn how to drink scotch in order to better fit in with the diplomatic community but was not finding its taste very pleasing. This would, we hoped, lead to DURAN expounding on his knowledge of the liquor, with Brenda feeding him additional questions to prolong the contact. Using her Case Officer Elicitation skills, she would then move the conversation into general social matters and, during the middle of the conversation, a few, subtle questions about his life in the city.

That was our plan, but it was only a general outline, and its success depended upon the interpersonal skills of the CO, who must constantly "read" the reaction of the target to the flow and tone of the conversation to keep it going without seeming to do so. Brenda was a disciplined and highly competent Case Officer, though without as much field experience as I would have liked. Nevertheless, I had full confidence in her abilities.

A short time later, Matt advised that DURAN had accepted an invitation to the National Day celebration at another Consulate in the city. This seemed like a good venue for the attempted contact because National Day parties are pretty open to local contacts of the Consulate as well as individuals interested in commercial activities with the country. Brenda's business cover would provide a natural entrée to the event. She arrived at the opening, probably unfashionably early, and placed herself in a location to monitor the official receiving line of senior host country officers. Arriving fashionably late, DURAN entered about halfway through the event. Allowing him time to proceed to the bar and greet a few diplomatic acquaintances, she watched him circulate around the room for about ten minutes before she approached him per our scenario.

When she first introduced herself, he seemed not to remember her, but quickly smiled and made a few remarks about the party and its refreshments. Brenda explained her presence at the event by stating that she was trying to break into the international business scene and had met the host country's Consulate's Commercial Attaché briefly in the past. However, other than him, she noted, she knew no one else at the party, so she was pleased to see DURAN once again. His remarks about the drinks being served provided Brenda the opportunity to move into the ploy regarding her lack of taste for scotch. DURAN quickly warmed to the opportunity to demonstrate his knowledge of the liquor. He took the bait completely. After a lengthy explanation of the various brands of scotch and each's unique taste, he insisted on getting Brenda a single malt scotch from the bar and then advising her on smelling and tasting it. By this time, Brenda was able to work on some elicitation regarding his interests while posted in the city and what type of leisure activities he enjoyed.

She broke off the engagement after about fifteen minutes, stating she had seen another business contact across the room. But, before departing, she thanked DURAN for providing his expertise on scotch and asked for his office telephone number in case she had any more questions, since she planned to give a big party in the next few weeks and wanted to get the best possible liquors to serve. DURAN provided his Consulate number, politely saying he would be happy to be of assistance. Brenda also gave DURAN her alias business card with her apartment/office telephone number and her title of Senior Business Development Manager.

For purposes of her cover story of attending the party to make business contacts, Brenda was obliged to introduce herself to a couple of other party guests before she could casually depart the scene. Upon returning to her apartment, she wrote up a complete review of how the contact went and her thoughts for the next contact. After a quick review and minor editing at the Station, the report was sent to Headquarters and in memo form to the Field Office.

Her assessment was that DURAN did not immediately remember her, and as the first meeting was so brief, there was little reason for him to do so. However, he was polite when she re-introduced herself, and he seemed to understand and believe her reason for speaking with him. The

CHAPTER THREE: DURAN

ploy of seeking his expertise on scotch worked as anticipated since it flattered his ego by allowing him to play the expert to an attractive young lady. In their general conversation, Brenda did not attempt much in the way of elicitation, but did learn that DURAN and his wife were finding it quite expensive to live in the city. Also, their child was sickly, as most young children often are, and medical services were expensive and not fully reimbursed by his government compensation. While not particularly expressing concern over local costs, it was apparent that he was concerned about the cost of living during this posting.

She also noted that she had set the "hook" for another contact by getting his office phone number and introducing a reason why she might re-contact him. The timing and substance of this next contact were to be discussed with Station management and local FBI SAs. The FBI noted that the office number he provided was actually the line into his communications room office, rather than the general line into the Consulate, where the operator would first answer and then direct the call to DURAN after having determined the name of the caller and the purpose of the call. This was considered a good omen by all concerned.

Soon it became the accepted routine with the Field Office, Winston and I met with Ralph and Matt and verbally discussed the contact at the same time we gave them the official memo. They were pleased that the contact had gone well and asked about our plans for the next meeting. This was, I thought, another good sign in terms of our relationship. Rather than offer up some scenario for the next meeting, they were satisfied to have us handle the operational planning as long as they were kept advised and given an opportunity to add their ideas.

I explained that Winston and I would soon meet with Brenda at a hotel outside of the city to plan our next move. I also noted that we were awaiting Agency Headquarters comments as well. Once we had developed a plan, we would meet with them to finalize it. Both SAs seemed fine with this approach.

Three days later, Winston and I met with Brenda in a suburban hotel room she had rented for the meeting. By that time, Headquarters had sent back a cable approving of how she had arranged and handled the contact. The cable also encouraged a bit more elicitation at the next meeting, and stated that FBI Headquarters had spoken with Headquarters and was on board regarding the operation

Now that a substantive contact had been made, planning for the next personal meeting involved several objectives, with the third meeting being one of the priorities. Other objectives involved learning more about his relationship with his wife and child, how he liked his work, how he was handling the higher-than-anticipated cost of living expenses, and how he would describe his official duties to an American businesswoman. But first, we had to consider the timing of the next contact, which would be a brief telephonic conversation with DURAN in his office.

Too soon a call could well lead to suspicion, or perhaps that Brenda had a personal interest in him, which would also be bad since developing a relationship along those lines seldom leads to a useful long term operational relationship, contrary to popular misconceptions of how spying is done. Waiting too long to telephone would call into question any remembrance, and hopefully positive feelings, about Brenda and her issues with selecting the right scotch.

So, what is the right time to make the telephone call? Well, there is no real answer. Usually, it depends upon the feeling of the CO and an assessment of how the target will react. In human operations, so much of the movement in a case, whether it be the degree or focus of elicitation or the request for the first small bit of tasking, depends upon how the CO reads the present condition of the interpersonal relationship. This is the reason that the CO's personality is so valued in the intelligence community, and applicants are so comprehensively tested for traits demonstrating this ability to read individuals' and relationship dynamics.

Brenda said, "About eight days after her contact with DURAN at the party would be the appropriate wait time." We reviewed her plan for the telephone conversation, which was cleverly thought out, and she subsequently made the call to the Consulate office. He personally answered the phone, and after she reminded him of their meeting, he was pleasant in tone and asked what he could do for her. This time the story line was directed at obtaining a luncheon meeting with DURAN. In the trade, we call it "buying a table" because, while to the uninitiated, this seems like spending more money than necessary on a meal. In reality, the entire point of the meal is to get "time on target" for assessment, development, and manipulation. The location and status of the restaurant must have enough interest or prestige to attract the target as well as speak to the status of the business cover of the CO. And the longer the meal lasts, which usually equates to the formality and cost of the meal, the more that can be accomplished. Thus, a leisurely meal, including dessert and coffee, is an operational priority. And, the weight that COs often put on in the service of their country is not necessarily enjoyable, and might even be considered a personal sacrifice by the officer.

Brenda explained her call by stating that she was in the final stages of planning an important business party at her apartment. It was going to be catered by an expensive and well-known local restaurant, and her company wanted nothing but the best to promote their image in the local market. She reminded DURAN of his assistance in advising her on scotches and asked if he would help her make some final selections for the party. She invited him to lunch at a local five-star hotel restaurant, noting that the restaurant carried a full liquor selection of the best brands and that his tastings and selections would be so helpful to her. DURAN responded positively, and accepted the invitation for the middle of the following week. The Bureau also confirmed the call and, in their opinion, DURAN seemed pleased to accept the invitation.

Brenda next made the restaurant reservation. She had taken a good look at the restaurant several days before, and asked for a table near the rear, in a discreet alcove. Selection of the appropriate restaurant is actually an important matter in more than just terms of the formality of the service and the length of time one can linger at the table.

There tends to be two types of seating design for high-end restaurants: those where people want to be seen and those where people wish for some privacy. Obviously, from an operational perspective, the latter is the best choice for assessment and development, as a CO tries to ingrain privacy, and then clandestinely, into a relationship as soon as possible. The first type of restaurant tends to have open seating space, and often large windows on a busy thoroughfare, with bright but subdued lighting in the evening. This environment allows individuals to be seen in public with others, sometimes just to enhance one's ego, but often to demonstrate association with the famous or powerful. The latter has a seating arrangement involving privacy for many tables, with high booths, curving table sequences, dim lighting in the evening, and various architectural features to further block sweeping views. This type of privacy serves several purposes, all directed at discreet meetings between participants.

Winston and I drove to the Field Office to brief Ralph and Matt and give them a copy of the contact report of the telephonic conversation sent to our Headquarters. After a brief discussion, we advised that we would soon have an outline of the scenario for the luncheon meeting.

The next day, Winston and I met with Brenda at a suburban hotel restaurant to plan the luncheon meeting. We first reviewed her plans for the scenario, objectives to be accomplished, ploys to enhance the personal relationship, and how to handle any reporting requirements levied by Headquarters. Brenda had a very sound plan: "Over lunch, after having DURAN taste and comment on several types of scotches and vodkas, I will praise his taste and accept his recommendations for the liquors, carefully noting their brand names in a notebook. Then I will engage him, as if he were a mentor, in explaining how my assignment in the city is my first big chance in the company. And, I really appreciated his advice as I am not as familiar and comfortable in the environment and atmosphere of international business and diplomatic circles as he is. I will then carefully express some other concerns about my readiness to handle such responsibilities. These comments will be used as a "mirror" ploy to stimulate the target to speak about similar feelings or issues. Finally, I will try to find an opportunity to get more information on his father."

After the meeting, we advised Headquarters of her plans and subsequently discussed them with Ralph and Matt. Everyone agreed the scenario was sound.

DURAN showed up at the restaurant at the agreed-upon time, and apparently, and luckily, did not spot the FBI's local Field Office surveillance unit in a car across from the restaurant photographing his arrival. It was Brenda who identified the surveillance, as would be expected of an Agency officer making an operational contact. When we learned of the surveillance photography, we were not pleased. It made no operational sense to draw any attention to the meeting by having photos taken. The Field Office knew the meeting was to take place, and whether he appeared or not would certainly be made known to them by Brenda.

After the fact, when we politely asked Ralph the point behind the photography, and questioned its value versus possible risk, we were advised it was an accident. He claimed the surveillance unit was not made aware that the luncheon was with an Agency officer, and the unit was just trying to monitor with whom DURAN was meeting. Maybe, but we had the suspicion that perhaps the Field Office was just checking up on us.

While responding in a professional manner, I made it quite clear that these types of actions were not helpful to the overall objective of making DURAN feel comfortable in his relationship. I might well have responded a bit more forcefully to this "accident." But, I actually did hope this was the result of a mix up.

Brenda reported that the two-hour-plus luncheon went quite well. As anticipated, DURAN enjoyed tasting and commenting on the several scotches and vodkas provided: The tastings, prior to the meal, also seemed to mellow him. When Brenda began the ploy regarding the conversational thread, he adopted a fatherly manner and assured her that she had the appropriate skills to function in international circles. When asked if he ever had such self-doubts, he replied, "My job has a great deal of responsibility, and early in my career, I had been carefully watched by my superiors to ensure I could handle them effectively. Now, however, as the senior official in his department, with a close personal as well as professional relationship with the Consulate General and his superiors in Bucharest, I have developed the self-confidence necessary to handle my responsibilities."

When asked if his father had played a role in his confidence building, DURAN responded:" His father had fought in World War II and was a physically weakened man after the war. His position in the Communist Party had gotten me into the Ministry, but then it was my efforts that had made me successful." He assured Brenda that with self-confidence, her personality, and good looks, she could certainly be successful in international business. She thanked him for his comments and for the personal compliments.

Through lunch, over coffee, and dessert, good progress was made in developing personal rapport with DURAN. He discussed, in general terms, his office routine at the Consulate and noted that besides supervising maintenance of the communication equipment, he was usually only really busy when the Consulate opened in the morning and closed at night. He noted that if the Consulate had been busy that day, his duties could last several hours after closing time, making him the last officer to leave the facility. He added that this is why having lunch worked better into his schedule than an evening engagement.

Brenda concluded the meeting by asking DURAN if he would accept an invitation to her party, since he was such an important factor in arranging it. He readily accepted, and she asked if he would bring his wife as well. He responded that depending upon child care, he would try to.

There were a couple of reasons we wanted to get the wife involved; one to cement the personal relationship with DURAN in a purely social context, another to see if the wife would provide additional insights into the couple's wants and desires, and finally to start to integrate Brenda into the couple's life for a better assessment window.

As DURAN was about to depart the restaurant, Brenda excused herself ostensibly to go to the restroom. This excuse permitted her to exit the restaurant several minutes after DURAN had departed the area, thus creating a time separation between the two. After conducting a discreet countersurveillance detection route, just in case someone from the Consulate had followed DURAN to see with whom he was meeting,

CHAPTER THREE: DURAN

Brenda went back to her apartment and wrote up the contents of the luncheon meeting. Early that evening in a downtown department store, she had a brief contact with another Station officer to pass him her written report.

As the operation seemed to be progressing well, we decided it was time to clandestinely install a secure electronic link between Brenda's alias apartment and the Station. We requested Headquarters support, and were advised they would send a technical team under the cover of a cable TV installation to her apartment to set up the communications link. This would enhance the security of the operation by reducing the need for physical contact between Station personnel and Brenda to a minimum. An appropriate concealment device, in a piece of furniture matching her apartment décor, for the electronic equipment, was also brought out by the Headquarters technical team to hide the equipment. Of course, her cable TV system was also enhanced to support the cover story of the team's visit to her apartment.

Now we had to consider what to accomplish regarding DURAN at the party, where we could create any scenario and social environment we pleased.

Headquarters responded rather quickly to the contact report of the luncheon meeting, and offer deserved praise for Brenda's efforts. Ralph and Matt also were pleased.

There were several objectives we wanted from the party, most importantly, a deeper personal rapport between DURAN and Brenda. However, we also decided to use this opportunity to introduce another CO into the equation. Winston and I discussed this with her for several hours in a rented hotel room in a different city suburb. She came with a list of local people, both business and foreign missions' contacts, she wished to invite to further her business cover, as well as the estimated expenses for food, drink, and service for the affair. The scotches and vodkas suggested by DURAN, expensive brands, were included in the costs. About twenty-five to thirty people were to be invited. It was agreed that another Station officer, in a commercial alias, would also attend to work on another approach for assessment of DURAN. This additional Station officer would also play a small role supporting Brenda's cover by telling those he encountered at the party various anecdotes about her successful business deals he knew of before she was sent to the city.

We also discussed how Brenda could create an opportunity to meet DURAN's wife at the party. If a separate relationship could be developed with the wife, valuable insights into their personal circumstances and desires could be obtained. To this end, it was agreed that a few days prior to the party, Brenda would call DURAN to try to determine if his wife was accompanying him, and if necessary, try to motivate him to bring her if he had not planned to.

The role of the other Station officer, operating in the commercial alias Stan as a financial trader from a West Coast firm just visiting the city, was a bit more aggressive. He was to set in action a ploy to start to determine DURAN's willingness to accept money for information obtained in the course of his official duties. This was to be done in a low-key manner. He would bump into DURAN during the party and strike up a conversation about oil exportation quotas from Romania, explaining his interest in terms of his job trading petroleum futures at his firm. He would attempt to get some vague bit of information that he would later claim had been valuable. If he was unable to meet and engage DURAN by himself, Brenda would introduce Stan as an old friend from graduate school to DURAN about an hour before the party was to end. Obviously, we preferred that Stan meet DURAN without Brenda's direct introduction. To facilitate this, we obtained several photos of DURAN taken by the Field Office's surveillance unit, and his driver's license photo. Stan was to study these so he could recognize DURAN at the crowded party.

With the party scenario established, our next step was to visit the FBI's office, bringing along Stan in a light disguise.

Sitting down with Ralph, Matt, and Larry, a member of Matt's squad with responsibility for monitoring activities at the Romanian Consulate, we went over our plans and objectives for the party. Larry noted that it would be unusual for DURAN to bring his wife to the party, as previously she had always stayed home to care for the child. He also wondered if DURAN might become suspicious of Brenda once Stan made his contact and went into his scenario regarding oil exportation. As this was our first introduction to Larry, we didn't know if he had any strongly held views about the operation or the Agency in general. We agreed that the wife's attendance was problematic, but we were hopeful that Brenda's specific invitation to the wife through DURAN would cause him to bring her along. We also assured him that Stan's ploy would be predicated upon his assessment during the conversation on DURAN's willingness to even discuss the topic of his country's oil export quotas. He did not seem to have his concerns eliminated by our explanations, but we moved on. Both Ralph and Matt asked some additional questions, but accepted our plans.

While Larry's presence and concerns were unexpected, the meeting seemed to have gone well to that point. So, I brought up a subject that the Bureau might deem as somewhat sensitive—their monitoring of the party through surveillance or photographic means. The surveillance photography at the restaurant had been a risk but luckily went unnoticed. A repeat of this at Brenda's apartment building might well not be as successful, and if noticed could well call into question her cover and actions.

I explained that several individuals invited to the party were from various foreign missions in the city. Some of these missions had security and intelligence personnel assigned to them, often with responsibilities to watch their own people for any indications of bad behavior. If any of these individuals were followed to the party, these security or intelligence agents might spot the FBI surveillance. I then asked why the Field Office wanted it for the party. This was a little tricky, as I did not want to even infer that the Field Office's surveillance unit was, in any way, unprofessional. I noted that they would have a complete report on the party after the fact, including details of any conversation Brenda or Stan had with any of the individual attending in whom they had an interest. Thus, photo coverage would be unnecessary.

However, Matt responded, "Surveillance photos would be useful, both for the Field Office's files and to use in support of their case reporting, and he had confidence the surveillance team could take the photographs without being noticed." We debated the risk versus gain equation for some time. Finally, Ralph decided that this time surveillance would not be necessary, and instructed Matt to be sure the surveillance team was so advised. I was most appreciative and made it a point to try to placate Matt and Larry by complimenting their squad's efforts in supporting us to date. Whether this softened their displeasure at being overridden by Ralph was not clear.

After the meeting, as Winston engaged the others in a conversation with a humorous war story about his activities in Paris a few years ago, I privately thanked Ralph for supporting our view. I reiterated that my request was not a slight on the professionalism of the FBI, only a desire to reduce any risk of exposure to an operation, and an operational cover platform, which was working well. As we parted with a handshake, I felt a bit more confident of my working relationship with him, but Matt and Larry were different stories.

The next day at the Station, Brenda and I spoke at length, over the recently installed communications link, about the party plans and the recent meeting at the Bureau. Then, she and Stan discussed their respective roles and interactions. Everything seemed in place, coordinated, and ready to go.

However, as humans are so unpredictable, events seldom go as planned. So, what we really had was the general concept of the scenario and what we wished to accomplish. While they were specific steps planned to attain each objective, the COs could only use these steps as guidelines, as they had to react instantly to how the target responded, whether or not it was as anticipated. I was quite comfortable with the plan and the capabilities of the CO involved. I even felt the Bureau was on board. But, having personally been in numerous situations, well-planned and orchestrated, where all Hell broke loose, I had little illusion that we needed luck as well as professionalism to make the party an operational success.

Four days before the party, Brenda telephoned DURAN and, under the guise of providing him with an update on the party details, mentioned how much she was looking forward to meeting his wife. He was hesitant

CHAPTER THREE: DURAN

at first, noting that she usually stayed home watching the child. Brenda countered with a plea that she really wanted to meet his wife and that his wife probably deserved to attend a lavish party after all her hard work caring for the child. She then discussed options DURAN might have for babysitting while he and his wife attended. DURAN agreed that his wife would enjoy the party, and he also noted that his wife had expressed an interest in meeting Brenda. So, it was agreed that the wife would attend along with DURAN.

The substance of the call was reported to Headquarters, and a copy was provided to Matt's squad.

Chapter Four: The Party

As the COS, my view of the results of the party would come in two forms; the contact reports and operational cables written by the COs Brenda and Stan, and debriefings of them after the event.

Brenda described the party as "quite successful from both her operational and cover objectives." Twenty-two guests showed up, and several lingerers remained after the formal end of the party. The quality of the refreshments and the service attested to her supposed business status, and from the comments of several of her local business contacts, her alias persona was being accepted as legitimate. She also obtained some additional assessment information on several of the foreign officials who attended, and received an invitation to an investment seminar to be held at one of the foreign Consulates later in the month.

As to Mr. and Mrs. DURAN, both did attend and apparently enjoyed themselves. In her contact report, Brenda noted that she was able, over the course of the four hours of the event, to have several conversations with Mrs. DURAN. She learned Constanta was born in the city of Oltenita in 1958. Her family came from the tradesman class of Romanian society, with her grandfather and father active in union politics. Her father was a secret member of the Bolshevik wing of the Socialist Party of Romania. He eventually became influenced by Comintern agents and took an active organizing role in the August 1944 coup against the Romanian Government, as well as the Communist effort to take over the government in 1948. He became a high-level trade union official for the Party, and she grew up in schools attended by the children of other Party officials.

She noted that after the war, the country was in horrible shape, but as a Communist Party official, her father was able to provide for his family.

Constanta met her future husband at a Communist Party Youth social event, and they dated for almost a year. Both families agreed on their marriage, and it was conducted by a senior Party officer. DURAN was in the early phase of his career at the Ministry, but due to the Party status of both families, they were authorized a one-bedroom apartment, with sitting room, kitchen, and bathroom; quite a bit of luxury by the standards of the time. They tried, but it took several years to finally have a child. They named their son Anton. He was a bright boy, and generally healthy, but had a glandular disorder that affected his metabolism.

Recognizing the child's illness as a sensitive issue, Brenda expressed empathy and inquired more about the details and what had been done to treat his illness. As one would expect, Constanta readily reviewed Anton's condition. She stated that health services in Romania were quite poor compared to the West, but as a government official, DURAN had been able to get himself treated by doctors who reserved their practices for Party and Government personnel. These individuals had access to more modern equipment and testing procedures than the common Romanian health services. However, based upon having lived in Paris when DURAN was assigned there, Constanta was aware that even these professionals were not as well-versed in the latest medical procedures as most Western physicians.

The Romanian doctors had diagnosed Aton's condition but had been unable to specifically identify which glands were involved and the specific effect on his metabolism. Part of the reason for seeking an assignment in the United States was the hope that an American doctor could do a better job of identifying the health issue, recommend appropriate treatment, and have the facilities with which to provide the treatment. While there was a doctor assigned to the Consulate, she was not even as capable as the doctors back in Romania. Constanta explained, " We hope to find an American doctor, but medical expenses in the city are very high compared to my husband's salary, so we are trying to save up to get an appointment with a specialist, once we find one. "

Brenda was able to move the flow of the conversation on health issues towards asking if both Constanta's and DURAN's were reacting well to the climate and food in the city. Apparently, both were particularly enjoying the wide selection of products and fresh vegetables, fruits, and meats available in the stores. While the Consulate had a small store for special Romanian goods, as well as tobacco and alcohol products, which were duty-free and therefore very affordable, most of the Romanian officials shopped at city supermarkets. She commented, as would be expected from Soviet Bloc residents, " that U.S. stores had such a variety and higher quality of items than even the special stores in her country for Party officials. "

More interestingly, Constanta also mentioned that "her husband did have one health problem which he hoped to address during this assignment in the U.S. Several of his teeth were in poor shape, and he wanted it fixed in the U.S. since Romanian dental practices were far behind those of the West."

As to herself, she noted, "My health is fine and I am looking forward to getting out more in the social scene." She explained that watching the child since arriving had not allowed her to accompany DURAN to the various business and diplomatic events. Because he spoke a high level of English, as did she, since they were taught the language for their posting in Africa, he was often called upon by the Consulate General to represent the Consulate at various events. For the past several weeks, Constanta had been sounding out the wife of a newly arrived Consulate junior officer, who had three children of her own, regarding babysitting for Aton. When DURAN mentioned that his business contact, Brenda, was having a large party and that she was specifically invited, Constanta decided this was her chance to get the women involved in babysitting. She asked DURAN to speak to the Consulate General and explain that in American society, bringing the wife to events is a common practice and would assist him in his efforts to make useful contacts for the Consulate. The Consulate General agreed, and the wife was instructed to act as a babysitter for this party.

CHAPTER FOUR: THE PARTY

Brenda noted that all this information was obtained during several five to ten-minute encounters during the party. In between these encounters, she noticed that Constanta actually blended quite well in the crowd, developing social conversations with several other guests, though mostly females. Brenda believed that Constanta's social skills were quite good. However, her dress was quite plain by American standards, as was her makeup. Since she was most likely noting the dress and appearances of the other females, she was becoming well aware of the contrast and probably would try to make some changes in her appearance if she could afford to.

Brenda also spoke with DURAN several times during the evening. She met him and his wife upon their arrival, and after a brief welcoming chat, she focused on Constanta to ensure that she felt comfortable. About halfway through the evening, she conversed with DURAN for about ten minutes, opening with the line that his choice of the liquors had been perfect and several of the guest had complimented her on their selection. He seemed quite pleased, and noted "the food is delicious and I have met several businessmen who had expressed interest in Romanian products and even investment opportunities there." Unfortunately, other than observing that DURAN was attentive to his wife when not engaged in conversation with others, Brenda did not have the opportunity to get much in the way of personality assessment on him during the party. She did note that he appeared quite poised in his manner and enjoyed playing the role of the Romanian diplomat, even though he really was only a code clerk.

Just near the end of the party, Brenda had another brief conversation with DURAN as he was finishing a dessert plate. She noted that both he and his wife had been quite active at the buffet table, and DURAN equally so at the bar. DURAN said that he was very appreciative of Brenda's special invitation to his wife to attend. He explained that while he had been quite active socially, the babysitting requirement had not allowed Constanta the same opportunities. This had been a small issue between them, but attending this event would help a great deal. He also expected that in the future, the babysitting arrangement would be much easier to handle.

The final contact of the evening was as the couple was about to leave.

While saying goodbye and thanking Brenda for their invitations, Constanta expressed the hope they would see each other soon. Brenda responded by noting that she would love to take them out to dinner in the near future, and, of course, would also like to meet Anton. Brenda noted that she really was not much of a cook, and rather than forcing frozen pot pies on them as a meal, her expense account allowed her to take whomever she wanted out to restaurants. In what Brenda described as a most sincere response, Constanta said she would be pleased to have Brenda visit their apartment and meet their son.

All and all, Brenda's contact report, with the atmospherics filled out by a conversation with her on the secure communications line, indicated some solid progress, especially in terms of information on the wife. She was also able to report that she had been able to do some elicitation and personal rapport building with a couple of other developmental targets who attended the party. Finally, she felt that the party had been beneficial in further establishing her alias commercial persona within the local international business community.

Stan's contact report was equally interesting, although much shorter as his role was limited to only a couple of tasks. He arrived at the party fashionably late, well dressed, and adopting a confident demeanor for his operational persona. Upon entering the apartment, he was greeted by Brenda, who discreetly advised him of what DURAN was wearing in order to make the target identification as easy as possible. First Stan circled the room while getting a drink to observe the other guests, wishing to be sure there was no one there who knew him in a different alias or persona. Of course we had cross checked Brenda's guest list with Stan's list of operational contacts. But, things happen in human operations that can never be anticipated, so Stan's initial casing of the room was a practical as well as standard procedure.

Once satisfied he was safe, Stan introduced himself to a couple of other guests, being sure that he was doing so within the vision of DURAN. After the third such chat, as he turned to head towards the bar, he "accidentally" bumped DURAN. While saying "excuse me," he also commented he was

CHAPTER FOUR: THE PARTY

on the way to the bar and asked if DURAN wanted a refill. He threw in that the choice of liquors at the bar was excellent. As anticipated, DURAN responded, and the ploy began to develop. Stan introduced himself as a financial investor in overseas commodities, and DURAN introduced himself as a diplomat from the Romanian Consulate. After some comments about the city and how DURAN liked it, Stan explained that he was based in San Francisco but had clients in the city so visited often.

Having laid in the basics of his cover, Stan and DURAN walked to the bar and got another drink. Stan then asked DURAN what he knew about Romanian oil exports to other Eastern European countries. He explained that with slightly more liberal economic policies in some of these countries, investing in hedge positions on oil futures had some profitability. DURAN responded, "I don't really understand much about this type of investment, but I do understand that Romanian oil production is about to increase because of the recent purchase of drilling equipment from Poland." Stan responded" this was very interesting," and then changed the subject to a discussion of the brand of scotch they were drinking. DURAN was very happy to discuss this at length, until Stan excused himself several minutes later to talk with another guest across the room.

Stan's second encounter with DURAN took place about forty minutes later, as Stan was about to leave. He approached DURAN and mentioned that he would be back in the city in a few weeks, and wondered if they might have a drink if DURAN was free at that time. He gave DURAN his alias business card. In return, he received DURAN's diplomatic business card. He then stated how much he had enjoyed their conversation and explained he had to depart because of an early morning flight back to the West Coast.

The next morning Winston and I sat down with Stan to get his verbal debriefing. His assessment was that his interaction with DURAN had been casual and innocent-seeming, and that DURAN would remember him if he made a re-contact within the next two weeks or so. He also gave his impression of the party and how it reflected positively on Brenda's commercial persona. Finally, he noted that in his observations of Brenda's interactions with Constanta and DURAN at the party, the body language and facial expressions seemed to indicate comfort and friendliness.

Obtaining Stan's impression of Brenda's relationship with DURAN and his wife provided another professional's view on how the relationship seemed to be developing, and it was not in any sense a means of "checking up" on her actions or reporting.

From the reporting and comments of both COs, I felt that the funds expenditure for the party had been well and productively used. Definite progress had been made by meeting the Target's wife as well as setting the scene to test the Target's willingness to go just a bit beyond the normal boundaries of his official duties by accepting some cash for information he provided.

Brenda's and Stan's contact reports were shared with Headquarters and the Bureau, as usual. Now the next steps were to get Brenda into DURAN's family life, and to have Stan reappear with "good news."

Chapter Five: Dual Assessments

It now seemed advisable that every time we had reporting on a contact with DURAN, Winston and I would meet with the FBI to provide Station's comments as well. Eventually we fell into a pattern where we would alternate meeting sites, gathering either at the Station in my office, or at the Field Office in Ralph's office.

At this early stage in an operation, Agency doctrine is that compartmentalization of the development operation should be somewhat loose, so that the other Station COs can provide advice and support to the officers involved. As the operation moves forward and matures in its potential, fewer individuals are involved, and information on it is held closer within the Station. The FBI tends to operate differently, because as a law enforcement agency, their mentality is to widely share information obtained for legal verification purposes and in case additional resources are needed quickly to assist in the activity. This cultural mentality also exists in their FCI efforts. For example, the Bureau usually sends two agents to debrief an informant to ensure the information, which could become legal evidence, can be verified by a second USG officer. The Agency's usual procedure is to have one CO as the primary individual working with an asset at a time.

This practice places a great deal of emphasis on the CO reporting comprehensively, and honestly, on the meeting. However, there are some checks and balances involved. Certainly the oral debriefing of the CO regarding the contact is one balance, for example.

The vast majority of COs are honest reporters, even when the meeting does not go as desired. But, there are a few bad apples in all professions, and management's careful monitoring of operations, as well as careful monitoring of the personalities and habits of the COs themselves, provides another level of verification of the operation and the information produced.

At the Field Office, its validation system for expenditures of resources and money was based upon demonstrated results as noted in periodic reporting. Thus, when we briefed them on the party, which was a significant event in the operation, we entered Ralph's office and found several more SAs than had previously attended our meetings. In addition to Ralph, Matt, and Larry, three other squad members were there. One of them, Frank, was a newly arrived SA, assigned to monitor the Consulate. A second, Bob, was in charge of the official file on DURAN's wife. The third, BJ, was described as the backup Squad Chief to Matt and therefore needed to be kept fully advised on the operation. Pretty soon, we were going to need a bigger room for our meeting. And, from an operational security perspective, since the Station was located under a commercial cover, I was somewhat concerned about a large contingent of FBI SAs tramping into our office. They do sort of stand out in public.

However, the meeting went quite well, and after describing how the party had gone, the conversation moved into a "give and take" discussion on how to move forward. I explained that our approach would be to test DURAN's willingness to provide insider information for financial incentives. We would do this through the ploy Stan would be using, while also further attempting to cement a personal relationship between Brenda and the DURAN family to exploit opportunity for additional assessment. The concept being that should DURAN reject Stan's attempt to provide a reward for the information on Romanian oil production, or in the worst case become insulted and react hostilely to the offered gift, Brenda's relationship would still remain intact.

The logic of this approach was not lost on Ralph. However, Matt and Larry voiced some concern that if Stan's offer was rejected, DURAN would also become suspicious of Brenda. Therefore, Matt suggested "Stan should

CHAPTER FIVE: DUAL ASSESSMENTS

make his reward a big one, as DURAN's acceptance of it would be a strong indication he was ready to be recruited." Matt reasoned that if DURAN did refuse, the Field Office knew of a few other illegal business activities in which he had been involved and could then threaten exposure and possible embarrassment to the Consulate. I countered that Brenda's relationship seemed solid enough, and due to the size and nature of the party, that she could, if necessary, feign surprise and anger if DURAN told her about Stan's offer.

Also, I explained "we wanted Stan's offer to be accepted, and therefore planned to make it appropriately small and easy for DURAN to take. The concept was to get DURAN to trust Stan and slowly provide more information in return for larger rewards." I added this was better than using a "negative hold," that is a threat of some kind, to force his cooperation. In our experience, threats did not create a willing and motivated partnership with an agent. Rather, it often created a strained relationship in which the agent provided only the minimum effort to avoid problems while demanding maximum rewards. We wanted a fully cooperative partner in the operation.

That last comment was apparently not well phrased, as both Matt and Larry took issue with my view. Matt insisted "that based upon their extensive experience with recruitment of informants, a well-documented threat produced an asset ready to take orders and produce what was required."

My first thought was to explain that we did not want just an informant; we wanted a willing agent who saw common cause with us for an operation running over a long period of time. However, Matt's sharp tone gave me pause to remember that law enforcement personnel do view informants differently than the Agency views its agents. A cultural issue, really, as law enforcement wants evidence and eventual prosecution and conviction from informant information, and the Agency wants plans and intentions intelligence that may never be known outside the classified world.

I thought about attempting some type of apology, but decided just to try and change the focus of the conversation. A trick that is very useful in dealing with touchy "cultural" issues and young children.

I told Matt that his experience was a valuable point, and that before Stan actually re-engaged with DURAN, we would have to decide carefully the value and nature of the reward to be offered. I then asked how soon the SAs thought Brenda should make a follow-up contact with Mrs. DURAN to start to build a relationship with her. Both Matt and Larry believed the sooner the better. And, we discussed possible scenarios for some time, thus taking a lot of the previous tension out of the situation.

To conclude the session, Winston gave a brief summary of the operation to date and what had been accomplished in terms of assessment and operational advancement of DURAN's development. He noted the value of these joint discussions with the SAs in planning future operational activities. We thanked everyone and departed, in one piece.

Within a few days, Headquarters' response to the reporting on the party and both COs' efforts came in. As expected, both the Romanian Desk and other Headquarters elements involved were complimentary of our efforts. The Counterintelligence element added its pro forma comment that we must continue to be alert to any surveillance of our interactions with DURAN by Romanian or other Warsaw Pact personnel assigned to the city. The Headquarters consensus was that we were off to a good start, and they looked forward to our plan for the next step in tempting DURAN with a small reward for what he would be told was somewhat useful information of a financial nature.

So, I arranged a meeting with Brenda, Stan, Winston and I to do some planning. Both Stan and Brenda had developed their own ideas, and after a discussion we agreed they were ready to proceed. The basic plan was that Brenda would telephone Mrs. DURAN and get herself invited over to the DURAN's apartment. She would bring a small gift for Mrs. DURAN and a toy for the son. During the social visit, she would try to develop a better feel for the relationship of the couple, as well as obtain any additional biographical information on the wife and DURAN. She would be very low-key and try to arrange a luncheon where she could undertake additional development and elicitation of the wife.

CHAPTER FIVE: DUAL ASSESSMENTS

At this point in the relationship with DURAN, Brenda began playing a supporting role. However, we were also hoping that in a worst case situation with Stan or one of his successors, her relationship with the family might enable her to hear about it from DURAN's perspective.

Stan's ideas were equally good. He wanted to wait almost a month before "returning" to the city and contacting DURAN for a lunch date. This would give Brenda a chance for at least one, and perhaps two, meetings with Mrs. DURAN. The timing would also fit with the comment he had made at the party to DURAN that his business trips from the West Coast were usually once a month or less. There was no need to have the Target think that Stan had especially come to see him—at least not at this point in the relationship. Stan's idea for a gift was also on target: he suggested a wrist watch costing a little over a hundred dollars. This was something that DURAN should like, and certainly was of value, yet was also an item DURAN could explain as having saved up for and purchased on his own if ever questioned.

Stan planned to telephone DURAN, knowing that the call was going through the Consulate's switchboard, and remind him of their brief meeting at the party. He would advise that he planned to be in town near the end of the month, and would suggest a lunch where he wanted to further discuss what type of business the Consulate might advise for a European-based client. This conversation, we assumed, would appear to fall within the activities that DURAN had been pursuing for the Consulate should it be monitored by security personnel. And, the restaurant selected was one which the Field Office had often heard DURAN described as one he enjoyed but was too expensive for him to go unless he was taken by a business contact.

Stan would arrange to meet DURAN at the restaurant, and would engage him in social niceties over a couple of scotches. After a leisurely meal at which Stan did much of the talking, explaining in appropriate jargon his investment and commodity hedging activities, he would thank DURAN for the information on the plan to increase Romanian oil production. He would explain in some detail how he had used the information to hedge a future position in European oil sales to make a couple of thousand dollars rather quickly. Since he was a fair businessman, he felt that he owed DURAN a small gift for providing him with this money-making opportunity. He would then offer DURAN the wristwatch.

If DURAN accepted, Stan would move the conversation to the benefit that both could obtain if DURAN was able to produce any additional business, trade or financial information from his position at the Consulate. Stan, or one of his European clients, could then use it to make an appropriate investment. He would emphasize that, as Romania was only slowly opening its trade relationships outside the Warsaw Pact and since little of its trade plans were known, almost any information could be of value. Stan would suggest that as DURAN handled his normal daily duties at the Consulate, he could stay alert o anything he heard that might be of business value. If DURAN seemed receptive, Stan would then establish another meeting within a few days at the same restaurant, setting the day and time so no additional contact through the Consulate would be necessary. At this meeting, he would listen to what DURAN had learned and decide if any was of value.

Should DURAN react negatively to the gift of the watch, Stan would apologize and explain that his offer was standard business practice among his colleagues and he had not meant to insult DURAN. He would then put the watch back in his briefcase and change the subject back to DURAN's views of what type of business the Consulate was attempting to promote. Upon completion of the meal, he would thank DURAN for his views and time and depart. His role in the operation would end at that point.

We coordinated our plans with Headquarters, and then had to decide how we would discuss our plans with the Field Office and obtain their agreement. Based upon Matt's and Larry's attitude at the last meeting, we had to tread carefully.

As the meeting was scheduled to be at the station, this allowed us to at least set the environment and tone to use in explaining the plan and the rationales behind it. We decided that rather than openly oppose Matt's and Larry's views, we would make our position that if Stan's ploy worked with DURAN we would see what other business information he can up

CHAPTER FIVE: DUAL ASSESSMENTS

with at the second meeting and plan from that. If, however, he rejected Stan's gift than we all would have to regroup and look at all options to continue the operation. That, we felt, was a position the Bureau would agree to. Luckily, and you need luck in any operation in addition to skills, fate intervened to make the meeting much more pleasant and harmonious than we anticipated.

When Ralph showed up for the meeting, he only brought Larry with him. Matt was busy with another case, of which we were offered no details. After Winston explained what Brenda would be doing, Stan provided a comprehensive explanation of how his operational scenario would play out with DURAN. At the conclusion of their presentation, I made the point that if the reward's ploy failed, we would have to rethink the operation and noted the input Matt and Larry had made at the last meeting. Rather than bring up the previous issues, Ralph was immediately supportive of the plans, and Larry was acquiescent, although his body language was decidedly less comfortable than Ralph's. Stan, sensing the mood, engaged Larry in a discussion of DURAN's personality as reflected in the Bureau's files. He phrased his questions to Larry in a manner of seeking some guidance regarding what he could expect of DURAN's behavior and reactions during their luncheon. Larry, while at first a little reluctant to provide many details, soon warmed to the subject as Stan asked more and more questions.

For over a half an hour Stan and Larry discussed DURAN. This really took the edge off the meeting and was actually the beginning of a solid operational relationship between the two. They would go on to run several successful joint operations in the next couple of years. Perhaps it was their closeness in age, or perhaps that they shared a common military service background, the U.S. Marine Corps, but whatever it was, their personalities jived.

As the SAs were to depart, I mentioned to Ralph, "Do you think the operation is moving in the right direction? I think this next phase of meetings might be a key test of the viability of the operation. If Stan's offer of the watch is accepted and DURAN showed up at the next lunch with any information he felt was of financial value, then we actually have a chance to fashion a full scale recruitment operation." I noted "considering his intelligence potential as a Warsaw Pact code clerk, I assume this operation will quickly become of high interest at both of our Headquarters as well as with some other U.S. Intelligence Community agencies." Ralph responded "we will see," which was a less assuring reply than I would have preferred. I concluded by once again thanking him for the level of cooperation the Field Office was providing, wondering to myself if Matt's absence and Larry's attitude may well have been part of Ralph's efforts.

Chapter Six: Brenda and Mrs. Duran

The day after the meeting, Brenda telephoned Mrs. DURAN and had a pleasant and friendly conversation, which included an agreement that the next week she would come to the DURAN's apartment for coffee. Once again, the timing was important: we did not want Brenda to call before we "officially" discussed our plans with the Bureau, but also did not want too much time to elapse so that Brenda's initial conversation at the party with Mrs. DURAN had been forgotten by her.

After the telephonic conversation, Brenda reported the substance to me over the secure communications channel. I suggested she wait on submitting a formal report for Headquarters and the Bureau until after she had her meeting at the DURAN's residence. But, I urged her to write down the important points of the exchange now as her report would, I suspected, be closely reviewed by the Field Office's SAs.

The next week was going to see both the meeting with Mrs. DURAN and Stan's reappearance in the city for the luncheon with DURAN. However, first, Stan had to make the telephone call, ostensibly from his West Coast office, to DURAN. He had worked out the conversation he would give DURAN, keeping it simple and seemingly innocent: he was following up on their brief conversation at the party, and interested in what business the Consulate might be able to promote.

Stan made the call with Winston and me in the room. The switchboard operator asked Stan's name and business after he requested to speak with DURAN, and there was about a two minute pause before DURAN came on the line. Stan reminded him of their meeting and gave his story regarding the reason for the call. DURAN at first seemed not to remember the contact at the party, but once Stan mentioned that he had clients with possible interest in Romania, and that he wished to discuss it at a lunch at the restaurant, DURAN's interest perked up. He said he needed to check his schedule, and placed Stan on a hold for a couple of minutes. Upon returning, he advised he was free and would join Stan for a luncheon discussion of potential business opportunities. Once the date and time were agreed to, Stan ended the conversation. We all felt the conversation had gone well. We later learned from Matt that DURAN had conferred with the Consulate General during the several minute hold, advising that Stan's business contacts might prove valuable to the Consulate and the Romanian Government. We were not told at the time how the Bureau knew this, but had long suspected that in addition to the telephone monitoring, they had also been able to penetrate the Consulate with audio collection devices. Later in the operation, we learned that they had some audio coverage of areas in the Consulate, and even ran a low-level human source with access to the facility on a daily basis.

Stan wrote up his report on the conversation and it was sent to Headquarters. He then arranged a meeting with Matt and Larry at a coffee shop some distance from the Field Office and gave them a copy of the report. Stan later mentioned that he had a good operational discussion with both SAs, and felt that his personal rapport with them was developing nicely.

Tuesday of the next week was the day Brenda went to visit the DURAN residence. It was an apartment; a two-bedroom and one and a half bath unit, in a small building located in a semi-urban residential neighborhood about five miles from the Consulate, which was located in the downtown business center. The apartment was on the third floor, and there was an elevator. Two apartments were located on each of the five floors, and in the basement, there was an apartment occupied by the building manager and engineer, along with the boiler and related building equipment. The building had street parking, which was heavily used by private cars,

CHAPTER SIX: BRENDA AND MRS. DURAN

probably owned by local residents, and commercial service vehicles. Brenda described the DURAN's apartment as somewhat sparsely furnished, with a well-worn sofa and chairs, a six-person dining table and chairs that had seen better times, and a half bathroom that looked like it had been done about twenty years ago. The son's bedroom was furnished with a single bed and an old chest of drawers, but it had quite a few toys and some children's books in both Romanian and English. The kitchen had a sink, gas oven, old toaster, and dishes and cookware in glass-fronted cabinets above the counters. They appeared to have been installed about twenty years ago as well. In addition to the bedrooms, kitchen, baths, and living room, there was an alcove between the kitchen and living room which served as the dining area. Brenda did not see the DURAN's bedroom or the full bath.

We knew most of the information about the building and the neighborhood from the Bureau's files, which they shared with us as soon as they knew Brenda would be visiting the apartment. Also, I had two other Station officers independently conduct a casing of the area and the building. This was actually good training for a couple of my younger officers, involving little risk as each did a one-time only pass into the neighborhood and building under appropriately constructed cover activities. Both officers also reported no indication of FBI surveillance of the building during their visit. Brenda, however, did note Bureau surveillance when she arrived at the building.

One of Brenda's basic tasks during the meeting was to make observationsof the apartment itself. And, she did a good job, which provided the Bureau with very useful information they had not yet obtained by their own methods. While it is always important to know and work within the environment of any operational site, both we and the Bureau also had other potential plans requiring a comprehensive understanding of the building, the apartment, and the general area: a future audio penetration of the apartment and an audio reception base to receive those transmissions. But, that would come later if the operation was moving forward and warranted the resource expenditure required to monitor what Mr. and Mrs. DURAN were saying about their relationships with our officers.

Brenda and Mrs. DURAN had a very enjoyable afternoon. Mrs. DURAN seemed very appreciative of the company and spoke fondly of the time she had at Brenda's party. Brenda began by presenting her with a small gift and then asking to see the son so she could give him the toy teddy bear she had brought for him. The child was very pleased with the stuffed toy and played quietly with it until it was time for his nap. Mrs. DURAN explained that he has been waking up very early, about 4 a.m., the last few weeks, and she has had to play with him to enable Mr. DURAN to stay sleeping until his usual 7 a.m. wake-up. But, the good aspect of this was that he took a several-hour nap in the afternoon, which usually allowed Mrs. DURAN to do the same. Brenda's description of Mrs. DURAN as looking drawn and quite tired gave credence to her story. And, the child's long nap offered the opportunity for lengthy conversation before he awoke and needed Mrs. DURAN's full attention.

Their conversation included several items of interest regarding the DURAN's family life, their interaction with other Consulate personnel, and how their Communist Party affiliation fit into their overall view of life. Mrs. DURAN's spoken English was quite good, though at a level well below that of a native speaker. Apparently, she had learned Basic English in school in Romania, and then improved her skills in France and during the Africa posting. Her accent did have a decidedly Eastern European accent, however. She said she also had some capability to speak French, but not as well as English.

Brenda started the conversation asking how Mrs. DURAN was enjoying the experience of living in an American city. She responded "that when compared to even Paris, the shopping opportunities and prices were wonderful." She explained" that in my country even common place goods might often be scarce; however, my family's status within the Communist Party ensured that I did not have the same difficulty as the common folk. "But, she added, "the lack of many goods was the fault of trade polices enforced on various socialist countries by others." Brenda noted that she stated this in an almost rote manner, without any particular emotion, and

CHAPTER SIX: BRENDA AND MRS. DURAN

in a manner not meant to blame Brenda for such policies. Mrs. DURAN went on to say, "My husband and I are planning to purchase a great many items such as kitchen appliances, clothes, and personal accessories before being posted back to Bucharest. Then, our apartment will have all the luxuries of the West." Also, she added, "it was a custom for those posted abroad to bring back gifts to not only family members, but also professional colleagues and superiors to thank them for the opportunity to be posted abroad. So, our family is saving all the money it can for these purchases, and thanks to various allowances provided to those posted abroad, we have some extra funds that can be saved." That said, she explained that by American standards, DURAN's salary, even with various allowances, was quite modest, so a tight budget had to be maintained.

Brenda commiserated with her and noted that even she, with a good salary and liberal expense account, found it often difficult to save money. Mrs. DURAN continued that, "another item for which they were saving was health care. Her son, Anton, had some health issues and since medical services were more advanced in the West, they wanted him to have treatment here before they returned home." Brenda responded by offering to provide a list of specialists in the medical field who might be able to assist Anton. But, Mrs. DURAN explained "as of yet we do not have adequate savings to start any treatment. But my husband is now in the first year of his posting, and we hope to be able to spend at least four or five years here. That amount of time would allow us to accumulate enough to have Anton treated and also make the purchases we wish for shipment back to Bucharest."

Brenda asked if a five-year tour was a standard policy for the Romanian Government, and explained she had business contacts at the U.S. State Department and they tended to be sent on two-year assignments overseas. Mrs. DURAN said, "Most overseas assignments were three years, but her husband and the Consulate General are good friends, so we hope to get an extension of assignment for at least two additional years if not more." She added," My husband is in a very technical and important position, and the field of individuals who could replace him is limited." Brenda wisely did

53

not seek further information on DURAN's duties, as Mrs. DURAN seems to be providing quite a bit of interesting information without any need to seem too inquisitive.

Brenda's next conversational subject was whether Mrs. DURAN had been able to make many friends in the city since her arrival, noting this within the context of how hard it has been for her, as a relatively newly arrived businesswoman, to break into the international business circles here. Mrs. DURAN explained that she and her husband had been introduced by DURAN's predecessor to several people in the local Romanian emigre community. However, both quickly found these people wanted special favors from the Consulate and weren't really interested in a social relationship. She then confided, "that even within the Consulate family, it was not always easy to develop personal relationships. Because my husband is a close friend of the Consulate General, many members of the Consulate envied his relationship. Also, many of the wives used their spouses' titles and diplomatic positions to create a social hierarchy that made it difficult for us, since my husband's official diplomatic ranking is somewhat low." Brenda responded with empathy, stating that she has often seen the same status consciousness in corporate circles, and really hated it. She said that what she cared about in a person was their personality and their willingness to be an honest friend. Mrs. DURAN agreed.

After discussing the values of real friendship for a while, Mrs. DURAN, with a wistful and somewhat sad look in her eyes, noted "that also because we are Communists and living in a city in a Capitalist country, this placed even more restrictions on interpersonal relationships. Within the Consulate, there are individuals sent to protect Consulate personnel from provocations and threats from local organs of the U.S. Government who might attempt to embarrass or trick us. While all Communist Party members understand the need for this and support their work, an unintended consequence of this does cause some strains within the Consulate family." Brenda asked what Mrs. DURAN meant. She responded "an atmosphere of suspicion is always present, in which certain people are constantly watching others and seeking opportunities to report

CHAPTER SIX: BRENDA AND MRS. DURAN

the behavior of others to the security personnel." She said she had not seen this atmosphere so developed in either assignments in France or Africa, and was quite surprised when she noticed that her innocent comments might be reported as indicating anti-Communist thoughts. "After all," she stated, "both my husband and I, and our families, are long-time Communist Party members and we even have family friends who are officials of the Party back in Romania. This type of atmosphere, along with the envy many staff members hold of my husband's close personal relationship with the Consulate General, makes it difficult to develop close personal relationships within the Consulate community. So, I actually have only a few people with whom I might have a close friendship." Brenda responded," I would hope our relationship might grow into such a close friendship."

One other topic was alluded to by Brenda that stimulated an interesting response from Mrs. DURAN. Brenda was asked how her social life was now that she was established in the city. She responded that it was always difficult for young and single women to integrate into such a new environment. Mrs. DURAN wondered if Brenda had a boyfriend, and whether she planned to get married and have children. Brenda said she did indeed want a husband and family, and loved children, but the right man had yet to appear. Her career, which was often quite demanding time-wise and often included a great deal of travel, further complicated the matter. Brenda then asked Mrs. DURAN whether she had found it difficult to keep family life stable and happy. She wondered if overseas postings, away from other family members who could provide material and emotional support, as well as demanding and time-consuming duties by her husband, added pressures to their relationship. Mrs. DURAN responded, "My husband is a caring husband and father, and throughout his career has made every effort to balance his professional responsibilities with his family life." She described how much he loved their son and the time he spent with him reading and playing on weekends. Every evening, even if he returned home late due to a heavy workload, he went in and read a story to Anton. Mrs. DURAN described him in equally glowing terms as a caring husband.

After a little over three hours, about twenty minutes after Anton had awoken from his nap and Brenda had played with him while Mrs. DURAN fixed him a snack, Brenda took her leave, expressing appreciation for the visit and offering a luncheon in the future. Brenda said she would call Mrs. DURAN in a few days and see how they could match up their schedules. She noted," I am not much of a cook, so I want to take you out for lunch." Mrs. DURAN said she would look forward to hearing from Brenda.

As soon as Brenda returned to her apartment, she called me at the Station. In describing the meeting, it was immediately obvious that she was experiencing the emotional high that COs get after a good operational meeting. I suggested she write up her report for Headquarters at once, while she still remembered all the details.

She was right, it had been a highly successful meeting and the possibility of developing a monitoring capability of DURAN's actions and reactions to his interaction with Stan and other COs as the operation moved forward was a few steps closer. The next thing to worry about was Stan's meeting with DURAN and the offer of the watch in return for the oil information.

Chapter Seven: The Opening Ploy

The luncheon meeting with DURAN had been set for that Friday, at 1 p.m., at an expensive French restaurant located within one of the city's five-star hotels. It was going to be a hundred-dollars plus lunch. It was becoming obvious that DURAN had expensive tastes when others were paying, and this worked to our advantage.

Stan arrived at the restaurant about ten minutes early; ensured he was seated at a table in the rear of the dining area, shielded from view from those entering the restaurant or anyone looking through the windows facing the street while passing by. He advised the waiter that he was expecting a guest and provided a general description of DURAN. Thus, when he arrived a few minutes late, DURAN was taken directly to Stan's table. While Stan and DURAN were still exchanging pleasantries, two men were shown to a table closer to the bar area, and immediately requested another table more to the rear of the restaurant. This all took place behind DURAN's back, as Stan had taken the seat with his back to the wall which provided a full view of all the action surrounding them. While perhaps nothing at all, Stan's CO training made him suspicious. These individuals could be security personnel from the Consulate, monitoring DURAN's meeting, or they could also be members of the Field Office's surveillance squad monitoring the meeting. However, Stan had not identified any static surveillance on the restaurant when he arrived, so if it was the Bureau, it must have been surveillance which had followed DURAN there.

Stan began the luncheon by thanking DURAN for taking the time away from his official duties. But before getting down to business, Stan insured

DURAN had a drink and a chance to look at the menu. So, for a few minutes they discussed which scotch to have, and whether it would taste better with or without ice and soda. Stan also highlighted a couple of the menu luncheon specials, including the lobster salad and the roasted lamb. After an appropriate discussion of the choices, and about ten minutes to finish their scotches, both ordered. Stan also selected a decent Sauvignon Blanc to accompany their meal. While drinking their scotches, Stan recalled that he had been impressed at the party by DURAN's knowledge of scotches. This was a rather obvious attempt at some flattery, meant to gauge how DURAN would react to flattery in the future: he seemed to like it.

As DURAN reacted to the flattery, Stan also noticed that the two men recently seated near to them did not order pre-luncheon drinks. Could this mean the Bureau folks are not able to drink on duty? Or, perhaps it was that the Consulate security personnel who did not have a large enough expense account to permit pre-luncheon drinks? Or, just two guys who did not drink alcohol at lunch? Not much to go on, but well worth filing away as further observations of their behavior should provide more clues to their actual purpose in the restaurant.

During the pre-luncheon drinks, Stan did the usual light, rapport building conversation: how are things going, I've been busy, have you been busy, etc. Then, after the food arrived, he moved into a well-rehearsed discussion of his recent international investment activities, highlighting his activities in the oil futures area. He asked DURAN if he had heard anything more about Romanian marketing or export activities recently. DURAN responded that he had not seen anything new on oil exports, and usually focused his official duties on other responsibilities.

While DURAN continued on, in a rather vague way about his official responsibilities, Stan observed what the two suspicious men had ordered for lunch. One, the older of the two, had ordered a fish dish and the other a steak with some type of sauce. Both were dishes in the high range on the menu.

When DURAN finished his rather vague discussion of his work, Stan began his explanation of the value of the information DURAN had

CHAPTER SEVEN: THE OPENING PLOY

previously supplied on his country's oil exportation planning. The explanation involved a great deal of technical jargon regarding timing and competing price guidelines utilized in computer-generated international futures speculation. Hopefully, the purposely complex explanation was enough to both impress and confuse DURAN, who appeared to listen intently as he ate his lobster salad. Stan concluded by noting "that while this effort had made a bit of money for my clients and a small percentage commission for me, I realize that you also deserved some reward."

DURAN responded quite quickly with surprise, and asked "how much money had been realized in Stan's complicated trading activities." Stan repeated "that the amount had been rather small, because, frankly, I did not know how accurate your information was." Stan explained this was not meant as an insult, but as they had just met and had only spoken briefly, he was not prepared to risk too much on the information. If he had had more confidence in the information, he could have made six or seven times the amount.

However, it was only right that DURAN receive some benefit for his part in the trades. So, Stan said," I have purchased a small gift for you as your "commission Now, noted Stan, he had no idea how a diplomat could handle business profits so the easiest way was to just give him this gift. He then discreetly passed a box across the table containing the wristwatch. Stan was fully prepared to rebuff any argument DURAN would make regarding why he couldn't accept the "gift." However, that was hardly necessary as DURAN accepted the box, quickly opened it, and beamed as he looked at the wrist watch. After trying it on his left wrist, he thanked Stan and stated that he had never owned as nice a wrist watch as this. He then expressed surprise that such common knowledge within the Consulate as he had casually mentioned to Stan should have such business value.

This presented the opening for Stan to go through his planned scenario: convincing DURAN that information he picked up in the course of his work at the Consulate could be turned into additional profit if they worked together. Stan's lengthy justification for future information sharing regarding business activities of the Romanian Government lasted from the end of the main course through most of the dessert. He provided numerous recent examples of Eastern European business activities, all well publicized in the press, where advanced notice would allow speculation in the futures market, resulting in significant profits. Over coffee and brandy, DURAN asked," What type of information could you use?" Stan responded that as a Consulate official, DURAN must see information from Romanian Government offices every day that included plans for economic and financial activities in the international market place. All he had to do was periodically provide this information to Stan, who would then use it to the financial advantage of his clients, and of course, to DURAN as well. Stan concluded his remarks with an assurance that in the Capitalistic World this type of activity, using insider information for profit, was a well-established business technique.

As DURAN asked a few questions about the type of information he should watch for, Stan noticed the two men had finished their meal and were about to depart the restaurant.

DURAN expressed one concern, however. He noted," Often, information I hear is considered to be confidential within the Consulate, and I certainly do not want to get myself in any trouble." Stan carefully reassured him that all he needed to do was discuss what current business information he had learned and Stan would handle the rest. There would be no need for DURAN to do anything but his normal job and keep his eyes open for information on his government's business plans and intentions.

Stan stated that he would be in the area for about a week, meeting with a few clients in nearby cities. He suggested that DURAN have lunch with him, same time and same place, in five days hence, and be prepared to discuss what he may have learned during that time period. DURAN agreed, but said he could not be sure of having any information of value. Stan said that might be, but as he enjoyed DURAN's company, a friendly lunch and talk was always a pleasant experience for him. Stan also asked DURAN how he wanted to handle the matter of any future "commissions." Did he want gifts or would he prefer cash? DURAN responded" while I greatly appreciated the gift, money would be more useful since I am saving up to

CHAPTER SEVEN: THE OPENING PLOY

purchase various items." Stan said he understood fully, and that any future "commissions" would be in cash.

With agreement for the next meeting established, Stan and DURAN ended the lunch, with DURAN leaving immediately but Stan excusing himself to use the bathroom. When he did leave the restaurant about ten minutes later, after having used the Men's room facilities to jot down several key points from their conversation, Stan made a point of checking the area for any sign of the two men from the nearby table. As he took an hours plus counter surveillance route back to his car, Stan did not observe any indications of being followed.

The next day Stan's report on his meeting with DURAN had been sent to Headquarters, and passed both orally and in report form to Ralph, Matt, Larry and BJ. Between the report of Brenda's interaction with Mrs. DURAN and Stan's success at getting DURAN to accept the watch and agree to future reporting, the FBI and our Headquarters were quite satisfied with our progress.

However, Matt and BJ were somewhat less impressed with our future plans, which they felt were too slow in moving DURAN into a relationship. Our plan was to slowly enhance DURAN's cooperation over a series of meetings where his information seemed to result in increasing financial compensation, while carefully getting him to reveal exactly how he acquired such information within the Consulate. Once he admitted he was the Code Clerk, planning to eventually task him for information on the Consulate's communication system could begin. We hoped the additional funds he would start to receive, along with the confidence he should develop that he could pass information without endangering himself, would draw him deeper and deeper into the relationship with Stan. We had some indication, based upon DURAN's expressed concerns about security at the Consulate and Brenda's conversation with Mrs. DURAN, that it would take time for DURAN to feel comfortable sharing information from his official duties. Also, we were not sure how strong a loyalty, or fear, of the Communist Party played in obtaining DURAN's cooperation. Certainly, he was willing to take small risks for money, but once we got down to tasks related to his Code Clerk responsibilities, that was an entirely different matter. Our long-term plan called for gradually bringing DURAN into a secret, high-profit, international non-governmental organization that could not only maximize profits on his information, but had the personnel and technical resources to assist him in acquiring the code information without fear of discovery. Thus, we envisioned a lengthy developmental time frame, which nurtured his cooperation and confidence, step by step, before gaining control over his reporting.

A rather lengthy period of assessment and development is a pretty standard operational scenario for the Agency, whereas the Bureau often preferred just to confront the individual after he or she had been taking money for a while and offer them a choice of cooperating or being exposed. Again, a cultural difference in the way one does business. Ralph was, as usual, the deciding factor at the Field Office, and he agreed with our approach. I should add, while I fully expected Ralph to understand the value of our approach, had he disagreed and pushed for an early recruitment attempt, I and Headquarters would have elevated the discussion to much higher levels at the CIA and the FBI.

Stan also included the information and descriptions of the two men in the restaurant in the security section of his Contact Report. We checked to ascertain if the Field Office had decided to surveil the meeting, and were advised they had not. Regarding the two men, the Field Office advised that based upon the descriptions provided by Stan, they did not seem to be from the Consulate or any other Soviet Bloc official establishment in the city. So, we assumed, at least for the moment, they were just innocent civilians having lunch.

However, the Bureau had surveilled Brenda's meeting at DURAN's home, and without questioning the Surveillance Squad's professionalism, we continued to see surveillance of our officers' meetings as a potential risk for these operations. This was a delicate issue from both an interpersonal and bureaucratic perspective. The Field Office considered this "their operation," even if we were doing the actual contacts, and as such, their use of surveillance resources constituted their involvement at this point. Yet,

CHAPTER SEVEN: THE OPENING PLOY

even the best surveillance can be identified, either by a mistake or simply by reusing surveillance individuals whom a target may have observed too often. I was able to discuss this with Ralph and explained my concerns, while he explained the issue from the Bureau's perspective. We came to a reasonable and practical conclusion: as soon as the operational scenario developed to the point that it was appropriate, we would use an FBI SA as part of the group in contact with DURAN. However, for the time being the Field Office would continue to use its surveillance assets as follows: monitoring DURAN's travel from the Consulate to any meetings with an Agency officer to ascertain if he was being followed by any Romanian security personnel. If the Field Office decided it also wanted to surveil an actual meeting, they would discuss it beforehand with me. That was a practical solution, and one which both organizations could live with.

One key fact always requiring the attention of the CO is the constant struggle with the agent's very human desire to enjoy the fruits of his clandestine labor vice while keeping in mind that such behavior will bring him to the attention of his country's security or counterintelligence service.

So, attempting to embed Brenda in a monitoring role regarding DURAN's use of his operational funds would provide an excellent insight that DURAN's handling officer, Stan, could use to both fashion his on-going guidance to DURAN and gauge the security of the operation.

Chapter Eight: Mrs. Duran's Insights

At this point in the operation, Stan would be the primary Case Officer for the operation, attempting to condition DURAN to provide sensitive information in return for money. During this phase, he was able to hold five personal meetings with DURAN while still maintaining the cover story that his office was located on the West Coast. By the third of these meetings, Stan had moved the venue from public restaurants to hotel suites, where he was ostensibly residing while visiting the city. During this period, our reporting and planning procedures with Ralph and his SAs remained the same. Ralph was, on the whole, pretty satisfied with the manner and timing of our progress—Matt and BJ a bit less so to say the least. Stan's other contribution was a developing personal relationship with Larry, which smoothed some discussions with the Field Office.

At the same time, Winston and I did our best to keep our Headquarters satisfied. Stan's reporting on each meeting was comprehensive and well written, clearly demonstrating that developmental progress was moving forward. In separate communications, I discussed the pace and future scenarios of the operation with appropriate Headquarters managers in an effort to reinforce their understanding of the overall strategy we were pursuing for the eventual acquisition of the Romanian encoded communications' tape disks. We all realized the strategic value these would have to the U.S. Government: allowing NSA to read all the Romanian diplomatic, and perhaps intelligence communications, being sent from Bucharest to the Consulate and from the Consulate to the Romanian capital.

CHAPTER EIGHT: MRS. DURAN'S INSIGHTS

Based upon an NSA assessment of the communications' traffic flow among Warsaw Pact countries, it was felt that the Romanian Consulate might also be receiving classified information on Warsaw Pact political and military planning communications.

A few days after Brenda's visit to the DURAN's apartment, she followed up by telephone with an invitation to Mrs. DURAN for a mid-week lunch at a restaurant in the downtown business area. Brenda was careful to choose a location where the Bureau advised Consulate, or for that matter Soviet Bloc officials, were never seen. Also, the environment of the restaurant was meant to demonstrate the meeting was social not business.

When Brenda and Mrs. DURAN spoke, she seemed quite friendly, but did note that she would have to get a babysitter for her son, as his age would make it difficult to enjoy a restaurant experience. She then explained that the Consulate spouse who would occasionally babysit might not be available as she had recently taken some part-time administrative work at the Consulate. This news was anticipated, based on information from the Field Office, and Brenda was ready with a suggestion: she had met a young girl just out of local business school who was seeking a position as an Administrative Assistant in a corporate environment. And, Brenda had been able to get her a part-time position with a local business contact. However, the position did not pay well, and perhaps this young woman would also consider babysitting to enhance her income? Mrs. DURAN responded with two concerns: how caring and responsible would she be to Anton, and how much would she expect to be paid? Brenda, after a suitable pause to consider these questions, responded that Mrs. DURAN would have to meet with the girl to interview her and observe how she interacted with Anton, and since Brenda was doing a favor for the girl in getting her some employment, her charges to Mrs. DURAN would be only a couple of dollars an hour." After all," Brenda concluded, "she would be making money at a time when otherwise she would just be sitting home unemployed." Brenda suggested that she contact the girl and determine if she was interested. If so, Brenda would re-contact Mrs. DURAN to arrange a meeting with the girl. Mrs. DURAN agreed.

We now needed a "babysitter," and this presented the opportunity I wanted to get an FBI SA directly involved in the operation. The day after the telephone conversation, I asked Ralph if he could provide someone to play that role. This request fulfilled my earlier promise to place an FBI officer in the operation, and would also save me from exposing another officer in only a small supporting operational role. Ralph readily agreed and selected an SA newly assigned to the Field Office, serving on a White Collar Criminal Squad. She would play the role of Alice Petsworth, the soon-to-be babysitter. Alice was quite young looking, despite being in her late 20s and just out of the FBI Academy at Quantico, Virginia. This was her first FBI assignment.

As it was considered a low threat undercover activity, and since she was new in the city and working in an investigative area removed from the FCI field, Ralph had little difficulty obtaining the SAC's approval and subsequently FBI Headquarters approval.

Alice was actually quite excited at the opportunity to play this role, and it was arranged that she and Brenda would meet at a suburban hotel to discuss her role in the operation. Alice was briefed on the general outline of the operation: that Mrs. DURAN was the spouse of a Romanian diplomat who was a target of the Bureau and the Agency, and that her role was to act as a young girl looking for a business career whom had been assisted by Brenda and therefore owed her a favor. She was to meet Mrs. DURAN and provide the cover story about herself and her association with Brenda. She was to be very caring upon meeting Anton and to express her deep affection and desire for children of her own at a later point in her life.

Brenda reported back that Alice seemed to have the right role-playing skills and attitude to fit the requirements of the task, and I conveyed this to Ralph. The next step was a two-day training period for Alice on how to be a good babysitter, including a bit of emergency First Aid training. After all, we didn't want anyone taking care of a young child without proper preparation. Ralph and I were hopeful that she might become a regular babysitter for the DURANs. This would provide us with two important benefits, one bureaucratic and one operational: an FBI SA directly involved

CHAPTER EIGHT: MRS. DURAN'S INSIGHTS

in the operation, which significantly enhanced its "jointness" in the eyes of the Bureau, and an SA with access to the DURAN residence in their absence. Brenda again spoke on the telephone with Mrs. DURAN and explained that the girl was interested in babysitting. A day and time for Alice to be interviewed at the DURAN Residence was set. Subsequently, the FBI was able to confirm that Mrs. DURAN had discussed the babysitting issue with her husband, and he had agreed. Also, he encouraged his wife to enjoy the lunch, describing Brenda as a kind and friendly young lady. He also made another remark of operational interest: he mentioned to his wife that, considering the "politics" in the Consulate, not letting the others know that she was having lunch with an American friend was a good idea.

We and the Bureau were well aware that Warsaw Pact diplomats were permitted official and business contact with Americans, but must report these contacts to their security personnel. Private relationships with Americans, unless authorized and reported in detail, were not allowed. Thus, DURAN was breaking the rules, knew it, and wanted to take measures to evade the rule. He was starting to involve himself and his wife in a conspiracy. He definitely was our type of person!

Mrs. DURAN and Alice met as scheduled, and their meeting lasted almost two hours. During that period, Mrs. DURAN did not ask too many questions about Alice's background, but was very interested in how she interacted with Anton. Her bona fides seemed to have been accepted. During her play time with Anton, Alice was also able to mention that previously she had taken a Red Cross First Aid course for her own general experience. Mrs. DURAN was duly impressed. Alice's interaction with Anton went well according to her, and she described him as a pleasant and inquisitive child. She felt his English language skills were a bit limited, and Mrs. DURAN explained that she and her husband spoke a mixture of English and Romanian in the residence. Alice responded that she would try to help Anton improve his English while she watched him.

From Alice's description of the meeting, she and Mrs. DURAN hit it off fine, and Anton also seemed to like her. That was good. And, subsequently, the FBI was able to report that Mrs. DURAN had told her husband that the young lady seemed mature and responsible, just as Brenda had said. Best of all, her manner and playing with Anton had been very gentle and kind, and she had even volunteered to try to teach Anton more English. Mrs. Duran also happily noted that since she was repaying a favor to Brenda, Alice was willing to babysit for only a couple of dollars an hour.

This was almost exactly the same story that Mrs. DURAN provided to Brenda, when she telephoned after the scheduled meeting to learn if Mrs. DURAN felt comfortable with Alice watching her young son.

Now with Anton taken care of, Brenda could have lunch with Mrs. DURAN. And, it turned out to be a very pleasant and interesting two-hour-plus outing. It was apparent from the start that Mrs. DURAN had not had the opportunity to get out to many restaurants in the city, and was enjoying the atmosphere and the food, as well as the company. As is the standard practice in such meetings where elicitation of assessment information is the primary objective, Brenda began the conversation with general social topics: a comment about the city environment, the food at the restaurant, how Anton is doing, the weather, etc. The elicitation questions would come later, in the middle of the meeting, so that Mrs. DURAN probably would not even remember them by the end of the lunch.

Mrs. DURAN explained that she really did not have much of a chance to shop in the downtown area as yet, but once she and her husband saved enough money, she was looking forward to seeing what furniture and appliances were available at some of the discount stores in the area. Also of assessment value, she mentioned that Anton's allergies had not been bothering him, but they still wanted to find a good doctor to look at his gland issue, which they believed was affecting his metabolism. However, as with the household purchases, they needed to wait a bit longer until they saved up more funds. A bit later, she also mentioned a few details regarding a dental issue affecting DURAN.

Apparently, DURAN had serious problems with his teeth. The problem, which involved an infected tooth, had occurred in Africa, and the local dentist he went to for treatment had filled the tooth with substandard filling material. Within a year, the filling had cracked, and unknown to DURAN

CHAPTER EIGHT: MRS. DURAN'S INSIGHTS

at the time, a gum infection had started. Back in Bucharest, DURAN had sought dental treatment to stop the infection, but those efforts had proven unsuccessful. DURAN blamed this on the poor training and treatment facilities in the country, even though, as a Communist Party member, he had access to services much better than those of the average Romanian citizen. At the moment, he was using a medicine from the Consulate's Health Officer to treat the infection, and this was proving successful in relieving the pain, but not in eliminating the infection. In fact, it appeared that the infection had spread, and several of his teeth were now infected at the gum line. While not the most pleasant subject to discuss in detail over lunch, Brenda listened carefully and, by offering sympathy and mirroring the topic by describing a similar dental issue supposedly affecting a relative, Brenda encouraged Mrs. DURAN to discuss it in detail.

During the main course, Brenda directed her queries in a manner to get a better feel for the DURAN's ideological positions and political loyalties. This was done in the mode of talking about world affairs as they ostensibly affected her international business interests. Mrs. DURAN repeated earlier points involving their status as members of the Romanian Communist Party, and the positions which both families had in Romanian political and social circles. However, other comments she made also indicated her recognition that the country was hardly a Workers' Paradise or an egalitarian society. Apparently, while they were afforded special privileges as Party members, they were not yet of the rank where they had access to the best stores, housing, and other facilities reserved for senior-level officials. She was hopeful that, based on her husband's professional career and some friends in high places, such as the Consulate General, they would eventually reach this level. Not so much for themselves, she stated, but because they wanted Anton to have all the advantages involved, including education and access to a rewarding career and comfortable lifestyle.

Mrs. DURAN also made mention of another previously discussed subject—the suspicious atmosphere in the Consulate's social community which made her feel uncomfortable around many of the other families.

While not going into great detail, her point was that she really appreciated the opportunity to have a friend outside that circle where she could relax and not have to be concerned about how her every comment might be interpreted and reported to the Consulate's security officer. Brenda expressed empathy for Mrs. DURAN's plight and reconfirmed her interest in maintaining a friendship with her and the family.

The lunch ended with Brenda confident that, in addition to obtaining useful additional assessment information on the family, she had also reinforced her personal rapport with Mrs. DURAN. Her written report to our Headquarters and the Field Office was well received. Even Matt was pleased at the new information about DURAN's dental problems. From the results of Brenda's meeting, we were most interested in exploring the DURAN's views on the unequal living standards they felt and how they viewed the future for themselves and their child. The health issues, like the desire for more spendable funds, could easily be addressed once we knew what we might expect from DURAN in return.

The timing of meetings during the developmental and assessment phase of contact with a Target is always a delicate matter. Too often, the relationship would seem too aggressive and staged. Too infrequently, and the personalization of the relationship would suffer. In this case, based primarily upon Brenda's sense for how Mrs. DURAN was relating to her, we figured that a meeting about every three weeks or so was the right timing. So, in addition to the first restaurant lunch, a total of seven additional meetings were held through the Christmas holiday season.

After the restaurant luncheon, Mrs. DURAN reciprocated with an invitation for a tea time get-together at her residence. That was followed by several hours of shopping and a luncheon date under the guise of Brenda needing new clothes for the oncoming winter weather. The meeting after that was a mid-morning coffee shop affair with Anton present. The next was a coffee get-together at the DURAN residence, most of which took place while Anton took his midday nap.

Then, at Thanksgiving time, Brenda played the old traditional American Thanksgiving Day dinner card and had the DURAN family over to her

CHAPTER EIGHT: MRS. DURAN'S INSIGHTS

apartment for that holiday. She invited Mrs. DURAN to come over in the late morning, while DURAN stayed with the son, to help her prepare all the dishes of the traditional holiday dinner. Brenda explained when she made the invitation that she really was not much of a cook and needed some assistance in preparing the food. However, she emphasized that she really wanted the DURANs to experience this traditional American celebration of friendship. Mrs. DURAN, who was actually an experienced if not great cook, enjoyed learning how to make and cook the traditional dishes. This environment was perhaps the most relaxed of all the meetings and yielded some useful assessment details on both of the DURANs. When DURAN and the child arrived late that afternoon, a pleasant dinner was held and the DURANs left with both full stomachs, leftovers to take home, and pleasant memories of their first Thanksgiving.

The final meeting of the year, since DURAN had numerous social engagements to attend within the City's diplomatic community at that time of year, was a more formal occasion. It was an early evening cocktail party held at Brenda's apartment for a large crowd of her diplomatic and business contacts in the city. The DURANs attended this party as part of the overall guest list, and there was little opportunity for any interaction more than brief social chatter. But, their presence demonstrated that Brenda and DURAN were "business" contacts within the Consulate's activities in city business circles.

During this period, Alice's role as the babysitter turned out not to be as effective as we had hoped. Mrs. DURAN used her for the first restaurant luncheon and then for the shopping spree with Brenda. However, the few times during the period when Mrs. DURAN accompanied her husband to various social events representing the Consulate, they used a Consulate officer's spouse as their babysitter. And, they also did so for Brenda's holiday cocktail party. In attempting to understand how they used, or didn't use, Alice, we decided that perhaps they did not want the Consulate to know they had an American babysitter due to the security guidance they were under regarding having a non-official contact with Americans. This made sense, and also played into our hope that they were developing a way of hiding any relationships that they knew were against the rules.

In any event, Alice never gained the acceptance as a regular babysitter that we had initially hoped for. And, probably from the position of the operational security of the operation, the fact that Mr. and Mrs. DURAN did not risk the exposure of an unauthorized American in their household was a smart idea. However, with her role having been so limited, I had to reconsider another way to get an SA directly involved with the Target. The Field Office continued to push this point, which, from both a bureaucratic and professional perspective, was a point of comfort for them.

Over the course of the several meeting with Mrs. DURAN Brenda had been able to probe into her personal feelings about her family's future, their relationship with their respective families back in Romania, her commitment to the Communist Party, a bit about DURAN's responsibilities at the Consulate and an assortment of other topics and issues which helped us to better understand DURAN and his situation as Stan slowly moved the commercial relationship into more sensitive areas of Romanian business and political activities.

Brenda learned that the DURAN's experience of being posted overseas had affected their view of what constituted a good life. They clearly recognized that even with the special privileges they enjoyed back in Romania as members of the Communist Party, life was better in both commercial and personal terms in the West. According to Mrs. DURAN, they both felt that Anton's future prospects would be greatly enhanced if they could continue to be posted outside the country and he could obtain a Western education, which would give him a significant advantage when seeking a position in Romania.

As to their families back home, the DURANs were well aware that their families' ties to the Communist bureaucracy had helped DURAN get his position and his initial posting abroad. But their actual connections were dated, and a new Communist oligarchy was now in power. Their best hope of future career success was with patrons such as the Consulate General and other senior Ministry officials DURAN had met and cultivated while working at Ministry Headquarters in Bucharest. And to accomplish this, they needed to be able to provide these contacts with "gifts" from their overseas posting—expensive gifts if they were to compete with others also seeking the patronage of those officials. Mrs. DURAN explained this process as simply the way it was in their country, and one had to recognize it and accept it.

From her comments, it also became clear that neither she nor her husband believed in the philosophical, political, or economic tenets of Communism. They had no personal or emotional loyalty to it as a political system, but to live the best they could, they had to learn to use the system as effectively as possible. Mrs. DURAN even expressed some concern, but in a decidedly careful way, that the living standards for the average person in Romania had not improved much since the war and that a frustration with the Communist Party elite was growing. While the Party had the Organs of State necessary to keep itself in power at the moment, in a few years, the situation might change. And, depending upon the outcome, the DURAN family's future might not be very bright.

Another of Brenda's elicitation objectives was to get a better idea of DURAN's duties at the Consulate. While we knew he was the Code Clerk, we and the Field Office were interested in more details about how he actually functioned and what type of communications' traffic he had access to—was it only the political guidance from Bucharest, or did it also include Warsaw Pact reporting? Also, did his access include communications from the Department of State Security, Romania's security and intelligence organization, to its representatives at the Consulate?

In regard to DURAN's communications responsibilities at the Consulate, Mrs. DURAN was willing to discuss her husband's job in a bit of detail. With a bit of gentle prodding, she eventually provided a useful description of his role as the senior officer in the Consulate's Communications Office. The most effective elicitation ploy that Brenda was able to use with Mrs. DURAN on this topic regarded whether DURAN had adequate professional skills that might translate into marketable job skills in the international market. Brenda used this approach as a base for more probing details of how his skills related to his responsibilities. According to Mrs.

DURAN, her husband was both the Communications Office manager and the senior communications technician. In the Romanian version of the technical institute DURAN attended, which was considered equal to a four-year college degree, he learned to maintain and repair radio transmission and reception equipment as well as related electronic devices. Upon employment by the Ministry of Foreign Affairs, he received additional training on the equipment used by the Ministry and other government offices to communicate both domestically and internationally. He also received special training in the handling procedures for the various types of radio communications, which involved his obtaining special permission to process radio traffic from a variety of organs of the state. This was a significant privilege and one given only to a small number of people in the Ministry. This meant that he was a member of a small pool of Ministry personnel able to be assigned to overseas facilities where these types of communications were handled.

Because of his responsibilities, DURAN was the only individual in the Consulate, except for the Consulate General, who had access to all the Consulate radio traffic, at least according to his wife. It was his job to read and direct all the incoming communications to the appropriate office for a response or action. Also, when the Consulate's communications back to offices in Romania, or elsewhere in the world, were sent to the Communications Office for transmittal, it was DURAN who decided how and in what form it would be sent out. According to Mrs. DURAN, this meant that her husband's busiest time was early in the morning when the Consulate opened for business and he had to read and analyze all the correspondence in order to send it to the proper office. For the same reason, the close of the business day at the Consulate was equally busy as DURAN decided how and where to send out the official communications. This corroborated a comment DURAN had made to Brenda early in the relationship while explaining why luncheon appointments fit better into his official schedule than a dinner or breakfast meeting.

Mrs. DURAN stated that if it was a very busy day, her husband might not get home until a couple of hours after the normal closing time for the Consulate. Often, he was the last one to leave the office. Other times, when an urgent message was received on the radio equipment after hours or on the weekend, an alarm would go off at the security guard's desk at the main entrance, and DURAN would be called to come in and review the message and decide who needed to take any action.

She felt that her husband's job was a very important one, with significant responsibility. Yet, because his career field was in the communications section, he was always assigned a low rank in the diplomatic hierarchy at the official installation. She felt this was unfair, and usually meant they received poorer quarters and fewer benefits than regular Ministry diplomats. However, she noted, here DURAN had a good friend in the Consulate General, and was given additional responsibilities to make contacts in the local business community because he had a better command of English than many of the other Consulate personnel.

While seemingly a slow period in the operation, these five months provided useful assessment information as well as the establishment of the "commercial" relationship with DURAN. Yet, it was also characterized by some all too frequent nagging from both our Headquarters and the Field Office to move the developmental process along faster. In other words, it was the middle of the assessment and development phase, and everyone not directly involved in the operation was in a hurry to get to the recruitment phase. Unfortunately, from the bureaucratic perspective, developing a solid feel for an individual and testing their willingness to commit more and more serious actions is not an activity that can be "bottom-lined" as in a production line process. Humans don't necessarily respond on a given schedule, and interpersonal trust and confidence, let alone careful manipulation of events and motivations, take time and the proper environment. Sadly, even when field-experienced COs at Headquarters become managers, they often forget these realities. So, while actually a very interesting and at times exciting part of a human acquisition operation, this phase in the process can also be greatly frustrating.

We Americans really do have a short attention span when compared with most other cultures. We want things done quickly even when we understand that patience is the best tactic to employ. Plus, the period involving the Thanksgiving through New Year's holiday season often means an operation has to take second place to other social and professional commitments by the target.

Brenda's role working on Mrs. Duran for details on the Target and their personal lives was providing useful assessment information without doubt, and this remained her primary responsibility in the operation. Her elicitation requirements continued to be to obtain additional details on the DURAN's financial desires, their dedication to the Romanian Communist Party, their personal goals and desires, and be alert to any feedback indicating how DURAN was responding to his "commercial dealings." Also, she was to observe if the additional funds DURAN was receiving from these dealings were being spent in any manner that might call attention to him from security personnel at the Consulate.

As noted previously, a basic rule every CO is taught is that once an agent accepts financial compensation, it is the CO's responsibility to see that those funds are not expended in a manner that threatens the security of the operation. Perhaps the most common indicator to any security or counterintelligence officer of potential disloyal behavior on the part of an individual is a sudden and unexplained level of spending beyond his or her accepted standard of living. So, every CO has "the talk" with the individual about being careful in how the funds are spent. And, after the conversation, the agent nods approvingly and expresses appreciation for the CO's personal concern for the agent's safety and security. Of course, the agent then argues as to why he needs the entire payment at once and promises to spend it slowly and carefully in a manner that represents no threat to his clandestine relationship. This is a promise that is seldom kept. And, one of the key points of personal conflict throughout any operation is the CO constantly struggling with the agent's very human desire to enjoy the fruits of his clandestine labor versus the genuine concern that such behavior will cause him security concerns.

So, we hoped, attempting to embed Brenda in a monitoring role regarding DURAN's use of his operational funds would provide an objective insight that Stan could use to both fashion his on-going guidance to DURAN and gauge the security of the operation.

Chapter Nine: Moving Duran Along

As the primary CO for the operation, Stan's objective continued to be conditioning DURAN to taking more and more risks by providing proprietary and classified information from the Consulate. During this phase Stan was able to hold five personal meetings with DURAN, all premised on Stan's supposed traveling to the city from the West Coast. To enhance the security of the operation, Stan had moved the venue from public restaurants to hotel suites, where he was ostensibly resided while visiting the city.

During this period, our reporting and planning procedures with Ralph and his SAs remained the same. Ralph was, on the whole, pretty satisfied with the manner and timing of our progress—Matt and BJ a bit less so. Equally important, Stan was developing a personal relationship with Larry, which was most helpful in keeping Larry somewhat in our corner.

Winston and I did our best to keep our Headquarters satisfied. Stan's contact reports demonstrated that developmental progress was being made with the target. In separate communications, I kept senior Headquarters managers informed. The one point I did not have to dwell on was how valuable the Romanian communications would be to the U.S. Government.

A few years earlier, a senior Romanian intelligence officer, Ion Mihai Pacepa, had walk-in to the American Embassy in Bonn, Germany, and wanted to defect. He had been the head of the Industrial Espionage Directorate of the Romanian intelligence service, and also had significant information in general about overall foreign intelligence activities by the Romanian Government. He was flown to the United States and

CHAPTER NINE: MOVING DURAN ALONG

comprehensively debriefed over the course of several months by Agency and FBI officers. His background in the Romanian intelligence service gave him access to so many of their activities that then President Nicolae Ceausescu ordered that he be assassinated. Thus, he was kept isolated and under heavy guard for several years, but his information on Romanian intelligence activities in the United States was made available to Agency Stations and FBI Field Offices where that country had an official or commercial presence. In my city, the Consulate did have Intelligence Officers, separate from the Security Officers, and they were involved in conducting collection and influence operations in the city and region. The senior Security Officer was in charge of both security and intelligence activities for the Consulate. The Field Officer believed it had identified the Intelligence Officers assigned to the Consulate and, by monitoring their activities, had a pretty good idea of their local agents and activities. However, they were not sure they had complete visibility on all the intelligence operations, thinking there might be another Intelligence officer at the Consulate working under the cover of a regular diplomat or trade representative, and there was a possibility that a non-officially covered officer, an illegal in Soviet intelligence parlance, might also be in the city or its environs handling particularly sensitive collection operations. If we were able to convince DURAN to provide the tapes, the Field Office would have full insight into all Romanian intelligence activities in the area. So would we, and we probably would have a slightly different approach as to how this information was translated into effective counterintelligence actions.

As we pondered this information and Brenda's insights provided by Mrs. Duran, Stan was busy working the Target. Five days after DURAN accepted the watch as his "commission" for the oil information, he showed up on time for his follow-up meeting with Stan at the restaurant. Stan followed the usual pattern for a developmental meeting: initial rapport building and social conversation only then to be followed by specific reporting requirements to be fulfilled. In this case, Stan spent about half an hour, from the pre luncheon drinks to the start of actually eating lunch, gauging

DURAN's mood and judging how their personal rapport had developed. Once he felt that DURAN seemed comfortable, he spent a few more minutes discussing in general terms some of the humorous interactions he had recently had with his supposed clients. After getting a couple of laughs from DURAN, Stan reaffirmed his interest in any information DURAN may have seen regarding purchases or sales of the Romanian Government.

DURAN responded that within the last few days, he had tried to pay attention to any such information that came into the Consulate, but very little had been received. He explained that while one of the main purposes of the Consulate was to promote trade, it also had responsibilities to promote and explain Romanian Government policies and to provide assistance to Romanian citizens in the city. And, the majority of theinformation from Bucharest involved these tasks. Stan said he understood, and personally hoped that United States relations with Romania would eventually adopt a more realistic international approach in trade and commerce.

DURAN then mentioned, "I have seen one piece of trade information that might be of some interest, a report that the Romanian Government is planning to purchase some East German military equipment, mostly armored vehicles." As he told Stan about the size and cost of the anticipated order, he appeared somewhat concerned. Stan noticed this and after getting the details asked DURAN if there was anything wrong? DURAN looked down at the table and said, "I am uncomfortable discussing military things because of their sensitivity in my country."

Stan responded with a variation of a CO's set speech on how carefully any information obtained would be handled, how the source of the information would be well shielded from anyone's knowledge, and how important it was in their relationship that DURAN's cooperation remained a secret between them. Now, while this is a standard response well practiced by all COs, it is also the truth: the protection of the identity of the source and the method of obtaining the information are both personal and professional obligations that the CO owes to the agent.

Stan speculated on how this information might be used to make a

CHAPTER NINE: MOVING DURAN ALONG

little money for both of them. He asked DURAN how widely known this information was, and DURAN said that within the Consulate, the communication had been distributed to senior officers in the trade and military sections, as well as, of course, to the Office of the Consulate General. He added that while it was not marked "officially" as a classified or controlled document, it was to be handled as a "protected" document. Stan took this all in and told DURAN, in a most sincere manner, that he would be particularly careful in his use of this information.

Stan than speculated on whether some money could be made on hedging against the stock of any other companies outside of the Warsaw Pact that might be involved in the order? Obviously, there was no way to invest in the East German company since it was state-owned. DURAN responded that he had no idea if his government had been considering the purchase from other sources. Stan said that he could check this out through his international "grey" arms contacts.

Stan then changed the subject to more rapport building topics and stayed on this theme through coffee and dessert. Just before paying the bill, Stan advised DURAN that he would be back in town early the next month, and at that time should have some news on whether or not the East German purchase information had been of any financial value. He suggested DURAN meet him for lunch, at a different restaurant he named a bit further away from the Consulate area. Stan said that he had heard this was a particularly good restaurant, with an excellent selection of rare scotches. DURAN agreed and noted the date and time in his pocket calendar. This caused Stan to make a mental note that at the next meeting he would have to reinforce the point that their "business relationship" must remain a secret between them.

Once again, DURAN departed the restaurant first, with Stan following about ten minutes later after finishing a coffee refill the waiter provided along with the paid check. Yes, COs are required to provide receipts for developmental meals.

This meeting was, at our request, surveilled in its entirety from DURAN's departure from the Consulate until he returned to the Consulate. The

Field Office's Special Surveillance Unit did not place people inside the restaurant, but did have both mobile and static positions. In fact, since DURAN knew the date, time and location of the meeting, surveillance had been placed on the Consulate since it opened that morning in case anyone there went to the restaurant and established themselves before Stan and DURAN met. Our reasoning for this, which in the past on occasion we had opposed as a potential risk, was basic counterintelligence concerns. Had DURAN become suspicious of Stan, or simply concerned about his own part in providing Consulate information, this meeting would have been an opportunity to have the Consulate's security personnel follow him to the meeting and then take additional measures to identify Stan and ascertain his true motives. No surveillance from the Consulate was observed—another indication that the operation was moving along nicely.

Once Stan forwarded his report to Headquarters, he began doing some research on the information DURAN provided. Since it was military-related, we hoped it was sensitive and represented an indicator of DURAN's willingness to provide such information. However, when Headquarters responded, it noted that this was well known in international defense circles. It had been mentioned recently in Jane's Defense Weekly publication, a publication reporting on military and corporate affairs.It was reported that the original purchase offer had been circulated to both French and Italian defense industry companies as well as to East Germany.

Did this mean that DURAN had been a bit more dramatic in his packaging of the information? Or, that within the Consulate this was considered sensitive information? Did it matter in any event? No. DURAN had provided information which he hoped would result in financial gain, and packaged it in such a way as to indicate that he was acting outside of his official capacity. This was good news. Now, Stan had to do some thinking as to how to explain making a couple of thousand dollars on the information, and rewarding DURAN with a few hundred dollars in cash.

However, to cover all the bases, I asked Matt to check his monitoring of "activities," meaning their electronic and human sources, in the Consulate to determine if he could find any indication of how the information on the East German military purchase was being considered. After a three-day wait, he advised that his sources had heard nothing about the subject. This information, or more appropriately, the lack thereof, only meant that, being optimistic, we could hope the information was as closely held within the Consulate as DURAN had stated.

After some thought, and some research on the French and Italian companies mentioned, Stan came up with a plausible story regarding how he had made money based upon DURAN's information. He would tell DURAN that he had taken a "short position" on the stock of a French company, which he had learned had made a bid on the Romanian military contract, on the French stock market. In effect, he had purchased an option that the company's shares would go down in value once the loss of the sale was known in the marketplace. What he did not tell DURAN, and we were pretty sure that DURAN would not have the interest to research on his own, was that the French company had also experienced a labor disruption months before and this several days shutdown would be reflected in its stock price when its semi-annual profit estimate was provided to investors. While the anticipated stock price drop would probably be only a few francs, Stan would explain that he had created a twenty-five thousand dollar profit by "shorting" on several hundreds of thousands of shares.

If this sounds like a story a con man would come up with to trick some greedy investor, that is exactly what it was. After all, good COs shares many of the same personality and intellectual traits of the con man—but, of course, they are doing it for good not evil. The type of research Stan did was also quite typical of the research a CO must use in any developmental operation. Targets vary a great deal: military, political, financial, etc. Yet, to interact in a manner to sustain contact with the Target, they must be able to discuss subjects of the target's interest and provide explanations for actions that fit into the area of expertise of the Target. Thus, after many years of operating in the field, a CO develops a wide, if perhaps not very deep, level of knowledge in a larger number of fields. An interesting corollary to acquisition of certain expertise is that during the reporting phase the Case Officer must continue to study and stay current in the field in which the agent is reporting in order to know what questions to ask, what information to have clarified for reporting, and if the information being provided by the agent does not seem accurate. While Reports Officers and analysts at Headquarters also carefully review all reporting for accuracy, it is still the CO's responsibility to constantly verify his agent's reporting.

Once Stan explained his proposed story, and I was sure I fully understood it since high finance is not my strong suite, we decided it was time to run it by the SAs. So, we invited Ralph, Matt, and Larry to the Station. As might be expected, stock market manipulation was not a topic well known or understood by these guys. Perhaps if they had been involved in white collar crime, they would have known a bit more. Thus, they asked some very logical and basic questions about how one "shorted" a foreign stock, how thousands of shares could be held for several weeks with only marginal expenses, and how an American investor could operate in the French stock market. Stan was able to explain all these issues to their satisfaction. And, this was actually a very useful exercise, just in case DURAN asked similar questions, which we strongly suspected he would not, since we hoped that his only interest was in his commission.

At the conclusion of the discussion the SAs expressed approval with the story, and Ralph complimented Stan on the thoroughness of his preparation. So, Stan was set for the next meeting as soon as we agreed on what other operational objectives we wanted accomplished and, certainly an important question, how much money he should offer to DURAN as a commission. We decided that the most important objective of the meeting was to get DURAN to accept the funds and desire more. To this end Stan would have to carefully explain to DURAN that the more sensitive information he could provide on a timely basis, then the more opportunity Stan would have to be able to profit from it. To what degree Stan would have to explain to DURAN how his role as the source would be protected was left up to Stan's perceptions of what was necessary to make DURAN comfortable.

The question of the size of the commission took a while to decide. It had to be large enough to motivate DURAN to provide more information, and be willing to take the risk necessary to do so, but not so large as to dampen future risk-taking requests without very high financial compensation. We did not want to price ourselves out of the market when we got down to the really sensitive tasking. So, we finally decided that two hundred and fifty dollars was an appropriate amount. Stan would explain the amount by noting that while the information had been actionable, it was not all that sensitive within the international defense industry. In fact, Stan had only been able to make a couple of thousand dollars in commission himself, which after his expenses, was not very much.

Not knowing whether DURAN would find the two hundred and fifty dollars acceptable, it was decided that Stan would make a point of explaining that bigger profits were available based upon the type of information DURAN could provide. He would be commensurate with DURAN regarding the small payback, and attempt to engage him in a discussion of what additional types of information might translate into more profitable stock speculations for them.

Stan had to be careful not to push too hard at this point. We still were not sure of DURAN's tolerance level for risk-taking, or for that matter, his personal sense of loyalty and ethics concerning the type of government information he was willing to pass for personal financial gain.

Thus, it was agreed our objectives for this meeting were specifically three: have DURAN accept the two hundred and fifty dollars' commission, involve him in determining how and what more profitable information he could provide through his official duties, and carefully try to gauge his acceptable level of both risk taking and willingness to provide sensitive information. An optional fourth objective, depending upon how DURAN reacted to the "commission" and the discussion of obtaining more profitable information, was to arrange the next meeting in a hotel room rather than a public space such as a restaurant. Stan would explain this in terms of the press of business he anticipated during his next visit to the city, also noting that he and DURAN could have lunch in his hotel room. Moving the site of their meetings out of public view was an operational security step, and DURAN's agreement might be seen as a subtle recognition of the "private" nature of their relationship.

The meeting at the new restaurant, this time an upscale Italian place about three miles from the Consulate, went pretty well. The usual pattern of drinks, appetizers, main course, dessert, and after-meal drinks kept the luncheon going for a bit over two hours. DURAN was relaxed and quite friendly with Stan, even talking a little about his relationship with his son. Interestingly, he also mentioned that he had been busy at the Consulate, doing both his regular work and assisting the Consulate General in handling some matters with the local Romanian community. He even noted that his expanding role in Consulate activities was causing a bit of friction with some of the other officers. When asked if this could cause him trouble, he brushed it aside by reminding Stan that he and the Consulate General were close friends.

Before the main course was served, and after DURAN had downed two expensive, single malt scotches, Stan began his well-rehearsed story about the rather small commercial value of the information DURAN had provided on the East German military purchase. DURAN listened intensely as Stan explained "The profitability of the information was rather small and your commission would only be two hundred and fifty dollars." Yet, DURAN actually seemed very pleased to receive that amount and happily accepted the cash, which was passed to him in the middle pages of a current copy of a local newspaper. Stan made a point of explaining that he did not want anyone to notice that DURAN was taking any money, as it might give even the most casual observer the wrong idea. DURAN agreed it was a necessary safety measure in their commercial relationship. While DURAN did not ask any questions about how Stan was able to profit on the information, Stan nevertheless provided a shorten description of his stock manipulations to booster his commercial cover story.

Stan then asked if DURAN had been able to acquire any more information that might prove profitable. DURAN responded, rather apologetically, that he had not seen anything that he felt might be in that category. He explained that he had read all the commercial messages since their last meeting, but nothing he believed to be of interest had been received. Stan adopted an understanding manner, noting that he knew DURAN had done his best and that he was sorry that nothing has turned up. He further explained that this was common in his business. He noted that he spent a significant amount of his time searching out bits of information and only a small amount of time actually working the stock market to generate a profit.

During the main course Stan began a discussing how they could improve their profits based upon what DURAN might be able to provide. Stan said "If you were to give me a better sense of what information you see on a daily basis, perhaps together we can figure out how to exploit it." DURAN responded somewhat defensively, stating that as the Consulate Communications Officer, he saw all the correspondence coming into and going out of the installation. However, because it consisted of a wide range of political, economic, personnel, and other topics as well as commercial issues, he hardly had time to read all of it. Stan expressed his understanding of the situation and empathy for DURAN's position which must be very demanding in terms of time and effort. He then suggested, "The economic and commercial streams of correspondence, along with any political information that might impact such issues, probably represented the most useful source for future profits." DURAN thought about this for several seconds before responding that this made sense. He agreed that he would concentrate his reading in these areas, and also expressed the hope that future commissions would be forthcoming. Stan replied that he also hoped so, but in reality it all depended upon the information and how quickly he could move to profit from it.

With the after luncheon drink, and DURAN preferring a cognac with his espresso, Stan suggested that they arrange their next meeting now so that both could place it in their schedules. He explained it would be another three weeks before he would return from the West Coast, and that in another step to keep their relationship discreet, perhaps they should have lunch in Stan's hotel suite, where there would be less chance anyone saw them. Stan further explained that he valued DURAN both as a friend and a commercial contact, and didn't want any of his business competitors in the city to know he was so involved with DURAN. The Target responded that it was probably a good idea, and then noted that it probably was best if no one from the Consulate observed their meetings as well, since he was "moonlighting" in this commercial relationship.

Stan gave DURAN the name of the hotel where he planned to stay, and advised him to call from the lobby phone when he arrived there on the date and at the time agreed upon. DURAN wrote it down in his pocket diary. Stan was able to observe that he did not use Stan's name in the entry—very good. Operational security was being slowly integrated into the relationship.

While no new information had been obtained from DURAN, I was pleased with Stan's report of the meeting. The Field Office seemed equally pleased.

From the Station's perspective, we wanted a better understanding of DURAN's activities with his friend, the Consulate General, and with whom at the Consulate frictions were developing over such activities. These factors could well have an effect upon the operation, yet the Field Office had not mentioned them during our planning sessions. It turned out that Matt simply did not realize we would be interested in this type of information until we explained why we needed it and why it was important in operational terms.

About ten days before the next scheduled meeting with DURAN, Winston, Stan and I sat down with Ralph and Matt at the Station to address these issues. I had spoken with Ralph a couple of days earlier, so the SAs were prepared to answer our questions once we explained our concerns.

Matt stated that surveillance of the Consulate General's and DURAN's interactions with the local Romanian community, verified by FBI "sources" not further defined, showed that in one case they had taken several crates of duty free liquor and sold it to a Romanian businessman who owned three neighborhood bars in the northwest suburbs of the city. In a second case, they had accepted several hundred dollars from another former Romanian citizen, now an American citizen, for promises of assisting a family member in Romania obtaining a passport for travel to the United States. In both cases, Matt explained, DURAN's share of the profits was in the less than a hundred-dollar range, with about two-thirds of the money kept by the Consulate General. This helped us better understand why the Target had been quite happy to receive two hundred and fifty dollars for the East German purchase information. We now had a much better idea of his perception of task versus profit.

As to the conflict within the Consulate, apparently the senior commercial officer was upset that he was being cut out of the duty-free liquor sale, and the head of the political section was angry that he had not benefited from the Consulate General's influence in handling the passport request. The Field Office felt that while these individuals were not happy with DURAN's closeness to the Consulate General, the Consulate was a nest of illegal activities, and incidents of personal jealousy among the staff were frequent. Matt noted that the Consulate General, while politically powerful thanks to senior "friends" both in the Ministry of Foreign Affairs and the Romanian Government, did make it a habit to spread around opportunities for his officials to make these types of private deals. So, Ralph and Matt doubted if the anger at DURAN was more than transitory.

Winston asked whether the Field Office had been able to use these illegal activities to their advantage in manipulating any of the Consulate officials. Matt looked at the floor, while Ralph seemed quite thoughtful before answering. He stated, "Many Eastern European Consulates are engaged in similar activities within their local immigrant communities." Apparently, it was a bureaucratically acceptable activity as long as some of the profits found their way back to officials' "friends" in their country's ministries and government. So, the local officials had little fear in terms of their careers, as their seniors already knew this was going on. "Also," Ralph noted, "since the officials involved had diplomatic status, any criminal prosecution for actions illegal in the United States would not be possible." He continued, "The only leverage the FBI has would be the public embarrassment and international propaganda value that such exposes would have on the countries involved. And, the Department of State, which is kept well informed of such activities, usually argued that the risk of punitive actions against American diplomats posted abroad in these countries was not worth the value of any exposure." " Obviously," Ralph noted," this is a constant point of friction and frustration between the State Department and the Bureau. "

Later, we were to learn that other crimes, such as shoplifting and traffic accidents resulting in injuries, were a different matter and might be exploited by the Bureau to induce cooperation by foreign officials posted in the United States. As specific to this case, Matt's squad had been able to use the threat of exposure of the wife of a low-level Romanian Government employee at the Consulate, who was not covered by diplomat immunity, who had been very active in shoplifting in the downtown area to induce his cooperation. His reporting on daily events at the Consulate provided a useful window for the Field Office, but his lack of status did not provide much access within the installation. However, this knowledge would later enable us to add certain carefully worded questions into Matt's SA's debriefing of his source in support of the DURAN operation.

As the site for the first hotel room meeting, Stan selected a four-star hotel located on the fringes of the city's shopping district. He called the hotel and made a reservation for two nights in his commercial alias, using his alias credit card to reserve a small suite, which consisted of a bedroom and a separate sitting room. I should add that he made the reservations only after we had checked with the Field Office to determine that the hotel was not a "hot spot" for any illegal or other kinds of activity that might suddenly bring it to the attention of the police, press, or public. This precaution reflected operational respect for Murphy's Law—anything that can go wrong will go wrong. More than one sensitive operation by the Agency was exposed to public scrutiny accidentally by conducting a meeting at a location where, for reasons in no way connected to the operation, the local police raided a criminal group or a local politician was exposed by the press as he departed after an inappropriate meeting with someone, usually a local businessman or young woman.

In this case, we also wanted to be sure no individuals worked at the hotel who were associated with the Consulate or the local Romanian community. We did not want DURAN recognized in the hotel, or to find that the room service waiter might recognize him. Ralph checked with the various units: Romanian Squad, Criminal Squad, White Collar Crime Squad, and Political Corruption Squad. He reported back that the hotel seemed "clean" based on Field Office investigations. He also had informally checked with the city police, in a discreet manner, and found they did not consider the hotel as a site under investigation.

Early in the evening prior to the meeting, Stan drove his car to the general parking area of the downtown train station and parked in the long term section. He took his one traveling suitcase, which he had carefully checked to ensure all identification material therein was related to his commercial alias persona, walked through the train terminal, used the various shops and corridors as a countersurveillance maze, and then proceeded to hail a taxi to the hotel. His check-in was uneventful, and his small suite was comfortable. The sitting area provided an area for a served lunch as well as a lengthy conversation. That evening, he went down to the hotel's bar and had a drink while casually engaging the bartender in a conversation about his train travel from the West Coast. He mentioned a funny story about an interaction with a fellow passenger. Upon leaving, he left a generous tip for the bartender. His behavior had a purpose: it was to strengthen his alias cover. Should anyone, for example Romanian security personnel from the Consulate, start snooping around the hotel and ask about him because of his meeting with DURAN, assuming the worst and that DURAN had either been followed or had reported Stan's activities, both the hotel's front desk and bartender would support the alias role Stan was playing.

The next morning Stan departed the hotel, and while dropping his key at the front desk mentioned he had a busy morning with a local client. He then conducted a previously planned counter-surveillance route for about an hour and a half. When satisfied he was not being surveilled, he stopped in a coffee shop and drank a cup of coffee, and read the local newspaper for about half an hour. He then returned to the hotel to await DURAN's arrival.

DURAN called the suite from the lobby phone almost to the minute of the scheduled time. Stan provided the room number, and the Target was soon knocking on the door. As DURAN took a seat in the sitting area, Stan produced a bottle of single malt Glen Haven scotch he had brought with him. He presented the bottle to DURAN for his inspection and comments. DURAN expressed his satisfaction with the scotch, and Stan pour two glasses, without water or ice to weaken the flavor, for them. After both took their first sip, Stan began the usual rapport building social conversation. He asked how DURAN was doing and if his responsibilities at the Consulate were as busy as ever. DURAN responded appropriately, then asking how the trip from the West Coast had been and how long Stan was planning to stay in town this time. After about fifteen minutes, and as Stan poured a second round of scotch, they got down to business.

Stan asked the Target if he had come across any commercial information of value to his clients since they had last met. DURAN responded that there did not seem to be much commercial activity at the moment by the Romanian Government or its State Industries. He had read all the commercial correspondence carefully and found nothing that he believed Stan would find of interest. DURAN continued that, realizing they were going to meet soon he decided to search the economic and political section correspondence as well, since he did not want to come to meet his friend empty-handed. However, even with this additional effort, he was not sure he had any information that might prove profitable to them. As Stan began to commensurate with DURAN's situation, internally he was also starting to wonder if the Target had developed second thoughts about working with him. DURAN then announced, "I do have one bit of information which may be of interest. In a political note, I read of a Soviet—Polish trade deal with India. The deal would involve Poland providing heavy machine equipment for flat mill steel production in India. The heavy equipment would be shipped by sea to India." DURAN wondered if this information might somehow be exploited? He noted, "The deal would involve a great many shipments over several years." Stan said he was not sure if he could use this information, but perhaps if he knew more about the Soviet role in the deal there might be an angle there which could provide an opportunity for profit.

As DURAN was about to respond, a knock on the door and the call of "room service" indicated that lunch was about to be served. This stopped all business talk until the waiter had set the coffee table and brought out the plates of food. Stan signed the check and ushered the waiter out the door.

Apparently, this brief interval had given DURAN time to reflect on what he was going to say. As Stan sat down, the Target took a swig of his scotch and proceeded to explain "The Soviet portion of the trade deal was actually a very sensitive matter." He looked Stan directly in the eye and warned that what he was about to tell Stan was a secret, and Stan must never reveal that he heard this from him. Ignoring his luncheon plate, the Target said, "The steel production equipment from Poland is only the pubic reason for the shipments to India. While some such heavy equipment will be sent, most of each shipment will be spare parts to update various pieces of military equipment for the Indian Armed Forces. This will include aircraft parts for navigation, radio, and defensive electronics for older MIG models which the Indian Air Force is currently flying."

At this point, as he later noted in his report, Stan was straining to look calm and pensive while internally feeling that rush a CO experiences when an operational threshold has been passed. Stan responded that he wanted to give this some thought, and suggested they eat their lunch while he considered how this information could be used. DURAN, whose body language seemed to demonstrate that he had just overcome a significant emotional hurdle, began to eat slowly. As he ate, his composure slowly became more relaxed. Stan also began eating, trying to mask the excitement he was experiencing at the news of the Soviet—Indian plan.

For several minutes, they ate in silence until DURAN asked if there might be something in the information that could produce some profits for them. Stan responded slowly and carefully, explaining that the shipping aspect of the deal, since it would be conducted over a lengthy period of time and require a significant number of ships, might be an exploitable position.

But, he added, he needed more details about the Soviet involvement to better gauge the total amount of equipment involved and the number and time frame of the shipments involved. DURAN said that he only had some general details, as the correspondence was a communication from a Warsaw Pact office and only sent to the Consulate because all the United States Soviet Bloc installations, including the offices at the United Nations, were instructed to carefully leak the news that the Polish State Industries had secured a profitable deal to supply Indian with steel making equipment. This was to be done to hide the actual transfer of military items.

As the meal continued, DURAN provided what few specific facts he had about the type of military equipment that was to be sent in the Polish shipments. Just as they started on dessert, Stan excused himself for a bathroom break. Entering the bedroom area, he went into the bathroom, locked the door, sat down on the bathtub rim, and hurriedly wrote down the specifics he could remember about the Soviet parts to be sent to India. Obviously, he had not expected such information, and wanted to be sure this memory was supported by at least some notes. He completed his notes, flushed the toilet, splashed about in the sink, dried his hands, and rejoined DURAN, who was now quite relaxed and enjoying his chocolate torte and coffee.

Stan offered DURAN an after lunch glass of the Glen Haven, and poured a small one for himself. He then went into a lengthy, and purposely complicated, explanation of how he might be able to identify the shipping company from international transportation records. If so, and if it were publicly traded on some exchange, this increase in business would result in a share price increase which he could capture with a futures trade assignment. However, if it were a state-owned company, he would have to look at another aspect of the deal. For example, what transportation firm in India would be involved in offloading the equipment and trucking it to the various end locations? Could this company be a potential source of profitability? Depending upon who owed it, or perhaps could buy it, these shipments might provide a good profit. Stan continued with several other potential options and interspersed his discussion with financial trading terms meant to further impress DURAN. This seemed to work, as DURAN's face began to glaze over as Stan's musings became more and more complex and intricate.

Stan completed his speech with the recommendation that DURAN continue to read all the Consulate communications related to this matter, as any additional information might assist in identifying how profit could be made. He then closed the meeting by stating his appreciation for the hard work DURAN had done to find something of interest for both their benefit. He told DURAN to be very careful in his searching for more details; since the information was secret Stan wanted to make sure that DURAN did not get into any trouble. In fact, Stan noted, they both probably should be careful in their future meetings in order to protect their relationship. In this regard, he noted that he would be back in town from the West Coast in a little less than two weeks. He suggested they again meet at this hotel on the 23rd of the month at the same time, with DURAN again calling from the lobby phone. At that time Stan should have a better idea of if and how this information might prove profitable. Recognizing that at this point in their relationship DURAN's greatest personal concern probably was that he not be exposed as the source of the secret information, Stan decided to answer the question before it was asked. Just before DURAN departed, Stan firmly stated that as personal friends as well as business colleagues, he recognized that it was his responsibility not to allow the information on the Soviet-India deal, or for the matter any information he received from DURAN, to ever be traceable back to DURAN. He noted that in his business, he often obtained sensitive information from people inside various companies who spoke without the authority and approval of their corporate officials. And, only by carefully protecting these individuals could he continue to be successful and profitable for all concerned. Stan stated, with a most sincere look in his eyes, that this was both a personal and professional responsibility that he could never betray.

This was, of course, very true, but DURAN did not understand the real context of the statement.

However, he was now in very deep and his willingness to continue would depend to a large degree not only on the rewards he received, but also on the confidence he had that he would not get caught. That meant he had to trust Stan. They were now engaged in a classic conspiracy, which would only deepen as the real objective of the operation became clear.

Upon hearing and reading Stan's report, we were "pleased" as Winston would say in true British understatement. His report was sent to Headquarters, with a request for comments on the validity and value of the information on the Soviet—India deal. The next morning a meeting was arranged between Ralph, Matt, Winston and me at the Field office. We brought a copy of the report and added some oral comments Stan had made about the atmospherics of the meeting and DURAN's personal reactions during it.

Both SAs were congratulatory of Stan's fine work. Matt, being his usual aggressive self, commented that now DURAN had committed to stealing secrets, we should focus on getting information from the Consulate's Code Room. After a lengthy discussion on various issues mentioned in Stan's report, I began to explain the Agency's perspective on the status of the operation.

From our perspective, we had an individual with probable access to communications at the local Romanian Consulate. DURAN claimed access to traffic of commercial, economic, political, and military topics, and his most recent information seemed to demonstrate he also had access to communications regarding the plans and activities of the Warsaw Pact. We believed he was the Code Clerk, responsible for encoding all outgoing communications and decoding all incoming communications. We did not know if he also handled communications regarding security and intelligence activities. We had information from both DURAN and indirectly from his wife that he was the senior communications officer and often the last to depart at night due to his responsibilities. His interaction with Stan clearly demonstrated a desire to make some additional money, and he seemed willing to take some risks to accomplish this. From the wife and a few comments made by DURAN, we had some general ideas regarding what he wanted and needed the money for. Thanks to FBI sources, we also knew that DURAN had established a pattern of making money on the side through illegal transactions, often in cooperation with his friend, the Consulate General. And, based upon Stan's most recent meeting, he appeared willing to share "secret" information in the hope of obtaining some financial benefit. This was, indeed, all good, and the operation was moving in the right direction.

However, (and I could see Ralph and Matt grimace when I said "however") at this point, we do not know if the information he provided on the Soviet—India deal is true, nor whether it is really considered to be sensitive by the Warsaw Pact. Our Headquarters should be able to give us a better perspective on this within a few days. DURAN could be inflating the importance of the information in hopes of a better commission, or he could have made the entire topic up as part of a counterintelligence ploy by the Romanian security service to manipulate what they had identified as an intelligence operation against one of their personnel.

I concluded by stating that I had no reason to think that DURAN was a counterintelligence ploy. Indeed, we had initiated the contact and taken thoughtful counterintelligence actions of our own as the relationship developed. Our operational security practices had also been professional. There were no indications of any security problems with the operation itself. Therefore once we learned what, if anything, the United States intelligence Community knew about this Soviet—India military transaction, and the Polish machine trade cover story to protect it, we would have a better measurement of DURAN's motivation regarding his relationship with Stan.

I then attempted to refocus the real operational objective in Ralph's, and Matt's, mind: we wanted access to the full range of the Consulate's communications' material. That was the prize. And, our activities to date were meant to test and manipulate DURAN's desire for additional funds within the context of motivating him to accept greater and greater risks.

I concluded by noting that one very important aspect of his motivation still remained a total mystery to us: how loyal, or at least committed, was he to his country and the Romanian Communist Party? So far, he had not provided any information directly harmful to either entity. From his wife's comments, both accepted their place in the Party and were well aware of the benefits their membership provided. And, even if any personal loyalty they had to the country and the Party was purely pragmatic, would DURAN be willing to risk betraying it? If so, what would be the price both in terms of the confidence he would demand that it could be done safely, and how much would it cost to pay for his risk?

My speech, after the excitement generated by Stan's report, gave the SAs some important issues to consider. To their credit, after some discussion, they agreed that while progress was being made, we still had a ways to go. Ralph then asked how we saw the operation moving over the next several meetings. I responded that the first thing we needed was to verify the truth and details of the Soviet–India deal. And, I assured them that just as soon as our Headquarters responded, we would get back to them with the information. Then, from a position of knowledge, we could plan our next moves.

Headquarters responded to Stan's report within a day and a half, praising his handling of the case to date, and expressing an optimistic attitude that the DURAN operation was moving along smoothly. Their correspondence advised that they were in contact with the operations support desks of India and the Soviet Union, as well as analysts in the Directorate of Intelligence. In this regard, they were pulling together all the information the United States Government had on this deal. They anticipated it would take several days to check with the various elements within the U.S. Intelligence Community that would have knowledge about this matter.

Two days later, we received a reply stating that knowledge about the military sale had been received from our Station in New Delhi, and the National Security Agency had collected some communications discussing it in general terms. Headquarters added that Agency assets were well placed to monitor the shipments, and even when the new equipment was installed and functioning. However, the information that the Romanian Government, and other Warsaw Pact nations, had been instructed to discreetly spread the Polish heavy equipment sale cover story was not

CHAPTER NINE: MOVING DURAN ALONG

known. Stan was asked to write a field intelligence report focused upon the Polish cover story aspect of the military sale. He did so quickly, and we were careful to cite a "social contact with proven access to the information reported" as the source of the information. At this point, we did not want to further identify DURAN by specific position or access as the intelligence source. His potential future value was much greater than reporting this type of information.

Headquarters also advised that we should pass the information they had provided to the FBI Field Office, and noted that they had already passed the information to FBI Headquarters. We immediately arranged a meeting at the Field office, hoping to be able to provide Ralph with the news before his own Headquarters did so. We also took along a draft copy of Stan's intelligence report.

That afternoon, when he arrived at the Field Office, Winston and I were greeted warmly by Ralph, who then called Matt into his office. Both SAs carefully read the communications apparently, we had beaten FBI Headquarters in getting the word to the Field Office. Once finished reading, Ralph expressed his satisfaction with the way the operation was progressing. And, I made a point of noting how cooperation between the two organizations was enabling our success to date. Matt was more interested in knowing what the next step would be now that we knew DURAN had provided accurate and sensitive information. I responded that we had developed a general concept of how to proceed, but first wanted to hear their views.

This was problematic because if they came up with anything we felt was ill-advised or presented operational security risks, we would have to find an acceptable way of negotiating these issues. But, asking their views was a necessary part of this "joint" operation. Luckily, or perhaps based upon his personal experience, Ralph noted that so far our plans had been successful and he was interested in hearing our future planning. Matt followed his boss's lead and only stated that it was about time to get an FBI SA involved in the operation in an undercover role.

We were well aware that bureaucratically life would be easier for the

Field Office if they had one of their personnel directly involved in this "joint operation." Our attempt at having Alice, the baby sitter friend of Brenda's, become a regular sitter for the DURANs had not worked out. So, we had to start thinking about how we could use another SA in some role-playing part as we constructed the recruitment operation by the fictitious international business entity.

Chapter Ten: The Plot Thickens

Winston, Stan and I spent the next afternoon huddled in my office discussing how to proceed. Should we reward DURAN at the next scheduled meeting, with Stan providing some complex story about how he was able to use the information profitably? Or, should he see if the target had been able to acquire any more information on the subject, and then have Stan later claimed he had been able to capitalize on the total information provided? There was also the matter of the timing of meetings. DURAN had not been compensated at the last meeting, but we did want him to get into the habit of expecting to be paid every time he was able to perform a task. Did we want to go to another meeting without rewarding him?

Also, it was about time for Stan to begin preparing DURAN for the next step in the phased recruitment approach—the eventual introduction to a business contact of Stan's who was better placed in the world of international business to use DURAN's information to produce even larger profits. Perhaps, we could use the information on the Soviet—India sales as a bridge to mention that Stan had to consult with "more experienced" international financial experts to profit from this information? There could be a risk that DURAN might be upset that someone else knew where the information came from, so Stan would have to be particularly careful in how he described his association with this individual. Perhaps, he could be a senior official in a large, privately own investment group that was both a client of Stan's and also a major player in international markets in its own right? Hard decisions to make since we were still testing DURAN's risk versus gain limits.

We had to find the right approach that stimulated his cooperation with the promise of increasing financial benefits, while at the same time not scaring him about the increased risks he would be asked to take. He had to be convinced psychologically that he was dealing with individuals who could be trusted and had the capabilities to handle his information in a completely secure manner.

We worked well into the early evening hours, talking through various scenarios. As should be the case, Stan's perspective was given primary consideration, as he was the only person in the room who actually knew DURAN on a personal basis. And, in the end, most of what he suggested did become the operational scenario for the next meeting with the Target.

The plan was that Stan would tell DURAN that he had not been able to as yet find a way to profit from the information on the Soviet—India military trade deal. He would add that he had contacted some other international businessmen, frankly much more knowledgeable in how to manipulate such information into profits, and sought their advice without disclosing how he had obtained the information. Since these were old friends as well as business colleagues, they advised him that what he had were useful bits of information, but that additional details on the types of military equipment, specific military units involved in both countries, and at what level of both governments the deal had been made were what would make the information really valuable in an international business context. He would then ask DURAN if he felt he could obtain any of that type of information. If DURAN said he would try, Stan would respond that he would add another couple of days to his stay in the city to give DURAN the opportunity to gather more information, and a second meeting's date and time would be arranged.

However, if DURAN stated he would not be able to supply any more information on the deal, or seemed hesitant to seek more information, then Stan would use a financial inducement to try and encourage his cooperation. He would say that based upon the advice of his friends, he now believed that he and DURAN could make some money. Perhaps

CHAPTER TEN: THE PLOT THICKENS

in this case there were not enough details to profit, but as long as they worked together carefully, Stan believed they would eventually find some information of value. He would state that he had decided that it would only be fair to place DURAN on a consultant arrangement: DURAN would receive $300 a month as a retainer to compensate him for staying alert at his job for information of potential profitability. And, when he was able to provide such information, and Stan was able to use it profitably, DURAN would also receive a portion of those profits.

We felt this approach would suit what we believed to be DURAN's financial motivation, while holding out the potential for larger sums of money based upon what he was able to provide. If the retainer ploy was accepted, Stan would use the next several meetings to guide DURAN regarding what type of information he should be alert to and emphasize how much specific details enhanced the value of the information. While we actually hoped DURAN would accept the first scenario and attempt to acquire more information on the Soviet–India deal, we also felt the backup scenario was workable.

After we discussed these scenarios with Ralph and obtained his agreement, we forwarded them to Headquarters for their comments. Their response was general acceptance of the plan, but with a note of caution that we should not push DURAN into taking too much of a risk at this point. They reminded us that the ultimate objective of the operation was the code material. Stan's reaction to the communication was that it was telling us how to "suck eggs," a term meant to indicate that this was such basic guidance that we had already considered it and didn't need to be told the obvious.

This comment from Stan was not unusual for a CO involved in a case. Had I been the CO handling the asset, I may well have felt the same way. And, indeed, as I recall, when I was running certain agents, I had bristled at some Headquarters' responses to plans I proposed. Stan was in a very stressful situation. He was working a potential recruitment Target with access of strategic value to the United States Government. He was the only Agency or Bureau, for that matter, officer actually in direct contact with the

Target. He felt he had the only true insight, on a personal basis, regarding how the target related to him and the operational scenario. He did not like to think someone sitting back at Headquarters was trying to second-guess him. By the same reasoning, Headquarters clearly recognized the potential value of the operation and did indeed state the obvious for bureaucratic reasons. My job here was to console Stan, keep his confidence up, and insure he was focused on what we needed to accomplish next with DURAN. He would soon get over his frustration with Headquarters.

Following the usual security procedures, Stan arrived at the hotel late in the afternoon of the 23rd. The next morning, he conducted his usual countersurveillance exercise, and at lunchtime, he returned to his suite and awaited the telephone call from DURAN. The previously scheduled time for the meeting was 12:15 p.m. No call. By 12:35 Stan was feeling that gut wrenching anxiety that any CO feels when a Target does not show up. Just as any salesman will tell you about the wasted time he has spent sitting in potential clients' waiting areas trying to see someone, any CO will tell you the same story about wasted hours in safe sites when agents either didn't show up or were late. In either case, the first thing thought in a CO's mind is that the operation has been blown. Maybe the agent was caught, or maybe s/he was injured, or maybe they had just quit. No matter, it was over, and had it been the CO's fault anyway? This is always a frightening experience, and, particularly in areas where promptness is not a cultural value, it can happen almost on a routine basis. Yet, it is always a traumatic event—every time.

So, when the phone finally rang at ten minutes of 1 p.m., Stan carefully answered in as calm a voice as possible and gave DURAN his suite number. After DURAN arrived and was given a glass of scotch, he apologized for his lateness. He explained that the Consulate General had called him in at 11 a.m. for a conversation about some equipment updates Bucharest was sending for the Communications Room, and he had to explain how they would affect the Consulate's communications capabilities. DURAN noted that the Consulate General was not a technically inclined individual, so it took a while to explain the details of the new equipment. As soon as he finished the discussion, he hurried out of the Consulate and came to the hotel

Stan said there was no problem and he completely understood that DURAN's official duties had to be dealt with first. He also immediately recognized that the installation of new communications equipment would be of great interest to both the Agency and the Bureau. So, he asked DURAN whether any of the new equipment was of European manufacturing and, if so, whether enough of it was being bought by the Romanian Government to make this information worthwhile? DURAN responded readily, seeming quite pleased to demonstrate his technical knowledge. He said, "The equipment is updated, high-speed, radio reception equipment which had been assembled in Hungary from various components, including some obtained from France. The equipment package included a new antenna array, a base reception station with a link to the current paper tape decryption machine, and a base sending station. The new system, once installed, and that would be done by a team of technicians sent by the Ministry of Foreign Affairs in Bucharest, would permit much higher speed transmission of radio communications. It would also enhance the radio traffic's security with the stronger encrypted algorithm."

Really warming up to the subject, DURAN explained the new system was a vast improvement over the one currently in use at all Romanian installations abroad. And, the installations in the United States were going to be among the first to receive it. The installation team would start on the East Coast and move across the country to the West, starting in about four months. He emphasized that this equipment was produced by Warsaw Pact technicians for eventual use in all Pact installations. Other member countries were also in the process of sending out installation teams. Even the Soviets, he noted, were planning to use the new equipment for Pact communications.

As the target continued to discuss the new equipment, Stan poured him another drink, and mentally tried to concentrate on all the details DURAN was providing. However, they were soon interrupted by the room service lunch waiter. And, the conversation had to turn to such topics as the weather and general business themes while the luncheon was set up. Inwardly, Stan was quite concerned that the break in the conversation might disrupt DURAN's enthusiastic discourse. But, there was nothing he could do.

Once the waiter left, and as they began to eat, Stan switched the topic to the information regarding the Soviet—India military deal. He asked if the target had been able to acquire any more details. DURAN responded that he had not seen any additional information and asked if what he had provided had turned out to be of any business value. In response, Stan went into his prepared story about checking with some of his business contacts with more expertise and experience in military and grey market arms deals to determine if he could make some money on the information. But, his contacts indicated that without additional specifics on the types and identifying details of the equipment, as well as loading and unloading locations, and the transportation agencies involved, there was no way to leverage the information into a profitable situation.

At this point, DURAN's facial expression noticeably saddened, and he softly expressed regret that he had not been more helpful. He took a long drink of scotch and said he had hoped his information would have been worth something. He noted, "My wife and I have been only partly successful in saving funds to buy some items to eventually take back to Bucharest. I had really hoped our association would help that effort."

As Stan contemplated these comments, he thought, as he later reported in his Contact Report, "there is a God and thankfully he is on our side." Every once in a while, things fall into place, and a CO is experienced enough to know when to modify the plan to take full advantage of the situation. Stan did so, and subsequently was highly praised for doing so, which helped eliminated any of his residual resentment at previous Headquarters comments.

Stan responded to the Target's comments with both empathy and sympathy. He said he understood DURAN's desire to purchase a few things to make life better for his wife and child. He mentioned that his

CHAPTER TEN: THE PLOT THICKENS

father had been a factory worker who used all the overtime and bonuses he earned to make life better for his family. He also stated that now that he knew DURAN as a person, he wanted to do what he could to help him. However, Stan noted, "My ability to financially assist you is limited and mostly based upon your ability to provide information from Consulate communications." But, he added, by pulling a few strings, he should be able to provide a monthly retainer fee to DURAN by charging the cost to one of his larger international client firms. He then took out his wallet and offered DURAN three hundred dollars in twenty-dollar bills, telling him that as long as they worked together, he would get this amount monthly, in addition to any profit made on specific information he was able to provide. The Target reacted with a smile and a whispered "thank you," placing the money in his inside suit jacket pocket.

For the reminder of the meal, Stan and DURAN discussed what he intended to purchase with the retainer. And, Stan noted in several different variations that the Target should be careful so as not to arouse the suspicion of others at the Consulate. DURAN responded that he planned to buy some items for their residence, and that he and his wife seldom had anyone from the Consulate visit their apartment. But should any of his colleagues see a few new items in his residence, he would simply explain that they were purchased with the money he had saved with his overseas allowances.

After DURAN had his dessert, and apparently, he was developing quite a taste for the chocolate torte, Stan poured them both a scotch and began to explain that he had been doing some thinking about the new communications equipment that DURAN had mentioned earlier. This, Stan said, might still represent an opportunity for us to make some money. Since the French communications industry is involved in some component sales for the project, its stock should increase in value. Now, the real question is how widely known this information is. DURAN responded that it was considered sensitive at the Consulate. In fact, DURAN said, were he and Stan not close friends he would not even have mentioned it.

"Fine," Stan replied, "then I think we have something we can move on quickly and seize the opportunity for some profit if you can help me identify the French companies involved. I can then purchase some stock futures of the companies, and we can benefit from the stocks' increased future value. Perhaps, I can even place us in a position to reap multi-year profits if you can give me an idea of how long component support for these new systems is included in the deal." Stan continued that while he could not guarantee how much they could make, as he would have certain expense involved in setting up accounts worldwide to disguise future purchases on the same companies, this deal might have the potential for several hundreds of dollars in commissions. Perhaps, even more.

DURAN's eyes noticeably widened at the mention of this much money, but his face quickly faded into a serious portrait of concern. Recognition of what he had told Stan in a careless moment to explain his reason for being late had sunk in. He was excited at the potential "commission," but also realized he was dealing in information of a secret and sensitive nature, closely held within his country's government and the Warsaw Pact.

In agent recruitment operations, this is one of those "moments of truth" where the Target actually realizes what he is becoming involved in. There can be many such moments in an operation, as the degree of risk increases or some ethical or philosophical barrier must be crossed or at least rationalized by the Target. In DURAN's case, it was the realization that to make the kind of money he desired, he had to provide sensitive information on the communications equipment. Should he be discovered, he could not explain it away as general business information he used just to make a few extra bucks. This was information he knew of based upon his official responsibilities, and he was well aware it was secret. His friend, the Consulate General, would not be able to help him were he to be found out, but would have to be in the forefront of condemning him.

Recognizing DURAN's situation, Stan sought to address the issue because DURAN could bring up his concerns. He began a lengthy explanation of the need to keep all this information just between the two of them. Explaining that since the information came directly from DURAN's official duties, he had to be careful not to let anyone know he was talking to anyone else about it. As he learned additional details on the equipment, the upgrading time frame, etc., he would have to be very careful. Stan explained they would have to hold their meetings in a more discreet manner. Also, if DURAN had told anyone about their relationship, he would have had to develop a story about it ending, probably using the excuse that he was not able to make any money from their relationship. Stan emphasized "That in order for him to make money he had to protect his sources of information, so no one but me and you would know the information came from you." "This is a secret between us, and as such, would protect both of us from any problems." He concluded his comments by noting that DURAN was a clever person and a respected professional in the Consulate. He was the head of the Communications Office. This would easily give him a safe and secure environment in which to obtain the details and information needed to enable both of them to profit handsomely on this deal.

DURAN took in all of Stan's speech, and from the concentration evident in his eyes, he was carefully reviewing and considering the points made. Slowly, he began to speak in a low and serious tone. He noted, "This is very sensitive information, not only affecting my Consulate but other governments in the Warsaw Pact. This means that even the Soviet Union is involved. If I were to involve myself in discussing something like this, the risk would be very great. Sure, my minor unofficial "business" deals could easily be ignored by Consulate security officers, especially if the Consulate General protects me, but this is something else. Should even a hint arise that I am the source of the information, the security services of the Warsaw Pact, including the resources of the KGB and GRU, would be tireless in their efforts to punish me."

"To take such a risk would require complete confidence that my role could be protected and that the compensation would be worth the risk," he stated. DURAN said that he respected Stan and valued their personal relationship, but could Stan guarantee that he could protect DURAN as the source of the information? Also, as Stan had mentioned earlier, the commission received in return for this information would have to be in the hundreds of dollars. The Target continued that he felt fairly confident that he could obtain detailed information on the French companies involved.

He would be given all the instruction manuals for the equipment upgrades and would assist in their actual installations at the Consulate. He would also probably be able to learn additional information from the technicians sent to handle the installation. Indeed, some of them might be former colleagues from the Ministry of Foreign Affairs. And, in any event, it would be his responsibility as the head of the Communications Office to take care of the technicians while they were in the city. But, he was concerned about protecting his role as the source.

Basically, he felt the risk of exposure was something he could handle within the Consulate, but he was not as sure if he could be confident of the same degree of protection in the world of international business. That seemed to be his basic argument. He didn't seem to have any ethical concerns, nor much in the way of security concerns with local Consulate authorities. And, it was quite clear that he was very interested in the money Stan had spoken of earlier.

With this explanation of DURAN's concerns, Stan began to address another aspect of his business. He started by noting that advanced information, usually well protected and often from government sources, was provided without official approval, and was a quite normal way that international traders made their big profits. After all, he stated, just look at the money traders make on Wall Street. He said, "Do you think that is because they are so much smarter than the rest of us? No. It is because they have established sources that provide inside information on industry activities and developments. These sources are well-paid and often make more than their regular salaries within their various private and public organizations. International traders operate the same way. I am only a small-time trader compared to the real power brokers, but I also have my sources, which I pay well and protect, that allow me to make a comfortable living. This is a system that works just a little below the public view. Its existence depends upon the ability of the traders to have a continuing source of non-public information, which in turn exists because the traders can protect the identity of their sources and pay them very well for the small risks they are willing to take. To be honest, I have been told that senior

CHAPTER TEN: THE PLOT THICKENS

government officials in many countries, both in the West and in the Soviet sphere, are involved in these activities. I am confident that, considering the type of information you mentioned, I would have no difficulty exploiting it with no fear that you would be exposed as the source. In fact, I would suspect that other traders are, or will in the near future, obtain the same information from their sources."

DURAN paid close attention to Stan's remarks and with a serious look on his face said that he would have to think carefully about this. Stan responded that this, of course, was the right approach to take. If he and DURAN were to work on this type of deal, they must be careful in all aspects of it. He then poured DURAN and himself another scotch and began to explain in detail the type of information that would be needed for money to be made. Stan said he wanted specifics on the types of equipment, their manufacturing data, how they interrelated within the Consulate's communications system, the components in the new equipment, and if DURAN could do it, copies of the operating manuals which could provide valuable data on maintenance features and offer other clues on possible related support foretelling of future contracts with French and other Western firms.

The Target listened carefully. And at the conclusion of Stan's list of requirements noted that the technical installation team, and the actual equipment and manuals, would not arrive for about five weeks. So, it was doubtful he could get much in the way of the specifics Stan wanted until that time. However,, there were a few details in the communication sent from Bucharest advising of the upgrade and the installation team's schedule. DURAN said "I can provide more details without great risk," but still expressed serious concerns about a more comprehensive degree of cooperation.

To conclude the meeting Stan reiterated his understanding of DURAN's concerns about his personal security. In a more limited way, he once again explained how the entire inside trading system worked on non-public sources, which had to be protected from identification within their professional organizations. He said that he could stop back in the city for a day in three days' time, and suggested that they have a luncheon at that time to settle the issue. Stan noted that as a sign of good faith, he would guarantee DURAN a commission of $500 for any additional information he was able to obtain on the upgraded communications equipment, sight unseen. While such information might have no business use at all, he explained that he wanted to demonstrate his trust in DURAN's cooperation. As he walked DURAN to the door of the suite, Stan remarked "I believe we have developed a close personal relationship and, regardless of your final decision, we will remain good friends." DURAN warmly shook his hand and departed down the hallway.

Stan stayed in the suite for a couple of hours, writing up his notes of the meeting and thinking carefully about what had transpired and how he would relate it to Headquarters. It certainly was a surprise, but he felt he had reacted to an opportunity with sound operational judgment. The operation was moving faster than anticipated, but it was the Target that had sped things up. In Stan's view, and one with which Winston and I both agreed, when DURAN brought up the sensitive information he automatically gave Stan the right to ask more about it and attempt to exploit it. Still, would Headquarters feel we had pushed too hard? Probably not, but a CO lives on insecurity in all operations.

Stan did an extra-long countersurveillance route between the hotel and the station. He alerted me at my home by a pager signal that he wanted to talk at the station, and I notified Winston as well. As the full moon shone in a cloudless sky that evening, we three met for what would turn out to be six hours of discussion of what took place, what it meant, and how to explain it to Headquarters. Stan was pumped up, as one would expect, and it took about an hour of his relating the events of the meeting to bring him down from his adrenaline high. During this time, we just listened carefully and asked a few questions to ensure we had all the details. The next step was to get Stan's views regarding the atmosphere of the meeting—DURAN's temperament, how their rapport fared, any indications of falsehood in DURAN's behavior, etc. We also quickly reviewed the security of the meeting. Had there been any suspicious incidents related to the meeting?

CHAPTER TEN: THE PLOT THICKENS

Did the hotel staff exhibit any unusual interest in your visit? Were there any suspicious incidents during your morning countersurveillance route? How about your route from the hotel to the station after the meeting? All of this would have to be addressed in a section of the meeting report sent to Headquarters.

Stan advised that he and DURAN had agreed on the time for the next luncheon in three days, and when he checked out of the hotel tomorrow morning, he would make reservations for one night two days hence, explaining to the desk personnel in a casual way that he was unable to make one appointment so he had to return to accomplish that.

We then got into the substance of the meeting, and more importantly exactly how Stan interpreted the events. I asked Stan to identify as objectively as possible the key points in the meeting. He said there were several:

1. DURAN had initially shared the information about the equipment upgrade because he felt guilty about being late for their pre-arranged meeting at the hotel.
2. Once he got into the topic, he probably saw it as a way of demonstrating his expertise and impressing his business contact. Also, by this point, when providing so many details, he must have realized he was sharing sensitive information in violation of his professional responsibilities.
3. His obvious concern over the lack of a commission for the information he had provided on the Soviet-India military deal, and his then rather long comments on the hopes he and his wife had for the use of the financial compensation, seemed real.
4. His reaction to Stan's suggestion that the equipment upgrade might be exploitable for profit seemed an honest mix of concern because the information was so sensitive and because of the possibility of money to be made. Stan emphasized that it was DURAN's demeanor and body language, much more than his verbal comments, which demonstrated his interest in the financial potential of the information.

5. DURAN's expressed concern about the sensitivity of the information was real, and perhaps was his first real recognition that his commercial relationship could generate significant financial compensation but would also require serious risks which could affect his future.
6. Stan's "answering the question before it was asked" scenario regarding how well the information could be separated from its source seemed to give DURAN some confidence, but not enough to make him agree to providing additional details or commit to a greater reporting role once the installation team and the new equipment arrived at the Consulate. When Stan then offered the $500 incentive bonus, under the guise of wanting to assist DURAN regardless of the future profitability of the information, once again DURAN seemed assured by the offer but not ready to make a full commitment to the deal.

Winston took the lead in questioning Stan on these points, separating where Stan's judgments could be supported by DURAN's actual comments or by his demeanor, and where Stan's analysis was based on his observations and CO experience.

An experienced CO is as skilled as any psychiatrist in analyzing the motivations, fears, and desires of a Target. And, for that matter, has an easier job in only trying to exploit the Target's personality traits and psychological issues in support of the operation's objectives. The psychiatrist, however, must actually try to help the individual achieve better mental health. So, the gut instincts or intuition of the CO always plays a major role in driving the pace and direction of the recruitment phase of the operation. However, in terms of reporting to Headquarters, it is necessary to parse clearly the target's comments and behavior as observed from the Case Officer's opinion of those actions.

Once Winston had sorted out what could be reported as fact, and what could be reported as analysis and interpretation of behavior, we started to consider the next step. Actually, I should say we started to plan for the next step since the onus really was on DURAN. Depending upon how he

CHAPTER TEN: THE PLOT THICKENS

reacted at the next meeting, we would either focus on the arrival of the installation team several weeks hence, or if he announced he was unwilling to provide more information on that issue, we would go back to tasking him to search for and provide less sensitive Consulate information.

So, we went over the details required to conduct another hotel luncheon meeting. We decided that since this was an occasion where, if so motivated, DURAN might have decided to protect himself by telling his friend the Consulate General of his situation—most likely by stating that he had accidentally gotten himself into a business relationship that was going into areas which his loyalty to his country and Party would not permit—that we wanted Field Office assistance all that day to get any advance warning that the meeting was being setup for some counterintelligence purpose. We also developed an emergency escape plan for Stan should the Consulate security personnel attempt any strong arm stuff. While not a great threat, such actions had been observed in the past with the Bulgarian service and the East German service in other cities.

Stan then sat down to write his report on the meeting, and a bit after midnight it was transmitted to Headquarters. I also sent a personal correspondence back to the senior officer on our support desk noting our counterintelligence perspective, and suggesting that Headquarters wait for the results of the next meeting, two days hence, before responding to Stan's reporting. While I was doing this, Winston had contacted the Field Office's Watch office and requested a meeting with Ralph at their location early the next, or actually by that time, this, morning.

After a few hours' sleep, the three of us drove to the Field Office. We had Stan wear a light disguise, and got the Field Office's permission to drive directly into their underground parking area so Stan would not be seen by the public entering the building. Once in Ralph's office, Matt, Larry, and BJ joined us. As usual, we provided a copy of Stan's report and then Stan gave his oral report. When he was done, the questions flew left and right. Matt was particularly excited about the communication's upgrade equipment, stating how valuable it would be if DURAN could be made to agree to let NSA place some of their devices into the new system. Larry echoed Matt's excitement. Ralph smiled approvingly, but said nothing.

I then explained that while we all were excited about the future possibilities, the results of the next meeting would be the best guide as to where and how to proceed. At this time, I asked Ralph for the support of their special surveillance unit, explaining our counterintelligence concerns. He agreed and subsequently brought in the head of the unit so we could personally brief him on the locations and objectives of the desired coverage of DURAN and the Consulate.

As the meeting broke up, Larry invited Stan into his office for a cup of coffee, and Ralph asked that Winston and I remain for a moment to talk with him. He wanted to give us his personal view on the status of the case. He noted that Matt's excitement over the possibility of bugging the communication equipment was understandable and that the Field Office would acquire a great deal of praise if it could assist NSA's efforts in this regard. "But," he noted, "you did not suggest this in your comments, and I was rather surprised. Why did you not think this was a good idea? "

I responded that "I understand Matt's perspective and that accomplishing such an operation would be a significant success for the Field Office, let alone for NSA's capabilities to collect radio communications into and out of the Consulate. However, should DURAN agree to cooperate by providing more details on the equipment and team, it was not a sure bet that he would be willing to actually try to place anything in the equipment. The installation team would probably consist of some highly trained technicians as well as some security personnel assigned to ensure the installation was accomplished securely. So, we could not assume DURAN would have the capability, let alone the technical expertise, to bug any of the equipment." I also noted that once installed, it was quite possible that security monitoring devices were implanted to identify any attempts to modify the overall system or particular equipment. My reasoning on these points was based on my knowledge of how most intelligence organizations protect their own communications systems in the field.

I then noted our thinking regarding the operation's ultimate objective, "While having the capability to monitor Consulate communications

CHAPTER TEN: THE PLOT THICKENS

would be of value to the USG, we are really after a greater prize—the Romanian encrypted codes which would allow NSA to read all Romanian Government traffic. Thus, we would not want to jeopardize the Target's potential cooperation and access on any lesser goal."

Ralph thought a moment, and then responded that he understood our position. He agreed that DURAN's greater potential was in obtaining the Consulate's communications tapes. However, there was no guarantee that we could accomplish this, he added. In fact, I knew from previous experience that this type of activity was a very complicated and high-risk operation. But, we both knew that if successful, the value to the USG's strategic intelligence capabilities was immeasurable. I added "in terms of dollars, that success in such an operation would justify both yours and my salaries and retirement compensation, as well, probably, as that of all the Agency and FBI personnel involved." "OK," Ralph responded, "let's see what happens." We smiled, perhaps a bit weakly, and shook hands. Winston and I then went to Larry's office to get Stan.

Once we collected him, he advised that Larry was also excited about the possibility of DURAN reporting on the new communication system. Larry had questioned Stan closely on his view of his relationship with the Target, and his understanding of the Target's motivations. Stan noted that he felt he had a pretty good personal relationship with Larry, and therefore believed him when Larry commented that Matt was starting to trust us. However, Larry also advised Stan that the sooner we could get an undercover FBI SA into the operation, the better. This was hardly a surprise to us. At this point, I viewed this as more of a bureaucratic issue than one of personal trust, at least between Ralph and me.

After we returned to the Station, Stan went to his office to continue his preparations for the next meeting. As I entered my office, our Chief Communications Officer came in behind me and gave me an envelope containing an "eyes only" message from Headquarters. It offered some compliments for Stan's handling of the meeting, and advised it was looking forward to the results of the next meeting. It also noted that senior officials at the Agency were watching this operation, and so were people in the

Counterintelligence Center. Good, so far, and as my old college professor used to say, "God willing and the creek don't rise," the next meeting would give us a clear indication of how to proceed. We had Headquarters and the Field Office on our side; we just needed the Target to cooperate.

Chapter Eleven: A Breakthrough?

Stan went through his usual drill of parking his car at the train station and taking a cab to the hotel, arriving about 10:30 a.m. In his reservation, he had noted an early arrival so the suite would be available well before the meeting. It has cost a bit extra due to the early check-in time, but it is obviously well worth the expense. At 11 a.m., after he had checked—in and prepared the room to look as if he was a traveling businessman—he received a phone call from Larry from a telephone booth in an office building about a block from the Consulate. Larry advised that the Field Office had monitored the Consulate since it opened that morning, and there were no indications that any known Romanian security officers had left the building after arriving for work that morning. He also advised that there had not been any indications that the morning was anything but typical in the way of official business. He concluded by reminding Stan that DURAN would be under observation from the time he left the Consulate until he arrived at the hotel. If there were any indications that he was being followed, Larry would telephone Stan's room, pretending to be a client asking a question about a payment due from a previous investment. Stan could respond anyway he wished, but he would have to handle the meeting within this context to protect the operation and his cover situation.

DURAN arrived promptly at noon, and as usual, he and Stan had a pre-luncheon scotch while DURAN looked over the room service menu deciding on his meal. About a quarter after the hour, Stan called down to room service with their order. DURAN had again ordered the chocolate torte as his dessert. Stan took this as a good sign that the target was comfortable and relaxed. Also, the absence of any telephone call from Larry gave him additional confidence to proceed with the meeting as planned: ascertain to what degree DURAN was willing to provide information on the radio equipment upgrade.

Over another scotch, Stan broke away from their social small talk and noted that yesterday he had completed a lucrative deal with another client on the sale of American agricultural machinery to an Asian agro-business corporation. Much of the cost of the machinery would be handled through a loan guaranteed by the US Import-Export Bank and financed by one of the Asian countries' state-controlled banks. Stan continued that by purchasing futures on the price of the agricultural product, whose quantity would significantly increase with introduction of the new farming equipment, a great deal of money will be made." This was starting to be a good week," Stan noted.

He then asked DURAN the big question: "Have you given any thought to whether or not you are interested in working with me on the about-to-be-installed new communications equipment at the Consulate? " OK, now is one of those moments of truth in any development operation. Does the target respond positively, and we all move along happily to the next phase of the recruitment? Or, does the target stand up, indignantly throw his drink in your face, accuse you of trying to turn him into a traitor, and stump out of the room? Or, worst case, thugs barge into the room and proceed to beat you up!

Well, standard operating procedures are that you do not ask such a question unless you are reasonably sure of the answer. And, Stan was indeed reasonably sure. DURAN had come to the meeting, no surveillance had been detected by the FBI, no unusual activities had been noted at the Consulate, and the Target had acted friendly and comfortable since he arrived.

DURAN responded slowly, apparently choosing his words carefully, "There are several risks involved in the type of business deal you are offering." He mentioned that when the installation technicians arrived, he would have to follow their instructions in terms of both the installation of the upgraded communications equipment and how it was to operate on a routine basis. Thus, he did not know exactly how much information he would be given about the technical components of the equipment. And, it would be dangerous for him to try to question the technicians beyond the information he required to do his daily tasks. "As to instruction manuals," he continued," certainly they would be provided to the Consulate so that proper maintenance and repairs could be handled locally. However, these manuals are probably marked secret, and therefore kept in a secure file system which I can only access when necessary to keep the communications system operating. "So, he wasn't sure exactly how much detail he could get on the equipment that would help Stan craft a profitable deal.

DURAN noted a second issue: "Over the past several months, I have come to trust you personally, and recognized that you handled our business dealings with great discretion. But, this information is considered very sensitive by the Romanian Government, and I might even be considered a traitor should my role in providing it become known. Should such a situation happen, not only would my family suffer, but also both our parents' families could lose all the special privileges they had as members of the Communist Party."

"Finally, on a personal basis," DURAN said," I have to decide if I am doing the right thing for both my family and my country. As a Communist Party member, I have been well rewarded for my loyalty and am in a position to acquire many Western household items to take back to Bucharest that would make his family's life even easier. My career, especially with the patronage of the Consulate General and the gifts I planned to acquire for other Ministry senior officials, is moving along well, and I can anticipate promotions and, perhaps, even another assignment to a Western country.
"

"But," DURAN continued, 'my ability to save money from my salary and overseas benefits is not as great as I had anticipated. Also, I have made little headway in saving for special medical care for Aton. And, I, myself, have some health problems I would prefer to have treated in the U.S. So, on a personal basis, the $500 monthly retainer, and certainly any additional funds that could be generated from any deals you are able to make, is very attractive."

Stan listened intently, as DURAN moved into his conclusion. Looking straight into Stan's eyes, DURAN said "I want to cooperate but I need certain assurances before I can agree. First, you have to recognize that I can only provide information that I have access to in the normal course of my Consulate responsibilities. I cannot take the chance of being caught doing anything suspicious." He explained that within the Consulate, there were Romanian State Security officers who monitored all the activities of the staff. Therefore, he would have to be the one to decide what he could and could not provide safely.

Secondly, while he had complete trust in Stan, he added he "would need your assurances that any information I did provide would, when passed along in a business deal, in no way be traceable to me as the source of the information. This was most important, and if you could not promise this, there could be no business relationship."

Thirdly, DURAN continued, "I am a Romanian diplomat and a Communist Party member. In this regard, you will also have to promise me that any information provided for business deals would only be used for making financial profit. In no way would any of this information be used in any manner that might harm either my country or the Romanian Communist Party."

Finally, and this was very important to DURAN on a purely personal basis, he wanted Stan to assist him in using the profits from their business deals to purchase the goods and services they desired without arousing the attention of others within the Consulate. DURAN explained that while various members of the local Romanian immigrant community had offered to help with various purchases, he did not trust them. And, since he would have a great deal of extra cash to spend, he would need guidance in how to do so discreetly.

Stan sat back, and began to respond when a loud knock on the suite's door interrupted his train of though. The knock was followed by the announcement "room service." It is worth noting thatn agent meetings the

CHAPTER ELEVEN: A BREAKTHROUGH?

"room service" knock always comes at a bad time. Stan took a deep breath, and went to the door. Both he and DURAN sat in silence, finishing their drinks as the waiter uncovered the dishes and rolled the service wagon back into the hallway; Stan closed the door and returned to DURAN.

In his professional empathy mode, Stan began to provide DURAN with assurances that his concerns were fully understandable, could indeed be met, and actually was the same concerns that he had in all his business dealing. And, with the exception of the Target's third concern, the Case Officer was being honest. The operation could only succeed and have long-term strategic value to the United States Government if DURAN's involvement and his access were protected. Not only did it have to be hidden from anyone in the Consulate, let alone the Romanian Government, it also had to be protected within the American Intelligence Community for both operational security and counterintelligence purposes.

After providing DURAN with these reassuring comments, Stan moved on to suggestions regarding how to implement them. He discussed how they would establish meetings in the future, how they might communicate if necessary to change meetings, where future meetings should be held to provide the best privacy from observation, and even some basic tips on how to ascertain if DURAN was being followed by anyone from the Consulate. Stan also made a strong argument regarding how DURAN was to handle the $500 a month retainer that he would start receiving at this meeting. He said that any household items purchased should be infrequent, so as to appear related to his savings schedule, and should be done discreetly without attracting undue attention at the Consulate. This meant that certain items intended to take back to Bucharest could stay in their boxes, placed away in his resident's closet or a bedroom rather than displayed in their dwelling. Of course, Stan noted, these precautions should also be explained to his wife, since she would not be able to tell other Consulate personnel about any purchases that could not be explained through their saving's plan.

DURAN appeared to accept this guidance thoughtfully, and the CO moved on to the next important point: how much did Constanta know about their relationship? In almost every operation I have been involved in, the spouse was at least partially aware of what was going on. However, in a majority of cases, the agent at first insists that he or she has not told their spouse, girlfriend, or whatever, anything about their relationship with the CO. They tend to do this because they know it is what the CO wants to hear from a perspective of the operational security of the activity. So, what Stan had to do next was emphasize that the best way to protect their relationship was to be honest about how to handle it. He did so by repeating the key points DURAN had raised about his own security concerns and applied each of them to how DURAN's wife's role in the Consulate community could either enhance his security if properly planned, or cause it great harm if not properly planned.

DURAN responded that Constanta was aware that he was involved in some small business dealing with Stan, as they both knew their saving's plan was not adequate to buy what they hoped to purchase in goods and medical services. She was concerned that he be careful, as she was well aware of the jealousy inside the Consulate community and that gossip of any negative or suspicious sort would quickly get back to the Consulate's State Security agents. DURAN stated firmly that he could convince his wife that he would handle the flow of insider information carefully enough to ensure no suspicion arose. Also, he had already advised Constanta of his personal trust in Stan's ability to use the information he provided in a manner that completely protected him as its source. DURAN added that he also make it clear that on a personal basis he trusted Stan to protect and help both of them.

This all sounded good to Stan—good but not necessarily totally true, perhaps. In any event, it was a good start. And, these issues would have to be reviewed and analyzed at just about every meeting.

Now the CO could get to the core of the meeting—what additional information, if any, did DURAN have about the communication's equipment upgrade? Since the reassurance of DURAN's concerns and the general discussion regarding security for their activities had taken place over the course of the lunch, DURAN was about half way into the torte when

CHAPTER ELEVEN: A BREAKTHROUGH?

Stan moved into this line of questioning. In a normal agent meeting the debriefing for intelligence would have taken place much earlier in the session, with the final time dedicated to providing requirements for future reporting and, especially important, enhancing the personal and operational rapport between the CO and the agent. However, even with DURAN's apparent agreement to provide the information, he was not yet a "controlled agent" but rather still in the developmental stage of the operation. Gaining "control" would still take a while. Once DURAN was fully committed to a conspiracy, which he could share only with his CO, and clearly recognized that his safety and future depended almost completely upon the professionalism of his CO, then he would be under "control."

I should also note that in human agent operations, "control" and "recruitment" are not the same thing. And, as in all issues when dealing with human beings, they can be applied differently to each individual and by each CO. This is an important point in the intelligence business. COs tend to be graded, and therefore promoted, on their recruitments and the information they produce from those recruitments. So, when a developmental target is moved to the status of "recruitment," it is a significant step in the operation. And, there are certain bureaucratic requirements set by Headquarters that supposedly must be met before the agent can be considered "recruited." However, often some COs and their managers can be quicker than others in declaring recruitment. I tend to take a harder line, which on occasion had led to disagreements with my COs and Headquarters. But, in this case, Station management, meaning me and Winston, and the CO were all in agreement. Stan's commitment to a strict definition of the term was yet another example of his professionalism. Considering our long term scenario for obtaining the encrypted tapes, we did not foresee declaring DURAN to be recruited during the time in which he was the CO.

In response to Stan's question about more information, DURAN reached into his coat pocket and brought out a small piece of paper with hand scrawled notes written in pencil. He placed the paper on the coffee table and proceeded to tell Stan the details he had been able to obtain so far. Within the first minute of the Target's comments, Stan interrupted him and noted that he needed to get his notebook in order to take accurate notes of the information DURAN was providing. While seemingly a simple and logical act, it was another step forward in the operation—recognition and agreement by the source that the CO was writing down his information, and thus by extension, that it would be shared with someone else.

With Stan taking notes and asking clarifying follow up questions, DURAN provided many details on the new communications equipment to be installed. Much of the information concerned how DURAN should be prepared to assist in either replacing or technically interfacing the new equipment into the Consulate's Communications Office system. So, the value of this information was useful, but not great. Of more interest were the details of the installation planning; its schedule, how it would be conducted, and how much training, and in what fields, DURAN would be provided to care for the new upgraded system.

The installation team would consist of three Ministry of Foreign Affairs communications experts from Bucharest, who would arrive accompanied by their equipment. The technicians would be officially listed as "visiting diplomats," affording them diplomatic protection under the Geneva Convention. They would arrive in mid to late January of the New Year, and probably be at the Consulate for between three and four weeks. DURAN would be their point of contact, and the Consulate General had advised DURAN that he was to arrange for their hotel rooms and generally to take care of them while they were in the city. Upon completion of the installation, they would move on to the next Romanian official installation.

Stan took careful notes on the technical details DURAN provided, as well as the names and backgrounds of the three Ministry of Foreign Affairs Communications Officers involved. The timing of the visit meant he and the target had about six weeks to wait.

When DURAN finished his reporting, Stan congratulated him on providing some very useful, information. He then gave the target an envelope containing $500 in twenty-dollar bills, adding that this was the

CHAPTER ELEVEN: A BREAKTHROUGH?

first of what he was confident would be the start of a long-term consulting relationship. He reminded DURAN that any profits he made from specific business information provided by DURAN would also be split with him on a fifty–fifty basis, after expenses, of course. He then once again discussed briefly the importance of DURAN and his wife spending any of this money in a careful and discreet manner in order to avoid any suspicion. He also suggested DURAN give him his scrawled notes, so they could be destroyed, as it would be terrible if, just by accident, someone saw them. DURAN did so, and Stan placed the paper in his notebook, stating he would burn it later in the bathroom and flush the ashes down the toilet.

Then, Stan suggested a final scotch to celebrate DURAN's entrance into the world of international business. He made a toast to future profits and shared business successes. In the ten minutes or so it took to finish their drinks, Stan focused his conversation on how DURAN planned to spend the upcoming holiday season. Just before escorting DURAN to the suite's door, Stan went over the arrangement for their next meeting in three weeks' time, right between Thanksgiving and Christmas. The location, a small hotel located in a suburb of the city near public transportation systems, and the time. The date was established, and the meeting was to take place at night, after DURAN had finished his duties at the Consulate. Should DURAN not be able to make the meeting, or needed to talk with him immediately on some other matter, Stan provided his West Coast office phone number—actually, a Station operational line monitored 24 hours a day, seven days a week aware of the cover story supporting Stan's commercial cover story. He noted that if he were out of the office, the secretary could advise a specific time for DURAN to call back when he would be in the office. He also noted that DURAN should only call this number from a public pay phone, not near either his residence or the Consulate.

After DURAN left, Stan immediately began jotting down notes on their conversation, focusing on DURAN's expressed concerns and how he had addressed them. Also, he noted in detail the operational security issues he had brought into the discussion. He then wrote down his perceptions of

DURAN's demeanor, state of mind, and the apparent state of rapport between them. Finally, using the notes he had taken from DURAN's comments and the information on the hand scrawled paper DURAN brought, Stan prepared the outline for an intelligence report on the planned Romanian Government's radio communications upgrade. In the middle of his writing, he was interrupted by a telephone call from Larry, advising that Field Office surveillance reported that DURAN had gone directly back to the Consulate after the meeting. The SA also advised that the Field Office would be monitoring activities at the Consulate for the rest of the day to determine if any unusual flurry of activity was observed.

This is a normal counter-security practice when the capabilities exist. The rationale behind it is that if DURAN, was acting in a double agent capacity then after a meeting such as this where he had agreed to tasking by an adversarial service, the details of the meeting would be discussed among various security personnel in the Consulate and then immediately sent to Bucharest. Or, if DURAN had been discovered by Romanian security officers from the Consulate, the same immediate discussions and communication would be done.

Stan worked on his reporting until early evening, and then as prearranged, left the hotel and a few blocks later took a cab to an Italian restaurant about four miles from the hotel. He ate dinner, and in the course of his meal, visited the restroom, where he gave his notes to another Station officer, and returned to finish his meal. He took a cab back to the hotel and settled in for the night. He departed mid-morning the next day, and after an especially rigorous countersurveillance route, ended up at his car at the train station. He was in the Station by noon, as Winston and I both eagerly awaited the opportunity to get a first-hand account of the meeting.

After the Station officer got Stan's reports, he returned to the Station that evening to secure them in the office. The next morning, Winston and I read over the draft reports and made a few notes on issues we wanted to address with Stan. Obviously, from the reporting, the meeting had gone very well. DURAN had agreed to provide classified technical information

CHAPTER ELEVEN: A BREAKTHROUGH?

on radio communications equipment that would be the new standard for every Romanian Government official installation overseas. The United States Government, specifically the NSA, would benefit significantly, in both time and money, in its collection activities against Romanian radio traffic with this information. Or at least it appeared so to us. Equally important, DURAN had willingly entered into a conspiracy that he knew was both wrong and dangerous. Stan's written report indicated that he had handled the meeting excellently.

When Stan arrived at the Station, he was as excited to talk about the meeting as we were to hear about it. Meetings like this are what COs live for. And, unfortunately, they represent only a small fraction of a CO's career. The vast majority of development operations end, usually after a great deal of effort over a lengthy period of time, with the Target either being judged as not willing to accept a clandestine relationship or turning down the proposal when it is made. Then, additional time is required to end the relationship in a manner that at least seems to indicate a measure of "friendship" still exists between the CO and the Target. Even when you know the operation is going nowhere, for operational security requirements, you still have to play out the game.

In my office Stan orally went through the entire meeting. We took notes, since no written report ever captures all the information discussed. Later any additional details Stan briefed, or more likely any additional meeting atmospheric or security elements he mentioned, would be included in the final report sent to Headquarters. The final report was sent out in the late afternoon. Then, Winston and I drove down to the Field office to brief Ralph and company.

Once again, the FBI allowed us to enter their underground parking area and take their security controlled elevator to their offices. This would become a routine, and represented a privilege extended to us. The gesturedemonstrated increased professional respect from the Field Office. Ralph met us at the elevator and took us into his office, where Matt, Larry and BJ were waiting.

We provided a brief summary of the meeting's results, stating in a restrained but optimistic tone that we seem to have reached a significant point in the operation. I praised the operational security support the Field Office had provided through its monitoring of the Consulate and on DURAN, and noted Larry's telephone calls as being very helpful. Matt then suggested that each of his officers should read the copy of the written report before we got into a serious discussion. He gave the report to BJ to make copies for them.

As the report was comprehensive and somewhat lengthy, Winston and I sat in silence for about fifteen to twenty minutes while the SAs carefully absorbed the information. Ralph was the first to break the silence, and did so with a smile on his face. He congratulated us on the successful meeting and wanted to make sure we advised Stan of his praise for the manner in which the meeting was conducted. Matt then joined in, stating "Now that we have DURAN recruited, my Squad can get a great deal more information on the activities inside the Consulate." BJ joined in, suggesting that at the next meeting, it was time to introduce an SA to start debriefing DURAN on Consulate matters.

I quickly looked at Winston, whose face was drawn up in a typical British nonchalant expression, and then glanced at Ralph. Our colleagues were moving too quickly and not seeming to understand what had transpired at the meeting. I had to refocus the conversation on the actual status of the operation, but without in any way insulting the SAs. You might think that with all my experience in role-playing situations, this would not be all that difficult for me. But, you would be wrong because in real life, I'm far from the most subtle and diplomatic personality.

As Matt and BJ continued to discuss how they could exploit DURAN's access for their counterintelligence requirements, I tried to decide how to respond. My first thought would be to simply say, "Hold it, if you read thecontact report carefully, you will see that all DURAN agreed to was to provide additional information on the new communications upgrade. He has not committed to reporting on anything else." However, my second idea proved to be less confrontational and a gentler way to bring everyone back to the realities of the situation.

CHAPTER ELEVEN: A BREAKTHROUGH?

When Matt and BJ came to a natural break in their discussion, I suggested that now that they had digested the reporting, we wanted to review the meeting with them to include the informal comments Stan had provided us. This was sort of a misdirection play on my part. Yet, it allowed me to review the meeting's events orally and place my emphasis on such key points as what was agreed to, what had been discussed, and more importantly, what had not been discussed or agreed to. I concluded by stating our assessment of where we were in terms of the relationship with DURAN. A great deal has been accomplished. DURAN has agreed to provide details on the equipment for the Consulate's communications upgrade in return for a fee. He knows that he is providing sensitive, nonpublic information entrusted to him by his government based upon his official position. He knows he has crossed a line, but only as a "businessman" seeing some profit—not as a traitor to his country. As you will recall, he specifically brought this up as one of his concerns. He has also committed himself to a discreet, if not clandestine, relationship with Stan, whom he trusts to protect him as the source of this information. "So," I concluded, "at this point we have an individual who has rationalized violating the trust of his official position to make some additional money to accomplish his long-term goals while on this overseas assignment."

"Unfortunately," I continued," while this is a significant step forward, it still leaves us far from the ultimate objective of the recruitment of a code clerk. All he has agreed to is a one-time provision of classified information." We doubted, based upon Stan's assessment that DURAN would be willing to talk about all the activities in the Consulate, yet alone be prepared to meet an FBI Agent. "But," I noted," we are in a good position to move the operation forward and introduce additional ploys and role players to get to our final objective."

Both Matt and BJ stared at me, and Ralph looked noncommittal. So, trying to sweeten the pot if possible, I then noted that while we had not really planned this out yet, that in the next phase of the operation, we would want an SA, from Matt's squad, involved in a role-playing part. Winston then began to explain our general plan to move DURAN into a deeper and more responsive relationship, but still within the concept of "business deals" since we still did not have a solid grasp on how strong his loyalty and personal ties to the Romanian Government and the Romanian Communist Party were. In our experience, he explained, Targets can rationalize doing something for personal profit, either out of ethical concerns or just fear of the consequences to their lives and families, many never get to the point that consider their action as betraying their government. So, we planned to increase DURAN's financial payments for information, assist him in using some of the funds discreetly, and slowly move him into meeting another "international businessman" who could use his insider information in even a more profitable manner than Stan could. Meanwhile, through Stan's meetings with DURAN, and Brenda's meetings with Mrs. DURAN, we would continue to try and determine whether he would accept a United States Government relationship or if all our dealing would have to take place under a business guise.

When Winston was done, Ralph commented that he agreed with our plan. He noted that we were making solid progress and that doing anything precipitous at this point would be foolish. He was also pleased that we were making specific plans to get an SA involved in direct contact with the Target. Matt agreed, quite a bit less cheerfully, and said that he wanted to discuss with us the specific details of inserting the SA. He asked, "Would it be in a formal undercover role? Would it be in an alias role-playing part? And, what actual function will the SA have in the overall scenario?" Winston responded quickly, noting that before we made such final decisions, we wanted to talk with Matt about his views on these subjects. He continued that we were not quite there yet in our planning layout, but perhaps we could meet next week to get Matt's views. Ralph interjected that this was a good idea, and Matt agreed, seemingly more because his boss had done so than because he was happy about it.

We left the Field Office feeling pretty good about the meeting. I think we got the point across, at least to Ralph, that we certainly did not feel that we had DURAN under our operational control as yet. The SAs all seemed pleased with the progress made, and hopefully, Matt was placated

CHAPTER ELEVEN: A BREAKTHROUGH?

by the notice that soon one of his people would be actively involved in the operation.

However, just to be on the safe side, I telephoned Ralph the next day and we scheduled a lunch for early the next week. We met at an Irish tavern and had a frank talk about how each of us viewed the cooperation on this case. Ralph was candid about Matt still having some doubts about our true intent on making this a joint operation. I explained how the Agency's culture affected its operational development approach, and that because we were moving along well, we would prefer to go slow and carefully. I was pretty confident that we were going to get information on the communications equipment that would prove valuable to NSA, and also expected that the Field Office would get their share of the credit for this information as well. We both knew that each of our offices would get credit for the same success in our own channels—that was the way the government bureaucracy worked. I also promised that, as soon as possible, we would create a role for an SA, so that the Field Office would have an independent observer involved in the operation. But, I also emphasized "that it was vital that we shared all of our reporting so that no misunderstandings developed either in the field or back in Washington."

Ralph reacted well. He stated that the Station had the confidence of the Field office management, at least for the most part. He said he would work with Matt in this regard. He also mentioned that as the operation was developing well, in the near future there might be a few more resources that the Bureau could bring in to assist Stan and Brenda's efforts. He provided no details. However, later it became apparent that he was talking about their low-level human agent in the Consulate and their audio coverage package there.

After the meeting, I felt pretty confident that the situation was in hand, at least as far as our relationship with the Field Office was concerned. We had come a long way over the months. Now all we had to do was build on our success, which of course depended much more on DURAN than on us.

Chapter Twelve: The Communications Upgrade

The next significant operational event would be the arrival of the communications equipment installation team. Meanwhile, Stan would have one meeting with DURAN where he could focus on assessment and rapport building, and Brenda could continue to try and monitor the DURAN family through her social relationship with Constanta.

From the assessment data Brenda had obtained from Constanta over the past months, we were starting to piece together a profile of the family's desires and concerns. Add to this the information Stan had obtained at his meetings with DURAN, and we did know a couple of strong motivation points: DURAN needed additional funds to purchase items to secure his future career in the Romanian Government and for health care issues affecting his son. It made sense that he was willing to accept a certain degree of risk to get money for these two purposes. However, we also eventually needed to know just how much money he needed to satisfy these goals, and what represented an acceptable level of risk in his mind to accomplish them.

Brenda believed that the DURANs were pragmatists and looked at their actions purely in terms of how they would enhance their future life. From their perspective, their loyalty to their Government and to the Romanian Communist Party was based upon the belief that this was the best path to a successful career and an acceptable lifestyle. Their families' positions within the Party were also an important part of their "security blanket" in Romania. So, while they weren't ideologically or philosophically committed to Communism as a political or economic system, it was the path they had to follow in order to move through life in the most comfortable manner. Thus, we suspected that DURAN was not ready to betray his country or the Party yet, because doing so would destroy his plan for his future personal and professional well-being.

Brenda also emphasized that both parents were sincerely committed to providing their child with the best possible future, and treating his health care issues was the priority for them. Later, his education would become the key concern, but first, he had to be deemed healthy. And, the best chance they saw for this was to get him treatment in the United States. From what Constanta had inferred in conversations with Brenda, the Consulate General was aware of their desire to use an American doctor to address the son's health issues, and had no objections as long as it was done discreetly. The major hang-up was saving enough money to pay for an American specialist. DURAN had attempted to get some recommendations from some of his contacts, both in the local immigrant community and diplomatic circles, but with no real success to date.

The purchase of various items for both personal use back in Romania and as gifts for various Ministry and Party contacts was also an objective that would require more savings. Mrs. DURAN never specifically mentioned that her husband was involved in "business activities" outside of his official duties. But it seemed obvious to Brenda that she was aware of them. When queried for the reasons she felt Constanta knew of these activities, Brenda responded that it was obvious the DURANs planned their lives as a couple and that realistically it is always doubtful that in a close marriage relationship one partner can hide much from the other.

As we began to blend our personality assessment information into a more formal personality assessment, we enlisted the aid of a Headquarters analyst, well-versed in Romanian culture, history, and current politics. As we added CO insights into DURAN, we sent it back to her, requesting any comments she might wish to make. Within days of the last meeting

Stan had with DURAN, she came back with additional questions about the DURANs' lifestyle. She also asked if Alice, the FBI SA who had posed as the babysitter briefly, could provide any insights into the interaction between Constanta and the son.

Ralph was very cooperative in this regard, and within a couple of days, Alice provided several pages of her observations, which we forwarded to Headquarters. At the same time, we also asked Ralph if his SAs, Frank and Bob, could provide their written views on the DURANs and their relationship based on the telephone calls between them. Their information was not particularly insightful, with the exception of the fact that several comments between the DURANs in telephonic conversations did made it clear that Brenda was correct—Mrs. DURAN was well aware of her husband's unofficial business dealings, at least those which involved the assistance of the Consulate General.

Stan was also asked to provide some follow-up information on his assessment observations, but the Headquarters analyst felt that because of the focus on "selling" his commercial cover to DURAN, their business meetings had not really produced that much insight into the target's personality. It was agreed that since we had one more meeting with DURAN before the communications installation team was to arrive, Stan would focus the meeting on elicitation aimed at enhancing our assessment of the target in some specific areas to include:

What were his future expectations for a happy personal and professional life?

Could he even conceive of a life outside of Romania?

With additional business compensation, what would be his priority purchases?

Risk aside, did he have any personal concerns about providing sensitive information for business use?

About three days before the next scheduled meeting with DURAN, the analyst provided us with a draft assessment of the DURANs. It pretty much stated what we had already figured out, which was not surprising since the only information they had to work with came from us. It did, however,

CHAPTER TWELVE: THE COMMUNICATIONS UPGRADE

suggest that the business approach was the safest route to continue to take while carefully moving the target towards more sensitive collection requirements. It also noted that while Stan had sold his cover story and commercial guise to DURAN, there did not seem to be any great personal rapport between them. Consequently, before getting to the most sensitive tasking, which meant getting our hands on the encryption tapes, someone had to be introduced into the operation who could be the "father figure" whom DURAN would see not only as his protector but also his mentor and guide to a better life. They were correct, and this had been part of our long-range planning. But, we just weren't there yet.

Stan bristled a bit at the analyst's remarks about his relationship with the target, but both Winston and I reassured him that he was playing out his operational role exactly as was planned. His role was a very important one in moving the operation along in the risk versus gain equation, and he was performing excellently. If we succeeded, his role would get all the credit it deserved.

Before we sat down with Stan to review his planning for the last meeting before the holidays and the installation teams arrive, I wondered whether or not we should again request Field Office monitoring of the Consulate and DURAN as he traveled to and from the meeting site. Such a decision is always a risk versus gain question. The decision hinged on whether or not we felt that DURAN was under suspicion within the Consulate. Strictly from a counterintelligence perspective, if he was actually working under the control of his government's State Security Service, there would be no point in his being followed to the meeting site. DURAN already knew the destination and would report in detail all that transpired if he were acting as a double agent.

In our counterintelligence analysis of the operation, there were still no telltale indications that DURAN was acting as a double agent. And, how he responded to the requirements once the installation team arrived would pretty much settle the issue, since it was highly doubtful the Romanian Government would be willing to provide the technical details on a worldwide new radio communications system just to identify an operation attempting to recruit one of their code clerks. I also saw no indications that he had attracted any suspicion within the Consulate. However, I did recognize that Ralph's SAs were in the best position to make that analysis. So, I arranged a meeting with Ralph and Matt to get their input on this issue.

In an hour-long meeting at the Field Office, Matt provided a general overview of the Field Office's monitoring capabilities against the Consulate and its personnel. Based upon these capabilities, it was his opinion that there were no indications that DURAN was under any type of suspicion. It was known within the Consulate that DURAN and the Consulate General were doing some "outside" business together, but others in the office had also been involved in similar activities, so it was not seen as unusual or suspicious. I thanked Matt for his views, and then thanked him and Ralph for providing me with a better "feel" for their analysis of the situation. Matt's reaction made it rather clear that I better figure out how to insert an FBI SA into the operation sooner rather than later as a reciprocal gesture of the "jointness" of the case.

After returning to the Station and speaking with Winston, I spoke with Stan to arrange a meeting to discuss this planning the next day, about mid-morning. He was still in the process of composing his planning scenario.

The next day, the three of us sat down for a long discussion. Following Headquarters directions, we agreed that Stan would craft some elicitation questions related to the points Headquarters had addressed in their communication. Since the meeting was primarily rapport-building, these questions could be phased into the middle of the meeting, after DURAN had drunk a couple of scotches and eaten most of his dinner. By placing them in the middle of the meeting, assuming a subtle line of questioning was developed, the Target seldom remembers them as well as topics brought up either at the start of a meeting or at its end.

Next, we agreed that since this was a new month, and to keep the financial momentum going, Stan would pay DURAN another five hundred dollar "retainer" fee, again in twenty-dollar bills. He would accompany the payment with two lines of comment. First that if the information the target

CHAPTER TWELVE: THE COMMUNICATIONS UPGRADE

was going to provide on the communications equipment was as good as he hoped, Stan would advise DURAN that an advance on anticipated profits would be available along with his usual retainer. The second point would be the standard guidance about being discreet and careful in how he spent the money so as not to attract any undue notice from his colleagues. Stan would emphasize this point by noting that he was very careful in this regard for tax purposes. He explained that he sent much of his compensation "offshore" in order to avoid federal and state taxes. So, he maintained a comfortable but middle-class lifestyle in order not to attract the scrutiny of any tax officials. At a later date, if we got to that point, when DURAN was being paid in the thousands for his cooperation, it would be suggested to him that placing portions of his compensation in an "off shore" account would benefit him in terms of his personality security as well as obtaining a higher rate of return on his investment.

Stan then raised an excellent point in terms of how to handle the fact that this next meeting was the last before the Christmas season—the issue of a gift for DURAN. Obviously the actual point behind the gift would be to enhance the personal relationship between Stan and the Target. But, what was the best approach to use? We could provide another personal item valued in the hundred-dollar range. Or, we could give him a "holiday bonus," claiming it was a normal business practice in Stan's industry. The question was what approach would best demonstrate Stan's supposed personal and professional closeness to the Target. The answer turned out not to be that difficult. The key emotional issue we had been able to identify was DURAN's love for his child, Anton. So, the gift would be for the boy. This would demonstrate that Stan cared about DURAN as a person, not just as a source of business information.

Based upon comments made by Brenda, with input from Alice, we knew that one of the DURAN family's goals was to improve Anton's English language skills while living in the United States. So, we decided upon an age-appropriate storytelling theme, a small audio and visual device that contained a series of stories which identified various items by name within the context of the story. Brenda felt that Anton was old enough for this concept, and was certain that Constanta would love the idea. While the item did cost close to two hundred dollars, it would not represent any threat to DURAN's security since it would be kept in his home, and there would seem to be no reason that its existence should ever be known within the Consulate. I dispatched one of the Station's administrative officers to make the purchase, which was done in an electronic's store in a shopping mall in a nearby small town. Payment was made in cash. The item was available nationally, so Stan would claim he had purchased it on the West Coast. It would be given to DURAN unwrapped, with an appropriate explanation about American customs of giving presents to children at Christmas time. Stan would explain the entertainment and educational benefits the gift offered. He would conclude that he had purchased a similar device for his nephew, a boy about Anton's age, to even further personalize the gift.

So, we had the scenario for the meeting covered. Stan would lead off with drinks, the payment of the retainer, and the gift for the son. Now we needed to talk about the elicitation portion and how the CO could obtain additional assessment information per Headquarters' request. We knew that we could not comprehensively cover all their requirements at one meeting, but we did need to make a start. So, we decided that Stan should use the "mirroring" technique to try and draw DURAN out on how he saw his future and whether he ever considered living outside of Romania. Over the meal, Stan would discuss his own business career and education, slowly shifting into asking DURAN whether his professional capabilities as a communications technician might be transferable to the international business sector. He would note that handling communications for an international company, particularly at a senior level such as the Target held at the Consulate, normally commanded a high salary and excellent lifestyle benefits with international firms. Then, he would query DURAN regarding whether he had ever considered the private sector, and depending upon the response, would either probe deeper in this area or move to the topic of how DURAN saw his future life. As in all elicitation scenarios, while a basic outline is developed as a guide, the CO has to analyze and respond to the target's reactions on a real-time basis. So, you never really know what you are going to get. Still, we did have a plan, and hoped we would get more insights than we currently had.

The final portion of the meeting was to be directed at reinforcing DURAN's motivation to bring out all the information he could once the installation team was on site. This would be done during the after-dinner scotch drinking, and as the last topic at the meeting, it should be the one most remembered by the Target. During the first phase of the meeting Stan had briefly mentioned his hope that the Target's anticipated future information would prove profitable to them both. Now, he would tell DURAN that he had done some research among his contacts in the international communications sector regarding the equipment that the Romanian Government might have access to in general. He learned that because of NATO sanctions on various items sold to Warsaw Pact nations, the communications equipment manufactured within the Eastern Bloc was not all that sophisticated. However, his contacts in the "grey market" for such equipment noted that various European firms, including American companies with overseas affiliates, were selling electronic components through third-country middleman companies, often in the Middle East, to Warsaw Pact nations. Stan noted that these companies had public stock trading on American, European and Middle East markets. And, this was the area where, if he were able to provide specifics on the equipment and its capabilities, Stan should be able to make some margin future bets on specific companies. To further demonstrate how he would do so in order to disguise his actions and the source of his information, Stan went into a lengthy and complicated explanation of how he would place these trade orders through second and third parties, with individuals whom he had used in similar schemes in the past. We figured this explanation to someone unfamiliar with international stock trades and the use of margin financing would muddy the waters appropriately in DURAN's mind. Having said that, because the story did have to ring true should by accident the Target was somehow knowledgeable of the procedure; Stan had done his homework on these details. Actually, by this point in the operation, Stan had developed a rather impressive knowledge of the stock trading and margin account business.

It is often surprising to those outside the CO profession to learn just how much knowledge in a variety of fields a CO absorbs over the course of a career. Particularly when operating in a commercial cover identify, a great deal of study, and often coaching by a professional in that line of work, goes into creating a believable alias persona.

Now that we had the plan for the meeting, we took it to the Field Office. Since Matt was out on another case, we ended up discussing it only with Ralph. While he had a few questions, he agreed with its organization and objectives. It is interesting to note that in law enforcement, and therefore the FBI, they emphasize only two of the five types of oral collection methodology: the interview and the interrogation. The Agency teaches all five: social conversation, elicitation, interview, debriefing, and interrogation. Therefore, Ralph was quite interested in how the elicitation scenario was structured and implemented. Winston spent about ten minutes providing a brief course in the concept and basic structure of an elicitation scenario.

Upon returning to the Station, we sent a summary of the plan to Headquarters, along with the notation that we had consulted with the Field office and they were on board. We did not anticipate any Headquarters' changes to the plan. The next day, we received Headquarters concurrence along with a compliment regarding the handling of the case by Stan. I was very happy to pass that along to him.

On the day of the meeting, Stan drove to the city's international airport, used its layout to conduct a countersurveillance route, and took a taxi from the airport to the hotel meeting site. He checked in, went to his small suite, and set the scene by placing several international business magazines and newspapers about the seating area. Then, just to ensure nothing of significance had changed within the hotel since his initial casing, he walked around the lobby and made a small purchase at the sundries shop as a cover reason to explain his presence in the lobby. Satisfied that all seemed as before, he returned to his room. After about half an hour, he donned his

CHAPTER TWELVE: THE COMMUNICATIONS UPGRADE

coat and went to the lobby, mentioning to the desk receptionist that he was going to be out for a few hours on a business appointment. From the hotel, he followed the previously planned countersurveillance route, which did include a stop at a local investment office where he made a general inquiry and satisfied himself that he was not under observation. He then returned to his suite and began to mentally prepare himself for his meeting with DURAN.

The exact meeting time was flexible, since it had to take into account DURAN's workload at the close of business that evening in his communications room. So, it was close to 7:30 p.m. when he rang Stan's room from the lobby phone and came up. He looked tired, and Stan immediately wondered if he had been under some stress because of the meeting, or perhaps it was just because he had a hard day at the Consulate. During the initial social small talk, Stan was able to determine that DURAN had, indeed, had a hard day because some of his radio transmittal equipment had broken down and had to be repaired at once as the Consulate General had some information on a local matter that had to be sent to Bucharest immediately. Other than that, the target did not seem to be particularly stressed about the meeting and began to relax noticeably with his first scotch of the evening.

However, there was a matter that he wanted to get off his mind, he stated, regarding how he would be able to provide the business details that Stan wanted. DURAN explained that a few days earlier, the Consulate General had briefed him on all of the details regarding the visit of the installation team. They were to arrive on 14 January, and spend no more than a week at the Consulate installing the new equipment, ensuring it was properly linked into the existing communications configuration, and testing all the equipment to confrim it was compatible and functioning. They would be bringing all the new equipment with them. However, the time frame for pulling out the old equipment and installing the new equipment is really quite short." DURAN continued that "rather than have any type of formal training on the new equipment, I am to learn while on the job, assisting the team with the installation. While complete instruction manuals for the new equipment would be left for future reference, I am concerned that this new gear is more complicated and technically complex than what I have been trained in and am used to working with. Consequently, I anticipated spending as much time as possible with the team learning how to do so."

And, he was also to be responsible for handling the administrative aspects of the team's visit that includedhousing, feeding, and whatever had to be done in terms of some social activities. So, DURAN anticipated that for the week or so they were in the city, he might be spending sixteen to eighteen hours a day with them. Thus, he did not think it was a good idea to meet with Stan until after the team had departed. He needed all the time he could get with them to ensure he could do his job properly, and even assuming some "down time" away from the communications room, he would have to be involved in socializing with them.

After listening carefully, Stan poured the target a second drink and calmly noted "I fully understood your position." He then spent a few minutes mirroring back to the Target why long hours would indeed be necessary, and agreeing that for DURAN's professional career, it was vital that he learn all he could about the equipment. "After all," Stan noted," the Consulate General counts on you to keep communications functioning, and you cannot afford to disappoint your friend and boss." "But," DURAN asked," would the delay in providing technical information on the new equipment lessen your ability to generate profits for them? "

Stan, adopted a pose of deep thought, and hesitated for about 30 seconds before responding," There is no question that the earlier I have this "inside information," the more we can profit from it." "However," he added,"there are other considerations as well. First of all, I am determined to keep your cooperation secret, and considering all your responsibilities during the visit, your getting away for even a brief meeting would be both difficult and even suspicious. Also, you are a respected professional Communications Officer both at the Consulate and at the Ministry, and in order to maintain this reputation, you have to become an expert on the new communication system. So, these factors, when balanced with the timing of any stock trades I can make, seem to clearly demonstrate that waiting is the most responsible

CHAPTER TWELVE: THE COMMUNICATIONS UPGRADE

way to proceed." DURAN appeared visually relieved and thanked the CO for understanding how important learning the new system would be to his professional future.

With this issue out of the way, Stan decided to interject a break in the business aspect of the meeting, mentioning that since he and DURAN were meeting in the evening, he had not been sure if DURAN would like to have a dinner brought up by room service. Perhaps, DURAN had eaten earlier or planned to eat back at his home with Constanta? The Target responded that his wife knew he would be at a business meeting, and so she did not expect him home until late. She and their son would have dinner without him. After a few minutes of discussion, Stan telephoned down to the kitchen and ordered their meal—chocolate torte once again ended up as the dessert. This was one personality characteristic we had nailed down.

With dinner settled, Stan went into what we refer to as the "requirements" portion of the meeting. Playing off DURAN's concerns about the timeliness of providing the equipment information, Stan noted that perhaps he could make up for this if DURAN could provide the actual equipment installation manuals and networking diagrams? These would provide adequate information to give Stan the best options in identifying component manufacturers. Now, Stan noted, he was no expert like DURAN in communications equipment. But, he had contacts with solid communications engineering backgrounds who would be able to recognize such details. And, as he had worked with these people for many years, they would not ask where he got his information, so DURAN's cooperation would be fully protected. DURAN gave this some thought, and mentioned that he had originally planned to take notes from the official manuals and then provide these to Stan. As the manuals, etc. would be kept in the Communications Office at the Consulate, DURAN thought he would have adequate private time to do so during his regular work hours. Stan responded "that notes would be useful, but the actual manuals would offer the best opportunity for profitable exploitation. Obviously," Stan added," you would have to take the manuals back to your office, so they would have to be copied at our meeting." While this was a bit unusual, the CO noted, he could get a camera which would probably be able to do the job.

DURAN appeared to agree, but noted that bringing out the manuals did involve some risk. "n what way?" Stan asked. DURAN responded that no one was permitted to take official papers out of the Consulate. Stan asked if people were actually searched on leaving, and DURAN replied that this was hardly ever done. Security personnel, he noted, were pretty lazy and as the Consulate community was pretty close knit, security in general was lax." In that case," Stan continued, "since you work late much of the time, and are often the last person to leave the Consulate in the evening, it seems there would be little risk if you bring out the manuals and then return them the next morning." "I assume," he said, "that you, as the senior officer, are in charge of all the sensitive items in the Communications Room?" "Yes" DURAN agreed, "I am." "Then I really don't see much of a risk factor here," noted Stan. DURAN agreed, but obviously with some reluctance.

Stan then asked if DURAN carried a briefcase or something similar to the office every day, perhaps to carry in things to read or personal business he would handle while in his office. DURAN replied negatively, and Stan suggested that DURAN purchase a cheap briefcase-like item, which he should immediately start carrying into and out of the office daily. This, he explained, would be an obvious, and therefore probably readily overlooked, method of bringing out the manuals. Once the pattern was established that he carried such an item daily, it would be ignored. DURAN gave this some thought and responded that it was an excellent idea. While he might carry the manuals on his person, depending upon how many and large they were, it might be awkward and suspicious even to a casual observer. However, if he was the last to leave, and the documents were concealed in the carrying case, there would be nothing suspicious. Stan agreed, and it was thus determined that at the next meeting the target would bring out the actual manuals for the new Consulate communications' system.

Finally, Stan asked DURAN if he was the individual responsible for securing the sensitive documents related to his communications duties. Obviously, the answer was yes, and DURAN said so. "Well then," Stan

CHAPTER TWELVE: THE COMMUNICATIONS UPGRADE

explained," let me suggest that you can have a good reason for taking home the equipment manuals in the oft chance that you are found doing so." This story, which Stan then discussed with DURAN, had both a logical and seemingly almost laudatory content to it. It had been developed just in case DURAN expressed some hesitation regarding bringing out the manuals.

Stan suggested that as the senior officer for communications at the Consulate, it fell upon DURAN to ensure the new system was both reliable and fully functioning. While his training on the new system had been with the installation team, and he had actually assisted in this installation, it was still a brand-new system to him. Thus, if he wanted to learn as much as he possibly could about the equipment in order to handle his responsibilities professionally, he needed to spend additional time studying the new manuals, and he decided to do so at home. Also, as he was the individual responsible for the security of the information in the manuals, since it would remain in his control at all times, there was no problem. DURAN listened carefully to this explanation and smiled slightly as he nodded in agreement. He said, "That is a good story, and quite believable since the Consulate General respects my professional work ethic." "At worst," the Target commented, "I might get a warning from the security officers if I were caught taking them out or bringing them back in, but I am confident that my friend, the head of the mission, would accept this story."

Room service arrived just as this conversation was ending, and Stan reverted to some elicitation topics while they ate a leisurely dinner. Stan referred back to their conversation about DURAN keeping his professional skills up to date, and asked if the target had ever considered using these skills in a private firm? Stan said he recognized that such opportunities in a Communist country were scarce, but if one looked at the international business community as a whole, someone with DURAN's professional experience and technical skills could probably command a large salary. DURAN sort of agreed, noting that he was actually quite well educated in radio engineering, and had attended the best schools his country offered. In addition, he had received training from both the Russian and the Polish radio services since being employed by the Ministry of Foreign Affairs. However, he did not think his Government would be very happy with him if he quit his position and tried to join a State-owned firm with international business activities. And, he added, in his country, unlike America, if the Government was unhappy with you, your lifestyle, and possibly even that of your extended family, could suffer significantly.

Stan then shifted his comments towards DURAN's experience living outside of Romania, asking if he enjoyed it or missed the familiarity of his homeland. DURAN commented that he had spent a few years in Africa, and found living conditions there for the general public to be worse than in Bucharest. He also found it difficult to understand the cultural aspects of the tribal personal and political loyalties that seemed to control all aspects of public life. All in all, while his access to diplomatic housing, food, and services ensured that he lived decently, it was not a particularly enjoyable place to be. However, he noted, his work there had gotten him recognized by the Ministry as a hardworking and bright technician. This helped him move up in his career. Seizing the given opportunity to ask for more details about his Africa posting, Stan did so, focusing on how his duties there demonstrated his future potential. DURAN, obviously warming to the subject, said that the radio equipment used at that Embassy was of a poor quality and its range was barely able to contact its repeater site at a larger Romanian radio communications facility at the Embassy in Cairo. It was almost a daily job just to keep the equipment operating. But, he did so, and apparently did a much better job than his predecessors. And, upon reassignment to the Ministry, he was selected for advanced training with the Russian radio service, which indicated that, professionally, he was being guided towards increased responsibilities.

DURAN continued that his next overseas post was Paris, where he was the second officer in a three-man communications room for the Embassy and also servicing the Romanian Trade Mission in the city. There, he worked with much more modern equipment and was actually in charge of maintenance for all the equipment. This, he explained almost proudly, even included some radio intercept equipment owned by the Romanian

CHAPTER TWELVE: THE COMMUNICATIONS UPGRADE

security service and used to follow activities of the French secret services monitoring activities at the Embassy. Stan decided not to follow-up on that interesting bit of information, as it did not fit into the subject matter he was supposed to be interested in. But, there was little doubt that down the road we would find some reason to get more information on this topic.

Instead, Stan asked how the target liked living in France. Well, of course, DURAN and his wife found Paris to be an exciting place to live. Their housing was better than their residence in Romania, and with the various privileges afforded diplomats, they were able to live well, if not lavishly, and save enough money to buy some items to take home. They also saved enough to purchase other items he subsequently gave as gifts to his superiors at the Ministry, which helped to ensure he was held in high personal regard there. The Target commented that Paris was really their first opportunity to experience life in a Western society, and it was very stimulating. The variety of items, food, household goods, and clothing, was almost overwhelming at first. Also, the few non-Romanians or Warsaw Pact diplomats with whom they socialized were friendly and very casual in their discussion of events. They did not have to be as cautious as Romanians are domestically to insure nothing is said or discussed that might be interpreted by the Government or Party as critical or derogatory. However, he added, because of his job, his social access outside of the Embassy was quite closely controlled: Resident Romanian security personnel monitored his activities, and compared to how he could behave in America, his freedom to socialize or even to wander about the city was very restricted. When Stan asked "why," as if he didn't know, the target explained that the French secret services were very active trying to hire Warsaw Pact diplomats to spy on their countries. And because he worked in the communications room, it was believed he and his wife would be priority targets for these services.

Sensing yet another area where he did not want to go, Stan brought the conversation back to how the DURANs viewed living in Paris. To focus the conversation, Stan mentioned French food. DURAN took to the topic immediately, discussing his favorite dishes and remarking that his wife made it a point to learn how to prepare some of these for him. He also spoke of a developed fondness for French wines, especially the full-bodied reds of the southern growing regions. Stan asked if he had been able to travel there while in France. "No," DURAN responded, but he was able to purchase a wide variety of French wines and cheeses at a diplomatic store at the Polish Embassy at very cheap prices. In retrospect, his liking of these products was probably a mistake because in America, their prices, even considering diplomatic prices which excluded all types of taxes and other charges, were more than he could afford except on special occasions. Stan commiserated, and said "Perhaps with your monthly retainer, you can now afford a good bottle of French wine periodically."

Just as DURAN started to devourer his dessert torte, Stan asked if the Target had ever considered leaving Romania to live in the West, since he had apparently so enjoyed its lifestyle. DURAN looked up at Stan, with a pensive gaze, and said that while the lifestyle was indeed enjoyable, his career and family was solidly based in Romania. While he probably would never enjoy the lifestyle benefits of the West in his country, DURAN hoped for an additional posting abroad where he could acquire various items to make his Romanian home more comfortable. "Again," he noted," you should understand that in a Communist country, an individual does not have the freedom to follow any career path or mobility desired. He is but a small part of a larger society with rules and discipline enforced by both the Government and the Party. And, one has to do all one can to make oneself and one's family comfortable within these circumstances. Perhaps in the future my son might have more options, particularly in the area of education, career mobility, and financial compensation, but for my generation, the situation is not very flexible."

Stan murmured that he understood, and then moved to the motivational portion of the meeting involving the new month's retainer and the gift for Anton. He began by noting that since this was a new month, he wanted to give DURAN his December retainer of five hundred dollars. He then removed an envelope containing the amount, again in twenty-dollar bills, and handed it to the target, commenting that he hoped this might help

CHAPTER TWELVE: THE COMMUNICATIONS UPGRADE

DURAN and his families enjoy the Christmas season a bit more. DURAN accepted the envelope, did not make any attempt to count its contents, and placed it inside his suit coat pocket.

As this was the second $500 "retainer" payment, there had been some discussion at the Station about the benefits of having DURAN sign a receipt for the funds during our planning sessions. As he was accepting this payment for a business transaction, obtaining a signed receipt for the money could be explained as a normal practice. But, at this point, a signed receipt did not seem to further the relationship to any great degree. So, what really is the value of a signed receipt? Sure, it is another step in formalizing the commercial relationship. But, frankly, it is the personal relationship between the CO and the asset which is much more important than any signed piece of paper. Now, some intelligence and internal security services from different cultural backgrounds often use a signed receipt for blackmail purposes. If they do not get adequate cooperation from the asset, they threaten to expose that individual using the signed receipt as proof of cooperation. , is not the Agency's way. Also, in the case of a blackmail approach, experience has demonstrated that the individual usually provides just the minimum information and cooperation required to keep them from being harmed by their handlers. Our hope is to develop an asset who willingly assists in moving the operation forward.

Anyway, after DURAN pocketed the funds, Stan began the explanation leading up to his presentation of the Christmas present for Anton. He noted that this would be the last time before Christmas that they would meet. And then gave a brief overview of his supposed holiday travel plans and visits with various relatives during Christmas and New Year's. Stan said that he had a favorite nephew, Wally, who was about Anton's age, and had been looking for just the right toy as a Christmas gift. He explained that he had found an electronic game that was supposed to help increase the child's language capacity while also enhancing his motor skills through the use of on-screen games. Stan admitted that he actually spent about ten minutes playing the game himself at the Sharper Image store. When he decided to buy it, it also occurred to him that this might be a suitable gift for Anton. While he had never met DURAN's son, Stan continued, DURAN had told him enough about the young man that he could picture him as much like Wally. So, Stan said that he purchased two of the games, and from behind the sofa pulled out an unwrapped box containing the toy. He gave it to DURAN, stating "Please accept this as a small present from me to Anton". DURAN looked quite touched by the gift and began to read the toy's description on the box. He noted that he and his wife were trying to increase Anton's English language vocabulary, and this device was definitely oriented towards that purpose. He appeared both pleased and sincerely appreciative of Stan's kind gesture.

After telling DURAN how happy he was that the Target felt the gift was both appropriate and suitable, he also noted that he would understand if DURAN felt it would not be wise to tell Anton, and perhaps also his wife, who actually gave the gift. After all, they were engaged in a confidential business relationship. Stan continued to then expand the conversation into how DURAN might use his retainer funds during the holidays, but should still exercise caution so as not to raise any suspicion. This was a variation of the same theme a CO uses at almost every meeting, since, as I noted earlier, one of the biggest operational security issues in every operation is trying to control how careful the asset is in spending his extra funds.

As Stan was finishing up his speech on discreetly handling the money, the room telephone rang. DURAN looked at it, and Stan, making every effort not to look equally surprised since no call had been anticipated, got up and answered the phone. The voice on the other end had a European accent, possibly Eastern European, and asked firmly if Serge was there. Stan answered that no one with that name was in this room, and end the call. He turned to DURAN and said the call was simply a misdirected call from the hotel operator. Obviously, the telephone call bothered Stan but he certainly did not want to show this to the target. For the time being, he had to forget about it and get back to closing out the meeting. But, the call might be just a wrong number, or it could be indicative of some operational security problems. This would have to be carefully investigated, probably

CHAPTER TWELVE: THE COMMUNICATIONS UPGRADE

with the help of Larry and the Field Office.

Stan asked DURAN what his plans were for the holidays, and listened politely as the Target noted that there would be rounds of holiday parties within the city's diplomatic community as well as among the members of the Consulate community. He noted, somewhat cynically, that at the official Consulate Christmas party, he could anticipate many gifts, mostly wine and liquor, from various members of the local Romanian emigre community who benefited from ties to the Consulate. He also mentioned that he had to find a suitable gift to give the Consulate General for Christmas, one that demonstrated his personal as well as professional respect. Now, he noted, he had a few more options considering the retainer funds.

DURAN concluded by noting that he probably also had to purchase some "gifts" for the installation team upon their departure, since he was their official contact at the Consulate. He explained this was common in his country and would enhance his reputation in the Ministry. Also, since these technicians were senior communications officers, it was quite possible that one or more of them could be his boss in the future. So, a little generosity now could pay solid dividends in his future career. Stan responded that he understood this aspect of "office politics" very well. It was, he noted, not totally uncommon in American corporate circles. He then suggested that since the information on the equipment was a business task, he saw no reason why such gifts to the visiting team could not be considered business expenses. He advised DURAN to keep receipts for the gifts and said he would reimburse him at their next meeting. DURAN readily and happily agreed.

While this was a spontaneous decision on Stan's part, it fit nicely into both the overall commercial scenario we were developing, and the personal conspiracy developing between DURAN and the CO. Our long-term objective was to have DURAN involved in a large, international business organization that operated on the fringes of, and often outside of, legal practices, and thus spent large amounts to insure even larger profits. Such an organization would expend funds to help its operatives' careers as long as that benefited organizational objectives. On a personal basis, Stan's willingness to assist DURAN with an expense he felt necessary was yet another demonstration that Stan was supportive of him and their relationship.

After Stan got a few more details on how DURAN planned to handle the family aspect of the holiday season, it was time to close out the meeting by going over the requirements for the next meeting. Pouring DURAN a "one for the road" small scotch, Stan suggested that the next time he planned to be in the city was in mid-January, and considering DURAN's responsibilities with the installation team, how would the 25th of January be for a meeting? DURAN responded that he expected the team to leave about January 21st, so even if some technical delay kept them a couple of days later, the 25th should work. The CO then reminded the Target that he was to purchase a medium-sized briefcase or similar bag and to start taking it to work on a daily basis. He suggested that DURAN include papers, a snack, or some personal business items in the bag, and several times between now and the 25th, he should take these items out of the bag in front of others at the Consulate so they knew what he used them for. For the January meeting, Stan once again noted that DURAN was to bring out all the technical manuals related to the new equipment, and that he would bring a camera to photograph them.

As to the meeting site, Stan said he would once again stay at this hotel and as usual, when DURAN arrived he should phone from the lobby to get the suite number. He also suggested that while he was confident that DURAN could bring out the manuals without risk, DURAN should arrange to have responsibilities the evening of the 25th so that he was the last to leave the Consulate.

DURAN confirmed his understanding of the meeting arrangements, finished his scotch and Stan escorted him to the suite's door. Just before opening the door, Stan firmly shook the Target's hand, saying "I hope you and your family have a very happy holiday season. I greatly value our personal friendship as well as our professional relationship. See you in the New Year." DURAN returned the holiday good wishes, and looking Stan

CHAPTER TWELVE: THE COMMUNICATIONS UPGRADE

directly in the eye said "You are a good friend, and one who I trust. In the New Year, I hope we will both profit considerably from our relationship."

Once DURAN departed Stan jotted down some notes on the meeting and placed it in a concealment section of his luggage. He then placed the room service dishes in the hallway and went to bed. He would depart the hotel early the next morning, casually telling the desk staff that he had an early flight back to the West Coast. After a decent countersurveillance route, involving two different taxis, he would return to the airport and pick up his car.

Chapter Thirteen: Waiting

As we were eager to hear what had transpired at the meeting, Stan came to the Station around 9 a.m., and Winston and I immediately had him come to my office and give us the details. The actual meeting with DURAN had lasted almost four hours, and it took us over two hours to hear all the details and ask the relevant questions. It was obvious that Stan had once again done a very professional job. He had obtained additional assessment data as well as shown sound operational judgment when some unexpected issues was brought up by the Target—concerns regarding meeting while the installation team was in town—and used his professional initiative in suggesting the briefcase device and paying for gifts for the visiting technicians as a business expenses rather than something DURAN had to absorb out of his own pocket.

Winston congratulated Stan on his elicitation technique, which had provided good insights into DURAN's feelings about the importance and reasons for his Romanian Government and Communist Party ties. As noted previously, once a Target begins to comment on a certain aspect of his life or feelings, a CO well-versed in elicitation techniques immediately understands that s/he has been given social permission to ask questions about those subjects. And, if phrased innocently and with some subtlety, it is natural for the target to respond with additional details.

Stan felt the meeting had been successful on several fronts: agreement to tasking, development of assessment information, continued development of personal rapport, and the movement of the Target deeper into a conspiracy that he knew was not acceptable in his official capacity. We

CHAPTER THIRTEEN: WAITING

were in agreement on all these points. The one minor concern we all shared was the unusual telephone call to the room during the meeting. We would have to speak with Ralph and his guys about that.

It was around noon when we broke up our meeting, and Stan went to his office to complete drafting his operational cables to headquarters. I wanted to get the information to Headquarters today, so this would mean another another late night for Stan, me and our senior Communications Officer. While I had no problems with Stan's writing style or how he presented the contents of the meeting, in the Agency anything that comes out of a Station is considered to have been released, and that means vetted and edited, by the Chief of Station. As a matter of professional responsibility, I always did a final read of any communications we sent out. In addition to keeping oneself up to date on all the operations by reading the traffic, there were also many occasions where some editing was required for grammatical or office politics reasons. By office politics, I certainly do not mean changing what a Target has said, but rather ensuring that the personal analysis of the CO is clearly identified as such and also that no personal affronts to any Headquarters personnel are included in the reports. After all, Agency folks are human and work under a great deal of stress, and tempers over opinions and perceived insults can occur.

In any event, as I settled into my daily reading board to see what else was going on, I knew it was going to be another late night away from the family. But, when an operation with strategic intelligence potential is going well, this is a great business to be in.

About 4 p.m., I called Ralph on our secure telephone line and arranged a meeting for the next day. In this conversation I briefly summarized the meeting and noted all the positive aspects Stan had reported. We agreed that he and Matt, and perhaps some others, would come to the Station about 11 a.m. for their debriefing of Stan and their copy of his reporting. I said that we would provide some lunch, since I anticipated the meeting would go for a couple of hours. I then returned to my other work, and waited for Stan's final draft report. A little before seven, he came in and asked me to look at his reports on my screen. As I did so, he stayed in the room to answer any questions I might have about the content or tone. It took me a bit over an hour and a half to review his reporting, make a few changes, and then release the reporting to our communications room for transmission to Headquarters. We left the Station close to 9 p.m. It had been a long day, but a good one.

The next day, Stan and I both slept in a bit later than usual, not arriving at the Station till a little before 10 a.m. In checking the morning's incoming correspondence, there were no replies from Headquarters on Stan's reporting. Understandable, since they would be carefully absorbing the meeting's content. But obviously, we were anxious to see their take on the meeting.

To fill the time until the Field Office SAs arrived, I also contacted Brenda via our secure communications link to ask her for an update on her relationship with Mrs. DURAN. She responded that she had not seen Constanta since the last reported meeting. So, I spent a few minutes bringing her up to date on the status of the operation.

Then, a bit before eleven, I walked into the office of the Station's Administrative Officer to ask him to go out and purchase some sandwiches and drinks for our lunch with our FBI colleagues. He suggested Chinese take-out as good value for the money, and as the person responsible for monitoring Station funds, I knew where he was coming from. However, the thought of five or six people trying to discuss an operation while attempting to eat out of small cardboard boxes, some with chopsticks but having only dubious success with them, was unappealing.

I remember doing so at Headquarters one night during a foreign crisis in a country for which I ran the operational support element. We were busy with the senior Agency analysts discussing what intelligence requirements we need to put out to the Station, and recommendations for the Department of Defense, in order to provide clarity of the situation to the President and his senior advisors. As one might expect during such intense discussions, focusing on your eating skills is not the main priority. A couple of us and I managed to spill Kung Pao chicken, soy sauce, and chili pepper paste on our shirts. Since we had to appear on a multi-agency

CHAPTER THIRTEEN: WAITING

televised conference within an hour or so to present our ideas to the senior officials, there was no time to go home and change into a clean shirt. OK, in theory, it would be the logic and clarity of our recommendations that would be judged by these individuals, as well as the Agency Director and his assistant, who would formally chair our delegation. But, there really was no way that heavily stained shirts were going to help us make our points. After the hurried rush to the bathroom sinks and scrubbing ineffectively with paper towels, some of the colors dissipated, but the stains did not. Only quick thinking saved us from some embarrassment. I got to the "tank," the secure television conference room on the seventh floor of the Headquarters building, about fifteen minutes before the conference was to begin, and spoke with a very helpful technical that dimmed the overhead lights above the seats of the three of us so we sat pretty much in shadows. Days after the crisis was over, I spoke with a National Security Council colleague who mentioned that he thought he had heard my voice during the conference, but due to the darkness in the Agency, he was unable to make out my face. Thus, I succeeded in hiding my messy eating habits from the President of the United States and other senior Government officials. However, I have often wondered whether being more visible to that level of national leadership might have moved my career along quicker.

Anyway, that was the reason that I had suggested deli sandwiches. I really didn't want to worry about spilling food on my shirt. And, I suspect, if they thought about it, neither would anyone else involved.

The SAs arrived a bit after 11 a.m. Ralph brought Matt and Larry along. I asked Stan and Winston to join us in my office. Stan began by providing his overview and take on the meeting. I then provided our report to them. As one would expect, they were all happy with the meeting, even Matt. Ralph asked if I had received any reactions from our Headquarters, and I responded "not yet." Stan brought up the one troubling aspect of the meeting: the strange telephone call to the room by a seemingly Eastern European speaker asking for an individual with an Eastern European name. He explained that this could be nothing but a wrong number, but at this point in the operation, it was worth checking to see if it had any connection to the meeting with DURAN.

Matt said he would check with his fellow Squad Chiefs at the Field Office to see if any of their coverage of Eastern European subjects of interest was in the area of the hotel. Ralph also said he would have an SA assigned to the local Drug Task Force go to the hotel and, under the guise of a drug investigation, ascertain if anyone named Serge had been registered in the hotel that night. We appreciated this security support, and I said so. I then brought up the subject of the next meeting, on January 25th. I explained that from our perspective, if DURAN did bring out the manuals, we were about halfway towards our objective of recruiting him. And, while we were quite confident that DURAN could bring out these documents without much personal risk, we still had to entertain the possibility that he had been under suspicion and found out or had reported his conversations with Stan and was playing a double game. If he provided the manuals, and the United States Intelligence Community validated them as genuine, then we could be pretty sure he was not a double agent. However, until that time, we thought it would be wise if the Field Office could monitor both the Consulate and the meeting site of the January 25th meeting. Ralph readily agreed, as did Matt.

The meeting ended in a most cordial manner, and I later told Winston that this had probably been the best meeting we had had with the FBI since I took over as Chief of Station. All concerned were pleased with the progress of the operation, and anticipated that we were moving steadily towards our ultimate objective of acquiring the Romanian code tapes.

Also, during lunch, no one at the meeting spilled anything on their shirts or trousers.

Saturdays at the Station tend to be more casual. We do pull our communications in the early morning and then again at noon, but mostly it is a half day exercise in catching up on reporting, talking with the COs about their operations, or often just sitting around in the bullpen area, where the more junior COs have their desks, and discussing tradecraft or general subjects. Since we were moving into the Christmas–New Year holiday season, for the next several weeks, we would probably make

CHAPTER THIRTEEN: WAITING

Saturday an optional day for most of the staff. Either I or Winston would come in to read the communications to insure there were no immediate actions required. But for the COs, who normally put in well in excess of sixty hours a week between planning, reporting and conducting meetings, let alone the time required to securely move to and from those meetings, it would be a little more time for them to spend with their families or on personal time to relax.

However, since it had been almost three days since we sent in the reporting on the DURAN meeting, we were hoping that the morning's communications would have some kind of response from Headquarters. It did not, and Stan was a bit concerned. I waited until I had seen the noon download of traffic, and then asked Stan to come into my office. I began by noting that I had hoped to see something from Headquarters by now, but considering the possibilities that could result if we do get the manuals for the new communications system, there was likely a great deal of coordination going on with other U.S. Agencies. Certainly, NSA had to be briefed on what was happening, and probably would want to provide some specific requirements regarding details in the manuals. Stan agreed, and admitted he was wondering why we hadn't heard anything back as yet. I concluded our brief chat by stating that I was sure we would have something early next week, and suggested we both go home and focus on our personal lives for a few hours.

As Stan left, I had no delusions that my pithy comments had been particularly comforting. But, I'd been there before, anxiously awaiting word about an operation I had put significant effort into. Yet, it must also be understood that Headquarters has a visibility throughout the U.S. Intelligence Community and knows a great deal more about the "big picture" than we do in the field. They might well have information already collected and not need the manuals from this Target. Or, through counterintelligence sources, Headquarters might know the operation has been compromised. Finally, there might actually be other operations with higher priority that might be taking their immediate attention at the moment—although any good CO would find that hard to believe as his or her operation should always be the priority.

Nothing from Headquarters on Monday, but we did get some useful information from the Field Office regarding the mysterious telephone call during the meeting. Apparently, Ralph had ordered an SA to check out the hotel's registration log under the cover story of a drug investigation. The SA was able to report back that for three days, which bracketed Stan one night stay, a Serge Tsvetnov stayed at the hotel. Based upon the information obtained at the hotel, including the credit card he used to pay for his stay, Ralph has run a quick name check through FBI Headquarters databases. He learned that Tsvetnov was a first-generation Russian-American businessman selling automobile replacement parts for both motors and brakes. It appeared he had been in town on a routine sales circuit, and some of his local customers were used car dealers in the city's Eastern European emigre community. He did not appear to have any connection to the Romanian Government. Apparently, the telephone call was simply misdirected by the hotel operator, or misdialed by the caller as Stan's suite and Tsvetnov's room shared two of the three room numbers. When it wants to, the Bureau can be very helpful.

Finally, in the Tuesday morning communications traffic, we got a reply from Headquarters. It was cautiously complimentary of Stan's handling of DURAN. However, it also openly hinted that there were other facts about this case that we were unaware of, and that we must be very careful to make certain we were getting accurate information from the target. Obviously, Stan was not satisfied with Headquarters' reaction. I will admit that neither was I. But, still, if we got the new communications equipment details, that would be valuable. Winston's reaction was one of equal puzzlement. Could this whole deal be a carefully crafted plan by the Romanians, or more likely the Soviets, to pass false information about a communications system in the hopes of causing the U.S. Government to spend money and human resources in a wasted effort on a system that did not really exist? This certainlyertainly wouldn't be the first time the Agency found itself involved in a well-crafted disinformation operation.

For the next couple of hours these thoughts continued to trouble my

CHAPTER THIRTEEN: WAITING

mind, as I reviewed how we had selected and approached DURAN, vetted his motivations, and did all we could to make sure he was not a double agent. If the operation was bad, it also meant that Brenda's cover was blown as well.

A little after 1 p.m., the Senior Communication Officer walked into my office and handed me a manila envelope marked "eyes only——COS." He said this message from Headquarters should make my day easier and left the room. It did.

The communication was from the Agency's Division Chief, the most senior officer in charge of U.S.-based stations. It was sent to the Station via a special privacy channel with only a few Clandestine Service senior managers copied. The Division Chief said that both Headquarters and NSA were very pleased with the DURAN operation to date, and Stan's skillful handling of the meetings was well appreciated. The time lapse between receiving his reporting and the response was the result of the need for a coordination meeting between the Agency, NSA, and FBI Headquarters. The instructions provided were:

If Stan was able to photograph the equipment manuals, the film, undeveloped, was to be hand carried to Headquarters immediately by an officer of my selection.

If DURAN brought the manuals, NSA believed they would be voluminous and that Stan may well not have enough time to copy them completely. If so, he was to have DURAN identify the pages containing the specs and diagrams for the reception updated equipment, and for the equipment which functioned as the interface between the encoded traffic and the decoding machinery used at the Consulate. NSA was not sure if the new equipment included the encoding and decoding equipment, but if so, these specs were a priority requirement.

The message concluded with a few words of praise for our handling of the case, and especially for the manner in which we were working with the Field Office. He mentioned that his bi-weekly meetings with his counterpart at the Bureau had actually become pleasant.

After digesting this information, I called Winston and briefed him on the new instructions. We agreed that within the Station our "need-to-know" compartmentation would be Stan, Brenda, Winston and me. At a later date, we also planned to introduce one more CO for a transition role, but would decide who closer to when the operation had matured to that point. I then went and got Stan. When we returned to my office, he took one look at Winston's smile and asked what was going on. I gave him about the same brief as I had given Winston, and really enjoyed his reaction. Every once in a while in life hard work is rewarded, and this was Stan's turn. After giving him time to enjoy the news, we sent him off to continue his planning for another of his operations. But, I doubted that for at least the next half hour, he would really be concentrating on that.

The next order of business was to figure out how to advise Ralph of the Headquarters' instructions. I assumed his Headquarters had told him of the importance that NSA, the Agency and themselves saw in the operation. But, the FBI has some different ideas on how to compartment sensitive operations and I needed to discuss this with him.

Consequently, since I wanted to speak with him alone, I called and invited him to lunch at a city tavern-restaurant we had visited before. We arranged to meet on Thursday at noon. I arrived early and took a booth in the back of the dining area. When he arrived, we ordered beers, and the first words out of his mouth were to congratulate me on the DURAN operation. Ralph said he had been called by his boss at the Field Office and told how excited NSA was about the possibility of getting all the details on the new Romanian communications system.

Accepting his compliments as casually as I could, I moved on to the subject of how to handle information about the DURAN operation in the future. I stated, "Our Headquarters distribution of DURAN reporting will be much more restricted, and at the Station, only those officers involved in the case would know it was still active." I then asked how he planned to handle the reporting in this new phase of the operation. Ralph responded, "Matt, Larry, BJ, Frank, and Bob will have to be kept up to date based upon their responsibilities with the Consulate and the DURANs. "I noted this made sense, but I would prefer that no one else be involved. Well, Ralph noted, he would have to keep the SAC briefed, but other than that, at the moment, no one else in the Field Office needed to know about the case. I really would have preferred a smaller number of SAs involved, but that could not be my call. We then had a pleasant lunch, talking about the upcoming baseball season and how the baseball gods would treat the rebuilt local team after their disastrous last year. While shaking hands goodbye before departing the tavern, Ralph casually mentioned, "We at the Field Office are looking forward to having one of our SAs involved in an undercover role in the operation." I managed to smile. The Irish are like elephants; they never forget and also aren't very subtle.

About a week after New Year, as our operational tempo began to rise, I spoke with Stan regarding the status of his planning for the January 25th meeting with DURAN. Since Winston was out of the city on another operation it was just Stan and me.

Obviously, the objective of the meeting on the 25th was to copy the communications manuals. We were not sure how many there would be, nor, for that matter, what size they would be. A few days earlier, we had asked Headquarters to query NSA regarding the size of Eastern European technical manuals and Warsaw Pact manuals. The response was that most were either standard 11 ½ inch by 8 ½ inch, but some were 16 inch by 8 1/2 inch. This helped us plan the type of camera equipment Stan would need to copy the documents. So, we sat down with the technical referent assigned to the Station and reviewed what we had on hand. We decided on a camera model to use and a tripod support frame that would hold the camera at a height to cover a copying area. We would use a high resolution film, and all of this would be folded into a package which would fit into Stan's suitcase.

So, the equipment was OK. However, this was going to be a relatively slow process, photographing page by page. If all the conditions were perfect, Stan estimated that he could photograph between five and six pages a minute. Yet, he could not hurry the process since blurry or out-of-focus copies would be of little use. So, assuming two and a half hours of copying, we could get about nine hundred pages of manual content. This assumed that DURAN could amuse himself while Stan concentrated on the photographing. This was probably the maximum number of pages under the best possible conditions, and we both knew that the best possible conditions never really exist in an operational meeting.

Recognizing the stress of the copying task the CO was going to experience, we decided that we would reduce any other operational objectives for the meeting to a bare minimum. In addition to some motivational reinforcement, both verbal and through payment of the January retainer fee, there would be mention of additional compensation once the document information was put to trading use. Along with the payment would be yet another mention of using the funds in a manner that would not bring suspicion on DURAN. And, plans would have to be discussed for the next meeting, probably about two weeks hence, when Stan could tell DURAN about the financial rewards connected to the manuals. Also, Stan would have to discreetly take several photos of the briefcase that DURAN used to carry the documents, as we needed to know what it looked like for future planning purposes. This was about as elementary a meeting plan as you can get.

We also discussed how we would get the film to Headquarters as soon as possible. It seemed to me that it made the most sense to have Stan carry the film there, since he could also provide a first-hand narrative of his meetings with DURAN and give his personal views on his assessment of the target and their relationship. Headquarters would appreciate this, and, frankly, from a bureaucratic career perspective, Stan could benefit from briefing senior Agency managers.

With agreement that he would hand carry the film to Headquarters, Stan went back to his office to write a report advising Headquarters of our plans.

A couple of days later, it was time to meet with the Field Office. In Ralph's office, the first question I asked was whether Matt's squad had noticed anything unusual happening at the Consulate. Matt responded that the installation team had arrived, along with a large amount of equipment.

CHAPTER THIRTEEN: WAITING

He said that activities in the Communications Room were very busy. Equipment was unpacked in the hallway on the top floor of the Consulate and then moved into the communications room. Old equipment was moved out of the room, and administrative personnel from the Consulate were packaging it for shipment back to Bucharest. He added that the installation team, four men of whom three seemed to be technicians and the fourth a security officer, was working long hours. They arrived at the Consulate before 7 a.m. each morning and often did not leave the building until after 8 p.m. The Team was staying at a low-budget hotel about six blocks from the Consulate, and was driven to and from the hotel in the Consulate van, with DURAN driving. The Field Office surveillance unit watched DURAN arrive at the Consulate as early as 6:30 in the morning to get the van, and in the evening, he had to return the van to the Consulate parking area before going home himself.

In a more direct response to the real point behind my question, Matt stated, "From all we are able to determine, DURAN is handling his duties well. He had even taken the team out to a local Polish restaurant late one evening, and he and the team had gotten quite drunk. So, everything looks good so far."

After I discussed our plans for the next meeting and received Ralph's and Matt's approval, I requested some operational support from their surveillance unit. This time I not only wanted the Consulate and DURAN surveilled, I also wanted Stan followed the next morning as he conducted his countersurveillance route. I wanted to be as sure as possible that he was not being observed by anyone. Ralph readily agreed to these requests. After about half an hour of social conversation, I went back to the Station.

With everything in place and all the planning completed, all we could do had been done. While I was certain that Stan was constantly reviewing his plans in his mind, we did not discuss it until the afternoon of the 25th. Just before Stan left the Station for the meeting, he came in for a brief chat. I asked if he had any final thoughts, and he asked if I had any additional information he needed to know. He didn't, and neither did I. I wished him good luck, with the full realization that we were counting on our planning and his professional expertise much more than luck.

When Stan arrived at the hotel, he immediately went to his suite and started to organize where he would setup the camera system. He first considered the bedroom area, so he would be separated from DURAN in the sitting room, and could better focus on one task at a time. However, the furniture arrangement was unsuitable. The large coffee table in the sitting room, where they usually took their meal, proved to be the best location. Stan set up the camera and tripod and practiced focusing on a hotel magazine. He then replaced the equipment in his hand-carried luggage. Now, assuming DURAN would arrive after 8 p.m., there was the question of providing some refreshments. He had brought a bottle of their favorite scotch. But, having their regular room service dinner would involve a lot of wasted time; he would have to remove the copy setup, socialize over the meal, and then remove it before once again using the camera. He needed to maximize his time to photograph the documents.

Looking over the room service menu, Stan decided to order four sandwiches and a couple of snack dishes, along with four serving of coffee, all to be delivered by 7:30 p.m. He would arrange the sitting area to look like a meeting was set, with four people, when room service delivered. So, the food would be there before DURAN arrived, and once settled in, there should be no interruptions. Once this was arranged, Stan sat down, turned on the TV and waited. He later reported, really, that the television show he watched was "Get Smart," a comic parody of a secret agent which certainly was not an accurate description of a CO's activities but did highlight the unusual things that can often occur in a clandestine operation.

This is always one of the tensest times for the CO: waiting. Will the target show up? Will he bring what he has agreed to? Or, will the door suddenly burst open and the operation be exposed? At least in the United States, the risk of the latter would not mean being roughed up and possibly put in a cell until some diplomatic effort got you out. It would only mean a blown operation—one in which the CO had vested a great deal of time and both professional and personal emotions and commitment.

DURAN called from the lobby about 8:20 p.m., and then came to the room. His briefcase, brown and rather cheap-looking, contained seven manuals. He explained that he was the last to leave the Consulate, having departed about a quarter to eight, and only the night security guard was there. He was not asked anything, nor was his bag searched. He said he had routinely been taking the bag with him to the officer for the past several weeks, and as Stan had suggested, it has become a routine and therefore normal. So, he felt confident that he could return the manuals to his files tomorrow morning and no one would ever be the wiser. However, DURAN added, he felt he could only fit seven of the eleven installation and maintenance manuals into his briefcase because of their size. He apologized, but added that the installation team brought with them a couple more manuals, primarily those related to maintenance and repair of the equipment, than he had anticipated.

Stan could only respond that he appreciated DURAN's problem, and that they needed to review what he had brought and try to determine which had the most profitable information in them. He also quickly explained that he had some refreshments available; he did not want them to be disturbed once they started working on the manuals. He poured DURAN a scotch and asked DURAN to start translating the various manuals. Four of the seven are related to the more powerful radio reception equipment. Each of the components was described in technical terms and with a schematic diagram of its internal circuits and connection applications. Stan had studied the subject well enough to know that the diagrams would be the best information for NSA use, so he prioritized copying these pages.

After setting up the camera system, and explaining how it functioned to DURAN, who actually seemed quite interested, the Target assisted by moving the various pages under the tripod as Stan focused each page and snapped the picture. In about an hour and a half, the diagrams from the four manuals relating to the reception upgrade had been copied. At this point, Stan called a break and they moved over to the food tray to eat. Stan also poured another scotch for them both, and in his own mind noting that the copying effort was about half over, took a few minutes to build some rapport by asking DURAN how his family was, how work was going, etc.

It was now after 10 p.m., and there were three manuals to go. These, DURAN said, concerned component upgrades to the transmittal capabilities of the Consulate's radio system. They involved incorporating more transmittal speed, a data compression capability to move data in packets, and a periodic and random frequency changing capability to make the transmission more difficult to track once it left the Consulate.

To Stan, certainly not an expert in communications engineering, this sounded like a most interesting set of capabilities. First, he copied the diagrams and circuit drawings, and then asked DURAN to identify the pages providing the narrative on each piece of equipment. He also copied these pages. This took somewhat longer than with the previous four manuals. They ended the copying about a quarter after midnight. It was late, and Stan knew DURAN was both tired and probably would have to explain to his wife where he had been, if he had not already advised her of the meeting.

He poured DURAN one more for the road, and put away the camera and tripod in the bedroom. He returned with an envelope which contained DURAN's retainer for January, and gave it to him. He then noted the expectation that based upon this evening's work there should be some profits forthcoming in the near future. And, of course, he briefly and casually reminded DURAN of the need to be careful with how he used the money.

Stan then asked what the subjects of the remaining manuals were. DURAN replied that the other four manuals concerned interfacing the radio data into the existing teletype machines that produced the written copies of the radio traffic, which were disseminated within the Consulate. This sounded like part of the operation required to decode the radio transmission data into plain text, and therefore was one of the key requirements for the NSA. If so, should he try to have DURAN bring out these other manuals tomorrow night, or in a few days, or what?

He decided to ask the Target for a few more details, explaining that he was no expert in anything mechanical and needed to understand things in the simple language of a businessman. DURAN explained, "After the radio

CHAPTER THIRTEEN: WAITING

traffic signals are received and broken down into text format, most of the messages are still in a coded context. This text is then sent through another machine that runs it against a set of tapes that contain the decoding keys, and the end results are message texts that are readable. Once decoded, the text is sent to the teletype machines to be printed out as individual messages for various departments or individuals within the Consulate. "

So, Stan said, the remaining manuals are for equipment that takes the clear message content and send it to be typed up for distribution. "Yes, you got it." replied DURAN. Trying to think quickly, Stan realized this did not seem to be a priority item, and frankly he was not sure of its values verses the security risk of pushing the Target to bring out more documents right away. Instead, he opted for a cautious approach and fell back on his commercial cover story. He said that the diagrams he had photographed probably identified components in adequate detail to permit business research to determine which were made by Western companies and by whom. So, he should be able to use the information he has already photographed to ascertain the type of stock actions he could take to make some money. At their next meeting, Stan advised, he would have a better idea if the remaining manuals had profitable information in them. So, at that time, they could decide whether there was a future need to copy these manuals. This was a cautious and smart approach—why create an unneeded risk for the asset until you knew whether or not the information justified it?

Looking at the clock in the sitting room, Stan noted that it was late and he was sure DURAN wanted to get home and to bed. He said that he would be back in town in about three weeks, near the end of February. He and DURAN agreed on a date and time. Once again, the hotel was to be the site. Stan concluded the meeting by stating that by their next meeting he was hopeful of not only having identified some profitable short term stock investment options, but also being able to estimate the anticipated profit from his activities. And, just before DURAN was about to depart, Stan suggested he check his briefcase to make sure he had all the manuals he had brought with him. DURAN did so, shook hands, and left.

The next morning Stan checked-out of the hotel quite early, conducted his countersurveillance route, and after a quick shave and shower at his residence came to the Station. He only had a half hour or so to describe the meeting to Winston and me before he had to leave for the airport on his courier mission to Washington. He told us enough to know it had gone well, and that he was carrying nine rolls of film to headquarters. It was agreed that he would write out his formal reporting after his return from Washington, but would provide an oral briefing on the meeting and his view of the state of the operation to senior Division officers while there.

Stan stayed at Headquarters for three full days, talking not only with Division officers, but also officers from the Warsaw Pact Operations Group and the NSA liaison element at the Agency. He was on his way back to the Station when I got a message from Headquarters. Again, it was in the form of an "Eyes-only" message. It instructed us to open a new operational file for the Special Handling asset CARAWAY. The Special Handling communications channel would now be used for all information regarding this operation. Stan was to submit all reporting from the meeting of the 25th in this channel for the target CARAWAY.

Chapter Fourteen: Caraway

Upon his return, Stan briefed me and Winston on his meetings at Headquarters. It seemed everyone was pleased with our efforts, and that our pacing of the case was right on the mark. We were moving slowly and carefully, creating a series of deeper and deeper involvements by CARAWAY in a conspiracy with Stan. We all recognized the ultimate objective was to get access to the encoded tapes, and that by building CARAWAY's confidence in providing increasingly sensitive information, we had the operational momentum moving nicely. And, while the joint Agency—NSA element would need time, probably a couple of weeks, to fully checkout the equipment diagrams and installation manuals, they confirmed Stan's views on what had been important in prioritizing the manuals' copying. As to the remaining manuals, they would later provide some guidance regarding whether or not copying them was worth the risk of CARAWAY taking them out of the Consulate.

Stan was excited about the movement of the case into Special Handling status. This was the first time one of his operations had been judged this sensitive. We agreed that his primary operational efforts would now have to be focused on this case. But, I noted that I also expected him to continue with his development of the Asian scientist, with whom he had started to build a personal rapport. The last thing you want is a CO feeling underemployed—they often get into trouble that way. A CO can often be like a three-year-old, keeping them busy and focused makes life a lot easier.

The next step was to get with Ralph and the guys to brief them on the meeting and what we saw as the next steps in the operation. It took Stan a couple of days to finalize all his reporting from the January 25th meeting so it could be sent to Headquarters and passed to the Field Office. So, by the time Winston and I actually went downtown to Ralph's office, we were sure that FBI Headquarters had already provided him with all the details from Stan's Washington visit.

And, we were correct. Ralph explained that our Headquarters had briefed his FBI Headquarters' boss on the details Stan had provided while in Washington. I accepted the compliments in an appropriately humble manner, both because that's always a good approach to take and because until we received the read-out on the diagrams from NSA, I really didn't know just how well we had done. I am not a pessimist by nature—far from it. But, there are just too many things that can go wrong in an operation. In addition to the always present security issues, such as CARAWAY being doubled, and the practical matters, such as the film Stan used somehow being defective, there is always the possibility that the information finally obtained simply is not all that valuable. Perhaps this new equipment was not really new to NSA. So, I do tend to be cautious in accepting or claiming credit until we have confirmation that we actually accomplished something.

Anyway, we provided the SAs with copies of the reporting, and all agreed that we needed to get NSA's comments on the value of the details of the new equipment, and if they also wanted information and diagrams from the remaining manuals CARAWAY had in his Consulate office. We then discussed the subject of our relationship with the Target. Here I was more optimistic. He had fulfilled a somewhat risky task and provided us with sensitive information. He had knowingly compromised the communications system of the Consulate. In return, he had accepted cash payments and anticipated receiving additional funds once the information he had provided was used for profit by an international businessman, whom he knew to be an American. It was safe to say that he knew he was involved in a conspiracy for personal gain.

After I made these points, Matt asked if I then considered CARAWAY to

CHAPTER FOURTEEN: CARAWAY

be a recruited agent. I responded "No," and this provoked some discussion as to why I felt this way. Matt repeated all the points I had made about the Target providing sensitive information for money, and knowing full well that what he had done was against the rules of his government. "It," he concluded, "sounds like CARAWAY is doing our tasking." Matt asked what more I really wanted from CARAWAY before I was willing to view him as an asset. Once again, a cultural issue was involved, as well as a professional one, which is even debated within the Agency.

By FBI standards, if an individual accepted their tasking and took compensation for it, while clearly recognizing there was a risk involved, they believed they had a source. I can see their point. Indeed, there was no question that CARAWAY had provided sensitive information in exchange for money. Hopefully, soon we will know just how valuable this information was to the U.S. Intelligence Community. However, he was doing so under a scenario with a limited range of tasking options because of the business cover story we were using. We certainly had developed some control over him, based on an assumed personal friendship and trust in Stan and motivated by personal gain, to acquire supposed "nonpublic" business information. We were able to manipulate this relationship to get communications technical manuals. But, could our tasking of him be advanced to the point that he would provide the encrypted tapes from the Consulate?

It would be difficult to convince him that the tapes had a readily profitable commercial value. To some degree, he must recognize that only State-type organizations could really exploit the tapes for some value. To be willing to take this risk, he had to have complete trust in our ability to handle the material without compromising it, protect him as he provided it to us, and have both a financial and personal alternative for him should he come under suspicion. And, of course, his compensation would have to be appropriately large. At this stage of the operation, he simply had an agreement with one businessman whom he seemed to trust to provide information for cash.

There were also the very serious issues of his personal commitment to the Romanian Government, the Romanian Communist Party, and his extended family back in Romania. To date, while he certainly recognized the seriousness of his providing the technical manuals, he could easily rationalize that all he had done was to give a businessman some information to use to make some money in the stock market. Certainly in his actions with Stan we had seen no indications that he was directly prepared to betray his country, Party or family. Thus, while we had the capability to motivate him with compensation and friendship, we had yet to develop a satisfactory psychological control over him, resulting in a shared conspiracy. In this type of conspiracy, CARAWAY would believe the financial compensation was worth the risk because we could protect him, and those important to him, and, if necessary, taking care of him if things went terribly wrong. Stan's image as portrayed to the target hardly supported such confidence.

The issue of psychological control, based upon a thorough understanding of the target's motivations and concerns, is the key to recruitment in the type of agent we wanted CARAWAY to become. Sure, some COs in the Agency would have already declared him a recruited asset, and his provision of the technical manuals would indeed be proof of his willingness to accept tasking and provide sensitive information. But, we had greater expectations in mind for him, and still had to create a scenario that would involve him in a long-term conspiracy with an organization which he could actually believe would be able to protect him. That would start with the next phase of the operation, assuming NSA was satisfied with what had been provided at the January 25th meeting.

It is worth noting here the big question usually asked by individuals at our Headquarters is why play around with the false commercial approach when, realistically, the information obtained, and certainly that which will be requested in the form of the tapes, is so obviously only of use to the U.S. Government? The answer in my mind is because, like most human Targets, this is a one-time opportunity. If we blow this one chance after getting this far with another Warsaw Pact code clerk, our odds of another opportunity are virtually zeroAccess to individuals like CARAWAY is difficult to say

CHAPTER FOURTEEN: CARAWAY

the least. With human assets, arguably the most difficult Targets in the business, there is no easy replacement process—if you lose the operation, you lose the access possibly forever. So, I was willing to go long into a commercial scenario, which either convinced or rationalized for the Target that cooperation was acceptable on his terms. You give the Target what he needs, in my book.

As I completed my little speech, both SAs looked at me in what seemed to be a puzzled way. Obviously, neither of them was impressed with my view of the status of the case. Matt asked, "Are you perhaps overthinking the operation?" He said that Stan had done a great job with CARAWAY, and now we had to exploit the relationship for all it was worth. Ralph was more circumspect and simply commented that, in his opinion, we actually had some good control over the target and had no reason to think he would not continue to respond to our tasking. These were not solid endorsements of my professional approach towardsthe operation. And, as it was a "joint operation," I was in no position to insist that my view was the only way to go forward. But, you better believe I felt it was.

So, I backed down a bit, noting that perhaps I had overstated the issues of control and tasking. I then suggested that, as soon as NSA sent us the results of their analysis of the technical data and any future interest they had in the manuals, we could plan for the next meeting. Thus, the meeting ended on a comfortable note.

Stan later told me that a few days after our meeting with Ralph and Matt he had lunch with Larry and the conversation at the meeting did come up. Larry said that Matt felt I was way too "academic" in my thinking, and that as a "street guy," he knew how to keep pressure on an informant once cooperation had been demonstrated. Matt also said that Ralph felt the case was under much better control than I believed. However, since the Station had the lead in the case at this point, and as long as CARAWAY continued to produce, the Field Office would just go along with the flow. Good feedback. As is true in most bureaucratic efforts, as long as things went smoothly, all partners would take credit. If they did not, Matt, at least, knew exactly who to blame.

And, to be perfectly honest about it, in the back of my mind, there was an alternative plan to claim him as a recruit should he refuse to get us the tapes, but be willing to continue to provide other information of value from the Consulate. In such an event, we would handle the agent jointly with the Field Office as a penetration of the Romanian Consulate. We would use him as aggressively as he would agree to. But, and this was a big but, I was determined to stay with our strategic objective just as long as we could.

Since the next meeting was set for the evening of February 18th, we had about two weeks in which to get NSA's readout on the value of the information and develop a scenario for whatever additional requirements were given to us. The wait was not restful. In the meantime, it was about time for another beer with Ralph to smooth over any troubled waters. We met after work, and after the usual social chatter, I said that in retrospect, I probably had been a bit too philosophical in my comments on the status of the operation. I continued that as this was a joint operation, the Field Office's input, as well as practical assistance, was vital to success. I understood Matt's points, and we would continue to push CARAWAY to establish control over him at every meeting. Ralph responded that he thought both Matt and I were saying the same thing. Hopefully, the horse was back in the barn at least for the moment?

The Saturday before the meeting, Headquarters finally responded with comments on the results of NSA's analysis of the manuals' diagrams, and some questions regarding how we planned to move ahead. So, we had four days to put together the meeting plan. Stan would handle developing the meeting scenario, while Winston would put together our plans for moving CARAWAY to the next phase of the operation. I would arrange a meeting with Ralph to get his agreement on the meeting plans. We would not bother the Field Office with our more strategic planning at this time.

NSA's evaluation of the diagrams was that they were authentic and functioned exactly as CARAWAY had described. From the photos, NSA also verified that some portions of the technical manuals were Romanian versions of Warsaw Pact manuals, which had already been acquired. We were told these communications equipment upgrades were closely held among Soviet Bloc communications agencies. That was very good news, as it supported our belief that CARAWAY was working with Stan as he had promised. From a counterintelligence perspective, because this was sensitive communications information, it was less likely to be "feed material" given to a double agent trying to impress his handlers.

NSA advised that while useful, both to validate other manuals obtained and to facilitate the collection of over-the-air radio traffic, this information was not helpful in terms of reading the radio traffic. So, we did good but not too good—yet. The only additional tasking NSA requested was quite general. Stan was to try and get CARAWAY talking about his position and exactly how he handled his daily duties.

Actually, in terms of our strategic plan, the details of which Headquarters had yet to be fully informed, we decided to use the next meeting to start the introduction of another personality into the mix. Stan could use the time for some elicitation and assessment, as well as build on the scenario regarding the additional contact in a manner intended to demonstrate future earning potential for the Target. This meeting would be more of a continuing developmental opportunity, without any specific tasking. I was not sure how Matt was going to respond to this, but from our perspective, it was just fine.

Monday morning, having worked in the Station most of the weekend, Stan had the meeting plan in draft form. I asked a few questions, which prompted him to modify a couple of issues, but he pretty much had everything covered in his planning. The meeting would evolve around a dinner meal, with good scotch before, during, and after. We both chuckled as I noted he did not mention the chocolate torte for dessert in his planning.

As was becoming usual, CARAWAY showed up at the hotel on time and called to get the suite number from Stan. Once into their first drinks, Stan brought up the fact that as a business guy he really was not very well versed in technical subjects, and after the last meeting wondered if he might miss some exploitative possibilities in the information because he did not understand the electrical engineering industry. "So," he explained,"

I ended up showing the diagrams to an expert in the field, and sought his comments regarding how to manipulate the information." CARAWAY looked surprised at this, and Stan immediately went on to explain that this was an individual whom he had used before. He also emphasized that he had not told this individual from whom, or where, he had obtained the pages of the manuals. Stan continued "This expert, Edmund, is a Canadian and heavily involved in the grey market for communications equipment. In fact, his activities often slipped over into the black-market area, working with companies involved in bypassing international sanctions on the sale of certain communications technology in Africa and the Far East." So, Edmund was the type of individual who did not ask any questions about the information. He simply analyzed it, got paid, and forgot about it. CARAWAY appeared to relax and seemed satisfied that his identity had remained protected.

Stan said that based upon Edmund's analysis, he had identified two European companies and one Japanese company whose components were included in the upgraded equipment. Further research showed a paper trail indicating that the European companies probably had sold their technology to the Soviets. However, in the case of the Japanese company, their components might have been obtained in a less formal manner— either stolen or sold in the grey or black market. With this information, Stan noted that he had made a leveraged options position on a bond held by one of the European companies, and as of yesterday has profited in the area of thirty-eight thousand dollars. However, he would not actually close out the option for another ten days. But, he intended to give CARAWAY part of his share of the profit now, and depending upon the amount finally made, would probably have more for him later. This raised a noticeable smile on CARAWAY's face.

Having given the target the "good news," Stan moved into the elicitation mode, which continued through the dinner and dessert. He began by asking if CARAWAY had experienced any problems while returning the manuals to his office, and then used the Target's response to move the conversation towards how CARAWAY spent his usual day at work. As

CHAPTER FOURTEEN: CARAWAY

CARAWAY described his duties, the CO was able to use the information provided to ask for additional details, all of which should seem normal in a friendly conversation. By the Target's third scotch, Stan was starting to get some specifics about the technical responsibilities of his position at the Consulate. Apparently, in the morning, CARAWAY and his assistant would download the radio data sent to the Consulate, interface it with decryption tapes stored in his office safe, and have the data decrypted and loaded on a storage disk on his communications system. They would then edit the data to ensure each separate message was addressed to the appropriate Consulate section, or if required, to a specific individual. Once this was done, he would move the traffic to the electronic printers for printing out in written form. His assistant, the junior Communications Officer, would then hand-distribute the correspondence throughout the Consulate. CARAWAY stated that on an average day, it could take them about an hour plus in the morning to process all the overnight traffic. He also noted that on occasion, there would be a piece of traffic that required special decoding processing, and this involved changing the decoding tape in the machine, which added about fifteen minutes to his morning's work.

Stan noted this, but did not seek any more details about it. That would come later. Rather, he asked if the morning was Target's busiest time. CARAWAY responded that actually it was in the evening, just as the Consulate was about to close for the day. Typically, the various section heads tended to wait until the end of the business day to authorize the communications from their people, which had to be sent to Bucharest or other Romanian installations. So, he would receive all the day's traffic usually in one large batch. Then, he and his assistant would have to process the correspondence onto tapes, load the tapes into the interface with the encryption tapes, then load the encrypted messages into the transmitter and send them. Stan asked if his assistant could actually handle most of these duties, so that CARAWAY did not have to do all the physical work. CARAWAY explained, "My assistant is capable of handling most duties in the Communications Room; however, as the senior officer, it is my responsibility to open and close the communications system daily. Also,

I am the Consulate officer responsible for storage of the decryption and encryption tapes, and as such, I have duties after the system is shut down." Stan asked the next logical question: "Does that mean you can never take a day off or a vacation?" CARAWAY said that with the exception of securing the encryption and decryption tapes, his assistant could perform all his duties on a temporary or emergency basis. But, besides him, only the Consulate General was allowed to handle the encryption and decryption tapes.

However, the Target said, in reality, he was not expected to take many days off or to take any extended vacations. His responsibilities were too important. Also, if a component in the system failed, it was often his previous experience that enabled him and his assistant to repair it quickly. While the technical manuals were there for reference, his assistant simply did not have the necessary experience to handle any but the simplest repair or maintenance problems—the Consulate General counted on him to insure a reliable and steady communications system.

By this time, as CARAWAY was finishing his dessert and Stan had asked a great many questions, carefully phrased within the context of the conversation, it was time to bring up the proposal. CARAWAY seemed in good spirits, well fed, and readily accepted an after-dinner scotch. To further insure his good, and hopefully receptive, mood, Stan brought out the money. He gave the target two thousand dollars, in fifties and twenties, explaining that based upon his current estimate of the total profits, this was a down payment on his share. He also reminded CARAWAY that as this was a new month, he was also owed his retainer fee of five hundred dollars, which was given to him in twenties.

This part of the meeting was a bit trickier than one may think. We assumed that CARAWAY would be pleased by the large sum he was receiving. However, there was also the possibility that as Stan had mentioned a potential profitability figure of about forty thousand dollars; he might feel his share was too small. If he readily accepted the payment, then it indicated that he was satisfied with his relationship with Stan and that was good. If he expressed a little concern that his share seemed small in comparison to the overall profit, Stan was prepared to list the various expenses he had underwritten to handle the deal. He would then agree with CARAWAY that he deserved more money, and use this as a way of introducing Edmund into the relationship.

But, in the worst-case scenario, if CARAWAY became quite upset, then the CO had to use his interpersonal skills to calm him down. While Stan had some general concepts to use should this occur, his success would depend upon his ability to address whatever reasons CARAWAY raised for his displeasure. Luckily, CARAWAY raised no objections and seemed quite happy with the payments.

After CARAWAY pocketed the rather thick packet of bills, Stan reminded him to be careful in how he spent it. And, then moved into his prepared speech about how his lack of technical knowledge might be a factor holding both of them back from greater profitability. He noted that his investment field of expertise was in financial trading, especially in international stock markets, where leveraged options trades could be manipulated due to local regulations less rigid than in the United States. Since CARAWAY was an expert in radio communications, it was quite possible that his expertise could be used in ways other than just inside business information obtained at the Consulate. But, as Stan did not really understand communications technology or that industry from a financial perspective, he was thinking about trying to use Edmund's expertise to help them determine if some better way to use CARAWAY's talents were possible. As anticipated, CARAWAY immediately looked worried.

He responded that he had to be very careful that no one knew of his "outside" business dealing with Stan. After all, he was not supposed to be providing "insider information." Stan responded with the carefully structured argument that he understood and shared CARAWAY's feelings. If Edmund were to meet with him to investigate what more could be done, it would have to be in a situation where CARAWAY's identity was fully protected. Not only was this important to the Target, Stan noted, but also to him as a businessman and not just as CARAWAY's friend. He explained that the "grey" market in "insider information" was very competitive, and depended upon the secrecy of sources for both legal and practical reasons. Should Edmund know that Stan's source of information was CARAWAY, he might either try to approach the Target directly and offer him a better deal to be his source, or he might sell CARAWAY's identity as a source to another international trader who would want to profit from the type of information he could provide. In either case, to protect his own business, Stan intended to ensure Edmund did not know CARAWAY's identity.

This argument, reinforced by Stan's additional comments regarding his personal concern for the Target's security and some stories of how he had learned to protect his business sources the hard way after others had stolen them, seemed to make CARAWAY comfortable. He and Stan then discuss how to structure a meeting where Edmund could meet and discuss how the target's experience and position might be more profitably utilized, while still ensuring his identity was unknown. It was agreed that they would meet in four weeks' time, at a different hotel in the city. CARAWAY would use the same procedure, arriving at a specific time and calling from the lobby to get the suite number. Stan would have Edmund already in the suite, and be sure to have him there a good half hour before CARAWAY was scheduled to arrive. They would hold their discussion, with the Target being addressed only as Bill. After the discussion, CARAWAY would depart and Edmund would not be allowed to leave the suite until half an hour after his departure. These conditions seemed to satisfy CARAWAY, though he still seemed somewhat nervous.

Since this meeting involved a third party, Stan noted that he would have to arrange for Edmund's travel and accommodation in a hotel in a different part of the city. So, the timing of CARAWAY's arrival had to be exact. And, if even up to the last minute, the Target was unable to make the meeting, Stan advised him to call the office number he had been given previously. His secretary would be able to get in touch with him and he could then adjust anything that needed to be done. With that, CARAWAY departed, apparently having accepted the scenario for the next meeting.

When Stan reported the results of the meeting the next afternoon, I spent more time talking with him about the atmospherics of the meeting and the level of rapport between him and the Target than about the actual content of his reports. CARAWAY was, apparently, following our script quite well. This could be because we are extremely clever COs, who have planned meticulously all aspects of our manipulation of the target, or just luck. Of course, it could also be that we are being played by the Romanian service. But, as I mentioned previously, the type of information he has already provided, now validated as accurate, would seem to preclude that possibility. Anyway, I was wondering how much of CARAWAY's cooperation was due to his strong desire for money, his belief that he could trust Stan's business persona, or any personal relationship he felt with Stan. Obviously, like any CO, Stan would believe that he had created a strong personal rapport with the Target. And, to a certain degree, this was true. But, for me, as we approach a switch, or turnover as we call it in the profession, to a new CO, I needed to feel confident that we were going to provide a scenario that satisfied both his motivations and his concerns regarding his personal security.

I listen carefully how Stan described his personal relationship with the Target, and had him then address how he felt CARAWAY viewed his international businessman persona in terms of trust and confidence that Stan could protect him. I also ask how the Target reacted when queried about his Consulate duties and when the subject of bringing in Edmund was raised. I was particularly interested in how Stan viewed CARAWAY's reaction, and apparent agreement, based upon his explanation of how and why he would protect the Target's identity. My understanding from Stan was that money was the key motivator for CARAWAY, and that he was willing to accept some risk as long as he could rationalize that he did have adequate protection from exposure.

Stan felt, and I agreed, that the Target's risk taking threshold depended upon his belief that he was dealing with someone who could protect him. I might add here that Targets from authoritarian cultures often instinctively view their personal and professional future as dependent on protection and assistance from an institution, such as the Communist Party, or a particular leader in power. Thus, our assessment had a cultural basis. So, if we were correct, we now had to build a structure that fulfilled both his motivational and his security goals to make him willing to get us the encryption tapes.

Stan submitted his reporting to Headquarters, and I took copies to Ralph at the Field Office as usual. I lucked out this time since Matt was traveling to an FBI conference in Washington. With Ralph I emphasized the information CARAWAY had provided about his Consulate duties, which Stan had made the subject of a separate report. I thought this was information that should be of use to Matt's squad, and thus represented specific value to the Field Office. I also spent some time explaining the brief but important role that Edmund would be playing in the next couple of meetings. Then, hopefully to preempt his suggesting that an FBI undercover play the role of Edmund, I explained that once CARAWAY was introduced to his actual final tasking, CO, I wanted to get two of his SAs directly involved in role playing in the operation. He liked that, and our meeting concluded with agreement on how to move forward.

As soon as I got back to the Station, I wrote a message to Headquarters requesting a visit by the Romanian expert. I explained the need to get an objective, outside opinion on the Target's motivation and the degree to which an authoritative and seemingly powerful figure would create the comfort and confidence the Target needed to take the risk of providing the tapes. I expected agreement from Headquarters, since the folks at the support desk always like to see the field asking for an "objective" opinion.

Chapter Fifteen: The Headquarters' Analyst

It only took Headquarters three days to agree to the visit by the analyst, butit took five to respond to Stan's reporting. The information on CARAWAY's daily duties was considered to mirror what Headquarters, the FBI, and NSA knew about Warsaw Pact code clerks. There were also some compliments for Stan's handling of the elicitation and, especially for the manner in which he convinced CARAWAY to accept meeting with the technical expert. And, through Larry, Stan was able to advise that upon his return Matt was even happy with the information provided on the Target's duties. With three weeks before the next meeting, we had two major tasks: select and train an officer to be Edmund and have the Headquarters analyst complete her assessment of CARAWAY.

Carol, the Headquarters Romanian expert, arrived the next Tuesday afternoon. I had worked with her on another operation a few years earlier, in an overseas location. She had some twenty years' experience in the Agency and knew how to handle herself in operational environments. That meant that she would be able to deal with the Field Office SAs without causing any "cultural" problems. I trusted her skills and instinct. We immediately set up a schedule of interviews for her with everybody at the Station and at the Field Office who had insights into the target.

I guess I should note that at this point in the operation, Brenda's role with Mrs. CARAWAY was not quite as valuable as in the past. We were now getting extensive "time on target" with CARAWAY, and using this access to probe for the assessment information we needed. So, Brenda had been slowly cutting back on her social meetings with hisr wife, claiming the press of her business dealings. Both we and the Field Office felt that monitoring of her telephonic conversations with CARAWAY would be sufficient in providing any indications of issues between them that might affect the operation. We thought that over the course of about five months, Brenda could break off all ties. Her commercial platform had successfully established her in the local international community, and from this cover had developed a couple of promising operations. I wanted her to focus on these operations instead of Mrs. CARAWAY. However, since she had been involved from the start of the operation and had some personal insights into both of the CARAWAYs, she remained on the Station's traffic distribution list for CARAWAY. If we were eventually successful in this operation, her role certainly would get appropriate credit.

On Wednesday, I took Carol down to the Field Office and introduced her to Ralph and Matt. She needed their approval to talk with the SAs who had been monitoring CARAWAY since his arrival at the Consulate. This would also include members of the surveillance unit, who had followed him around. It also included Alice, the short-term SA babysitter for Anton. In our meeting with Ralph, Carol explained her objective of trying to piece together a picture of what CARAWAY's motivations were and trying to establish some perspective on his risk-taking limits. She also casually mentioned that her old friend, who just happened to be a senior SA in the Behavioral Science unit of the FBI, asked her to pass along his best regards to Ralph, with whom he had worked previously on a New York City case. This, of course, was not an accidental comment. Carol had done her homework and sought out contacts at the FBI who could prove useful. She concluded by noting that this was a joint operation, and whatever she was able to ascertain would be shared with the Behavioral Science unit at FBI Headquarters as well as with Ralph.

As things were going well, and Carol's interpersonal skills were in full swing, I suggested we all go out for lunch on me, since I wanted Carol to visit a local restaurant I had told her about. Ralph agreed, and the three

CHAPTER FIFTEEN: THE HEADQUARTERS' ANALYST

of us had a pleasant lunch, made more enjoyable by Carol's stories of past assignments and some humorous incidents she had experienced overseas. She also related a couple of particularly good stories of joint activities with the FBI that had resulted in successful outcomes.

When we returned to Ralph's office to establish a schedule to interview the SAs, he surprised us by stating that now that the case was at this point, there were some other SAs that Carol should also talk with. He then told us that the Field Office had several microphones located inside the Consulate, as well as an asset, a local Romanian–American source, who did maintenance work in the building. So, he noted that BJ, who ran the Consulate audio operation, should also be on Carol's schedule. And that she should also question Matt about his human source at the Consulate. We readily agreed. Months later, Ralph made a point of telling me that early in the operation, he had not been able to tell me about all the collection capabilities the Field Office had at the Consulate, but had passed along any information from them that he felt was relevant to the operation.

Over the next four days, Carol interviewed all the SAs involved. Perhaps they had been specifically instructed to cooperate by Ralph, or maybe it was just Carol's personality, but she found their comments very helpful and in some cases obtained information and observations which she had not gotten from Station officers. Of particular interest to her were the comments regarding CARAWAY's personality and lifestyle.

Carol then spent the next several days, and they were long days, when she stayed at the Station late into the night, according to the Station's entry control log, completing her report. Upon its completion, she wanted to let me see, and perhaps comment, on it before she sent it to Headquarters for inclusion in CARAWAY's file. She also mentioned that she intended to do some research back at Headquarters on Warsaw Pact and Soviet Block archives to see what she might be able to dig up regarding the Communist Party culture in Romania after World War II, and how this may have affected CARAWAY through his parents' Party connection or that of his wife's parents. I asked how long that would take, and she replied that she believed she could get all she needed in a few days' research.

When Carol brought me her draft report, I found it contained an analysis of CARAWAY's motivations, how his priority of loyalties broke down, how he viewed himself within his professional status, his relationship with his wife and child, his relationship with his parents, his views of the Romanian Communist Party, and how these issues affected his decision-making in terms of risk taking. I tended to agree with her analytical points, and did not feel it was appropriate to add any comments. I then released her report for transmission to Headquarters, took her to lunch, sincerely thanked her for her efforts, and in mid-afternoon dropped her off at the airport for her flight back to Washington.

Chapter Sixteen: Enter "Edmund"

While Carol had been researching and preparing her draft report, Winston and I had been busy deciding which CO to use as Edmund. We finally decided on a first tour officer assigned to the Station who actually had an undergraduate degree in engineering, which was about as close as we could get to CARAWAY's specific field. We planned to introduce him as an "international" businessman, with no further specifics about his nationality. His American English accent was not a factor in our decision-making sense he did not have a regional accent.

Once we advised him of his role, which we anticipated would be only for two or three meetings at the most, we had him spend some time reading the entire DURAN and CARAWAY files. Previously, we had asked our Headquarters support desk to have NSA prepare a detailed description of their understanding of the physical setup and equipment at the Consulate. Edmund would have to study this, as well as absorb some general knowledge on long-distance high-frequency radio transmissions and the current status of the technology. The young officer was instructed to consider educating himself for this role to be his top operational priority. When first advised of this role, while excited to be part of this type of operation, he was also just a little apprehensive—actually, he was probably quite apprehensive if not actually scared. We were placing him in a difficult operational role: a transition role, which would require role playing and interpersonal skills as well as an ability to learn a great deal, in a short time, in a rather complex technical field. He had only been at the Station for a few months, but had already demonstrated his aggressiveness by starting up several assessment and development operations. His planning and reporting on these operations demonstrated both personal discipline and a solid grasp of tradecraft principles. But, the key reasons we selected him were some skills identified in his training report from the Farm, which highlighted his interpersonal and role-playing skills as being quite advanced. He was also a quick learner. This was exactly what we needed in this situation.

Our training facility, the Farm, provides all potential COs with a long and comprehensive training period where tradecraft is taught both in the classroom and through role-playing exercises. Unlike most military and civilian entry-level classes, it is as much a "selection out" exercise as it is a training class. Usually, at least one quarter to one third of the class does not meet certification by the training staff as COs. The realistic exercises allow the teaching staff, most of whom were or are COs with field experience, to observe not only how quickly new officers absorb tradecraft concepts and use them within the context of the operation, but also what natural talents they bring to the game. Thus, if a new officer can only learn the tradecraft practices in an academic sense, and cannot naturally translate them into scenarios suitable for each exercise, they will have problems passing the course. In the Agency, your Farm training evaluation can play a strong role in where you are stationed in your career, well into your middle grades within the bureaucracy. Needless to say, those individuals who struggle at the Farm usually have a much harder time getting assignments than those who, early on, demonstrate a knack for utilizing the skills. The CO business is a tough career, and even with a solid training report and previous successes, when you come into a new Station, you always have to prove yourself again.

Edmund spent a couple of days, including the weekend, studying up on the technical aspects of the Consulate's communications system and the specifics of the recently installed upgrades. We then had him and Stan spend the good part of a day just talking about the operation, and specifically how they would explain their professional connection to the

CHAPTER SIXTEEN: ENTER "EDMUND"

Target. This was a key issue if the transfer from Stan to Edmund was to be successful. CARAWAY had to believe that, for various reasons, and we planned to emphasize the illegal aspects of their activities, that Edmund would protect his identity as the source of the information. He also needed to believe that Stan, in whom some trust and rapport had been created, had used Edmund in other similar situations without any risk to the source of any information. So, it would fall on Stan to weave this story into his conversation with CARAWAY at the next meeting where Edmund would be introduced. The two COs also had to decide how to play their roles throughout the rest of the meeting. And, finally I asked them to prepare an outline of their entire scenario for Winston and I to review.

While my academic background was purely Liberal Arts, I also did a quick review of the technical briefing provided by headquarters and noted down a few questions I wanted to ask Edmund during our operational review. I have found that while one cannot be an expert in all fields, a fairly accurate judgment regarding whether the "expert" you are talking with really is one is to ask a few basic questions, the answers to which you have developed a fair grasp of. If the 'expert" can provide an answer which is understandable to the non-technical individual, it means the "expert" understands the issue. I have found this approach to be especially helpful in my previous tour at Headquarters, where I had responsibility for the funding and creation of a mainframe computer penetration operation. As someone who started in the Agency when copying documents were done on machines that literally burned a copy onto special paper, understanding the technology involved in computers and their networks did not come naturally or easily to me. However, determined to keep the developmental funds at scheduled levels, and in the face of computer technicians who insisted on spreading network diagram sheets across the floor of my office, asking some questions and listening carefully to how well the techies were able to answer them to my satisfaction and understanding, the project was completed on budget and implanted successfully against a foreign target.

When I called in Stan and Edmund to review their operational planning, I was quite pleased with the scenario they had developed. I was equally pleased with Edmund's responses to the technical questions I posed. Winston and I had very little to add to their plans. We did, however, carefully go over the logic and target appeal of their scenarios regarding both Edmund's capability to protect CARAWAY as the source of information, and the reasoning why Edmund's technical and business skills could bring greater rewards for the target. After this meeting, I met with Ralph and Matt to advise them of our planning and obtain their concurrence. We then sent the scenario to Headquarters and quickly received words of encouragement from them. Considering the importance that this "turnover" meeting had in terms of the operation's future success, the operational scenario had been surprisingly easy to coordinate.

Three days before the meeting, Carol's formal assessment of CARAWAY arrived at the Station. Winston, Stan, Edmund and I all sat down to read it and then discuss its value for the upcoming meeting. Its conclusions were as in the draft, and therefore supportive of what we had come to regarding the Target's motivation and the level of confidence he would have to have to take the risks required to bring out the tapes. Its conclusion was that CARAWAY was looking to enhance his family's lifestyle and career future without moving beyond what he considered acceptable boundaries within his cultural system. He had little in the sense of any loyalty to his government as an entity or to the Romanian Communist Party. However, he viewed both as organizations that would protect him and provide him with benefits unavailable to the general population of his country as long as he played by their rules. And, these rules accepted minor personal business dealings involving government privileges.

To CARAWAY, his family came above all other organizations. His first priority was his wife and their son. His second priority was his and his wife's parents and families. Beyond that, his actual commitment to any other entity was situationally dependent. He would support the government, the Party, and his Ministry when it benefited him personally or professionally to do so. It was the same way with his mentor, the Consulate General. If he could benefit from his association with the Consulate General, he would be both loyal and cooperative. But this loyalty

CHAPTER SIXTEEN: ENTER "EDMUND"

extended only to when it benefited him personally. While we believed this based upon Brenda's and Stan's assessments, Carol reinforced this point in her report. Apparently in conversations with his wife, and through other comments he made to others, his personal closeness to the Consulate General also came into a better perspective. CARAWAY viewed that official as a social friend who could be very helpful in his career, and who could even provide assistance in areas such as future postings overseas. However, the Consulate General's personality and attitude towards CARAWAY were not always collegial. He expected the Target to be constantly grateful for his patronage and ready at any moment to undertake any extra work, both official and personal, for him. Field Office sources identified several times when the Target assisted the Consulate General in some questionable business deals, but then felt that his share of the profits had not been forthcoming. There was also an incident during the holiday season when the Consulate General "suggested" to CARAWAY the specific and expensive "gift" he would like from the couple.

That CARAWAY did not feel any real personal loyalty to the Consulate General was of key importance to us, as was the lack of any philosophical or personal loyalty to his government or the Communist Party. This confirmed that our next objective was to create an entity to which he could have a loyalty, and this would depend upon our capability to manipulate him into believing that his future, both professionally and personally, was directly tied to that entity. It would also require the creation of an entity that could compensate him adequately and protect him from exposure or, if necessary, remove him from harm's way should he be exposed.

Carol's report also addressed an assessment of CARAWAY's perspective on government organizations versus private business organizations, and his own confidence levels regarding risk taking. Most individuals view organizations based on their own interaction with them. The Target was no different, and seemed to view all governments as functioning in the same manner as did the Romanian Government. Basically, he saw all governments and government officials as self-serving and corrupt. This meant that he would probably view the U.S. Government in the same way.

Trying to educate and motivate the target to change these perceptions would be both a difficult and time-consuming task. So, continuing the relationship under the guise of a commercial entity was the most effective way to proceed.

Carol also made a final point that we had recognized: CARAWAY responded well to an authoritative 'father" figure type. He apparently had that type of a father, whom he respected highly, and had initially viewed the Consulate General in that role until he became disenchanted with that individual's treatment of him. Carol noted that culturally, this was common among Eastern Europeans and that the Communist Party system had created a series of "father figures" within its structure that reinforced this perspective. So, we had another element to weave into our final commercial entity—a father figure with a heart. Or, a senior business figure whose character and personality radiated forcefulness and also kindness: A leader of a wealthy and powerful international business organization, with capabilities akin to a nation-state, who was able to instill confidence in CARAWAY that he would be rewarded and protected in all his business activities. OK—we can do that.

Since the Target's personal experience outside the Soviet Bloc was really limited to the diplomatic community, and mostly to Warsaw Pact countries, our first task was to expose him to the concept that such commercial organizations existed. Stan had made it clear that he had international contacts that could assist in placing stock trades. He had also briefly referred to gray market activities. But, he had not gone into any details about the supposed power and capabilities of certain international businesses. It would be Edmund's role to start CARAWAY's education in this regard.

As the two COs sat down to review their plan, Winston and I pondered where we were going to find the CO to play the role of the father figure/business boss. Could an FBI SA be that person? No, not anyone we had met to date. However, this was not a difficult decision on my part. The obvious choice, both in terms of image and experience, was Winston; his British gentleman persona, complete with accent, mannerisms, and

CHAPTER SIXTEEN: ENTER "EDMUND"

physical appearance, made him perfect for the role. That he was already read-in to the operation was a bonus.

So, we were ready to start planning the introduction of the powerful international business organization that operated just on the borders of, if not outside of, the law. But first, Stan had to convince CARAWAY to work with Edmund, and Edmund had to make the case that CARAWAY's best interests lied in working with this organization.

Chapter Seventeen: The Turnover

After his usual countersurveillance activities, Stan arrived at the hotel and established himself in the suite. Edmund arrived about thirty minutes later. Exactly on time, CARAWAY telephoned from the lobby and was given the room number. When he arrived, Stan introduced him to Edmund as "Bill." Stan offered drinks, and the social conversation phase of the meeting began. Edmund opened the conversation by stating that he was impressed with the technical diagrams he had seen and asked about the Target's professional background. CARAWAY responded slowly and carefully, stating in general the type of academic and engineering training he had received, but not identifying where. The Target then began to probe Edmund's background, asking where he was from and his professional training. As we had anticipated, this line of questioning, Edmund had a response meant to impress the Target's sense of personal security. Edmund stated his professional education in rather specific terms, citing several international institutions where he had studied. But, in response to the Target's query about any personal information, he responded that in his business, one does not discuss personal details. He continued, "My expertise and advice are provided in international business circles where discretion is the rule." He did not want to know anything personal about CARAWAY. His only interest was in CARAWAY's expertise and ability to provide information of value. And, he expected CARAWAY to respect the need for discretion. The Target readily agreed.

Stan moved the conversation to how experts like Edmund operated. He

CHAPTER SEVENTEEN: THE TURNOVER

explained that Edmund operated on a "consultant" basis, receiving a fee for his advice and guidance on technical issues related to communications. In their particular case, Stan had approached him to identify the manufacturers of various components from the information available in the diagrams and other documents CARAWAY had provided. With Edmund's input, Stan had made trading decisions which had produced a gross profit of about thirty-four thousand dollars. Edmund's fee was twelve percent.

However, Stan explained, Edmund had expressed interest in knowing what additional manuals and communication's equipment diagrams Stan's source might be able to provide. He said that he had other clients interested in this type of information, and perhaps both he and Stan could get a "finder's fee" if CARAWAY's capabilities fit the requirements of this client. Stan agreed, and looked CARAWAY directly in the eye, and said "Frankly I am not sure if you have other information which could be profitably used. But, if I can steer you towards some additional compensation, I would be happy to do so. "

At this point, Edmund noted that as a "consultant," he dealt with a variety of corporations and businesses. He knew what was needed in the international communications' sector to make money, and while he understood Stan's approach with leverage based stock market positions, it was not the most profitable way to utilize the type of information that CARAWAY had provided. For example, knowing in advance of the need for technical upgrades in communications systems was a much more lucrative approach to profitability. Or, even more profitable, but an approach that had to be conducted in a very discreet manner, was to plan the capabilities of the new equipment needs in a manner that pointed the equipment in the direction of a specific manufacturer. This approach could produce very high profits for all concerned, perhaps even for the government or organizational officials involved in placing the bid contract specifications and requirements. Edmund concluded by noting that these types of activities were quite common in international business, and while perhaps a bit in the grey area, were an accepted standard of practice around the world.

CARAWAY, having listened intently to Edmund, noted, "Providing this type of information sounds very dangerous." And, he added, "At least in my personal experience, this type of information is restricted to only a few people and certainly carefully controlled when bid contracts are issued." Edmund responded that CARAWAY's perspective was exactly what the public believed. However, in reality, in most cases, international business firms had contacts that provided the information well before it ever became public. He noted "Outside of the public view an entire class of powerful and wealthy businessmen operated in an environment where government officials cooperated "under the table" to not only enrich themselves but also to facilitate commercial deals that would quickly and effectively accomplish national goals."

At this point in the conversation Stan interrupted, stating "My method of business is predicted completely on the premise that the general public, and this usually included small and mid-level investors, actually believed such information is restricted only to those involved." This, he noted, was foolish. Large and powerful international business operated for both profit and efficiency. Individuals with insider information wanted to profit from it—this was basic human nature. And, if they were responsible governmental and corporate officials, they also wanted their business objectives to be accomplished successfully. Stan advised CARAWAY to think about how business was really done in his country.

Edmund then added some general stories about business enterprises which had benefited from advanced information on projects which were completed faster and better than could ever have been accomplished if less capable firms had been allowed to win bids. He ended his stories with a question to CARAWAY: "Have you not noticed that in all countries it is the political leadership and the wealthy businessmen who make the country run?"

Stan mentioned to Edmund that now that he had explained how CARAWAY could probably assist him, CARAWAY would need some time to think this over. As he ushered Edmund to the door, he advised that once CARAWAY had decided, he would phone Edmund at his hotel as to

CHAPTER SEVENTEEN: THE TURNOVER

whether or not they might work together.

After Edmund departed, Stan poured another drink for them both, and asked him what he thought about Edmund's comments. CARAWAY responded that he was not naïve about individuals in positions of authority using their power to assist businessmen in obtaining various contracts. He noted that he had seen similar activities within his own government. But, he was unaware of the degree to which this was a common practice. He also admitted that he had not considered that this practice may also have a benefit to the actual project. But, it did make sense that ensuring a company with the right capabilities and skills actually got the business would benefit everyone. While nodding his head in agreement, Stan was thinking "human rationalization is a wonder thing."

Passing CARAWAY the room service menu, Stan advised he was hungry and that they should order dinner. CARAWAY agreed. And, after the meals were ordered, Stan moved into the next scenario of the evening. He told CARAWAY that based upon the net profit from the stock actions he had been able to manipulate, the Target was due an additional one thousand seven hundred dollars as his share of the deal's profit. He continued that the actual gross profit of the transaction had only been in the area of about twenty-two thousand because of the expenses related to research identifying the actual components manufacturers, the cost of brokerage and trading fees in a couple of European countries to hide the actual purchaser, and related communications, travel and miscellaneous costs." It turns out," Stan continued," that the component sales are not larger enough to make a significant difference in the firm's profit profile and thus their stock did not rise as much as I hoped." However, since this was a new month, he also had CARAWAY's retainer for him. So, all in all, CARAWAY was to receive thirty-two hundred dollars.

As usual, Stan was not sure how the target would respond to his share of the profits, and was prepared to provide more fake details on costs if so required. However, rather than upset, CARAWAY only seemed a bit disappointed. So, he and Stan had a short discussion on the limitations that affected stock options trading, particularly the unknowns involved in not knowing the size of sales in order to properly gauge how these reflected profits would affect stock prices. Stan explained that if CARAWAY had been able to provide information on the number of components involved in the overall Romanian Government's upgraded communications equipment purchase, he would have been able to structure his leverage purchases more accurately. CARAWAY said he understood, but never had access to that kind of information as it would be handled by his Ministry, and not provided to the Consulate General.

Then, CARAWAY, with some hesitation in his voice, mentioned that he also had some others bills which Stan had told him would be considered "business expenses." He gave Stan four restaurant receipts and a receipt from a sporting goods store for several track suits decorated with the city's professional basketball team's logo. He noted that the restaurant receipts included three lunches and a farewell dinner he hosted for the Ministry's traveling communications upgrade team. The tracksuits were a parting gift for them as well. Stan took the receipts and was immediately pleased to see that they were quite modest in nature, and that he had enough extra operational cash with him to pay CARAWAY right then. The meal costs were a total of $287, and the track suits cost $165. He quickly paid CARAWAY the additional $452, commenting only that such expenses were often just the cost of doing business. CARAWAY looked quite relieved upon receiving the reimbursement.

The meal arrived, and once they began to eat, Stan said that he wanted to give CARAWAY his view, both as a friend and as an international businessman, about what would be best for him in terms of future profitability. He explained, "I can only afford to keep you on a retainer for another couple of months because this summer I will be moving to the Philippines to assist a Manila-based financial firm, which plans to trade only in options in the Southeast and Northern Asian region. My position in this firm and my salary is exactly what I have been looking for." Stan anticipated being out of the country for as long as five or six years, until that firm was fully established and profiting. And, he noted, to be frank from a business perspective, the Target had not been the source of much

CHAPTER SEVENTEEN: THE TURNOVER

information of value. However, he understood CARAWAY's personal situation and wanted to give him every opportunity to earn as much as possible. This was the reason he introduced him to Edmund, who had indeed expressed an interest in CARAWAY based on the official diagrams he had been shown.

CARAWAY was obviously concerned by Stan's notice of a coming end of their business relationship. He had become used to the extra cash each month. Though, he did not respond in a bitter way. Rather, he stated his disappointment while also confirming his respect for the personal relationship they had developed in the past months. He noted that he was trying to find business information that might prove useful to Stan, but as socialist country there was just not a lot of international business outside the Soviet Block. CARAWAY concluded by thanking Stan for both his friendship and the business funds he had received to date.

Stan responded that the lack of information was not CARAWAY's fault. He could only provide what he saw, although perhaps with a better concept of the whole environment in an international business sense, there might be more information in the communications than the Target realizes. In any event, Edmund, as a specialist in communications systems, is a consultant to several very powerful international businessmen. Stan said he could not provide names, as Edmund was very careful to protect the identities of his clients for exactly the same reasons Stan protected his clients and sources. But, if Edmund believed CARAWAY's expertise could be useful, Stan was confident money could be made.

So, Stan said, he believed that the Target should accept a business role with Edmund. He could insist on a monthly retainer, similar to what he now had, and negotiate a fixed fee for any specific work he did with Edmund. But, of course, this would mean that CARAWAY would also have to provide Edmund with his name and his position at the Consulate so Edmund could figure out how best to employ him.

Over the meal, and a couple of after dinner scotches, CARAWAY and Stan discussed the situation form various perspectives. Stan seemed able to convince the Target that Edmund was very security conscious and would be as protective of CARAWAY's identity as Stan had been. He also continued to emphasize that with Edmund's special expertise, he might well uncover profitable uses for CARAWAY's skills that had not occurred to either of them. Stan also questioned the Target about what other opportunities he might have to make additional money if he did not accept an offer from Edmund. CARAWAY considered this question carefully and admitted, "I have no other options to make even a few hundred dollars a month." "And," he noted somewhat woefully, "my wife and I do want to make some large purchases before we return to Romania, and need some funds for our son's health care."

By the conclusion of the meal, CARAWAY agreed that a position with Edmund was probably his best option. So, Stan suggested that he call Edmund at his hotel and advise him of CARAWAY's decision and arrange a meeting between them to work out the details. The Target agreed, and Stan placed the call to the suburban hotel where Edmund was staying. Edmund picked up the telephone on the first ring, as he had been anxiously awaiting it. Per the previously established scripted conversation, Stan advised that CARAWAY was willing to entertain an offer but the exact details would have to be worked out between them. He noted that he was due to fly back to the West Coast the following morning and asked how long Edmund intended to be in the area. Edmund responded that he would be in the city for another two days. He added that since it was late, a meeting that evening would not be suitable as he had an early morning appointment. Instead, he suggested that tomorrow evening at his hotel would be the best opportunity for him and the Target to have a comprehensive discussion regarding the creation of a working relationship. Edmund suggested that CARAWAY come to the hotel about eight in the evening.

While Edmund remained on the line, Stan passed the contact information to CARAWAY and confirmed with him that an eight o'clock meeting time was acceptable. He also gave the Target the name and address of the hotel and instructed him to use the house telephone to ask for the room of Mr. Edmund Harrison. CARAWAY agreed to the arrangements. Stan then told Edmund that all was set. Edmund ended the call by asking Stan to tell

CHAPTER SEVENTEEN: THE TURNOVER

the Target that he was looking forward to their meeting, which he hoped would prove to be mutually beneficial and profitable.

After having completed the telephone call which hopefully sealed the turnover of the Target to a new Case Officer, Stan had one more operational task—to leave the asset laughing as we say in the business. While the degree may be debatable, there was no doubt that personal rapport and trust between CARAWAY and Stan had been a key element in the operation. Thus, it was important to the future of the operation that CARAWAY continue to believe that Stan had been his friend even after their relationship ended. So, Stan spent the next hour engaging the Target in friendly conversation about his family, his future plans, and, of course, reinforcing the idea that he had made the right decision in agreeing to work with Edmund.

Stan brought the meeting to a conclusion by noting that he did have any early flight the next morning. Then, he went into his bedroom and returned with a bottle of scotch, Royal Salute, bottled in a ceramic vessel and encased in a velvet drawstring bag. He presented it to CARAWAY, describing it as the finest scotch he was able to find, and stating that it was an expression of their personal friendship and symbolic of their shared love of the liquor. Before showing CARAWAY to the door, Stan gave him a solid hug and once again expressed the strong friendship he felt for the target. He also said that if, for some reason, the relationship with Edmund did not work out, he would still be at his West Coast office, and CARAWAY should contact him. Also, should he have the opportunity to return to the city before his departure for the Philippines, Stan said he would certainly contact CARAWAY. The Target seemed quite touched by Stan's gift and comments, and responded with his own expression of sorrow at not knowing when he would see Stan once again.

Thus ended, we certainly hoped, Stan's phase of the operation. He had left the target with an expensive bottle of scotch and nearly three thousand dollars in cash, as well as the kind words of a "friend." But, since you never know what is going to happen, he also left the possibility of future contact if for any reason the relationship with Edmund did not work, or in a more remote possibility, something happened to Edmund that did not permit him to carry on with the operation. We always plan for Murphy's Law because in dealing with people, it happens quite frequently.

Stan's last responsibility of the evening was to telephone me from a pay phone in the lobby. He simply told me that his business trip was proceeding as scheduled and that he anticipated meeting with me late afternoon of the following day. The message was that the meeting had gone as planned, and the Target was to meet with Edmund the following evening. As Edmund had already prepared the scenario for this meeting, the only thing I had to do was wake up Ralph with a call to his residence. We had agreed, when I coordinated Stan's meeting's scenario with him, that if CARAWAY accepted the meeting with Edmund the FBI surveillance unit would monitor the Target's activities throughout the day until CARAWAY arrived at Edmund's hotel. The Field Office's translators would also monitor "real time" the conversations inside the Consulate as well as any telephone calls made by CARAWAY or his wife for the entire day. We wanted to be as sure as possible that nothing unusual was taking place at the Consulate or with the Target. With the call to Ralph completed, I went to bed feeling pretty satisfied.

The next day, CARAWAY went about his Consulate responsibilities in his usual manner, and neither the surveillance folks nor the translators found anything suspicious in his behavior or conversations. This was also true of the security officers at the Consulate, whom the Field Office was monitoring. The Target left the building about six o'clock, a bit early but not unusual, and went home. He had dinner and left his residence about an hour or so later. He walked to a bus stop, and took the bus to the commuter rail station, where he boarded a train to the suburban location where Edmund's hotel was located. Purposely, Edmund was staying in a less expensive style: he had a living room—kitchen—bedroom configured suite in a long term residence—type of hotel suited for middle level business persons. We wanted his professional image to reflect someone who operated on a consultant basis rather than that of an independent, wealthier, international businessman.

CHAPTER SEVENTEEN: THE TURNOVER

CARAWAY arrived at the hotel just a few minutes late, phoned from the lobby, and proceeded to Edmund's room. When Edmund answered the door, they shook hands and moved to the sitting area/living room. Edmund began by thanking CARAWAY for agreeing to meet. He said that his business activities were quite different from that of Stan's, and he wanted to make this clear so that the Target would fully understand what Edmund could offer in the way of a business proposal. The CO then went into his scenario regarding his role as both a technical consultant and talent spotter for various international business clients. In both cases, he worked for a set fee per task. His interest in CARAWAY was sparked by the diagrams he had reviewed and analyzed for Stan. He knew that these related to government communications' systems, and that they were from Romania—not only from seeing the identification notes were in Romanian but also from the way the components were structured within the system. So, he immediately knew the source of the diagrams must be a communications official with a good level of professional expertise from the Soviet Bloc.

CARAWAY seemed a bit startled that Edmund had already learned so much about him, and said so. But, then after thinking about it for a few seconds, he mentioned that actually it was pretty simple to figure out. Edmund said that he had been looking for an individual with this kind of technical knowledge and access for some time for a business client from Europe. This was a very wealthy individual, who managed a personal investment firm that had connections to senior trade officials in the Soviet Bloc. As such, he was involved in both trade and investments, which often had to be conducted around certain international restrictions and sanctions imposed by various Western governments. And, because he had been dealing with various Warsaw Pact Governments for many years, he was a trusted and valued contact by many Communist Party and Eastern Bloc senior officials. Thus, he was one of a handful of businessmen, operating in the grey area of international commerce, who could make profits from trade within the Socialist Bloc.

However, even with his good contacts, Edmund continued, his client still had competition from others and needed to stay constantly ahead of his competitors in terms of knowing what the various governments were planning in terms of purchases and structural upgrades, as well as anything they were planning to sell. Edmund later noted that CARAWAY took this all in with little expression on his face, but a noticeable widening of his eyes when the relationship of the client to Soviet Block leaders was mentioned.

Edmund waited for CARAWAY to respond. The Target did so, but only after a period of seemingly deep thought. CARAWAY said he fully understood the necessity for a confidential and discreet relationship in the type of business that Edmund had described. He explained, "I am well aware that in any country, political and governmental connections enable certain individuals to benefit through the use of insider and advanced information on business deals. "This," he notes," is certainly true even with the Communist countries." "And I am involved in sharing some minor information outside of proper government regulations. But, in all honesty I have not been able to provide a steady stream of commercial information to Stan which enabled him to generate a flow of profitable stock trades. So, I am not really sure I have the capability to suit the needs of a client such as you described. Yet, I am willing to try as long as it is not too risky, my efforts are compensated properly, and the client understands the type of information I might be able to provide."

Edmund responded that all of these conditions made sense, and that considering the breadth and scope of the client's business dealings, CARAWAY might be surprised at what he had to offer. But first, he said that the Target had to give him an accurate account of his professional background, to include specific academic and career training, his current position, and the responsibilities, and, of course, his true name. Edmund continued that his client is not going to interview just anyone he offers up as a candidate, so the information he presents is very important. He ended by stating that all this information was for the eyes of only one client, the international businessman he had described earlier. In return for providing his background, which Edmund would then prepare in a

CHAPTER SEVENTEEN: THE TURNOVER

resume' format, Edmund was prepared to pay CARAWAY an 'interview fee" of one thousand dollars. This would be a one-time payment, and any future compensation would come from the client, if he were so disposed. Edmund said that his compensation, both the retainer he was working on to identify a candidate and the sum he would receive when/if the client accepted a candidate, would be paid directly to him by the client: CARAWAY would not owe him any money for writing up the resume' paper or handling the introduction to the client, if that were to occur.

CARAWAY, rather quicker than we had anticipated, accepted Edmund's proposition and said he was ready to provide all the background information Edmund needed. He started by stating his real name and explained his position at the Consulate and the range of duties he handled there. Edmund wrote the information down, and then went to the kitchen area, and returned with two glasses, a bottle of middle-grade scotch, and a bowl of ice. Drinks were poured, and CARAWAY began to lay out the academic and governmental schools he had attended, the specific equipment he had been trained to operate and maintain, and his previous field assignments. Edmund carefully posed follow-up questions which added valuable information about CARAWAY's training, and helped to fill in some details of which institutes and schools in Romania were utilized by the government for their communications training. Also, in his description of his duties as the senior officer in the Consulate's communications room, he did state that he handled responsibilities for the tapes used to encrypt and decrypt classified radio traffic from other Romanian offices, Bucharest and other Warsaw Pact offices.

Edmund's debriefing of CARAWAY took over an hour, since he had to pretend that he knew nothing about the Target. During this time, Edmund did not offer CARAWAY a meal, only several glasses of scotch. We wanted this meeting, in terms of its operational environment, to stand in contrast with the way Stan had treated the Target. And, even more importantly, in contrast to the way he would be treated when he was introduced to the wealthy and politically well-connected international businessman.

At the conclusion of the debriefing, Edmund went to his briefcase, placed the yellow pad with all of CARAWAY's information on it inside, and removed an envelope. He then returned to the table and gave CARAWAY the sealed envelope. He said it contained a thousand dollars. He noted that he did not want a receipt for the money and that CARAWAY should feel free to open the envelope and count the cash if he so desired. CARAWAY accepted the envelope and indicated that he did not feel the need to count it. This seemed a good indication that CARAWAY had completely accepted Edmund's alias persona and commercial cover story.

Edmund then moved into the details regarding how future communications between them would be handled. He explained that his office was in Vancouver, but he also had a commercial answering service and mailing address in New England for his East Coast American business, and provided CARAWAY with his business card containing that address and telephone number. Due to the discreet nature of many of his clients, he preferred that all telephonic conversations be equally discreet and not done across international boundaries. So, he suggested, "You should call my New England number in the early evening, ten days from today. By that time, I should have an idea of the degree of interest his client might have in you. "He explained that it would take him a couple of days to write up CARAWAY's resume in an appropriate format, and structure the oral presentation he would use when offering it to his client. Then, he would need another couple of days to actually make his presentation to the client. He suggested that the Target not use his home or office telephones to make the call, once again reminding him that their relationship should remain confidential.

CARAWAY asked if Edmund would be in his New England office to receive the telephone call, and was told "no, but there will be a message for you. Just tell the individual answering that you are Bill, and have called to pick up a message." The Target agreed, but also noted that if his resume was accepted, he assumed the next step would be to meet the client. However, it would be difficult, if not impossible, for him to travel outside the city unless he had a great deal of notice and could pass off the trip as a vacation of some sort. Edmund indicated that he understood this problem and

CHAPTER SEVENTEEN: THE TURNOVER

would make sure his client also understood the issue.

To close out the meeting, Edmund gave CARAWAY another splash of scotch and told a few humorous stories about some of his past business experiences dealing with unusual clients and their specific demands. He was careful not to mention any of them by name, and when noting a particular location, he always referred to it as in a geographical area rather than identifying a specific country. We hoped this approach would further impress CARAWAY with both Edmund's discretion as well as reinforce his understanding that he was entering an environment where names and specifics were carefully protected.

After Edmund escorted CARAWAY to the door, and they ended on a firm handshake, the CO felt quite confident that the meeting had gone very well and began jotting down his notes from their conversation.

The next day in the office, Winston and I debriefed both COs. Stan had been able to write up his reporting the previous day, but Edmund was still working from his notes taken down after CARAWAY had left. Everything seemed to have gone quite well, and both COs felt the Target was firmly in hand and ready for the introduction to the powerful international businessman—the Father Figure. We decided to send both Stan's and Edmund's reports to Headquarters as a package, along with a broad outline of our operational planning for the introduction of the next phase of the operation.

After both reports had been sent, we took copies down to Ralph at his office. Ralph and Matt were both pleased with the results of the meetings, and our session was actually quite pleasant. I added to this atmosphere by telling them that Winston, whom both of them liked, was to play the part of the international businessman. Also, we wanted one of their SAs to play the role of the driver and personal bodyguard of the businessman. We specifically asked for a big guy, someone who looked tough. I explained that the role would not involve much of a speaking part, but that the mannerisms were very important in conveying the importance of the businessman. I then broke the news that I felt might not be as well received: that I would also be playing the role of the North American representative of the businessman.

Since in the past I had been so insistent on ensuring that my officers were not placed in positions where they might accidentally be associated with the FBI, I anticipated questions as to whether my frequent visits to their office should also disqualify me from a role in this operation. I went on to explain that I was not involved in any other operational activities in the city, and that I had made it a point in my off-duty time not to frequent the area near the Romanian Consulate or other areas where Field Office SAs had advised that CARAWAY frequented. Also, my role-playing would take place within the isolated environment of a hotel suite, where access was under our control. Somewhat to my surprise, none of the SAs voiced any concern about my involvement in the operation.

They were, however, very interested in the bodyguard role and specifically what it would entail. Winston explained that this role would function in three ways: as the driver, the personal Assistant/butler, and the bodyguard. As the driver, he would pick up CARAWAY at pre-arranged locations and drive him to meetings. Dressed in a dark suit and driving a luxury sedan, he would convey the image of the employee of a wealthy individual. Also, from an operational security perspective, by picking CARAWAY up at a specific location and then controlling his movements to the actual meeting site, we maintained control of that site and, if necessary, could use surveillance points along the way to verify that the Target was not being followed. Once in the hotel suite, the butler's role would involve bringing drinks, lighting cigarettes, and generally providing the businessman with whatever he needed. His role as the bodyguard would actually be explained to CARAWAY during the first meeting, and he would be armed in a manner obvious to anyone in the room with him. Most of his oral interaction would be along the lines of "yes, sir" and "no, sir."

The SAs were satisfied with Winston's description, and I suspected they would be quite pleased to advise their Headquarters that now they would have their own man directly involved. The next obvious question was which SA they wanted to use. Because of the limited role to be played, there was a minimal need for any backstopping required to maintain this

CHAPTER SEVENTEEN: THE TURNOVER

individual's cover status. His legitimacy was based on his association with the businessman—if CARAWAY believed in one, he would also believe in the other. So, the SA did not have to officially become an undercover operator, saving the Field Office a significant amount of bureaucratic paperwork.

After some consideration and discussion of what image we felt best suited to the role, Ralph suggested an SA from the city's Organized Crime Squad named Patrick. Matt readily agreed. Ralph described Patrick as a six-foot-four, about 220-pound, mid-forties SA with about fifteen years' experience in the Bureau. He had a college degree in Accounting from the University of Cincinnati, and had been a linebacker on the university's football team. Ralph said he really looked the part we had described. It was arranged that Ralph and Matt would discuss the role with him the next morning, and if all went well, we could speak with him shortly after that.

We returned to the office and began structuring our planning for the next meeting while awaiting our Headquarters' comments and the Field Office's permission to meet with Patrick. We first undertook the rather dull but still important issues of the window dressing for the scenario. Winston took some operational funds to go shopping. The next morning, he brought in two new dark, pin-striped, two-button suits. Both were cut in the British style. He had also purchased a two-hundred-dollar pair of dress shoes and three expensive dress shirts in the striped design popular among those in British society. We saved a few dollars in terms of underwear, as we didn't anticipate any situation where CARAWAY would observe that particular article of dress. Also, Winston already owned a collection of British club ties, so we were in good shape in this regard as well. It is said clothes make the man, and in terms of dressing for a stage, which was actually what we were doing, everything about the wealthy and powerful international businessman had to exhibit the proper image.

There were also the details surrounding the international firm that Winston owned that had to be finalized. We had studied how international corporations operated and decided that the company, Bluestone Venture Capital Enterprises, would be based in the Cayman Islands for tax purposes but also have a United States subsidiary in Wilmington, Delaware. Both locations permitted registration of business entities with minimum fuss and maximum privacy. Winston, in the alias James Helmsley-Haight, was listed as the Chief Executive Officer and Chairman of the Board of Directors.

Another element within the Agency provided high-quality business cards for me, as Robert Rose, the Senior Executive Officer for North American Operations, with the Delaware address and phone number. The phone was actually located in the vacant office in Wilmington, but all calls were forwarded to the Station. I should note here that the practice of Delaware-registered corporations having a local office containing only an active telephone is the norm for most of the registered corporations. All of our stage settings were falling nicely into place.

Later that morning Ralph called to say that Patrick had agreed to play the role, and we arranged a meeting at the Field Office for the next morning. We still had not heard back from our Headquarters, but we needed to keep the momentum of the operation going and had to have the meeting details for the message to CARAWAY from the supposed New England office fully thought-out within the next few days.

Winston and I met Patrick in Ralph's office. He was all that Ralph had described to us: big, broad shoulders, with a slightly weathered face that spoke of some serious life experiences. A full head of dark black hair completed the picture. His voice was deep, but smooth in delivery. Beyond the physical features, he turned out to be a very sharp guy and quite a good role player. We spent about an hour talking with him and explaining how his role would interact with both the Target and Winston's characters. It quickly became clear that Patrick was going to be a good part of the team.

After we returned to the Field Office, Ralph and I discussed the clothes Patrick would need, since he also had to be suitably, and that meant fairly expensively, dressed. He would need at least one dark two-piece suit, a bit tight in the back to ensure that his weapon and holster were discernible, and some white shirts and a couple of conservative single-color ties. Ralph said that he had spoken with his superiors at FBI Headquarters, and he was authorized to pay all expenses regarding the SA's role in the operation. I also noted we would need a luxury dark town car to use to pick up and drop off the target before and after the meetings. I assumed he would decide how Patrick would obtain the vehicle. "Of course," he responded.

There was one other detail we needed to discuss, an important one: the hotel suite that would be used for the meeting between CARAWAY and Winston. This was an area where the Field Office's assistance was going to be very important. As part of their general community and business outreach program, the Bureau maintains contact with hotel managers in order to be aware of who is in town and of any unusual activities by hotel guests. In certain situations, they also enlist hotel managers as cooperative assets who can provide access to various rooms for audio and video monitoring of guests' activities and nearby rooms as monitoring base locations. For this operation, we wanted the Field Office to find us a five-star hotel with a luxury suite that conveyed the wealth and power of the persona that Winston was to represent. And, knowledge of the reason for the suite and the activities that took place there had to be kept completely confidential.

When I discussed this in with Ralph, he smiled and stated that this would not be a problem. He said he would look at a couple of options, and let me know what location he thought would be appropriate for our needs.

Before departing for the Station, I advised Ralph and Patrick that we would be conducting some planning and practice scenarios at the Station in the next couple of days and would want Patrick to participate. They had no problems with that, and Ralph noted that Patrick's professional priority would now be his role in the case.

By the time we got back to the Station in the late afternoon, we had received two responses from our Headquarters. Our support desk approved our plan for the introduction of the wealthy international businessman, and passed along congratulations on the meetings conducted by Stan and Edmund. The second communication was from the special Headquarters unit, which acted as liaison to NSA. As we moved closer to our ultimate objective, this unit would be taking the lead in supporting our efforts. As their expertise was in areas a bit removed from agent recruitment and handling, it soon would become apparent that they would have little to add regarding how to conduct the operation and affect the final recruitment of the Target.

In this particular communication, the technical unit lauded the success we had experienced to date, praised the degree of cooperation we had achieved with the Field Office, and advised they looked forward to the results of the next meeting.

The following morning Edmund, Stan and Winston began planning for the meeting. And, I got a telephone call from Ralph on the secure line regarding the hotel we would be using. His smile at the time I made the request should have been an obvious sign that he knew he could provide exactly what we wanted, but I was still surprised, and frankly impressed, by what he was able to do.

Ralph suggested that we use a downtown hotel, one of the very high-end national chains that featured a top-floor, penthouse suite, with a private elevator from the underground parking area. He noted that this suite was often used by visiting foreign and American senior government officials as well as famous entertainment personalities. He explained that the hotel manager was a long-term cooperative source, who had assisted the Bureau in his previous management assignments in other locations as well. This manager personally controlled the booking for the suite, and often listed the bookings in false names to protect the privacy and the security of the occupant. In addition, the head of the hotel's security office was a recently retired FBI officer from the Field office, and a personal friend of Ralph's. Thus, he stated with confidence, the Field Office could control all identification and access at the hotel when we used it for meetings. Finally, he advised that, as stated previously, the FBI would pick up the costs of the suite and sedan. This cost was not insignificant, as the regular price for a suite of this nature would run into several thousands of dollars a night. However, I assumed Ralph managed to get some type of discount based on his relationship with the manager and the fact that a suite like that was not always occupied every night. One other key advantage of this arrangement was that, with few exceptions, we could have first call on the use of the suite so that our future meeting schedule could be based on the flow of the momentum of the operation rather than the availability of a meeting location.

The next morning, we began to concentrate on the structure for the meeting. We spent several hours talking about what image and relationship we wanted to convey, and what results we should expect from this meeting. After this discussion, I sent a message to Headquarters alerting the unit operating Edmund's business answering services regarding the exact message we wanted CARAWAY to receive when he called. The message was: "Please stand on the corner of Central Ave. and Post Street at 7:30 p.m. the evening of the 23rd. You will be picked up by Edmund." I asked Headquarters to confirm when that exact message had been passed to and confirmed by the answering service. Once again, because of my respect for Murphy's Law, we would check the next day to ensure the exact message was on file.

With only a few days to go, Ralph reserved the hotel suite and obtained a black, current-year model luxury town car, which he parked under a tarp in the Field Office's underground parking garage. For our part, we held the first of a couple of rehearsals at the Station to go over the scenario. Patrick joined Winston, Edmund and I as the role players, while Stan sat in to offer any comments he thought might be helpful. Unlike a stage play, we did not memorize lines as much as plan various responses to how the Target might react as the meeting progressed. Thus, there was a need for each role player to understand their character in terms of their interaction with each other as well as the Target. For example, Edmund was a mere functionary who would introduce CARAWAY and then politely but firmly be dismissed from the gathering. He, as a consultant working for Winston, had to be deferential to both Winston and me. Patrick, as the personal assistant, was deferential to everyone. I was deferential only to Winston, since eventually I would be the person directing CARAWAY's activities for the firm.

We spent a couple of hours practicing interactions and mannerisms that would create the environment we wanted to convey. Not surprisingly, Winston had the easiest time mastering his role and demonstrating the proper relationship with the rest of us. With his accent, British upper-class physical appearance, dress, and mannerisms, he was the part. Patrick also quickly adapted to his role. Apparently, he and his wife were keen watchers of British television shows on Public Television, and he was readily able to do a decent impression of the Butler. The one modification we had to make, based upon an observation from Stan, concerned the fact that in addition to being the formal personal assistant, he also had to clearly function as Winston's bodyguard. Therefore, he had to be a bit more menacing in his body language and more obviously aware of those surrounding Winston than a Butler might be.

My role wasn't that difficult to master. I would be the "executive officer" for the corporation's North American operations, providing details of reporting requirements, guidance, and assistance to CARAWAY as he started his work for the firm. As a CO who had handled numerous recruited agents, many with high-level access within their governments, I had developed the practice of being confident and firm while instructing assets in how to undertake collection activities. Also, as an American employed by the firm, my behavior and demeanor could be that of an American. I did however, have to remember to wear my best suit and to actually polish my shoes—which I have hated to do ever since I left the Marines.

On the morning of the 23rd, we gathered at the Station for one last check that we were all ready to go. Winston would drive his car to a parking lot in a nearby shopping mall, where he would be picked up by Patrick, who would then drive him to the hotel in the town car. They would arrive at the hotel about four in the afternoon, with a couple of suitcases. Once settled in the room, Winston would unpack the several bottles of expensive single malt scotch from one of the suitcases and look over the room service menu to ascertain what snacks he would have on hand for the meeting. There would be no meal this time. We wanted the target to clearly understand he was dealing with someone with whom he had to establish his usefulness before he could consider himself as accepted. Winston also unpacked several newspapers and magazines, purchased earlier that day at a news stand at the city's airport by the Station's Administrative Officer, including the Wall Street Journal, the New York Times, The Washington Post, The Financial Times, the Economist, Time, Newsweek, and the Guardian, and placed them around the sitting area.

Patrick, meanwhile, would make arrangements with the hotel parking attendant, reinforced by a generous tip, to ensure that when he drove in with CARAWAY, the elevator would be ready to take them to the penthouse suite, leaving the town car to be parked by the attendant. He then joined Winston in the suite to await the time to go out and pick up the Target. I would arrive by taxi at the hotel about an hour before the scheduled meeting, and handle ordering whatever room service items we needed, so their delivery would be made before the Target arrived, and thus would not interrupt the flow of the meeting.

Ralph and I had also agreed that it would be sensible to have Matt and Larry position themselves in a coffee shop, at a window table, across from the pickup point, to observe how the pickup went. While we doubted that CARAWAY would be followed or that anything unexpected would occur, having eyes on the pickup would also allow Winston and me to be alerted by pager that we could expect the Target to arrive in about seven to ten minutes, depending upon downtown traffic.

At seven, Patrick left the suite and drove the car to a parking lot about two miles from the hotel, where he picked up Edmund, and then proceeded to the pick-up location. As he arrived in the area a bit early, he double-parked the car a few blocks away and waited until a couple of minutes before the established time. Patrick had checked out the route to and from the hotel in his own Bureau car several times that week during similar traffic times to best calculate how to be at the pickup point exactly as scheduled. We wanted CARAWAY to start understanding that when you worked for this firm, you followed instructions perfectly and on time. If he did happen to show up late, Edmund would make this point to him in the car while they drove to the hotel.

However, CARAWAY was on time. As Patrick pulled around the corner, Edmund rolled down the back window and told him to get into the car. The Target did so and shook hands with Edmund, who explained that they were being driven to meet his client at a nearby hotel. He also explained that the client was the head of an international firm and that he might have other members of his staff present for the interview. His resume, Edmund continued, had stimulated the client's interest, but this personal interview would be the key decision-making event as to CARAWAY's employment. He advised CARAWAY to be open and frank about his professional expertise and what value he could bring to a consultant position based on his position in the Consulate. Edmund later reported that the Target was both nervous and anxious during the ride to the hotel and that was exactly what we hoped for.

Upon arrival at the underground parking entrance to the hotel, Patrick stopped the car at the elevator bank and got out of the car to open the rear door for Edmund and the Target. The parking attendant had called for the elevator to the penthouse, and Patrick held the doors while the two entered and then joined them. He pressed the button for the penthouse, and the elevator sped upwards, opening in a small hallway facing the front door of the suite. He knocked on the door, which I opened, and held the door open for both Edmund and CARAWAY to enter before entering himself and closing the door. He then took up a position by the bedroom door of the suite, in a manner resembling that of a security guard.

After the Target and Edmund both entered the suite, Edmund immediately introduced the Target to me in his full true name. I shook his hand with a firm grip, looking him directly in the eye. This not-too-subtle initial intimidation was intended to keep him in a defensive mood, and from his body language, it was working. I then directed them to sit down around the large coffee table in the sitting room section of the suite. Once seated, I asked Patrick to go to the bar at the other end of the room and bring us some drinks. I noted that I understood from Edmund that CARAWAY took his scotch straight, as did Edmund, but I always preferred a bit of soda water with mine. As Patrick moved towards the bar, I casually asked him

CHAPTER SEVENTEEN: THE TURNOVER

to also remove the newspapers and magazines from the table, noting that the boss had been doing some reading earlier this afternoon. Patrick did so, and then moved to the bar and poured three drinks before assuming his position near the bedroom door.

As we sipped our drinks, I explained that my role in the organization was that of the North American senior official, responsible for all of Bluestone Venture Capital Enterprises' activities in the United States and Canada. I provided a brief, investment jargon-filled description of the nature of the organization and its business interests. I particularly emphasized that because much of the work we were involved in was based upon personal relationships with political, military, and business senior individuals, we valued discretion above all. I then again looked CARAWAY directly in the eye and asked if he clearly understood this. He responded that he did, and I said, "Excellent, as anything we talk about in this room is to be considered confidential to the company. And, I mean anything; even the most innocent comment or discussion might have value to our rivals." I concluded by noting that what I had told him about the structure of the company, which in reality was almost nothing, was to be considered in this light.

I next explained that Edmund had provided us with CARAWAY's resume, and the boss found the background information on professional expertise and past experience to be of interest and possible value. When he had completed some overseas business telephone calls he was conducting in the other room, and I nodded towards the door Patrick was so ably protecting, he would discuss what his interests in a commercial relationship might be. CARAWAY nodded his head in understanding, but there was little doubt that he was nervous and intimidated by the scene so far.

Edmund spent a few minutes highlighting his confidence in the Target's professional capabilities, while also emphasizing that CARAWAY was a man of great discretion and well understood the need for loyalty in any commercial relationship. On cue, since Winston had been waiting at the bedroom door for the conclusion of Edmund's comment, Winston entered center stage.

He entered with the poise and confidence of a man who owned the room. His facial expression had the bored look of worldliness that is often associated in films and plays as characteristic of the British upper class. He just looked exactly like what anyone would expect a member of the aristocracy to look like. Patrick turned to face him and offered a slight but discernible bow of the head. As he approached, Edmund and I stood up, followed at once by CARAWAY, doing likewise. He gave a subtle nod of his head to Edmund, who responded with "Good evening, Sir," and then looked at me. I looked at him and said" Sir, may I introduce Mr. Dusko Bazna," and then faced CARAWAY and said "Mr. Bazna, may I introduce the Honorable James Helmsley-Haight, Chairman of the Board and Chief Operating Official of Bluestone Capital Venture Enterprises." Winston extended his hand and passed a faint smile as he shook hands with the Target. He then sat down and motioned to Patrick, who approached him. He told Patrick to make him a drink and to see if anyone else needed a refill. He then turned to CARAWAY and asked him to provide details of his technical background. The Target did so, explaining his technical education and the schools he had attended. Patrick first provided Winston with his drink and then refilled the glasses of the rest of us. Winston took out a cigarette after tasting his drink, and Patrick hurried over to light it for him. He then returned to what would be his post for the rest of the meeting; standing with hands clasped in front, halfway between the bar and where Winston sat.

Winston demonstrated a faint but polite interest in CARAWAY's description of his professional skills and particular areas of technical expertise. When CARAWAY had finished, Winston asked him to describe his current Romanian Government assignment and responsibilities. And, Winston demonstrated more interest in this subject as the target explained his Consulate duties. When CARAWAY had completed his description, Winston noted that he had been impressed with the resume' Edmund had submitted and found CARAWAY's description of his responsibilities to be interesting.

He turned to Edmund and said, "I believe you may have found me

CHAPTER SEVENTEEN: THE TURNOVER

the right candidate for my needs. Robert will provide you with your consultation fee and will be in touch with you should we need your further assistance." At this point, Edmund and I both rose to our feet, and Patrick moved towards the suite's door. Edmund said, "Thank you, Sir; I look forward to being of assistance in the future." I removed an envelope, stuffed with paper meant to represent cash, from my suit coat's inside pocket and gave it to Edmund. Patrick opened the door, and Edmund briskly walked out of the suite and, we hoped, the operation. His only future role would be in the case that, for some reason, CARAWAY did not accept the "consultant" position with Winston, and we need to get back in touch with him to try a different approach. But, it turned out not to be necessary.

Once Edmund left, I sat back down, and Winston instructed Patrick to refresh everyone's drinks. We sat in silence as he did so. Then Winston took a sip of his drink and told CARAWAY that his background and technical expertise were well suited to his future needs. However, he also needed to know if CARAWAY's loyalty and trustworthiness was as strong and deep as Edmund had claimed? Winston explained, "All my business dealings are sensitive in nature as they involve individuals who are not willing to have their names associated with his firm." "Over the years," he continued, "I have developed relationships which cross political and ideological lines. Business deals are made, profits are shared, and personal confidences are respected. Thus, everything the company does is hidden from public view." Winston noted that only a few senior company officials knew the details, and CARAWAY should expect that if he were selected to join the company, he would only know about activities in which he was personally involved. Individuals like Edmund were brought in only when a special type of skills was required—in this case the technical knowledge to vet potential business possibilities. His role was now completed, and CARAWAY was not to contact him again unless so instructed. "Do you understand that?" asked Winston with a firm tone in his voice. The Target replied, "Yes, I do."

Winston went on to explain that the people who worked for him were well paid, and could expect that in whatever activities they undertook for the company, they would be taken care of. The company was like a family, and loyalty was the binding ethic that made it run smoothly and profitably. On occasion in the past, Winston noted, there had been individuals who had wavered in their loyalty, often due to enticements by a competitor or a human weakness such as greed, and these situations had ended badly. "Betrayal," Winston noted, "is not a behavior that I can accept as I take it personally, as would any head of a family." He stated that he would never instruct CARAWAY to involve himself in an activity unless there was complete confidence that it could be brought to a successful and profitable conclusion for all concerned.

Having completed his speech, he asked CARAWAY if he felt that he had the necessary loyalty and commitment to join the company. He added that initially, until the particular enterprises they were developing were ready to implement, he would pay CARAWAY a monthly salary of fifteen hundred dollars. It would be in cash, as the company found the government regulations on taxes and other employment benefits cumbersome. In addition, arrangements would be made to provide health care benefits at company expense for CARAWAY and his dependents. Provisions would also be made, after an appropriate time with the company, for a separate, company-funded investment plan which the employee could claim upon a mutually agreeable retirement. And, of course, his salary would increase as his projects succeeded, and bonuses based upon overall company profits would be frequent occurrences. "Bluestone Capital Venture Enterprises is a family, and all of its members benefit from its successes," Winston concluded.

CARAWAY responded almost immediately. In a nervous voice, he stated that he was honored to be considered for such a position but wasn't sure that he had the knowledge and experience to be able to contribute to such an organization. He said he was only a middle-level Communications Officer in a rather poor Soviet Bloc country. While he had access to all the information coming into the Consulate, there seemed to be very little in the way of financial or commercial data that might benefit any commercial organization. He added, "I am an honorable man who is loyal to his friends, and I would be faithful to the company. Though, I am not

CHAPTER SEVENTEEN: THE TURNOVER

sure I can provide services to justify what seemed like a generous set of benefits. Yet, I am prepared to submit my resignation to the Ministry of Foreign Affairs as soon as you give me guidance on how I should transition into an international business role."

Well, that came as a bit of a surprise!

We had not anticipated the Target's willingness to quit his current position to take our commercial offer. However, a trait of a good CO is the ability to maintain the thrust of the scenario and adapt it as necessary. So Winston had to firmly dissuade CARAWAY from leaving his current employment, since obviously it was the whole point of the operation.

Winston began by stating that, based upon his technical background and the nature of his character, CARAWAY may well have the necessary skills for several projects the company had in mind. However, he added, as in any serious long term relationship a period of testing and suitability matching is necessary. So, CARAWAY should not plan on any immediate resignation from his official position. In fact, Winston noted, his position might prove to be useful in pursuing the development of some of these projects. Rather, he should consider himself in a trial period of employment with the company. His ability to assist in various business development projects will eventually indicate if a long-term career is beneficial to both parties.

At this point, Patrick bent over and whispered into Winston's ear, and Winston stood up, saying, "I am scheduled to take an international conference call in a few minutes. Robert will provide you with your initial month's retainer and discuss what we would like you to accomplish in the coming weeks. I am confident you will do well in this task. Good evening." CARAWAY and I stood up as Winston went into the bedroom, followed by Patrick.

I motioned for the Target to sit back down, and went to the bar and brought a bottle of the scotch back to the coffee table, pouring both of us a healthy drink. I then told CARAWAY that the boss seemed to like him, but that he was a cautious man and it would take time for CARAWAY to demonstrate his loyalty. That said, I noted that he should consider himself as an employee on a probationary status. As such, he would receive full company benefits, but must also show that his expertise and skills could profitably benefit the company. I stated that, as he must know, Winston was a busy man and frequently traveled to pursue various business opportunities. So, as the North American Senior Manager, I would be providing him with instructions and tasks on a routine basis. However, based upon my years of experience with the company, when Winston came to fully trust CARAWAY, he would probably take a direct role in assigning projects for the Target to work on.

I then gave him his first project, which was to provide me with a comprehensive list of all the communications equipment under his control at the Consulate. I explained that one project of the company involved the sale of advanced state-of-the-art radio communications equipment to Warsaw Pact countries. Some of this equipment was not legally transferable to these countries due to regulations imposed by NATO. However, there were ways around this, and the company had contacts that could make this happen. Yet, because of the legal issues and the expense that would be required to bypass certain restrictions, we had to know exactly what we could offer at a price that would make it a profitable venture.

I casually mentioned that some of the component boards whose diagrams Edmund had provided actually had been sold to the Polish Government through a Middle East company with Bluestone's acquisition and transportation assistance. Edmund, I added, was not aware of this, but when he identified you as a potential candidate for our company, he provided some of the diagrams as a representative of the type of information you could provide. "So," I said, "I have a fairly solid understanding of the type of information you can provide through your position at the Consulate, and with your technical expertise I think the company can gain some useful insights into the type of communications equipment your country and other Soviet Bloc countries need to keep their communications' systems up to modern standards."

"There are some other projects that the boss is working on that could have even greater profits for the company, but for the moment I want you to concentrate on providing us with specific identifying information on the current equipment in use at the Consulate, and what you know about the equipment at the Ministry of Foreign Affairs. We also need to know when plans are being made for upgrades, and if any particular equipment is proving ineffective, experiencing more than normal breakdowns, or requiring excessive maintenance. If we know what new equipment is needed, we have the contacts necessary to sell suitable upgrades. And, we can use our contacts to ensure a good profit for the company as well as a good product for the customer. Everybody wins, as long as it is done discreetly and carefully."

CARAWAY listened carefully as I explained that Bluestone had acquired and sold some of the components in the new communications equipment installed at the Consulate. That piece of information seemed to really impress him. He also seemed to readily accept the story that the company could provide equipment banned from export in most Western countries to his country and others in the Soviet Bloc. The concept that this was a win-win situation, from which he might well make money, seemed an important rationalization point for him.

In his response, CARAWAY agreed to provide a complete list of all the communications equipment, as well as comprehensive descriptions of how the various parts of the system interfaced. He would also try to remember as much as possible about the equipment he had worked on at the Ministry. He felt that it would take about a week to prepare his reporting on these subjects.

I responded that my duties in North America caused me to travel a great deal, and I would probably not be back in town for at least two weeks. However, I did maintain an administrative office in Delaware, managed by a trusted company employee. I gave CARAWAY the office's telephone number, noting that any message he left there could be relayed to me within a few hours. However, I emphasized that discretion must be the key in all our communications and meetings. If you call this office, use a pay phone and not one near either the Consulate or your residence. After all, it would be unwise for your Consulate colleagues to know you were involved in business activities outside of your official duties. Remember, the boss insists on confidentiality and discretion in all of his business activities. CARAWAY copied down the number and nodded his head in agreement.

I then told the Target that there was one other matter I wanted to discuss." In Edmund's profile of you," I noted, "there is mention of a health issue with your child as one reason for seeking outside employment. As the boss mentioned to you, we have a good health plan for our employees and their families, although in your case, as a probationary employee, we may have to take some extra steps to provide you with the care required. At our next meeting, I would also like details on your child's health issue. Try to be as specific as possible." CARAWAY looked quite surprised at my comments, but quickly assured me that he would do so. And, thank me and the boss for being so considerate of a potential new employee. I responded that the boss saw his employees as family and that hard work and loyalty in the company worked both ways.

I also explained that my current schedule might also change. I told him to work on compiling the list of equipment and call my Wilmington office in the evening, ten days from today, to confirm my return to the city. The office manager would also be able to provide information on where and when we would meet. Also, if for any reason he was unable to make a meeting we had established, he was to call this office and make arrangements for another meeting.

I then gave him his fifteen-hundred-dollar retainer, noting that until and if he became a regular corporate employee that would be his monthly retainer as a "consultant." I also gave him the standard warning to be careful about how he spent the money in order to avoid undue attention among his colleagues. In explaining this, I used references of a commercial nature, while making it clear that this was behavior the boss expected of all his employees.

As I led him to the door, I shook his hand and patted him on the back, assuring him that he was on the path to a very successful and profitable career. I told him to take a taxi to a spot near his residence and walk the rest of the way home. I explained that Patrick was busy assisting the boss.

CHAPTER SEVENTEEN: THE TURNOVER

CARAWAY departed seemingly happy and cheerful.

I waited until the elevator had left the floor, and went and got Winston and Patrick from the bedroom. We then sat around and discussed how the Target had reacted and how the meeting had gone. We agreed that CARAWAY seemed to have bought the commercial scenario, and that our various comments had helped him rationalize his commitment to providing the information requested. His first assignment was not really much of a leap since he had provided the diagrams and some technical manuals already. The monetary payment, and especially the offer to assist with his child's health issues, had been solid reinforcement tools in enabling him to accept our offer. As the requirements we ask of him became more and more sensitive, we would continue to provide him with additional motivational reasons to rationalize his cooperation.

We spent a couple more hours in the suite talking, writing up our notes, and then repacking everything we had brought to the meeting. It was near midnight when Patrick drove Winston first to his car at the now pretty much deserted shopping mall and then me to mine. He was careful to conduct a countersurveillance route before dropping us off. This was a procedure I insisted upon, even though we had no reason to suspect that anyone had followed CARAWAY to the hotel or that anyone else was suspicious of us. He then took the car to the Field Office and returned it the next morning.

I decided that the best way to provide Headquarters with a comprehensive picture of this meeting was to submit a composite report from all the participants: me, Winston, Edmund, and Patrick. The Field Office was happy to have Patrick write a brief report on his take of the event.

In my subsequent discussion with Ralph, it seemed that the injection of their SA into it had really cleared the air. Apparently, Patrick had reported back that our planning and implementation of the role playing was well organized and professional. Actually, I liked to believe that Ralph had become easier to work with and friendlier because of my great personality and professional image. Still a possibility, however, more likely it was having their own SA now operating as an inside member of the

229

operational team that made them more comfortable.

The requirements I had given to CARAWAY for the next meeting were partly to make it easy for him to respond, and also to provide some additional information of value to the U.S. Government. From my perspective, if CARAWAY's report differed from what NSA knew, we would have to determine if he was either holding back information or actually was being instructed what to provide. While I did not have any serious concerns at this point that CARAWAY was being used as a double agent, professional discipline dictates that counterintelligence concerns must always be a part of any operation.

As to the FBI, the list of communications equipment would also benefit them in terms of how the Consulate operated. We understood that upon receiving the information, just as we would report it to our Headquarters, the Field Office would make it into a report for their technical Headquarters unit. As noted, a pragmatic and bureaucratic value of a joint operation within the Intelligence Community is that all members of the joint team can report the same information and get credit from within their own organizations. This may seem self-serving, but the same information can be used differently by various organizations. For example, while we would use the details on the communication's equipment and their interaction as validation of the target, the FBI might use it to determine how to enhance their collection efforts against Warsaw Pact installations in the United States. That said, duplicative reporting of the same information can, on occasion, lead to false confirmations of information. Thereare cross checks performed within the Intelligence Community to avoid such problems. Usually, they are effective.

However, the most important reporting requirement given to the Target was the one he probably did not recognize as tasking—detailed information on his son's health issue. With this information we could start to providemore of the "carrot," which we hoped would insure CARAWAY's continuing cooperation.

As I noted before, in a slightly different context, in operations, you always prefer to ask a question to which you already knew the answer.

CHAPTER SEVENTEEN: THE TURNOVER

This is especially true when the question is whether the asset is willing to undertake the task, which is the objective of the operation. Thus, a smart CO never tasks an agent unless s/he is confident that the Target is ready to agree. There is nothing more professionally, as well as personally, embarrassing than having a Target stand up in the middle of a crowded restaurant and yell, "What, you want me to be a spy and traitor to my country!" Not only is such an incident a hard one to report, but it is also a hard one to ever live down. Needless to say, if this happens while operating overseas, other ramification usually occurs, which are not beneficial to your career!

Once we understood the nature of the son's health issue, we could figure out a way to address this issue, which we had known for many months to be one of the major concerns for him and his wife. If we are able to demonstrate both an interest and a capability to do so, human nature and family self-interest should further reinforce the Target's loyalty to the corporation. More importantly, it should convince him that his commercial relationship can provide what he desires, and therefore help rationalize taking greater risks as our tasks become more sensitive.

Chapter Eighteen: The Carrot

Ralph was fully on-board with the concept that the next few meetings would emphasize firming up the corporation's relationship with CARAWAY. And, I counted on the Field Office's contacts in the local medical community to provide the necessary, but discreet, assistant in the diagnosis of Anton's physical issue. Ralph assured me that this would be no problem, and that the Bureau would handle the financial aspects of the medical activities.

Our Headquarters responded to our reporting on the meeting with satisfaction. They agreed that all seemed on track, and, as usual, complimented us for involving the Bureau in a manner that demonstrated effective partnership in a joint operation. We were being given pretty much free rein in terms of our operational planning. That suited me just fine.

Since the Headquarters special unit in liaison with NSA was focused on technical issues, they seldom commented on our handling of the human end of the operation. That said, it would take a while before we fully understood the skills and types of activities of this unit—in my career to that point I had never worked with them. Based upon their title, I understood that they were the interface with the NSA on "human-assisted" acquisition of foreign code and equipment operations. The usual terminology used to describe their function was "liaison with NSA to coordinate human acquisition of technical data." We would soon learn they did much more, and once we learned about the range and scope of their activities, their impressive, unique skills and talents became apparent.

CHAPTER EIGHTEEN: THE CARROT

Our preparation for the next meeting was mostly in the administrative field: identify a meeting location, get the meeting's time and date sent to the commercial answering service, and ensure that appropriate tradecraft was included in travel to, at, and from the meeting with CARAWAY. The meeting itself had a simple scenario: get the list of Consulate communications gear, get details of the son's health issues, and continue to build confidence and rapport with the target.

As scheduled, CARAWAY called the Delaware telephone number and got the meeting details. The scenario called for me to pick up CARAWAY at a street corner about five blocks from his residence, and drive him to a suburban steak house, cleared by the Field Office as a site not patronized by Warsaw Pact officials or any of the local immigrant population in touch with the Consulate. Over a quiet dinner in a booth in the rear of the restaurant, I would get his reporting and set the scene for assistance for Anton's medical issue. Also, I would tell Target a few stories that demonstrated the loyalty and concern that the boss had for his employees.

Casing the restaurant and getting a car rental reservation in my alias identity took less than half a day, so we had adequate time to get the contact instructions message transmitted to Headquarters for the Target's telephone call to my "office." Then, we actually had a couple of days to let our planning formulate and be tinkered with.

However, a cultural difference between us and the Bureau did raise it head. Two days before the scheduled meeting, Ralph called to advise that his Headquarters wanted photo surveillance of the meeting in order to document their records. He stated that, as I knew, in the Bureau, resources are allocated based upon demonstrated progress over a set time period. I understood this but asked why photos were necessary, since that meant close in surveillance, which might be detected by the Target and frighten him. Ralph responded that even with a Government Discount at the hotel, the cost of the suite for one night ran near a thousand dollars, and expenses of this size did have to be justified. Also, he was planning ahead, and requesting allocation of several thousand dollars in additional case funds for future hotel suite rentals and anticipated high medical costs related to addressing Target's son's health issues.

Actually, this all made sense, knowing how the Bureau operated. It also, once again, made me very thankful that the Agency recognized that human operations required a great degree of flexibility because we are dealing with individual personalities. While we do have strong established accounting procedures to document and monitor expenses, we also have the cultural mentality that you have to "spend money to make money." Why? Because when one of the recruitments succeeded, the results were usually of such value to the USG that it saved many times over the funds spent on the unsuccessful operations. For example, consider the cost of sending a Navy aircraft carrier task force into the Pacific to conduct a blockage operation. Well, the costs of, say, thousands of dollars to obtain a foreign government's plans to ship certain materials deemed dangerous to a third country, and the use of that information to privately advise that government of our knowledge and stopping the shipment that way, really is a lot cheaper.

Ralph and I agreed that Larry would take a photo surveillance SA in an unmarked car near the point of the planned pickup, and photograph CARAWAY before and during his entry into my rental car. They would also photograph CARAWAY and me entering the restaurant, and eventually exiting the restaurant, and my dropping him off within walking distance of his residence. We agreed that photographs inside the restaurant would be an unnecessary risk. This agreement satisfied their documentation concerns and would involve long-range photography. I was really only concerned about any photography inside the restaurant.

About three in the afternoon on the day of the meeting, I drove to the airport and parked my car in the long-term lot. I used that lot because it is bigger and thus easier to hide the car in. I took the shuttle bus to the departure area and performed a planned countersurveillance pattern within the airport. Upon its completion, I walked down to the arrival area and took the rental car shuttle bus to the rental car office. There, I showed my alias driving license, used my alias credit card, and took a dark colored four door sedan out of the parking area towards the city. The auto color and style was, of course, one of the most common of all cars on the road. You never want to stand out as anything but common when making a car pickup.

I drove the car to a suburban library and spent a couple of hours reading up on thyroid diseases, figuring that having at least a basic knowledge would help me understand what CARAWAY was about to tell me about his son's health issue. I left the library, giving myself a half-hour time window beyond what we had estimated as the time required to get to a parking garage within three blocks of the car pickup point. Even with the end of rush hour business traffic, I made it to the parking garage about fifteen minutes early. And, parked the car, turned on the radio, and mentally reviewed my plans for the meeting. At ten minutes before the pickup time, I departed the garage and drove around the block to use up another five or so minutes. My goal was to be at the street corner exactly on time. Later in the operation, exact timing would be necessary and, as before, we were trying to program on-time discipline into CARAWAY's activities.

It is always a judgment call as to how close you can come to the pickup time in decent traffic. This is much easier when you are on foot and have a meeting. Traffic lights, double parked trucks, and the rest of the clutter of busy streets can easily screw up your timing. So, the CO is usually sweating a bit as he or she tries to arrive on time without leaving the target hanging around too long.

In this case, even with one large Federal Express delivery truck double-parked a block from the pickup location, I made the pickup only a few seconds after the car clock hit 7:30 p.m. I did not observe the FBI's photo surveillance vehicle. CARAWAY was standing exactly where he should have been and quickly entered the front passenger side. I shook his hand, and we drove almost directly to the restaurant, while I engaged him in some bland social chatter about the weather and the city's traffic.

I did not feel it was necessary to conduct a full countersurveillance route on the way to the restaurant, since the FBI was providing countersurveillance support. Also, in busy traffic, a significant number of resources, personnel, autos, and communication systems, were required to tail someone unnoticed who had even minimal training in spotting surveillance. I did a box pattern set of turns involving north and south one-way streets, explaining it to the target in terms of being a bit confused as to the directions to the restaurant since I had not been there before. Being unable to identify any other vehicles following my strange driving pattern, I proceeded to the restaurant. Upon arriving and giving the valet the car to park, we went inside. Once again, I was unable to identify the FBI photo surveillance activity.

Once seated at our table, we ordered drinks. CARAWAY, as usual, ordered an expensive scotch, and I followed his lead. We chatted pleasantly as we drank and discussed the menu. Once we decided on a true American red meat dinner, I asked him if he had been able to complete the report the boss had requested. He said he had, and from his coat pocket produced a several-page report, handwritten and including two diagram pages showing how the various components in the Communications Room were interrelated within the communications system. I took the report and spent the time we took on our first pre-dinner drink reviewing the report and asking some clarifying questions.

His report was really quite good. He identified each piece of equipment by brand name and function, and when able, listed the manufacturer of various components in each machine. He also provided both in-text descriptions and through the diagrams details on how each piece of equipment interacted to form the entire system. The one area where his description of both the equipment and how they interacted was less detailed was in the encoding and decoding process. This was the most sensitive portion of the system, and it appeared that CARAWAY was not yet sure enough of his relationship with us to share all he knew about how these procedures worked.

I was not surprised—these were the real secrets and he knew that just as well as we did. So, while I questioned him on several other parts of the system, I did not push him on that process. That would come later.

As we ate, I complimented him on his detailed report and noted that the boss would be very pleased. "From the information you provided, I

CHAPTER EIGHTEEN: THE CARROT

anticipate that the corporation," I said," would be able to identify some newer, but probably restricted technology, that the Romanian Government or other Warsaw Pact countries would probably want." I then told him a story about how the boss had been able to identify and then procure certain technical equipment needed by some Asian countries even before their governments were aware that such updates were available. Needless to say, I noted, we made a significant profit, and the governments receiving the equipment found themselves much further advanced in that technical field than they had anticipated. I concluded by stating that much of what the corporation did was a win-win situation for everyone concerned. Our advanced knowledge of what might be needed simply allowed us to establish channels to procure the technology and have it on hand when an organization or government needed it. And, while this sometimes meant finding ways to circumvent international restrictions or overly restrictive national copyright regulations, everybody deserved to share in modern technologies. After all, science and its technological creations belong to all of mankind, not just a portion of it claiming a certain political philosophy.

Unfortunately, that rationalization theme came from previous experience I had while debriefing numerous American scientists and technical experts upon their return from foreign exchange visits. Time and time again, these individuals would rationalize their discussion of American science and technical breakthroughs with foreign scientists using the concept that "all science belongs to everybody." Even after pointing out that the "foreign scientists" were specifically trained to elicit sensitive information from their visiting American counterparts, and that abundant evidence exists of the militarization of scientific information provided in such "free and open" discussions, very few of these professionals believed they had done anything other than share scientific knowledge among peers. We really are a naïve culture when it comes to being manipulated by our foreign adversaries.

When I finished my comments, CARAWAY nodded his head in agreement, and I changed the subject. I explained that I would be catching a late flight out of the city to Miami, where I was in the process of handling a negotiation for some military-related technical range-finding equipment with representatives of a Latin American country. Thus, I would have to leave the dinner by 10 p.m. However, the boss had specifically asked me to be sure and get more specific information on his son's health issues.

So, as we finished our meal and moved into coffee, dessert, and an after-dinner scotch, CARAWAY told me about his son's health issue. Anton had been diagnosed with hypothyroidism, a condition in which the thyroid gland produces a smaller than required dose of hormones. This can affect a child's physical growth as well as his mental agility. The doctors in Bucharest had believed that a lack of vitamins in Anton's diet may have caused the condition, and accordingly, he had been given medicine to correct the balance of the hormonal flow. However, CARAWAY and his wife did not believe this approach was working. Anton continued to be small for his age, and was far less physically active than his counterparts and less quick in his learning skills. Both thought that an American doctor would have more up-to-date knowledge of how to treat their son's problem. But, the cost of a specialist, known as an endocrinologist or a thyroidologist, was very expensive, and the family did not yet have the funds on hand for a consultation and ongoing treatment. CARAWAY had made some telephone calls and asked about the cost of basic services. He learned that the initial consultation and related basic tests to identify the cause of the issue would easily run into the thousands of dollars, even before any treatment required might be undertaken. He then produced from his coat pocket a wad of papers, which he described as the medical notes and diagnostic details provided to him by the Bucharest doctors, whom he described as being accessible to him only because of his Romanian Communist Party status.

I took the papers, but of course, they were written in Romanian, which did me no good. However, I said that one thing the boss clearly understood and valued was the concept of family and its loyalty. I advised that I would get the notes translated and have them reviewed by an American medical specialist in the field. Based upon his analysis, a course of medical action could be discussed and arranged. CARAWAY responded with a look of

CHAPTER EIGHTEEN: THE CARROT

pure joy in his eyes. He rather profusely thanked me, and said that this was the family's greatest wish—that their son could be cured and enabled to live up to his full potential.

I smiled benevolently and assured him that his son's health was now a corporate matter. I should add here that, as cynical as this may sound, the health of the Target's son was indeed to become a priority in the operation. When a CO enters into an operational relationship with an asset, he or she also enters into a series of professional responsibilities that include protecting the well-being of that individual and fulfilling all the commitments made in the agreement. In this case, we were about to spend a significant amount of money, the FBI's in this particular instance, to get the best possible treatment for CARAWAY's son. Our professional reason for doing so was to further bind him into a clandestine relationship and enhance his motivation to respond to future tasking. We wanted a cooperative and involved asset. That said, even the seemingly hardened Agency CO and FBI SA much prefer to provide assistance that actually benefits someone positively, such as health care. Rather than just give money to pay gambling debts or purchase material goods to satisfy the s agents ego issues.

After paying the check, CARAWAY and I got the car from the valet, and I drove him back to the pick-up point. Before saying goodnight, I noted that as this was a new month, he was due a salary of fifteen hundred dollars. I gave him an envelope containing the money. I noted that based upon my quick review of his report on the Consulate's communications system, he could anticipate a bonus from the boss along with next month's salary. I also reaffirmed that the corporation would start having its people work on Anton's health problem, and that he should call my Delaware office about 8 p.m. on the 28th of the month. I would have a message for him at that time about when we would next meet. I would also expect to have some information on the medical issue. I concluded by advising him that the boss next wanted a report on who actually worked in the Consulate and what their specific duties were. I explained that the boss wanted a better understanding of the work environment and areas of responsibility in the

Consulate. I suggested it would also be useful for him to provide a brief personality profile of his colleagues as well. I asked that he have his report completed by our next meeting.

CARAWAY accepted the funds and the tasking without comment, and said he looked forward to the information I would have for him on the 28th. We shook hands, and he exited the vehicle and quickly walked into the shadows of a parking lot towards the street leading to his residence. I immediately locked the door after him, a habit from foreign assignments, and slowly drove away. I actually took the rental car to my residence, parking in my garage, in order to turn it in the next day. On a one-day rental, returning the car the next morning is much less conspicuous than doing so late at night.

The next morning, I turned in the rental, claimed my car from airport parking, and drove to the Station. As I had written up notes from last night's meeting at my home, it took me only a couple of hours to prepare a full report to Headquarters, which included CARAWAY's notes on the Consulate's communications system and the information on his son's health issue. By noon, the report was on its way to Washington, and I was ready for a working lunch at the Station with our Field Office colleagues. Winston, Stan and Edmund all had a chance to read my report prior to the meeting, but we did not have time to discuss it in detail. I left the arrangements for the lunch to an Administrative Officer, so we could focus on our meeting with the FBI. That would turn out to be a mistake.

Matt and Larry arrived a bit after noon, explaining that Ralph was involved in a meeting with the Field Office SAC on another case, but would try to make the meeting if possible. No problem. It appeared that we were past the point where we needed the assistance of the ranking FBI FCI officer when discussing this operation. I began with a detailed review of the meeting, and thereafter provided both SAs with copies of my report and the papers provided by CARAWAY. Most of my comments related to the atmosphere of the dinner. As our primary objective had been to enhance the trust and confidence of the Target in our relationship, describing how he reacted to various ploys such as the stories of the corporation's business

CHAPTER EIGHTEEN: THE CARROT

activities, the boss' specific concern for his son's health issue, the suggestion that he could expect a bonus for his communications' system report, etc. held the most interest to the SAs.

Everyone agreed the meeting had gone well, and our objectives had been accomplished. Matt skimmed the report on the Consulate's communications system and stated that it would be a useful document for the Field Office. And, he noted, NSA will probably find it even more useful. I did note, up front, that the least amount of detail CARAWAY provided was on the most sensitive part of the system: the interface for decryption and encryption of the radio communications. But, we had every reason to expect that he would hold back on this as it represented the most sensitive information his government had trusted him with. When he was ready to provide this information in response to a tasking, I expected he would do so.

The health information was the focus of a lengthy discussion. Matt assigned Larry to speak with a local endocrinologist who was a Field Office contact and could be trusted to handle CARAWAY's son's health issue with complete discretion. It was agreed that this would be a priority effort, so that appropriate information could be given to the Target during his call to my Delaware office on the 28th. We then discussed some security measures we needed to build into the CARAWAY—doctor relationship. It was agreed that the doctor would have to know CARAWAY's true name as the medical records had to be usable in the future if that became necessary. But, that information should only be in that doctor's files. If out-of-office medical testing was required, a slight variation in CARAWAY's true name would be used on the prescription for that service. All medical charges other than those of the doctor were to be sent to the doctor's office and paid through that office. The doctor was to explain to the CARAWAY family that he was on retainer to handle all the medical work in his field of expertise, and that he would bill the corporation directly for all charges. He would emphasize that the relationship between a doctor and his patient, and the patient's family, was both a legally and ethically protected confidential relationship.

Administratively, the Field Office, through Larry, would provide the doctor with all the funds required for his services and whatever medical tests and medicines were necessary to treat Anton. We would expect the doctor to keep us informed on the progress of the treatment, but would respect his professional responsibilities regarding the doctor–patient relationship. Our goal was to see Anton cured, which would deepen CARAWAY's psychological debt to the boss and further entangle their relationship. Since the Field Office had a great deal of experience in these types of arrangements based upon their own cases where true identities had to be protected, we could anticipate that it would be handled smoothly. However, it was up to me and the boss to ensure that CARAWAY understood the confidentiality involved in the medical treatment. And, of course, he clearly recognized that this benefit was the result of his loyalty and complete cooperation with the corporation.

Larry also brought along the photos taken by the Field Office of the car pickup, the restaurant entry and exit, and the drop off of the target. These photos were not particularly interesting to us, but Matt explained they would be used as documentation for additional funding requests for this case. Larry also noted that no evidence of surveillance of the Target had been observed.

We concluded the meeting about midafternoon, agreeing to meet as soon as Larry had contacted the doctor. Meanwhile, the Field Office would make its requests for additional funds, and we would focus on planning the next meeting, the time and date of which would also be given to CARAWAY during his telephone call on the 28th.

As the SAs departed, the Station's Administrative Officer came into my office to complain that the conference room was one hell of a mess. So, we walked back into the room, and he was right. We had been rather messy eaters, and the choice of Chinese food by his assistant had not been the best. The gooey sauces from the various Chinese dishes had spilled onto the table. Along with a mix of the sweet and sticky Chinese sauce packets and the steamed rice, quite a coating had developed. While he had been the one to order and pick up the food, it was not his responsibility to clean up after us. So, I thought about calling in Stan and Edmund and having them clean up the room. But, along with authority goes responsibility. It took me well over half an hour to clean the place. Note to me: no more Chinese food for lunches as there are simply too many problems related to inexperienced chopstick users eating the food.

Headquarters responded to my report the next day, noting the attachments were sent to NSA for its comments. Later that day the COs and I gathered to start planning the next meeting. The boss was to be present at this one, as we wanted to make some strong points about CARAWAY's responsibilities to the corporation as well as note how his employee benefits were being handled. After sketching out a general concept of the objectives we wished to accomplish, the COs went back to develop a scenario for further discussion.

We still had almost a week before CARAWAY was to call my office for the message, so we did not feel rushed in our overall preparations. Larry visited the Station a few days later with all the information on the endocrinologist. This doctor was on the staff of a suburban research and teaching hospital associated with the local university. He had not previously been used in the diagnosis and treatment of government subjects who required identity protection. But, in his other role as a noted specialist in his field at the hospital, he had been involved with the Field Office when a group of Soviet medical doctors had visited the university and hospital to discuss certain treatment procedures recently developed there. After the visit, the Field Office sent SAs to speak with the doctors who had been involved in the visit, to get a perspective of what the Soviet doctors had wanted and what particular medical areas they were most interested in. All the hospital doctors involved were immediately able to identify the "senior doctor" as the security officer assigned to the group, since he was unable to discuss virtually any medical subject with ease. And, when in the research facility where a new virus-resistant strain was being developed, this individual continually asked to see research notes and test results. He was politely refused, much to his displeasure. The other doctors all seemed to be from the field of personal health and, quite apparently, from their comments at dinners and the other social occasions, their clients were senior Soviet

Communist Party officials and their families.

The endocrinologist had been particularly helpful in his interview, and a review of his background found that his parents were originally from Hungary. At the age of six, his parents had fled the country during the brief Hungarian Revolution against the Soviets. His family had gained special immigration status to enter the United States, and a local Hungarian community group in the city had helped the family become established. The father, previously a college professor, had a fair command of English and was soon able to find employment, with the assistance of the Hungarian community, at a local junior college. His son learned English in school and, supported by his parents, did well enough to obtain a scholarship to a small but respected college upstate. Upon graduation, he decided to apply to medical school, was accepted, obtained a medical scholarship as well as a supplemental scholarship from the city's Hungarian community, and became a doctor. He then specialized in thyroid disorders and had a sound reputation in the field. His family's background created an understandable dislike for the Soviets, as other close relatives had died in the revolution, and his smooth and supportive transition into American culture had given him a solid respect for the American ideal that everyone had an equal opportunity to achieve professionally.

Based upon Larry's information, we subsequently ran our own traces on the doctor and found pretty much the same information the SA had provided to us. The only additional piece of information we got from Headquarters was that the doctor's father, in addition to being a college professor, was also one of the leaders at the college of a group involved in the political planning that led up to the revolution. It was lucky that he and his family got out, because the Soviets were definitely after him once they had destroyed the revolution. This also helped explain why the family was able to get settled in the U.S. so quickly and with so much help from the Hungarian community, which was firmly anti-Communist in its politics.

Larry would be the only link to the doctor, and would provide him with any guidance he required on protecting CARAWAY's identity and handle all aspects of payment for treatment. Larry's performance in his selection and handling of the doctor was very professional, and made me think that he might be able to play yet another role in the operation as it continued to mature.

The initial response from the NSA, passed to us through the Agency liaison unit, was received prior to the Target's call to the office. It stated that CARAWAY's information and his description of the Consulate's communications system were accurate based upon their files. But, some of the components he identified were not previously known in the detail he reported. It was also noted that the key weakness in his report related to the equipment and interface of the encryption and decryption paper tape system used in the radio communication traffic. Since I had noted this point in my operational reporting, I was slightly upset that Headquarters stated it as if it was new to everybody. Guess this is yet another indication that we COs are often quite sensitive human beings.

Most importantly, from the perspective of management and control of the operation, there were their comments about the sensitivity of the information CARAWAY had supplied. NSA advised that the Romanian Government, and indeed the Warsaw Pact, considered most parts of their communication's system described to be their equivalent of "top secret." Only Communication's Officers at a certain professional level- those trusted by their goernments- were granted this degree of insight into the system. In most official installations, only the Senior Communications Officer would know this much detail, and his or her employees would know only what was needed to handle their more mundane maintenance and repair responsibilities.

NSA concluded that as the system described by the target was the current, and to the best of their knowledge, most modern communication's system in operation for Warsaw Pact countries, it was highly doubtful that information of this detail would be allowed to be given to a hostile intelligence organization as part of a dis-information program or a classic double agent operation.

While nothing is ever absolute in counterintelligence, NSA's pronouncement came close. We could now assume CARAWAY was indeed who we thought he was, and that he had the access we believed him to have. We could now create the scenario to get the next piece of the puzzle: portions of the actual encryption and decryption paper tapes.

The day before the evening call was to be made by CARAWAY, we sent the specific message to Headquarters for passage to the telephone unit. It had two parts: CARAWAY would have to have the capability to write down some information. The first part advised him that at eight in the evening of the 10th of June, he was to wait at the corner of 26th Street and Bridge Ave., about seven blocks from his residence. Patrick would pick him up exactly at eight and drive him to the meeting. The second part of the message concerned his son's health issue. CARAWAY was given the telephone number and office address of the doctor, and told to call the next morning to arrange an appointment for his son. He was advised that the doctor was expecting his call and knew that all expenses related to this new patient were to be paid by the corporation. The end of the message told him to repeat the key points of the message to ensure that he had understood them correctly.

The next morning, we repeated the same message to Headquarters and asked them to verify it with the telephone people. They did so. It was procedural that once CARAWAY made the telephone call, we would be advised of it. He did, almost exactly on time.

Now we needed to get the administrative arrangements set up, and this simply meant advising the Field Office of the need for the car, suite, and Patrick's assistance. Our role was to flesh out the meeting scenario, which at this point was primarily to develop the sense of mutual loyalty in the target. While he would also be given some tasks to justify his monthly retainer, we would also start to lay the background for acquiring access to the coding tapes. The clear message he was to take from the next few meetings was how he benefited from his association with the corporation.

The role players at this meeting on the 10th would be me, as Robert, Winston, as the boss, and Patrick, as the boss's personal assistant. It would include a dinner, with CARAWAY, Winston, and me dining, while Patrick served in attendance. Winston would provide most of

CHAPTER EIGHTEEN: THE CARROT

the dialogue, querying about the son's medical condition, explaining how CARAWAY's report on the Consulate's communications system had commercial benefit, and playing up his status as the wealthy and politically powerful international businessman. After dinner Winston would retire to his bedroom area under the pretense of international telephone calls to make and I would read and discuss CARAWAY report on Consulate personnel, pay him his monthly retainer and bonus for his previous report, caution him on how he spent the money, and insure he was handling the medical treatment of his son in a discreet manner which did not bring suspicion upon him from inside the Consulate.

Winston developed his script within a day and a half, and I had mine set in about the same time frame. We ran them past Stan and Edmund, and then discussed them with Ralph, Matt, Larry and Patrick. Nobody had any issues, but there were a few suggestions of value to add an emphasis here or a staging posture there. We and the Field Office were working as a team.

At the meeting with the Field Office, Larry gave us a report from the doctor on his initial examination of the son. CARAWAY had called as instructed, and an appointment had quickly been arranged for that Saturday morning at the doctor's office. CARAWAY arrived, as expected, with his wife as well as their son. The doctor reviewed the previous medical diagnosis presented orally by CARAWAY and his wife, and asked appropriate questions about the son's behavior, activities, and overall health. He conducted a general medical exam of the boy and had blood samples taken for lab testing. He then explained that, based upon his initial examination and the boy's medical history as it had been related to him, the next step would be a series of tests to determine how the thyroid gland was functioning. Also, he planned to look beyond that particular area and do a comprehensive examination of the boy's overall physical condition. This would probably involve further tests, he advised the parents.

He advised CARAWAY to bring his son back in a week, when the blood sample results were ready and he had scheduled additional testing based on the blood results. He concluded the first visit by reassuring the parents that he was especially well equipped to handle thyroid issues, and the initial impression he had based upon his examination of the boy was that his condition was treatable. The doctor also noted that he understood CARAWAY's corporation was directly covering all treatment costs, and that its policy enforced one of the strictest standards of privacy concerning the medical care of its employees and their families. The doctor later advised Larry that CARAWAY and his wife seemed sincerely appreciative of his services, and appeared to be somewhat relieved as they left his office.

Larry also noted that the doctor did pick up on the Eastern European accented English of the CARAWAYs, and asked him about it. Larry responded that, as the doctor could figure out from his patient's family name, they were indeed Eastern European, and this made their association with the FBI particularly sensitive. He suggested that the doctor could best help the Bureau and his country by focusing on treating the boy and ignoring anything else about the family. The doctor responded that he understood and would not ask further questions. So, all seemed well, and, of course, Larry also understood that he must keep a careful eye on the doctor to ensure he did not become too interested in the family beyond his medical duties.

There was little doubt, considering his family background and his previous work with the Field Office, that the doctor was a patriotic American. But, keeping CARAWAY's association with the Bureau secret was paramount to the operation's success, and any casual mention of this patient to colleagues, family, or friends would be dangerous. One of the key problems with compartmentalization in an operation is that people just have a hard time keeping a secret. I guess it may have something to do with ego, i.e. "I am involved in something really important but can't provide details." Or, since their involvement is often more interesting than their everyday activities, perhaps it is just the excitement that stimulates a casual comment to an acquaintance. In any event, when you let another individual into the operation, particularly a non-intelligence professional, you also take on the burden of monitoring and constantly reminding them of the need for discretion and caution in their participation. So, Larry, under the guise of checking on the results of the medical testing and future treatments, would also be ensuring the doctor behaved appropriately.

Our objectives for the June 10th meeting were primarily psychological. We wanted to establish Winston as the "father figure" who exercised a personal interest and concern for his employees. In addition, we needed to keep emphasizing the vast resources, political connections, and "power" that the corporation had in its worldwide dealings. In other words, we needed to make him feel like a member of a "family" that could protect him from harm if future tasks were of a risky nature. And, it was soon to get quite risky.

Once this portion of the meeting was completed, I would give him a task that would make it perfectly clear that the quid pro quo for his corporate relationship was going to be sensitive information he knew from his duties at the Consulate. His reaction to this reporting requirement would go a long way in determining if our ultimate objective was attainable. This time I would instruct him to provide details on the encoding and decoding machines in the Communication's Room at the Consulate.

Winston's role in the meeting was somewhat complex, as he had to philosophize on his view of loyalty and his personal interest in the welfare of all his people. And, he also had to explain in broad terms, with some examples, how powerful the corporation was and how well connected he personally was with political and financial figures worldwide. He would portray himself as a member of a small group of international businessmen who, behind the scenes, controlled a great deal of international financial transactions. While this may seem like some fantasy story out of a movie script or novel, you would be surprised how many people really believe that groups like this really exist. A great many people like to explain their own inability to succeed as the result of greater forces being in control—sort of an extension of the "victim mentality" whereas one fails not because of their own inability, but because of others who are out to get them. And, when you come from the political system in which CARAWAY grew up, knowing that a small group of powerful individuals controls your country and therefore your future, believing such an international group exists makes a great deal of sense. That is exactly how the Romanian Communist Party ruled.

My role would be to reinforce the boss's rhetoric and provide logical and comforting arguments regarding why CARAWAY should give us detailed information on how the encoding and decoding equipment at the Consulate operated. If Winston was convincing during his portion of the meeting, my job should not be that difficult.

With our scripts set, Winston and I met with the Field Office to get any last-minute input, and were provided with a very useful update by Larry on the results of the initial tests of the son and the doctor's conversation with the family at their second meeting. The blood tests indicated a low secretion rate from the thyroid gland, as well as a possible issue with the son's kidney functions. The doctor had advised CARAWAY of this, stating that medical technology in the United States was well suited to address both problems. He set up some tests required to analyze why the gland was not functioning normally and also to determine if the kidney was malfunctioning. The doctor told the family that the results of these tests would be available within a few days and that they should return the next Saturday for another appointment. Also, he concluded his comments by stating that additions to the son's diet were not going to solve the problem. Rather, looking closer at the functioning of the gland and determining why it was malfunctioning was the solution. He added that both his personal research and that of others at the hospital on the functioning of the thyroid gland represented American "cutting edge" knowledge. Thus, based upon the results of the initial blood work, he was confident that the cause of the problem would soon be identified.

These details were very important, as Winston would play them back to CARAWAY over dinner, thus demonstrating just how personal an interest the boss took in his employee's life. He would also casually note that while the costs of the additional testing were significant, it paled in comparison to the importance of loyalty within the corporate family. I would also reinforce this point in my post dinner conversation with the target.

Thus, with the Field Office's agreement to the scenario, we were ready to

CHAPTER EIGHTEEN: THE CARROT

proceed. But, not before one last-minute problem: Late in the afternoon of June 9th, I got a call from Matt advising that the hotel suite, the same one used for the first meeting between CARAWAY and the boss, had mistakenly been booked by the hotel for the next evening. He wanted to know if we had to cancel and reschedule the meeting or whether he and Ralph should find another location. They needed an immediate response if another location was to be arranged.

I told Matt I would get back to him in a few minutes and tried to think through the various issues a change in venue would have on our plan. First and foremost was the matter of operational security. If we moved to a new location, more people would know, either officially through obtaining their cooperation or unofficially just by observing what activities were taking place. Considering the sensitivity of the operation, keeping compartmentalization of it as small as possible was a security and counterintelligence necessity. Secondarily, whatever location we eventually used had to reflect, at least in the Target's eyes, the wealth and importance of the boss. So, I phoned Matt back and suggested that Ralph get the next best suite at the hotel we had used previously. Since it was a high-end international chain, I was pretty confident that it had at least a couple of suites that would appropriately reflect the image we wished to convey to the Target. I also reminded him that the site had to have a separate dining area, since we were planning a dinner for that meeting.

Ralph called back about an hour later with the good news that a second suite had been arranged through his contact at the hotel, and it was almost as luxurious as the other suite. Its separate dining room was somewhat smaller, but since only three of us were having dinner. That was not a problem. I also asked Ralph to have his contact insure that fresh flower arrangements were provided for the suite and that proper dinner place settings for three were provided. Another small problem solved.

The next morning, after a brief meeting with Winston, Stan, Edmund and me, to review any last-minute thoughts or concerns, Winston and I started our security procedures to separate ourselves from the Station.

251

Winston drove to a local suburban shopping mall and took in a movie, a spy thriller, I believe, and did not emerge until it was time for Patrick to pick him up in the limo. I drove to a local town's library and once again attempted to bone up on my medical knowledge, especially in the kidney area. After a couple of hours of difficult research, as I am a Liberal Arts kind of guy, I drove to the airport, parked the car, and spent about an hour at a coffee bar inside the arrivals terminal. From there, a taxi to the hotel about an hour and a half before CARAWAY was scheduled to arrive. Patrick and Winston had arrived about an hour earlier, and the suite was set up and looking as desired.

Patrick left to collect the Target, and returned just a bit late due to the end of business traffic in the city. This time the boss was in the suite's parlor area, sitting with a drink when Patrick brought in CARAWAY. I was near to the door, standing and extended my hand to him. Winston, who was seated and did not get up, raised his hand in a slight gesture of recognition. I then indicted to CARAWAY to take a seat.

Winston began by noting that recent activities in the exchange rate between the British pound and the French franc were causing problems for a couple of the purchase agreements he had recently made from a French-based company. He noted that he would have to speak with the French Deputy Minister of Finance about this. I jotted down his comments and said I would place a call to the Minister on his schedule later in the week. He then said, "Enough about business, Robert has advised me of the results of the visit to the doctor regarding your son's illness. I understand that additional tests are being run?" CARAWAY responded that this was correct and that the doctor was planning more tests and had identified the problem as a malfunctioning thyroid gland and a possible problem with his son's kidney. He concluded that he was very grateful for the doctor's assistance, and emphasized that both he and his wife were impressed with the doctor's expertise and the aggressive manner in which he was addressing the illness. He said that the doctor's behavior of explaining in detail exactly what was going on was quite different from the behavior of Romanian doctors. It was clear that CARAWAY and his wife were more

CHAPTER EIGHTEEN: THE CARROT

than satisfied with the son's care.

Winston listened carefully, allowing the Target to respond completely before speaking. He smiled benevolently and said that he had been advised this doctor was one of the best in the region for these problems. He then looked at me, and ordered that the doctor was to conduct whatever testing was required, regardless of the cost, and that I was to keep him fully informed as the diagnosis and treatment continued. I made a note of his instructions in my memo book.

By this time, Patrick had provided a drink for the Target, and Winston noted that a few years ago, another valued employee had experienced a similar family health crisis. His wife had developed a cancerous growth on her neck, probably from too much sun during a vacation in the Italian Riviera. At the time, the individual was the corporation's country manager in Rome, handling business relations with Italian defense manufacturers and the Italian Government. His personal connections to several senior Italian Government officials, based upon their earlier association at the Saprienza University of Rome, made him most valuable and productive. But, as the wife's cancer became evident, the Italian doctors, the best money could buy there, failed to inspire any confidence in the couple. "Well," Winston stated, "I had to step in." He explained that he instructed the employee to fly his wife to Switzerland and make an appointment with the cancer specialists at the Centre Suisse du Cancer at Lausanne. As anticipated, the Swiss specialists were much more professional and developed a treatment plan involving both isotope treatment and minor neck surgery that eliminated the cancer. While expensive, both in financial terms and the employee's absence from his Rome office, the results were well worth it.

To this, CARAWAY quietly responded that the boss's personal interest in his son's care was greatly appreciated by him and his wife. Winston responded, "Nonsense; it was the right thing to do both as an individual and as a corporate Chief Executive Officer." He explained that this employee had been loyal and hardworking, making significant profits for the corporation, and that loyalty must always be a two-way street. Money was not the issue, rather it was that he and the corporation demonstrated that we are a family that always looks out for our members.

Winston then noted that he had been briefed on the information CARAWAY had previously provided on the communications system at the Consulate. Corporate engineers had advised that the equipment noted did have certain components that could be upgraded. And, marketing personnel were looking at how a couple of Warsaw Pact countries could be advised that upgrades for their communications system were available. "Of course," Winston noted as an aside." There were some legal issues to address, but he was confident that workarounds could be found to get the components into the countries. He commented that CARAWAY had done well in his reporting, but additional information would be necessary to ensure maximum commercial utilization of his information.

At this point, room service arrived, and conversation shifted to a discussion of favorite scotches while Patrick supervised the placing of the dishes. Upon completion of the setup, he escorted the room service waiters to the door and provided them with their tips. He returned to the table and opened a bottle of the wine, gave it a few minutes to "breathe," while he carefully arranged the utensils and napkins. Then, he poured a small amount of the wine into a wine glass and brought it to Winston to sample. To keep the atmosphere "high class," we had ordered two bottles of the 1958 vintage Cotes du Rhone, Chateau D'remoue, with the meal. Obviously, we could have brought the wines ourselves at a significantly cheaper cost, as we did with the scotch. But having the wine come with the meal, was yet another demonstration of Winston's status.

Winston did the whole bit with the wine, taking a small sip, rounding it on the tip of his tongue, and finally sliding down the back of the tongue into his throat. He then gave a slight questioning expression, before advising Patrick with a slight smile that the wine could be served. Of course, the funny aspect of this is that Winston, his actual background notwithstanding, couldn't tell a decent Rhone red from an Annie Greensprings sparkling Rosé. But, CO training teaches you that all you need to be an expert in any subject is just a bit more knowledge, and perhaps some dramatic flair, than

CHAPTER EIGHTEEN: THE CARROT

anyone else in the room.

With the wine accepted, we moved to the table. Obviously, Winston sat at the head, with me and CARAWAY flanking him on either side. Patrick stood behind Winston and, always first attending to him, served the prime rib meal with all the usual accompanying dishes. During the meal, Winston, with my occasional comments supporting his remarks, discussed various business deals and issues of a current nature. Periodically, he would ask CARAWAY's opinion on how the Romanian Government or other Warsaw Pact countries would respond to a certain business approach. Within the context of the conversation were references to "contributions" and "consultant fees" paid to various officials, both in the Soviet sphere and in the West. We were hopeful that none of this was being lost on the target.

However, the most meaningful moment of the meal came when CARAWAY bit down on the crust of a piece of French bread, and instinctively uttered a muffled cry of pain. He immediately apologized and explained that for some time, he had been having a problem with a back tooth. Winston, remembering that there was a comment in our operational files about a dental problem, asked CARAWAY what the problem was. The Target explained that, unfortunately, dental care in Romania was not as advanced as in the West, and several fillings in his mouth were eroding. He planned to see an American dentist just as soon as he had saved up enough money to do so.

Well, almost angrily, Winston stated that no employee of his needed to endure such discomfort. He stared directly at me and stated, "Robert, you will arrange for Dusko to see a local dentist with whom we have a current contract. I want this handled immediately." He then went into a several-minute discourse on how decent food and good wine were one of man's few pure pleasures. At the conclusion of his remarks, I said that before CARAWAY departed that evening, I would arrange with him how we would address his dental needs. I added that he should understand that dental care for himself and his family was included as part of his corporate health plan. The Target, while silent throughout the conversation, offered a nod of appreciation to Winston.

Through coffee and dessert, Winston regaled us with some funny stories of his supposed social interactions with senior Hungarian and Polish Communist Party officials. He concluded his remarks by noting that he had yet to meet a Communist without a strong streak of at least personal Capitalism in his blood. We laughed appropriately. At that point, Patrick moved to Winston's side and noted that his schedule listed a telephone call to the Singapore office regarding the transshipment of some chemicals to North Korea. Winston nodded, arose, and said, "I enjoyed our dinner, but you must excuse me as I have some business to handle. Robert will discuss some tasking with you and handle any other administrative matters necessary. I am impressed with your knowledge and your disciplined response to our needs. Keep this up, and I see a very productive future for you. Good evening." He then walked into the bedroom area, with Patrick taking his place outside by the door.

Both CARAWAY and I had stood up as Winston departed, and I then motioned to the Target to follow me into the sitting room area and sit on the sofa. I took the wingback chair facing him across the coffee table. I started the conversation by noting that it was obvious that the boss was favorably impressed with CARAWAY's work to date. In particular, the boss's personal interest in the son's health issue was a good sign that he anticipated a long-term relationship with CARAWAY. I then moved into the business of evaluating his past report.

I said that as the boss had noted, corporate engineers had studied the various communications equipment used in the Consulate system and found that several components in the system were outdated. So, there were some opportunities for sales to various Eastern Bloc countries, which would benefit them as well as provide a decent profit to the corporation. However, in deals like this, there was a great deal of what we call "overhead costs" because careful communications and shipping arrangements had to be made to elude knowledge of the deal from various Western authorities. But, the boss had authorized you a bonus based on your part in developing the deal. So, in addition to his monthly retainer of fifteen hundred dollars given to him at our last meeting, I gave CARAWAY an additional two

CHAPTER EIGHTEEN: THE CARROT

thousand dollars.

Although I was prepared for any complaints by the Target regarding the size of the bonus, he once again accepted the money with a polite "thank you." Obviously, there was always concern that he might get greedy and question why the bonus was so small compared to the size of the business deals that the boss was always referring to. But, that never happened. We later concluded that the amount of money he was receiving each month was so much greater than his Romanian Government salary that he was simply overwhelmed by this level of disposable income. Also, the values of the health care, first to his son and then for his own dental problems, were not lost on him. Finally, as it was always made clear that the bonus figure was decided by the boss, we felt that his respect for the "father figure" authoritarian leader also played a role.

With that matter out of the way, I asked CARAWAY for his report on the duties of the various officials at the Consulate. He produced a several page report which I rather quickly read, while still stopping at a few paragraphs to seem to ponder certain of the statements. After completion of my reviewing of the report, I advised that I would forward it to the appropriate corporate officials.

Now came the hardest part of the session—levying the requirement that he prepare a report on how the encryption and decryption communication's system at the Consulate interfaced with the other equipment. I began by stating that the boss had another task for CARAWAY to handle in the coming weeks. I explained that our corporate engineers commented that while your diagram and narrative of the Consulate's communication's system was useful, a key part of it was missing—the interface of the encryption functions. As that portion is the most sensitive from the Romanian Government's perspective, and thus the most valuable, the corporations most profitable business would be if we were able to provide improved capabilities in that area of communications. Therefore, we needed to know exactly how the encryption interface worked.

A slight expression of concern quickly passed over the Target's face, and slowly he responded, "The encryption system is the most sensitive part of my responsibilities, and the security procedures surrounding the system are very strict. I am the only Communications Officer at the Consulate with full access to that equipment, and only the Consulate General and the senior Consulate security officer have any access to the system, and their functions are to check and verify that I am handling the equipment properly. Thus, knowledge of this type is very closely held."

I looked him straight in the eye and said "We are aware of this." I continued that, as I had just noted, the sensitivity of the equipment is what made it so valuable from a commercial perspective. I then explained that by now, he must realize the corporation's business activities were in areas not usually thought of by the public. The reason our engineers identified the absence of the encryption interface was that they were well aware of how a Warsaw Pact country conducted its communications, both in terms of the equipment in use and in the interface of that equipment for encryption and decryption of sensitive information. Who did he think sold them the equipment he was currently using, which he certainly knew was manufactured based upon Western-designed technology, I asked.

I asked him if he really thought the Poles had developed the equipment on their own. He quickly responded that while he was officially told the equipment had been developed by the Polish Government for Pact use, his professional background did cause him to recognize that it was very similar to the equipment he had studied, which was produced in the West. With this admission, I plowed ahead, emphasizing that the real money, for the corporation and by the way for him, was in selling his Government and other countries' updated encryption systems. And, to accomplish this, the boss expected him to provide comprehensive information on his current equipment and the interface mechanism. I reminded him that he was not dealing with some local salespeople, but with a disciplined international organization with the money and political connections to handle matters like this in a discreet and secure manner. The fact that it was he who provided this information would never be divulged, even within the corporation. Our engineers worked on the information they received from our corporate headquarters, which included details, diagrams, and reporting from dozens of individuals in governments all over the world. "Surely," I said, "you don't actually think you are the only Eastern Bloc government employee earning a consultant salary from us"?

I continued in this line of reasoning for several minutes, and then told him that if he intended to continue his employment with the boss, his loyalty and full commitment was necessary. I than got up, moved to the side bar area and poured CARAWAY and myself another scotch.

Upon my return to the chair, the Target looked up at me and said that he understood and was very grateful for the financial compensation and the personal interest the corporation had shown in him. "Perhaps," he said, "I have been a bit naïve about how things really work in the world. I want to continue to be employed by the corporation, and only ask that you keep in mind that whatever you ask me to do has to also consider how I can protect myself from suspicion and exposure within the Consulate." I gave the Target a confident look and said that in our business, the security of our employees was a priority . I noted that, like the compensation package and health care, the boss insisted that the protection of our employees was a loyalty issue as well as a business necessity. I concluded by stating that he really had no idea of how comprehensive our security apparatus was, and that the boss's personal association with senior government officials worldwide also included individuals in the government security services.

Now that we had that settled, I gave him a very clear tasking: a comprehensive description, with a diagram, of the equipment and interface details, for the encryption and decryption functions at the Consulate. I advised him to write this only while at his residence, and to have it ready within two weeks. I explained that I would be traveling back to the city in fourteen days and would expect the report at that time. I would only be in town for one night. I would once again pick him up, and we would go to a restaurant for dinner. As my schedule was always fluid, I instructed him to call my Wilmington office after seven in the evening on June 20th, and he would be advised when and where I would pick him up.

With our business settled, we had one more drink, and I spent the last fifteen minutes of our meeting discussing how Winston's keen knowledge of wines developed because his family owned several wineries in the Loire region of France. I noted that he would be surprised how many senior French officials would willingly discuss confidential information while being served some excellent, and expensive, vintages.

Thereafter, I instructed Patrick to take CARAWAY back to the pickup point. After they had departed, Winston and I discussed the meeting. We both felt that by accepting the tasking, CARAWAY had advanced to yet another stage of acceptance in his "employee" role. To ensure the suite use seemed normal to the hotel staff, we had decided that Winston would stay the night and check out the next morning. So, as he prepared to go to bed, I went downstairs and started my trip back to the airport, and subsequently, my car.

Chapter Nineteen: Reinforcement and Testing

Since both our Headquarters and the FBI Field Office were in synch with our planning and development of the case, submitting our reporting and briefing the SAs on the meetings was becoming a routine matter. In our discussion with Ralph and Matt regarding the next meeting on the 24th, the only real issue was finding a dentist to see what was wrong with CARAWAY's tooth. Once again, this task was given to Larry. However, it proved to be more difficult than finding a doctor. Apparently, the only dentists with whom the Field Office was involved had legal issues, such as acting as money laundering channels for the city's organized crime elements or selling prescription pain medication. So, Larry had to look to other law enforcement agencies for some suitable prospects, but at the same time, carefully protect the real purpose he had in mind for the dentist. After a couple of days of little success, he found some assistance from the local office of the U.S. Marshals.

Since the U.S. Marshal Service is in charge of the federal Witness Protection Program, they often need all types of personalized services for their clients, including dental. So, they have a number of "cleared" contacts who will provide services without attempting to learn anything about the individual. While it is assumed that these individuals do so to assist the Federal Government, they are also paid at the high end of their professional rate to further facilitate cooperation and complete discretion.

So, after reviewing a list of local dentists "cleared" by the Marshals, and it was a short list, Larry selected an individual with an office in a residential part of the city some distance from the Consulate, CARAWAY's residence, and the local Eastern European neighborhoods. He then arranged an appointment by telephone without identifying himself. He subsequently met the dentist, "badged him" as an FBI SA, and generally explained the services that would be required and how contact with the individual must be conducted. He also noted that he would personally handle the dentist's bills and that, in addition to his regular fee, he could expect a ten percent premium for the additional administrative burdens of servicing the individual. The dentist agreed and signed a Secrecy Agreement, which outlined his legal responsibilities regarding protecting the identity and dental information of the patient.

After Larry was able to provide us with the biographical information on the dentist, we conducted our own research on him. With that completed, we worked to develop the procedures we wanted CARAWAY to use for his dental services. Since there were still several days before CARAWAY was scheduled to call to get meeting details, we decided to provide him with contact information for the dentist when he called in. We figured this would be another reinforcement of the fact that the corporation considered the health of its employees to be a priority matter.

We had also provided the Field Office with a copy of CARAWAY's report on the duties and responsibilities of the various officials at the Romanian Consulate. While accurate, it did not provide much new information.

With our local coordination duties complete, my next task was to identify an appropriate restaurant, case it, make reservations, and add this information into the "message" which we would send to Headquarters for use when the Target called in. It was good tradecraft not to use the same restaurant twice at this point in the operation. Yet, I needed one with the same type of high-class environment, away from the downtown business area, and from any of the clusters of Eastern European residential neighborhoods. I also wanted a restaurant that could provide a relatively isolated booth, near the rear of the restaurant, and, of course, not on the route to the restrooms. I decided it was time to run a basic

CHAPTER NINETEEN: REINFORCEMENT AND TESTING

"trustworthiness" operational test on CARAWAY, and that would require some degree of privacy.

I asked the other COs at the Station if they knew of a restaurant that matched my needs, and they had several suggestions. I finally decided on an Italian place located in the southwest suburbs of the city. The neighborhood was full of townhouses, low-rise apartments, and condominiums, all with prices or rents in the high scale. The restaurant itself, which I cased over a long lunch with another Station officer, had a small frontal area facing the street with two large windows. But, it then evolved into a backspace of dark tables and side booths. Several of the booths were in a second room at the back, while the restrooms were upfront by the bar. It also had valet parking. The menu was Northern Italian. They also served several expensive scotches from the bar.

The art of selecting the appropriate restaurant based upon the operational issues required for a particular meeting, status for the target's benefit, operational security, physical structure to assist in an operational task, etc., is one every CO must learn. That was the purpose of bringing another CO along on the casing. This was an opportunity to give a first tour officer some training in restaurant selection. However, there was also a secondary reason: if I wanted to spend more than an hour in a restaurant without looking unusual, I had better have another person with me. Single diners seldom linger, and a restaurant knows this well.

With the restaurant selected, my last step was to call Ralph and ask him if, from the Field Office perspective, the location was suitable for my operational meeting. He got back to me within a couple of hours with a positive response, and I made reservations for eight o'clock on the evening of June 24th. I advised the reservation taker that I required a quiet booth in the back room, as I was planning to close an important business deal over dinner.

Late that afternoon, I composed the specific message that was to be provided to CARAWAY when he called the evening of the 20th and sent it to Headquarters.

The next morning I made car reservations at the airport for a town car, with a pickup in midafternoon of the 24th. I used a different rental company than previously, but the same alias identity. I then scheduled a meeting with the CARAWAY "Ops Group," consisting of the usual suspects from the Station and the Field Office for the afternoon of the 21st. By that time we would be able to confirm that he had called into my "office," and received the details of both the meeting and how to handle his dental appointment.

I was in a relaxed mood over the next couple of days while I wrote out my operational scenario for the meeting. It was a draft of course, because I knew there would be changes after the group provided their input, and since I had yet to receive any reply from Headquarters, there was always the possibility that some additional requirements would be forthcoming. Also, I needed an update on the son's medical testing from Larry. I wanted to be sure and use that information, as well as the dental appointment, as motivators demonstrating what the corporation could do for him.

On the morning of the 21st I received confirmation that CARAWAY had called-in, and received the information regarding the meeting arrangements and how to contact the dentist to arrange an appointment. I also received messages from Headquarter concurring with our plans for the next meeting.

The meeting with our FBI colleagues was once again held at the Station. Since both Winston and I were now a regular part of the operation, it was agreed that operational security was best served by our not going to the Field Office. This time I decided that coffee and some small pastries would be adequate refreshments—less mess to clean up. Winston, who grew up in British society before becoming an American citizen, actually suggested donuts as we had a donut shop nearby. However,, I explained to him that culturally, providing donuts to law enforcement types might be seen by some as playing too much to a caricature. And, considering the fine degree of cooperation we were experiencing with the Field Office, the last thing we wanted to do was either pander to or stereotype our colleagues.

Ralph, Matt, and Larry arrived on time, and I began by explaining that my objective for the meeting on the 24th was to continue to emphasize the

CHAPTER NINETEEN: REINFORCEMENT AND TESTING

benefits CARAWAY could expect from responding to corporate tasking. I also planned to explain how I got into the corporation, using that narrative to further convince the Target that a few individuals and corporate entities internationally worked financial and trade deals that crossed political and ideological lines. Secondary objectives would be to discuss the need for personal security on CARAWAY's part in his handling of his money and his meetings with myself and other corporate officials. We would also discuss how he was planning to handle his dental work with his Consulate colleagues, as it might well become physically apparent that such work was being done. Finally, I said, "I plan to introduce a basic operational security test to see how CARAWAY reacts."

We discussed how I intended to use my supposed entry into the corporation to emphasize its benefits and how its activities were part of how the "real world" operated. Ralph actually had a couple of good suggestions. He really seemed to be on the team now. All agreed with the objectives I hoped to accomplish. We then spent about half an hour considering how I would respond if the Target had not brought a comprehensive report on the encryption interface of the Consulate's communications system. We agreed that my displeasure should be apparent, but that I should simply note that I would inform the boss. That would give us another opportunity, with Winston playing the leading role as the "father figure," to try again to convince CARAWAY that he could handle the task without concern about his personal safety and security. I would also advise him, supposedly on a personal basis, that he was making a mistake by not following the boss's orders. However, we all agreed that CARAWAY would bring the report.

The subject the SAs were most interested in was the operational test I planned for the meeting. So, I explained, "I will bring an unlocked briefcase full of bogus business contracts and studies supposedly related to corporate business with me. I will explain the briefcase contents in the context of my being on a multi-city business trip before flying to London to meet with the boss. I will note that the documents are very sensitive due to the individuals named in them. Then, later in the meal, I will excuse myself, claiming to use the restroom. I will leave the briefcase in the booth. While the briefcase and the material inside it appeared normal, actually, it is arranged in a very specific manner. So, if CARAWAY does open the briefcase, and presumably look at the documents, I will know that it has been looked at."

Ralph asked exactly what it would mean if CARAWAY did sneak a look inside the briefcase. I responded that it could mean several different things. It could mean he was curious about me and the corporation, and wished to confirm that we were what we said we were. It could also be an indication that he was working under the control of the Romanian security service and seeking additional reportable information, along with the results of our meeting. Or, it could just mean that he was the type to take advantage of a situation to learn something he did not know. However, it would definitely be an indication that we could not fully trust him at this point. My last point to Ralph was to address a cultural point I had experienced previously in my career working with the FBI. All too often, I found that after acquiring the services of a Confidential Informant, SAs over time came to accept whatever they provided as true and accurate. The Bureau did not have a system where another layer of analysis, done by Reports Officers in the Agency, looks at the information and compares it to other available information to judge its value and accuracy. An experienced CO never fully trusts an asset, and operational testing of various sorts is a standard part of the agent handling protocol.

I concluded by explaining "The test is planned to have a beneficial impact on the operation even if CARAWAY does sneak a look. What he would see would be further "proof" of how well connected the corporation was and the level of cooperation it was obtaining from senior government officials in various countries, both in the West and in the Soviet Bloc. So, regardless of whether or not CARAWAY looked into the briefcase papers, the operation would benefit."

Now it was Larry's turn to brief us on the son's health. He had seen the doctor yesterday in order to have the most recent information available. The SA stated that the CARAWAYs had now seen the doctor a couple of times. Several blood tests had been run, X-rays taken, and an ultrasound had been done over the course of a couple of Saturdays and a Sunday. The results indicated that the son had a small enlargement, medically referred to as a Goiter, on his Thyroid Gland. The doctor felt that with the use of a series of treatments with radioactive iodine, the enlargement could be eliminated. The doctor felt a series of treatments could be performed on several Saturdays over the coming weeks. The doctor would then monitor the boy's condition periodically thereafter to ensure it did not redevelop.

As to the kidney problem, the boy did have an infection, caused by a small tear in the lining, in his left kidney. He had prescribed an oral antibiotic, and gave the son an antibiotic injection to aggressively attack the infection. He believed this treatment would defeat the infection within a few weeks. The doctor told Larry that both CARAWAYs were profuse in their appreciation for his efforts.

Honesty, we were all pleased that the boy's health issues had been taken care of. Also, from an operational perspective this good news came at just the right time as our tasking requirements became more and more sensitive.

Larry also reviewed the arrangements made with the dentist. As we had previously discussed, the dentist would not know CARAWAY's true name or anything about him. CARAWAY would make his first appointment by calling the dentist's office and advising that he was an employee of the corporation and wished to make an appointment. At the appointment, the dentist would advise that all services rendered would be paid to him directly by the corporation. Also, the corporate policy was that it was not necessary for him to know the name of his patient. Larry had told the dentist to casually mention that while this type of patient handling was unusual, he did have contracts with several international business organizations that use the same procedures. He would also note that in many cases, he would only see the patient once, and give them the results of his exam or treatment to carry with them back to the corporation. He would then surmise that the corporation probably paid him so well because he was prepared to handle its employees on a priority basis when they were only in the city for brief business trips. The dentist had telephoned Larry the previous afternoon to advise that CARAWAY had telephoned the dentistry office and arranged an appointment for the following Thursday, around the luncheon hour.

So, we were now ready for the dinner meeting the next day. While optimistic, as I always am, that CARAWAY would bring an accurate report on the encryption system at the Consulate, there is always a bit of doubt in your stomach as you get this close to the actual meeting. I was prepared, should he not provide the information, with rational and emotional arguments to try and convince him to do so. But, knowing full well that the ultimate objective of the operation was the tapes themselves, we were still quite a bit away from where we needed to be.

I had a restless night mulling over and over again in my mind how I would handle a less than responsive CARAWAY. I was told as a young officer, and indeed have passed this along to young officers, who have served under me, that if you do not wake up in the middle of the night worrying about your operations you are in the wrong profession.

The next morning, I still had several hours to kill before starting the cleaning process of separating myself from the Station and my real identity before arriving at the hotel. I took a while to review my plans with Winston, just to get any last minute reactions he might have—he didn't. I then busied myself with some usual administrative responsibilities required by my position. But, regardless of the matter upon which I was trying to focus, the meeting was the main thought in my mind.

After lunch at my desk, I left the Station and went through the usual procedures of leaving my car at the airport and renting another car there. Then from the airport I drove to a suburban mall, which included a movie theater. I walked around the enclosed mall for a while to check for any possible surveillance, and then took in a movie to kill a couple of hours before testing my driving time to the pickup point with CARAWAY from the garage where I would wait to start my run to the pickup point.

Subsequently, I drove from the mall to the garage and then onward to the pickup point. The car "run" was "clean" from an operational security

CHAPTER NINETEEN: REINFORCEMENT AND TESTING

perspective, but nonetheless interesting. Downtown's end-of-business-day travel is always challenging, and I had several hard braking stops and near fender benders with aggressive taxi drivers and even a couple of municipal buses. I tend to be a careful driver, with good focus and well-developed peripheral vision, no doubt based on having driven in cities like Manila, Saigon, and Taipei, where common rules of traffic behavior simply do not exist and traffic flows like interrelated schools of fish. But, since it would be too obvious to arrive at a clandestine car pickup point in a recently damaged auto, a CO has to be extra careful.

As I finally arrived at the street corner within the acceptable time window, CARAWAY was there and immediately got into the front passenger side of the car. At the next block we hit a red light, and this enabled me to look directly at him, shake his hand and start a meaningless social chat about how he was and if he had any problems getting to the pickup site. I also asked if he had noticed anything unusual while he waited for my arrival. He said he had not.

Within less than ten minutes, we arrived at the restaurant, turned the car over to the parking attendant, and entered the reception area. We were promptly seated in a circular booth in the rear room, which was adequately situated to provide us with the desired privacy. I placed my briefcase between us in a position where it would open facing me. I should note that at the station, we had spent several hours preparing material which included contract agreements with several large European weapons manufacturers, private agreements regarding sharing of profits on various chemical shipments, and some personal letters from the corporation to government officials in several countries in Europe and Asia. Near the top of the pile was a copy of a letter marked "confidential" and addressed to a senior Romanian Ministry of Foreign Affairs official, whom we were pretty sure CARAWAY would know by reputation if not personally.

After we ordered our scotches, I placed my menu on the side of the table and asked CARAWAY the status of his son's health examinations. I stated that the boss was very interested in this and wanted a report on how the treatment was going. The Target responded that real progress was being made. He told me in some detail about the various tests the doctor had run and the results. His comments closely followed the details that Larry had provided the day before. Upon completing his report, he asked that I express to the boss the deep and sincere appreciation both he and his wife felt for his support in getting their son the treatment he needed. I advised, "This news is most welcome, and I will communicate it to the boss." I concluded by noting that loyalty to the boss was always a two-way street.

I then asked about his dental issue and whether or not he had contacted the dentist. CARAWAY responded that he had called the office as instructed, and the dentist had immediately scheduled an appointment for later this week. I said that I hoped his dental issues would be handled just as satisfactorily as his son's health issues. And, noted that I was sure the boss would also want periodic updates on how this treatment was going. CARAWAY responded that while he had not yet met the dentist, his office was in one of the expensive downtown office buildings, so he assumed that he must be quite good. "Of course," I responded," anyone contracted by the corporation must be one of the best in their field."

I then picked up the menu and we discussed the selection. It was heavy on pasta as one would expect. The thought passed through my mind as to whether CARAWAY simply did not eat for a few days before our meetings. Oh, the extra weight I put on in the service of my country!

Then, we moved to a serious discussion of the wine list. Here, the pretentiousness that usually passes for expertise comes out fully. I quickly glanced at the list and mentioned that even though I was having chicken, I always prefer an Italian red wine. He agreed. I then said a few words about various vintages, and even admitted that quite often my preference is for a rough Sicilian red such as a Villa Pozzi Negro D'avola. However, I decided on a Tuscan Chianti, with the Target's whole-hearted approval, as our choice for this meal. When the waiter returned for the wine and dinner order, I emphasized that the Chianti was to be served at room temperature. When he returned with the bottle, I checked the label and was careful to touch the cork to ensure it was moist. I then instructed him to let the wine

CHAPTER NINETEEN: REINFORCEMENT AND TESTING

"breathe" for about seven minutes before pouring it. My performance completed, we returned to a conversation that now focused on how he had been able to complete his assignment of describing the technical details and equipment involved in the interface of the radio traffic and the coding procedures.

CARAWAY reached into his suit coat and pulled out a sheath of papers, which he handed to me. As he sipped his wine, I glanced at his handwritten notes and two pages of hand-drawn diagrams. While no technical expert, our NSA Liaison Unit (NSA/LU) had sent me some general comments on what to look for in CARAWAY's reporting. His narrative of how the radio traffic was encrypted and decrypted through the use of a special set of paper tape spools, which contained the one-time encryption or decryption codes, seemed both comprehensive and clearly stated. His diagrams show how the communications traffic was recorded and then interfaced with the encryption tapes to produce encoded messages sent from the Consulate. I advised CARAWAY that I would forward the papers to our corporate engineers and see if they found it useful. With that, I open the briefcase and place his report on top of the pile of papers, closing the lid but not the two side clasps that secured it.

Then, as the waiter poured more wine and announced the arrival of the appetizers, I went into my prepared script regarding how I had benefited from my association with the boss and the corporation. I explained my own background—I had started in a Wall Street brokerage house after obtaining a Master's in Business Administration and was being well paid to handle international trading. But, within six months, I found the pressure and competition, let alone the long hours required, to be quite stressful. One of the house's clients was an investment arm of the corporation, and its portfolio was primarily based in foreign exchange Letters of Credit, working the exchange rate for additional profitability. I happened to meet the corporation representative a few times, and it turned out he liked to play squash, which I had taken up in my undergraduate days. We played a few times and developed a social relationship that included squash and the occasional dinner when he was in town to check on the account.

I had actually done a pretty good job, with some luck to be truthful, in manipulating exchange rates for him. And, one evening after confiding that I was not happy with the environment, he suggested that there might be a chance of employment with his corporation. He emphasized to me, as I have with you, that the corporation values talent highly. But, it also values discretion and loyalty. He confided that the CEO of the corporation, the boss as he called him, viewed his employees as family. He expected complete loyalty to the business and to him personally, and in return, the compensation package would easily outshine my current salary and benefits. However, he warned that the boss operated in international circles at a level which most people never even knew existed. He explained it as "working well beyond normal legal frameworks" and "within an environment based upon personal and political alliances outside of the usual international business structure." I was intrigued, and within several weeks, I was invited to meet the boss during one of his visits to New York City.

"Like you, I was picked up by Patrick and taken to the boss' suite, where he informally interviewed me over drinks. I was appropriately awed by him—as you know he has a certain persona which radiates power, wealth and influence—yet he is charming and immediately seems to be interested in you as a person. I left that evening not knowing whether or not I had impressed him, but very much aware this was the type of corporation I wanted to work for, and especially the type of boss I could trust and respect. Several weeks later, I was told to be prepared to fly to Rome the following weekend for a meeting with the boss. Airline tickets, first class of course, accommodation details, and all other details would arrive by messenger the next morning. They did, I flew, and had a brief meeting with the boss, was hired, and quit my job at the brokerage house the following Monday morning."

CARAWAY was listening intently to my story as I continued that during the second year of my employment I became part of the boss' corporate family—even staying for a weekend at his family estate in Scotland. I stated that the more I learned about the boss's connections, the more I realized that international business was actually conducted on a much different basis than I was led to believe during my academic training. From my experience at the brokerage house, I knew that international regulations and imposed sanctions by international bodies were more statements of political desires than enforceable procedures. But, only after working for the corporation for several months did I realize the collaboration that existed between influential international businessmen and political leaders to circumvent these paper restrictions to benefit their nations, and also make a considerable profit for themselves.

I noted that frankly, the boss liked me, and I readily admitted that I have a talent for planning how to get around various restrictions and similar issues in the acquisition and transportation of various equipment and materials. So, I had risen rather quickly in the corporation, and in the process became quite wealthy. However, as I remain an American citizen, I have to be careful in how I handle my money and corporate benefits. This was the tag line I would later use to lead CARAWAY into a discussion regarding personal security and its corporate benefits. "You see," I said, "even though the boss is well connected within U.S. political and, therefore, governmental circles, the key is never to flaunt these ties. We keep a low profile and he only calls in favors when he needs them, and even then always in a discreet and polite manner."

At this point, I asked CARAWAY if I was boring him with my personal story. He responded, "No, I must admit that I had no idea that business was conducted like this." He continued that from his own experience in Romania, he knew that personal relations and influence controlled political and economic decisions in the country, but had no concept that it also extended to the international world. I responded that few people really understood this, and it worked to the advantage of people like us that the general population remains ignorant. I concluded by noting, "I wanted to tell you a bit about my background and corporate experience because I think the boss feels you have a future with us. So, I wanted you to understand what you were involved in, and particularly that regardless of what tasks you might be given, we can protect you because we have the influence necessary to solve any problems that arise."

By that time, the waiter advised that the entrees were about to arrive. As he poured each of us another glass of wine, I mentioned that my overnight stay in the city was part of a full week of international travel to complete several agreements on the sale of various items to countries in Europe and the Middle East. I noted that my briefcase was stuffed full of these documents.

Then, before the main course arrived, I mentioned that I had to use the restroom up front in the restaurant. I excused myself and proceeded towards the bar area. I then went into a stall in the men's room and sat there for about five minutes to give CARAWAY adequate time to look through the briefcase if that was his choice. I then returned to the table. The briefcase seemed to be in the same place as when I left, and I noticed CARAWAY's wine glass was half empty. The entrees had also arrived, but he had not started eating, apparently waiting for me to return.

As we ate, I began to discuss his personal security. I started by noting that while several senior Romanian Government and Party officials were working with the corporation, his employment was, of course, completely confidential. Therefore, it was important that in his behavior at the Consulate and in his family life, he did not take any actions that might seem suspicious. CARAWAY nodded his agreement. I said that we can provide him advice on how to handle his corporate reporting responsibilities in a manner that attracts no special attention. I explained that we had a great deal of expertise in this area based upon our association with other employees or consultants in government positions worldwide.

The first issue I raised was whether he felt his collection of information so far had been noticed by anyone in the Consulate, for example, his Communications Office assistant or the Consulate security staff. CARAWAY responded that he did not think so, as he knew most of the details of the communications' equipment and its functioning from his normal, daily activities, and then prepared his written reports at his residence. So far, he continued, the only time he had taken material from the office was when he brought out the technical manuals for the communications upgrade. He

CHAPTER NINETEEN: REINFORCEMENT AND TESTING

had simply placed them in his carry bag, which everyone in the Consulate knew he brought in every day, and waited until he was the last official to leave that evening. He had the manuals back in the office's files early the next morning, before his assistant and other Consulate officers came to work. I congratulated him on his actions and moved on to the point about the money he had received from the corporation.

I noted that in the past several months, he had received thousands of dollars, which he could not explain to his colleagues. I asked how he was handling these funds. He explained that he had spent about a thousand dollars on some electronic items and home furnishings so far. He did not advertise these purchases at the office, and while he has had some colleagues and their families at his residence for social events, no one has commented on these items negatively. "It is," he continued, "common practice to buy all the Western goods you can when on a foreign assignment, and it is generally known that I have assisted the Consulate General in some business activities from which I have made a little extra money." He said that he planned to buy some additional electronic items, but these would be for family and Ministry contacts back in Romania. So, once purchased, they would be kept out of sight at the residence and never unpacked.

Again, I complimented him on his careful handling of the funds and asked where the other money was kept. CARAWAY said that he and his wife kept the money hidden in their residence. He did not want to open a bank account, since they were paid from the Consulate's Finance Office and could keep funds in an account there. I then asked if he had continued to take adequate funds from his salary to indicate he was paying for the everyday expenses, such as groceries and other normal family costs. "Yes," he replied," I have been careful to do so and use my official salary for household and living expenses."

I stated that while I knew he wanted to get various Western items, he must continue to do so slowly. And, to develop some stories for his office about special deals and local contacts he had made that were allowing him to get a good price on various items. He could also even hint that he knew some people who could sell him items that "fell off the back of a truck" on occasion. If anyone noticed that he had acquired more than seemed reasonable based upon his official salary, those stories might explain how he was able to get them before he was ever asked. I added that if his employment with the corporation became permanent, we could work out some financial arrangements that would address his desires to obtain various items. CARAWAY nodded enthusiastically at my comments.

I then asked how he was managing to keep his son's medical appointments discreet, as well as how he intended to handle his dentist appointments. CARAWAY said, "My wife and I are taking Anton to see the doctor only on weekends when I have no official responsibilities. I have not mentioned the doctor at work, and do not plan to." I then asked if his colleagues, and especially the Consulate General with whom he was close, knew of the boy's health issues and had been aware of his plans to seek American treatment for their son. He said the Consulate General did know about it from a conversation several months ago, but doubted that the issue was very important to him. I suggested that he slowly spread the story that he had taken the son to a doctor at a local city hospital, obviously not the one he was actually using, and that the American doctor advised that the Romanian doctors were correct: the boy's condition would improve, but slowly, as he digested more iodine. Eventually, the gland would be functioning normally. And, he could even add to the story that while he had only seen the American doctor twice, it had been very expensive.

As to his dental appointments, I noted that once fixed, his face and smile would probably be a very public indicator that work had been done. Thus, he needed to develop a cover story to explain how he was affording this dental care. We discussed a couple of approaches he could take in creating such a cover story. He could say that through a local contact in the Eastern European immigrant community, he had found a dentist who worked cheaply, yet still he was having his dental problems handled slowly because it was still expensive by Romanian standards. Another approach would be to claim that a neighbor in his building had recommended a dentist who was willing to do the work and accept payment over time rather than at

CHAPTER NINETEEN: REINFORCEMENT AND TESTING

each appointment. CARAWAY thought that story would work with his office mates.

The final security point I wanted to discuss was that of operational security for our meetings and the communications that led up to them. First, I discussed how contact between CARAWAY and the corporation must be conducted in a discreet manner. Obviously, he was never to contact us from the Consulate or his residence. My office would continue to be the central point of contact. And, he was to use it if he had a message for me as well. I noted that he was to use a different public telephone booth, not one too near either his office or his home, for each call. I explained that as a foreign official, even the local police might be interested in him, and as many of our dealings were "too complicated" for local police to understand, we needed to keep our relationship truly confidential. As to the actual meetings, picking him up at designated locations was working quite well, and we would continue to do so. I then asked if he fully understood the corporation's security concerns and the business reasons behind them. He replied, "I do, and from my perspective, should my government learn of my moonlighting with the corporation, not only would my government career be over, but I might even face criminal charges." He said that he had no illusions that what he was asked to do was considered illegal by his government. I responded that while this was probably true at lower levels in the Romanian Government, I was confident that our corporate contacts in senior levels of the Government and Communist Party could be called upon to keep him out of trouble. However, I added, if we were careful, there is little chance that our business relationship will be visible to anyone. This seemed to reassure CARAWAY somewhat, but the real point was that he did, indeed, fully understand the reason that our contacts and communications must remain secret.

By this time CARAWAY had finished his main course, and was prepared to order dessert. I, having spent the major of the dinner talking rather than eating, had the waiter removed only a partially eaten plate of chicken, and asked for the dessert menu. The waiter quickly returned with the menu, and, surprise, surprise, CARAWAY ordered the tiramisu. I then prepared to give him his tasking for the next meeting.

As he finished his cake and we sipped coffee, I told him that the boss was also concerned that his cooperation with us should never get him in trouble with his own officials. Thus, for our next meeting, I ask him to think about what procedures he has to follow at the Consulate while conducting his daily activities that might have security implications. What relationship does he have with the security officers, both professionally and personally, that might affect his ability to gather information? Also, what are the security procedures that impact his regular duties, and do they pose any threat to his corporate tasks? I noted that we needed to discuss these details in the future.

While the Target had not asked about his "consulting" funds during the meeting, at this time I removed an envelope from my suit coat pocket and passed it to him. It contained his monthly compensation, which he did not count. He simply said "Thank you."

As we left the booth, I picked up and locked the briefcase, and we went out to the car. On the way to the drop-off point, I told him to telephone Wilmington on July 13th, as I anticipated we would next meet in the third week of that month. I also noted that I would want an update on his son's health and his own progress with the dentist. I reminded him that the boss was very keen on ensuring both these issues were being handled successfully. As he was about to leave the car, we shook hands firmly, and a smile was on his face.

I then went through the standard countersurveillance procedures, traveled into my neighborhood and parked the car on a well light street several blocks from my home. I worked till the early hours of the next morning writing up my notes while my memory was still fresh. The next day I returned the car to the airport, got my car and drove to the Station.

Once inside the office, Winston came over and asked how the meeting had gone. I replied that I think it all went well, but we would need an NSA opinion on the information CARAWAY provided on the encryption interface. I then opened the briefcase and compared the position of its contents against several photos taken when it was loaded with papers.

CHAPTER NINETEEN: REINFORCEMENT AND TESTING

There seemed to be no change in the papers' position. So, it appeared that CARAWAY had "passed" this test.

While I was preparing my report for transmission to Headquarters, the senior Communications Officer walked in and handed me an "eyes only cos" message. It stated: "If CARAWAY's reporting on encryption interface appears accurate, do not forward reporting of the meeting. Prepare your report, and along with the report from the Target, proceed immediately to Headquarters for consultations. Send notice of your travel plans, and hotel accommodations, and Headquarters parking arrangements will be made." I immediately called Winston and showed him the message. We then discussed what CARAWAY had reported, and agreed that from a non-specialist perspective, the information seemed logical. So, I sent Headquarters the message "COS will arrive Hqs area evening June 22nd and be in office early June 23rd. I then spent the day typing up and polishing my report.

Later that afternoon I called Ralph on the secure telephone line, and advised that I was called back to Headquarters for consultations. But, for his ears only, I thought the meeting had gone well. I briefly mentioned that the Target had apparently passed the briefcase ploy successfully. I would give him a full brief after my return, which I anticipated would be no later than the following Monday.

Chapter Twenty: Headquarters Consultations

The next morning I packed, picked up CARAWAY's information at the Station, and was on my way to Washington, DC. I arrived a few hours later, picked up the auto reserved for me by Headquarters, and drove directly there. It was after normal business hours, and my appointments were not scheduled until the following day. Nonetheless, security procedures called for me to ensure that CARAWAY's information was secured in an approved storage site once available. After having done so by leaving the material with the Duty Security Officer, I drove to the motel in Arlington, Virginia, where reservations had been made for me. Needless to say, my room was not a suite, and the place wasn't a five-star location.

The next morning, I arrived at Headquarters and spent about fifteen minutes finding my parking space. In the old days, a COS back for consultation would get a parking space in front of the Headquarters Building, in the small parking lot reserved for important visitors. However, apparently, we were now getting a great deal of important visitors on a daily basis, and I ended up several spaces from the West entrance in F Lane of the West Parking Lot. Well, walking is always good for you, and at least it wasn't raining or snowing.

After "badging in" at the security checkpoint inside the West Entrance, I proceeded to the Security Duty Office and picked up my CARAWAY reporting and the original of his handwritten report on the encryption

CHAPTER TWENTY: HEADQUARTERS CONSULTATIONS

interface information. I then went down a couple of floors to my Division's Front Office. There I was greeted by the most powerful person in the Division—the personal secretary to the Chief of the Division. And, she knows it too. I said, "Good morning, Susie, very nice to see you. Is the Chief in?" Looking up and slightly acknowledging my greeting, she noted that the Chief was at the morning Deputy Director of Operations (DDO) staff meeting. She instructed me to sit down and wait; quietly, it was made clear, while she attended to more important business. Having been intimidated by Susie for many years, I did as I was told.

The Chief appeared less than ten minutes later, and after providing instructions to Susie about some other appointments and telephone calls he needed to make, he motioned me into his office. He took his place behind his desk, told me to close the door, and pointed to a chair. I had worked at Headquarters for the Chief before I was sent out as the COS. In fact, I had handled one particularly tricky task for him: going out to relieve a COS who had fallen in the habit of drinking too much—and in those days drinking too much really meant drinking too, too much. I had apparently done it well and had functioned as the manager for a support section for all the East Coast Stations for almost two years as well. These accomplishments got me the COS position. He knew me, and I knew him.

After a couple of minutes of polite small talk, the Chief complimented me both on the progress we were making with the CARAWAY operation and also on the degree of cooperation we were attaining with the city's FBI Field Office. He said that he had briefed the Deputy Director for Operations on the operation, along with the Chief of the Soviet and Eastern European (SE) Division and the Chief of the Technical Services Division which conducted liaison with NSA. Everyone was pleased with the operation to date.

He explained that at this point, the specific reporting requirements were coming from the Technical Services folks, and the SE Division would be providing operational guidance on occasion. However, in terms of basis support, funding, logistics, and additional resources, our Division would still take the lead. He said that today I would meet with the SE Division folks involved, the Technical Service Division's NSA/LU, and at the end of the day, brief the DDO on the status of the operation. He commented that it was going to be a busy day, so I better get started.

As he walked me out into the Front Office reception area, he asked Susie to give me the printed list of my appointments, with room numbers but no names of any of the officers I was to meet with. Susie did so, this time with a slight smile which quickly vanished as she returned to her important duties. Off I went into the bowels of the building, about to meet some very interesting people whose duties and expertise I had not known existed in the Agency.

Agency doors are marked with floor numbers and then office numbers—no signs to indicate which office are behind which door. And, within certain areas behind one door, you will find that a quarter of the entire floor is actually one large section. So, even to someone who had worked at Headquarters, outside of one's own Division, the geography can get very confusing, even with room numbers.

My first appointment was with the Chief and Deputy Chief of the SE Division, Herbert and Paul, two officers with reputations in the Operations Directorate for tough personalities and particularly colorful vocabularies. After the initial compliments on the progress in the operation, Herbert proceeded to tell me how valuable access to the Romanian Consulate codes would be to the USG. He stated that NSA believed that the Consulate codes might provide a unique insight into the plans and intentions of not only the Romanian Government, but also the Pact and the Soviet Union. Paul then took over the conversation, discussing the security concerns involved and providing a great deal of information on how Warsaw Pact intelligence and security officials operated in my city. In a narrative heavily dosed with adjectives, nouns, and gerunds I had not heard since the Marine Corps, Paul described the extensive activities and capabilities that the Pact had in the city. I will admit that I was surprised, since I thought I had a solid knowledge of the counterintelligence scene here. But, Paul was providing an insight based upon very sensitive reporting. He advised me not to mention any specifics of his briefing to the Field Office, as much of the reporting came from sources unknown to it. His point, echoed by

CHAPTER TWENTY: HEADQUARTERS CONSULTATIONS

Herbert, was that operational security had to be perfect. I was to use all the capabilities I had, including the use of Field Office surveillance units and sources, to protect the operation. Paul stated that throughFBI channels, the Field Office would be advised to provide all the support I requested.

I left the SE Front Office somewhat intimidated, both by the amount of information I now had on hostile capabilities in my city, and, frankly, by the shall I say strong personalities of the two senior officers. Luckily, I had briefly worked with Paul previously and thus had some familiarity with his personality. In fairness, I subsequently found both officers to be extremely helpful not only in this operation but also supportive of my career later on. Like many COs, their tough exterior mannerisms were professional personas, used to enhance leadership and management efforts. Paul was actually a very kind and considerate individual.

My next stop was literally in the sub-basement of the Headquarters Building, off a seldom-used corridor near the small exercise gym. Upon entering, I found myself in the office of the NSA/LU of the Technical Services Division. As I mentioned, I knew very little about these people and had no idea what type of support they provided. I soon learned they were the unit that provided on-the-ground operational support for human-assisted code acquisition operations.

I met Fred and his deputy Betsey, who began by complimenting the Station on the CARAWAY operation. I gave them a briefing on the results of the last meeting with the target and provided a general description of how Station and FBI Field Office officers were playing out their roles. They explained their functions in general and then discussed how they were prepared to support our operation. They also noted that providing requirements would be their primary function at this point. However, once the encryption tapes were acquired, they would have to come to the Station to work with them. They were also interested in the Station's assessment of CARAWAY's character, personality, and motivation for working with the corporation. Fred stated quite frankly that they had never worked with a foreign code clerk who was not aware that he was dealing with an intelligence agency of the USG. This led to a lengthy description of how we had built the reputation of the corporation, and specifically the "Father Figure" of the boss, up in the Target's mind over the course of several meetings.

I ended up spending several hours with Fred and Betsey, learning a great deal about the responsibilities of a Warsaw Pact, code clerk—specific details which we had not gotten from CARAWAY, frankly because we probably didn't know the right questions to ask him. It seemed obvious that CARAWAY was not the first code clerk they had worked with, but it certainly would not be professional to ask them about this.

I was then introduced to several other members of the Branch, although apparently some were traveling in support of other operations. So, I spent about another half hour in small talk with them. Fred also told me that while NSA was very interested in this operation, his Branch would channel any requirements or comments they might have. So, I would not be meeting with any NSA officials at this point. I noted that CARAWAY's report on the Consulate's encryption interface between the radio traffic and the encryption process was now with my Division, and that we wanted an expert evaluation of it as soon as possible. Fred responded that he would have the report by that afternoon and share it immediately with his liaison folks at NSA. He felt that they could communicate with us within a few days on the accuracy and value of the information.

It was midafternoon when I left their office and returned to the sunlight of the above-ground hallways of the building. I had about an hour and a half to myself before the meeting with the Division Chiefs and the DDO. I used the time to talk about a couple of other operations with members of the Branch that supported the Station in our Division. I also visited with the Division head of Personnel and Assignments, who was a CO, assigned to that role as part of management development. His office controlled all Division assignments and managed the performance evaluation system and its promotion and awards panels. While trained and experienced human resource and budget officers comprised the Office, a CO headed it because of its role in selecting which officers were promoted and where they were assigned. Evaluating COs' Performance is not an easy job. Human recruitments and the intelligence they produce cannot be measured in any numerical manner. Rather, the COs' efforts and skills as applied in each operation should be the elements that demonstrate expertise, sound judgment, and a mastery of the tradecraft. It is not an objective process, and often leaves non-promoted or non-recognized Case Officers frustrated with the system. However, no one has yet been able to devise a better system.

My conversation with the Office Chief focused on discussing the talents and areas needing some improvement of a couple of young officers working at the Station. I also included some comments on the strong work of Brenda, Winston, Edmund and Stan. I knew that in his position, he did not always see the regular operational reporting from the Station, let alone communications handled in the more limited distribution channels. So, without going into specifics and without identifying the operational details, I praised their efforts with generic tradecraft examples. When the time came for these officers to be placed before promotion or awards panels, the Division Chief would be the one to brief the panel on their specific roles in any operations that were too sensitive to be detailed in the official annual Performance Review that Station management submits to Headquarters.

A few minutes before 5 p.m. I returned to my Division Front Office and waited in the reception area while the Division Chief concluded a closed-door meeting. Susie acknowledged my presence and somewhat sternly advised me to straighten my tie as I was going to brief the DDO. About five minutes later, the Division Chief came hurrying out of his office, motioned to me to follow him, and off we went. While awaiting the elevator to the 7th Floor, where the DDO's Office is located, my Division Chief commented that we were late. Without providing any details, he complained that a personnel matter had taken more time than anticipated.

At the DDO's office, we were ushered into his private conference room, and gathered around a conference table were his Deputy, the SE Division Chief, and the Technical Services Division Chief, whom I had not met previously. I did know the DDO and ADDO from previous assignments.

The Clandestine Service was actually small enough in those days that most officers knew each other, at least by sight if not by having worked together at some point in their careers. The DDO and his Deputy nodded at me, and my Division Chief introduced me to Bob, the Technical Services Division Chief. The DDO then took over the meeting.

He began by providing a summary of the operation and concluded with the comment that senior officials at NSA were very hopeful that we would be able to get the Romanian encryption system. The SE Division Chief added that he was confident that if we got the system, we would also have access to Warsaw Pact traffic because the Romanian regime was considered a "trusted partner" which operated under Soviet control. The ADDO then asked my opinion on our chances of success. I replied that our operation was proceeding nicely, and I believed we had convinced CARAWAY that he was working with a powerful and well-financed international corporation that could both protect and reward him for his assistance.

At that point, I was interrupted by the Technical Services Chief, who questioned how we could expect to ask CARAWAY for the encryption system when we were pretending to be a business rather than a government entity. He said that it made no sense for a private company to want the system, and that only a governmental body, most likely one unfriendly to the Romanian Government, would both want the system and have the technical capabilities to actually exploit it once obtained. At this point, all the focus in the room was on me.

I was not exactly unprepared for this line of questioning. Commercial recruitments are often difficult to make productive, exactly for the reasons he stated. But we knew what we were doing and why we were doing it. So, I started by noting, "This was a targeted operation from the start. The FBI had identified the Target, and we had approached him and had moved him through a very comprehensive assessment and development scenario, involving several Case Officers. The important point here is that we are working with the motivations and concerns that the Target has shown over a lengthy period of assessment, evaluation, and testing. We believe we understand the Target's personality, his prioritized values, and perhaps

CHAPTER TWENTY: HEADQUARTERS CONSULTATIONS

most importantly, what he needs to have in the way of confidence and security to take the risks we want." I quickly reviewed the key points of our psychological assessment of CARAWAY, noting that the Field Office agreed based upon their monitoring of his behavior and actions, and that a Headquarters Romanian expert analyst had also interviewed all the Agency and FBI officers involved and agreed with our conclusions. I noted that we had built a support scenario fitted to the Target's needs, from providing health for his son and now himself, to paying a monthly salary far beyond anything he would be able to make in his side business deals from his diplomatic status at the Consulate. Finally, we had created a "father figure" with the power and influence to protect him if necessary.

We had created this scenario with performances by various Case Officers and appropriate trappings to help the Target "understand" the realities of international business in the grey area of technical and military sales. We based his rationalizations within the context of his own knowledge and experience of how his government's and Communist Party's systems work. I concluded by emphasizing "this is a scenario tailor-made specifically for this individual, and in the opinion of everyone in the field involved in it, the operation is working. "

My Chief, the SE officers, and both the DDO and ADDO seemed satisfied. However, the Technical Services Chief remained skeptical, stating that he just did not see how we could convince CARAWAY that a private corporation, no matter how wealthy and powerful, could handle this type of operation. He continued that we know that Soviet Block code clerks are well briefed on security matters and know well the sensitivity of their knowledge of the radio codes and systems.

Once again, all eyes were on me. And, I responded, "Our plan is not to tell CARAWAY that the tapes will be opened. Rather, the corporation's technical engineers have created a device which can read the encryption tapes through the sealed packaging without breaking any of the security features in the packaging." "But," the Technical Services Chief stammered, "That is impossible. No such equipment exists, or we would be using it." "Correct," I responded, "but CARAWAY doesn't know that. If CARAWAY believes that he is working for a corporation that can pay him over a thousand US dollars a month, provide excellent health care to him and his son, and conduct business through the personal connections, both personal and political, of the corporation's head, why wouldn't he believe that its engineering staff can do whatever he is told they can do?" "Also," I added," we will have a logical and technical description of the process to be used, provided by a suitable role player with appropriate technical jargon, when we actually task him to bring out the tapes." I concluded with a point that all COs could relate to: "Remember, we are creating a perception acceptable to the Target, and the truth has nothing to do with this."

"OK," said the DDO. "That's it, I'm convinced you know what you're doing, or at least seem to." He then said that the Station would receive instructions regarding how to communicate future information on this operation within a few days.

As the DDO dismissed the others, he motioned me back into his office along with the ADDO. In a firm but friendly manner, he advised me that this operation would have very limited distribution in the Agency, at NSA, and at the FBI. He mentioned that he was not particularly fond of commercially covered operations, but understood my reasoning in this case. He and the ADDO wished me the best of luck, but also noted Station's actions would be closely watched. He also instructed me to tell all of the Station officers who had been involved in the operation that they had performed well and he was aware of their activities. That, I thought, was a nice gesture and I believed a sincere one. I returned to my Division Chief's office, told him what I had just been told, and was advised to get back to the Station and get to work.

Chapter Twenty-One: Lemon

I took an early flight from Washington back to the Station the next morning, and by midafternoon, I was in my office briefing Winston on what had transpired at Headquarters. Halfway through my rendition of what occurred in the DDO's office, the senior Communications Officer knocked and came in. He had an "eyes only" message for me from Headquarters as promised. It contained the instructions the DDO had mentioned: effective immediately, the new code name for the Target was LEMON, and all traffic on this operation would be sent in the Limited Distribution communications channel, which afforded dissemination at Headquarters to only those few individuals directly involved, based upon a "bigot list" created and controlled by the Agency Counterintelligence Chief.

After sharing this information with Winston, I decided it was time to meet with Ralph and his guys to discuss the new approach the operation was taking in terms of compartmentalization. We still had a bit less than two weeks before LEMON was to call my business office to get information on the next meeting. But, considering the critical tasking to be ordered at this meeting I wanted all the logistics setup well in advance so we could focus on the scenario and not the stage.

When I spoke to Ralph on our secure telephone line, he mentioned that he had received a communication from his Headquarters and was looking forward to my take on how the case was to proceed. We arranged for the SAs to visit the Station in the mid-afternoon of the next day. While meeting here was better operational security, anyone observing our colleagues coming to our office would immediately recognize that they were FBI Special Agents, what with their high-performance autos complete with above-the-dashboard and rearview mirror police emergency lights. Luckily, the parking area for our building offered the opportunity to park some physical distance from our office, and the FBI was usually polite enough to take advantage of this. Also, our location was somewhat hidden away in the suburban business park, in a nondescript office building, which also contained two other small USG offices. The good news was I did not have to worry about refreshments, other than the standard coffee upon which SAs apparently live on an hour-by-hour basis.

By the time Ralph, Matt, and Larry arrived, Winston and I had talked through our agenda for the meeting. We also had a copy of my report of the June 24th meeting to give them. We used my office for the meeting, and after passing out the coffee, Ralph stated that he had received a communication from his Washington Headquarters advising that the Agency had decided this case had progressed to a more sensitive stage. He was told that both the Agency and NSA now saw definite potential for obtaining the Romanian Consulate's encryption system through Briarpatch, which was how they continued to identify LEMON. So, Ralph had been instructed to limit all information on the case to only those in the Field Office with direct involvement. Then, once again, based upon different organizational cultures, he explained that this meant he would restrict all reporting on the case to his Field Office SAC and the members of Matt's Romanian Squad, about eight or nine people. I had actually hoped for a more restricted distribution locally. However, Ralph reassured me, the FBI had never had a Soviet agent in its organization, and all his people could be trusted to protect the security of the case. I had no choice but to smile and accept this since FBI procedures within their organization were beyond anything I could control.

It is worth noting, as I subsequently learned after the meeting, that both Winston and I had the same thought when Ralph made his statement about no moles within the FBI: we both added in our own minds "that you know of." Any experience officer in an intelligence organization must always assume that the organization has been penetrated by a foreign adversary. After all, considering the time, effort, and money we spend in penetrating other foreign intelligence organizations, it would be just plain foolish not to expect them to be doing the same to us. The FBI, as a law enforcement culture operating in its own country, apparently does not have that same mindset.

I then proceeded to provide an oral brief of my perception of the meeting and LEMON's state of mind during it. I also gave a brief description of my consultations at Headquarters. I concluded by noting that once we got NSA's evaluation of the Target's reporting on the Consulate encryption system, we would be able to frame tasking for the next meeting. Our FBI colleagues had little comment on my presentation, and we moved on to Larry's update on the health treatments for LEMON and his child.

Larry advised that, according to the doctor, the son's condition was stabilizing, and at this point, with continued medication, he anticipated periodic monitoring to be the proper course of treatment. However, the news on LEMON's dental problem was much more serious. He had his first visit with the dentist, and had an oral exam and a full set of X-rays. The results were "horrible" according to the dentist. Apparently, the target's previous dental treatment was either nonexistent or just so primitive as to be useless. The dentist described his mouth as "an open sewer, with infections and gum disease abounding." The dentist said that he was very frank with LEMON, explaining to him that extensive work would be necessary to remove several diseased teeth, repair severe gum disease, particularly in the upper mouth region, and then replace the missing teeth with bridges or similar surgeries. LEMON was upset, as one would expect, but became calmer as the dentist discussed the course of the treatment and what the eventual results would mean in terms of his overall health. According to the dentist, the gum disease was so bad that it was actually affecting other areas of the body's immune system. In fact, during his discussion with LEMON, he learned that several other issues, such as sinus pain and throat rawness, were probably related to the terrible dental condition of his patient.

Well, first, I was glad the Field Office had decided to cover all the medical and dental costs. It wasn't that the Agency wouldn't cover the cost — they would — but the thought of the paperwork Station would have to file, just to justify an expensive procedure to rebuild a Target's mouth, made me shudderLarry said the dentist advised that LEMON's total treatment plan could cost in the neighborhood of as much as thirty thousand dollars, perhaps even a bit more depending upon the extent of the surgery required, and the type of teeth replacement finally installed. It would take at least several months to complete the extensive work required, which had to be done in segments, allowing a portion to heal before another segment was addressed. However, treatment for the gum disease had been started at once. LEMON had been given a prepaid prescription for a heavy dose of antibiotics, and the dentist anticipated that the patient should start to feel the results of the medicine within a few days' time.

Overall, this was actually very good news from our perspective. Assuming LEMON was pleased with the dentist's treatment approach and that the antibiotic medicine would start taking effect shortly, his appreciation for the dental work should further enhance his willingness to continue to cooperate.

I thanked Larry for his efforts handling the dentist, and noted that we would provide our Headquarters with a full report on the health issues of the LEMONs based upon his briefing today. We then spent about half an hour discussing whether the Field Office had picked up any indications through their monitoring of the Consulate and its personnel that LEMON was under any suspicion or that anyone had noticed that he was acting strangely, or whether anything of an unusual nature was taking place within that installation. Matt responded that nothing related to the target had been noticed. However, they were aware that the Consulate General had once again sold several cases of duty-free liquor to a local Romanian bar owner. LEMON was not involved in the transaction; instead, the Consulate General handled the deal with the Consulate's Administrative Officer. Matt also noted that the head of the Consulate's Economic Section had just learned that his wife was having an affair with the head Security

CHAPTER TWENTY-ONE: LEMON

Officer, and that she had been caught, but not arrested, shoplifting in a fashionable women's store earlier in the month. So, they were carefully watching how the Economics Officer was going to respond.

They felt that he could not directly challenge the Security Officer because of his politically powerful position in the Consulate. So, if all he could do was let his temper and embarrassment burn internally, perhaps they might try a friendly approach to him to see if he wanted some revenge. And, if the wife had another incident of shoplifting, the local police had been advised to hold her until an FBI SA had a chance to talk to her about the potential embarrassment to the Consulate, which would probably result in sending her and her husband back to Romania.

These were interesting insights, and the fact that Matt was telling us all the details further endorsed the fact that trust existed between us. Therefore, I made a significant effort to be unusually tactful as I first expressed admiration for their monitoring capabilities and their possible future operational planning for that information. Then, I suggested that since we were in a very sensitive phase of the Briarpatch case, I hoped that before they took any offensive action against the Economic Officer or his wife, they would analyze whether such action might create a more aggressive counterintelligence atmosphere at the Consulate to the detriment of our joint efforts to get the encryption system.

I must have handled this well, as both Ralph and Matt understood exactly what I meant and agreed that any offensive activity made against the Consulate would have to be balanced against any impact it might have on the Briarpatch case.

As we concluded our meeting, I said that as soon as we got feedback from NSA and any guidance on moving the operation forward, we would set another meeting to jointly plan our next meeting with the Target. The SAs departed, and Winston and I both felt it had been a successful and useful meeting. Now, we just need to get some NSA feedback to plan our next step. We had about ten days until LEMON would make his call for instructions, and then at least another week to finalize our plans for that meeting.

It took a few days, but Headquarters did respond: both with an NSA analysis of LEMON's information on the encryption interface details and a very strong suggestion regarding what our next move should be. The NSA report discussed LEMON's description of the encryption interface on a point-by-point basis. Probably way too much detail for us, since it took us almost an hour with our Station Communications Officers to fully understand all they were saying. The bottom line was that his information matched what they knew about Warsaw Pact countries' encryption methodologies, which, for the most part, was based upon Soviet designed systems, developed with Polish engineering and encryption expertise. This system used a one-time paper tape system to encrypt and decrypt radio traffic which carried all the classified communications between the various official installations. There were two types of these paper tapes. One of the tapes was described in an English translation as "point-to-point" and used for traffic only between two locations, such as Bucharest to the Consulate. The second tape was known as "circulars" and was utilized when a message was meant to go to more than one specific location, such as general instructions or guidance which would be provided to all Romanian diplomatic installations abroad.

While the "point to point" tape would only allow NSA to read all the messages sent to and from the Consulate General, the "circular" tape would allow NSA to decrypt all the messages sent to multiple Romanian official installations worldwide. NSA believed that communications could provide valuable insights into Romanian diplomatic and military plans and intentions, as well as details of their intelligence and security activities. Also, NSA noted that because of the close cooperation between the Romanian intelligence and security services and those of the Soviet Union, Poland, East Germany, and other Eastern Bloc nations, it was possible that valuable information on their intelligence collection and counterintelligence activities might also be communicated within this system.

NSA experts believed that LEMON had accurately reported on the entire interface mechanism, thus providing information that he knew to be some of the most sensitive information of the Romanian Government. So, at least on the face of it, our Target had already taken an irreversible step over the line in his reporting relationship. However, as in most things in life, truth and logic are not always a part of a person's thinking. The question was to what degree LEMON actually realized what he had done and the probable consequences should he be exposed? And, we had to ascertain his true understanding of this issue without causing him to question his actions or to lose any faith in the fact that the corporation could protect him regardless of his actions.

Considering that the NSA/LU was not directly involved in human agent acquisition, their operational communication accompanying the NSA read-out was right on point as to tasking. The tasking was that LEMON was to bring out at least a one inch segment of both the encryption and decryption tapes for both "point to point" and "circulars." They needed these samples in order to determine if they had the proper materials on hand to reproduce the tapes once acquired.

Their correspondence also contained information regarding the role of the code clerk and the security procedures which were standard practice at most Warsaw Pact facilities regarding the storage, opening, handling, use, and destruction of the encryption and decryption tapes. LEMON had not been queried in detail about these procedures as yet, and this would have to be accomplished at the next meeting as part of the discussion about his providing a small used portion of each tape. We were advised that both the Consulate General and the senior Consulate security officer played a role in the handling of these tapes. The junior Communications Officer did not handle the tapes at all unless there was an unusual incident, such as the absence of the Senior Communications Officer.

NSA/LU advised that the tapes were removed from the safe in the Communications Office twice a day: once in the morning to decrypt the incoming radio traffic and again at the close of business when they were used to encrypt the outgoing radio traffic. If portions of them had already been used previously, then the senior Communications officer was responsible for logging them out of the safe into an Office log book and subsequently logging them back into the safe after use. However, if a new tape was needed, either the Consulate General or the senior security office had to witness the opening of the new tape, and was responsible for examining the packaging of the tape before opening to ensure that all its seals and the packaging itself had not been tampered with. A similar procedure took place when a used tape was to be destroyed—one of those two had to witness the destruction in the incinerator located in the Communications Office. The name of the witness and the time and date of the event were also noted in the Office log book, which was periodically sent back to Bucharest for review and retention at the Ministry of Foreign Affairs.

While this system seemed structured to ensure the security of the tapes, its weaknesses were readily apparent: only the senior Communications Officer was responsible for placing the opened tapes back in the safe after use. He did have to sign a log with the time noted, and one of the many specifics we had to learn was whether or not the safe had a timer in it that recorded the date and times of its opening and closing on an internal log. As to the taking of the actual samples of each tape, we would have to discuss with LEMON how best to do this—before the witnessed tape destruction took place or during it. This probably would depend upon whether the witnessing official actually stayed for the entire destruction process or left after the tape was placed in the incinerator. We felt that the actual removal of the small segments of the tapes from the office and building would not be an issue since LEMON was often the last to leave the building and he had never been physically searched upon his departure.

With the receipt of the NSA report and the tasking, I once again arranged for the SAs to come to the Station for a planning session. We still had a few days before the Target was scheduled to call my "office", so I wanted an agreed-upon operational meeting plan set before the call. I also wanted to give the Field Office another opportunity to play a firsthand role in the operation: I wanted an SA to play the role of the corporation's technical expert. This individual would be introduced to the target at this next meeting, treated as an equal within the corporate structure to me, and would handle the technical explanation to LEMON regarding the why and how we were going to use access to the encrypted tapes for international business benefit. For this particular role, I had Larry in mind. I hoped that Ralph and Matt would agree.

The planning meeting went smoothly. I explained in some detail the content of the NSA report and provided them a copy of it. Then, I brought up our ideas for the objectives of the next meeting in late July. I gave Ralph a copy of the operational correspondence from Headquarters and noted that LEMON's tasking was to be small segments of each of the used tapes. I suggested that this should not be too difficult to obtain, considering the procedures for destroying the used tapes at the Consulate. Matt responded that the operational information on security procedures for the tapes was new information for them. He asked how we knew this. I answered that it was also new information for us, and that I assumed it came from NSA files. After some additional discussion, it was agreed that obtaining these tape segments probably could be accomplished without great risk to the Target. However, we would carefully work out with him how he planned to accomplish this. We all felt that with the proper reinforcement and motivation at the meeting, LEMON would accept the tasking.

Next, we discussed the tone and environment of the meeting, and which role players would be present and how they would interrelate. As usual, I put forth the general outline of the meetings as Winston and I had prepared it prior to this session. We felt the meeting would include a dinner, and more indications during the meeting that the boss was gaining confidence in LEMON. The boss would start by questioning LEMON on the status of his son's health and then move into the issue of LEMON's dental treatment. After discussing these issues, the boss would transition into complimenting the target on his recent reports on the interface between the encryption system and the Consulate's communications system. He would note that this information was going to be very helpful in developing a new project for the corporation, which had great potential profits. At this point, he would also mention that as the information was going to be so useful, he had instructed me, Robert, to provide a two-thousand-dollar bonus to LEMON. I concluded by noting that between the personal concern expressed by the boss on the health issues for both LEMON and his son, and the mention of an additional large bonus to be provided along with his monthly retainer, the Target's motivation should be satisfied.

I then mention that we believed it was time to introduce another role player into the equation—one to represent a technical expert for the corporation who would provide rationale and technical explanations for future tasking including obtaining the small used tape fragments. I explained that we would need an officer who was willing to do some studying on the Romanian government's communications system and its equipment. Ralph asked if I planned to use a Station officer or bring in someone from our Headquarters. He was surprised, and indeed very pleased, as was Matt, when I answered that I felt it was time to get another SA involved in the operation. I suggested that Larry would be an ideal candidate for the role, assuming the Field Office approved.

Both SAs agreed that Larry would be a fine choice since he was already fully aware of the case. Also, Matt noted, he was spending time handling the doctor and dentist involved in the family's health issues, so in recent weeks, more and more of his responsibilities had been connected to this case. I noted that this new corporate official would be of equal rank to me, Robert, and would be treated as such by the boss. We also hoped that introducing someone who would have a logical commercial reason to know about the Romanian communications system would provide even more assurance to the target that the corporation knew exactly what it was doing.

I said that Larry would have to do a bit of studying regarding the encryption tape system so he could provide LEMON with a scientifically sounding story explaining how we would be able to copy the data on the tapes without the need to physically open them. I added that experienced engineers from Agency Headquarters would be sending out details to support this story, as well as other information that might prove useful to Larry in establishing his role as the expert.

Matt responded that he was sure Larry would be pleased to take this role,

CHAPTER TWENTY-ONE: LEMON

and Ralph agreed. And, early the next morning Larry was on the secure telephone between our offices to confirm that he did want to play the role and was looking forward to it. It was agreed that Larry would come to the Station to study the information provided by Headquarters engineers, and hence forth would be included in all Station planning sessions for the operation.

We concluded this planning session by confirming that Ralph would obtain the hotel suite and town car, and provide me with all the details within a day, so I could prepare the appropriate message for the Headquarters' telephone unit playing the role of my office. We would set the date for the meeting as the evening of July 15th, with a car pickup time of 8:15 p.m. at a location several blocks from LEMON's residence and in an area with some, but not heavy, pedestrian and vehicular traffic. We also agreed upon a meeting to review final scenarios for the meeting on the afternoon of the 13th, at the Station. In addition to Ralph and Matt, both Larry and Patrick would attend.

Within a day, Ralph provided details of the meeting's location. Once again, he had arranged the suite at the first hotel we had used and acquired an appropriate town car for Patrick to use to pick up LEMON. So, with a few days to spare, I sent a message to the telephone unit with the specific instructions that were to be provided to the Target. Subsequently, the Station was advised that LEMON had called in as instructed, received the message, and repeated it back to confirm accuracy of its content.

The next step was to get Larry, known as Franklin Bouranski in the scenario, up to speed on his role and how he fit into the overall cast of characters and the scenario. This involved working with him to create a background that would explain his familiarity with Warsaw Pact communications procedures and equipment, as well as other aspects of his cover story regarding his association with the corporation. In addition to several hours of discussion with Winston and me, he was also able to spend some time reading background material on procedures known to the U.S. Government regarding Romanian—Warsaw Pact communications procedures, security practices, some general information on the use of encryption and encryption paper tapes, and security measures used to ensure their protection from unauthorized handling and opening. While Larry's academic background was in accounting, he had a very organized mind and was a quick learner, thank God, because some of the papers seemed pretty technical to me. All in all, with a couple of role-playing sessions included, he mastered his new personality quite well within a couple of days.

On July 13th, we held our final planning session. Larry was well read in on his part, and Winston and I had fleshed out our roles. Ralph and Matt seemed very comfortable as I outlined the chronology for the meeting: the boss asks about the Target and his son's health issues, the boss says encouraging words about LEMON's reporting, at dinner the boss tells stories regarding his political and business contacts and activities, after dinner I explain Franklin's role, Franklin explains the need for tape segments, we discuss how LEMON can accomplish this, the boss retires to his bedroom and I pay LEMON and handle any issues he may have.

I emphasized the positive incentives we were relying on to ensure LEMON agreed to supply the tape segments. The SAs agreed that these factors should be adequate to insure his cooperation. I then further explained that both I and Larry would engage him in a comprehensive discussion regarding how his normal activities as the Communications Officer would also provide him the opportunity to physically get the tape portions.

Ralph agreed with the plan and added that he was confident that the meeting would go well. However, just before they departed, Ralph asked if we could have a few minutes alone to discuss another matter. We went from the conference room into my office. I really did not know what to think, as the operation was going smoothly and all recent indications were that the Field Office was completely satisfied.

Happily, there were no problems. Ralph simply wanted to explain that he and the Field Office SAC were aware of the sensitivity that his Headquarters, Agency Headquarters and NSA attached to this case now that we were about to actually obtain portions of the tapes. He said that

CHAPTER TWENTY-ONE: LEMON

while the Romanian Squad would continue to be aware in general terms of the Briarpatch case, only he, Matt, Larry, Patrick, and the SAC would be fully knowledgeable on all the activities being undertaken. Ralph also mentioned that he appreciated involving Larry in the case. This would give the Bureau its own "eyes and ears" in the case, and would put to rest any remaining concerns within the FBI bureaucracy that the Agency was not sharing all the information obtained from the case. He added that while trust and confidence had been established for quite some time in the field, there were still elements at his Headquarters that questioned the Agency's commitment to a "joint operation."

Since Ralph made these last comments in almost an apologetic manner, my reaction was to express understanding of the Bureau's position. I noted that I was well aware of some past operations where Agency officers may not have been completely candid in their sharing of details and information with the Bureau. I added that I understood my predecessor had not had a good professional relationship with the Field Office, and that meant that the burden of proof of our commitment to a fully" joint operation" was on my shoulders. So, I understood why some FBI elements were suspicious. However, I stated, from the start of this operation, the Station had worked hard to ensure that your SAs were fully informed of our activities.

With these mutual confessions of love and respect completed, Ralph and his guys departed. Now, all we had to do was wait until it was time for the meeting. Of course, waiting is never easy since anticipation, and worry, of problems unplanned for, is a career trait in COs.

The morning of July 15th was a bit anxious around the Station. We handled routine business, but the importance of this evening's meeting was constantly on my mind. If LEMON agreed to bring out the tape segments, we were much closer to our ultimate objective. If he had objections, we could probably deal with them because the actual risk of discovery was very small. But, depending upon the basis for his objections, we might need to modify our "employee" benefits or the manner in which we work to convince him that the corporation has the capabilities to protect him and his family regardless of the risks he takes. A CO, especially at this stage in a recruitment operation, likes to think that he has the Target all figured out. He wants to feel he is in psychological control of the relationship and knows what "buttons to push" to ensure the Target's cooperation. Yet, in real life, we can't control all the variables outside of the clandestine relationship that affect the Target's behavior and emotional attitude on a daily basis. Humans, regardless of nationality and cultural background, are like that, and our relationship with them can be just as volatile as any relationship between an individual and a spouse or an individual and a close friend.

About mid-afternoon, all of our people started to move out and begin the lengthy process of "cleaning" themselves. Patrick drove to pick up the rental town car and subsequently drove to a suburban shopping mall, where he met Winston. He then drove Winston to the hotel. With commercial rush hour traffic, the trip from the suburbs took a bit over an hour, so they arrived in the underground parking garage about a quarter to 6 p.m. They took the elevator to the penthouse suite and began checking the room and preparing it for the meeting. Patrick took the liquor bottles out of Winston's luggage and placed them in the bar area. The usual current copies of several international magazines and newspapers were placed in the reading area. Winston checked to confirm the suite looked appropriately lavish, and checked that a floral display had been placed on the table in the dining area. The table had been set for four places: the boss, me, Larry as Franklin, and LEMON. Patrick would stand behind the boss as before, serving the dinner from the room service carts. Once their inspection of the suite and their preparations were complete, Winston, with some advice from Patrick, decided on the dinner menu and the wine. Once again, we would sacrifice our waistlines for our country.

Now, the wines—three would be appropriate: a light white with the chowder, salad and clams, a Sauvignon Blanc with the entrée, and a slightly sweet rose with the dessert. Since wines were not Winston's strong point, Patrick provided some useful suggestions. He apparently was partial to southern French wines. Once the decisions were made, Patrick, as appropriate to his role, called room service and placed the order as well as

CHAPTER TWENTY-ONE: LEMON

verify that the meal would be delivered exactly at 9:30 p.m. That would ensure we had at least an hour to drink a few scotches with LEMON and also complete the social and motivational portions of the meeting.

I departed the Station about half an hour after Winston, and eventually drove to another suburban shopping mall, where I met Larry outside a men's shop. He had also parked at the mall. Like me, Larry had dressed up for the occasion. I always kept a couple of Brooks Brothers' suits aside in my wardrobe for operational purposes when I had to dress like a well-compensated businessman. Typically I dress like what I am—a USG employee of modest but comfortable means. In my previous encounters with Larry, he had always dressed in dark grey, somewhat baggy off-the-rack suits. To me, this seemed to be the FBI uniform, with the coat jacket's bagginess required to hide the sidearm that most wore on their right hip. While I considered asking if the Field Office had purchased the suit for him, I decided against it.

We exchanged greetings, checked our watches, and decided we had about half an hour to kill before we took a taxi to the hotel in the city. So, we had some coffee at a small café inside the mall. For the next twenty-five minutes, we engaged in some social conversation, perhaps with just a bit of elicitation on both of our parts, as we attempted to get to know each other a bit better. It turned out Larry was a good family man, with a wife of many years and a couple of kids, of whom he was very proud. Since his kids were nearing the end of High School, the subject of college costs came up, as did the related subject of government pensions, and when it was best to take them so a second career could be started to handle costs such as college. At 6:30 p.m. sharp, we left the mall in a taxi for the hotel and arrived almost exactly at 7:15 p.m.

Upon entering the suite, we exchanged comments with Patrick and Winston about the city's traffic. Our taxi driver, apparently a recent arrival to both the country and the city, was very aggressive in his determination to see every space between vehicles as an invitation to move quicker to his destination. I mentioned that it reminded me of my driving experiences in several Asian cities, where the traffic flow demands strict attention and a 180-degree perspective.

At 7:40 p.m., Patrick left for the garage. He had timed his route from the hotel to the pickup site the evening before in his personal vehicle and was confident that by taking a pre-arranged route, he would hit the pickup point within a minute's window of the scheduled time. If LEMON was not there, he had a circular route established that would bring him back past the pickup point in four minutes or so.

As Patrick left, Winston suggested that we have a drink while we wait, as it should look to LEMON as if we had been in the suite for some time discussing corporate business. He went over to the bar and broke out the scotch—an expensive one as LEMON would expect. In addition to helping to create the scenario's atmosphere, the drinks helped calm our slight, or maybe not so slight, anxiousness as the time for the meeting approached. We were all confident that we knew our roles and had the proper timing down for our various "speeches" during the meeting. However, and I assume that this is true of professional actors, the time just before one goes "on stage" is one of some anxiety and nervousness. But, once the meeting begins, that all seems to disappear quickly as one becomes one's role.

We subsequently learned that LEMON was at the pickup point exactly at 8:15 p.m., and Patrick arrived within half a minute. LEMON entered the backseat of the town car quickly, evoking only a few horn blasts from frustrated motorists trying to get home. Patrick drove directly to the hotel, entered the parking garage, stopped by the elevator bank, and escorted the Target into the penthouse elevator and up to the suite. At 8:28 p.m. LEMON entered the suite.

Winston was seated at the head of the coffee table in the sitting room, and I rose from my seat to greet LEMON. We shook hands, and I escorted him over to Winston, who extended his hand in a gesture of welcome without rising from his seat. I then introduced him to Larry, as Franklin Bouranski, another corporate senior officer who was involved in a special business development project in which LEMON might well play a role. As I handled the introductions, Patrick moved to station himself behind the boss's chair in the traditional bodyguard-man's servant position. Franklin

CHAPTER TWENTY-ONE: LEMON

and I also took our seats, withLEMON seated to the right of the boss. All the players were in place—curtain up—the meeting was to begin.

Winston began by instructing Patrick to provide drinks to all. He then began inquiring in general terms about the health and well-being of LEMON and his family. This conversation quickly moved into a discussion of the state of his son's health care. The target described several of the tests the doctor had previously conducted and the results of them. As LEMON went through a comprehensive review of the tests and treatment analysis, the boss listened intently, keeping his eyes focused directly on the Target's face. Franklin and I did likewise—hopefully from the Target's perspective he felt that all of us were keenly interested and concerned with his comments. Of course, since we had previously been briefed as to the results and status of the son's health, his remarks came as no surprise.

During this narrative, on several occasions, the boss made an appropriate utterance or gesture further demonstrating his interest in and personal concern with the topic. When LEMON gave the doctor's conclusions, we all reacted with visible relief and satisfaction. LEMON summarized his remarks by noting that the medicine provided by the doctor seemed to be working already: Anton had been acting more active and mentally alert in recent days, according to his wife. However, he mentioned, the doctor felt that in addition to the medicine being used, the family should bring Anton back to the doctor's office periodically to check on how the gland was returning to its normal functioning. As to the kidney issue, the doctor was confident that it would be quickly cleared up with the medicine prescribed.

The boss responded to LEMON by stating his satisfaction with the doctor's professional efforts and the successful results of the treatment to date. He cautioned the Target to be sure to schedule the required follow-up appointments. The Target seemed to take this pronouncement as sincere and thanked the boss rather profusely for providing the excellent, and he realized expensive, health care to his son.

The boss next asked about LEMON's personal dental issue, which had become apparent at a previous meeting during dinner. The Target responded that he had already had three appointments with the dentist. At the initial appointment, the dentist did a physical examination of his mouth and a full set of X-rays of all his teeth. Then, the dentist advised him that he had some very serious dental issues involving both his gums and some of his teeth. LEMON admitted that he was surprised at the seriousness of his mouth's condition. He then noted that dental care in Romania is not all that great, and he admitted that he had been somewhat casual about dental checkups during most of his adult life. Even when posted abroad, he had not bothered to get much in the way of preventative treatment. He continued that during the initial visit, the dentist had explained and demonstrated using the X-rays the various tooth and gum issues affecting him. The dentist's conclusion was that his gum disease was so advanced that it was affecting his overall health. So, it was agreed that he would immediately start a treatment of antibiotics to address the gum disease. Apparently, there were several teeth whose roots were rotted and would have to be removed. That would be the first step. Then, there were several others with cavities and degrading fillings that would have to be either repaired or perhaps removed due to their condition. The dentist felt that he would be treating LEMON for several months, since there was so much work to be done. However, at the conclusion of the treatment plan, the dentist said that he was confident that the target would have not only a healthy mouth, but also a great smile. The dentist added that once the dental issues were resolved, LEMON would feel a new, overall sense of wellness. The Target concluded by noting that he had been on the medication now for several days and already noted more comfort in his eating, and generally less fatigue overall in his daily activities. However, he said that he must honestly say that he is not looking forward to all the dental work, but knows it is for the best. He concluded by wondering if he could have his wife and son also see the dentist?

The boss expressed some surprise and empathy for the degree of LEMON's dental problems, but encouraged him to continue the treatments as directed. He explained that from his own personal experience, since British dentists were not internationally recognized as being among the best, if one does not keep up their dental checkups, problems can mount

CHAPTER TWENTY-ONE: LEMON

up quickly. He also made it clear that his employees' dental health coverage extended to their families as well, just as the medical coverage did.

I quickly gave Franklin a glance, as he would now have to advise the dentist that he could expect two more "corporate" patients. Hopefully, neither of them had dental problems on the scale of those of LEMON's. But, we would soon find out. I don't know if our dentist has a kid going to college or has an expensive hobby like sailing, but I suspected that, however he spends his money, his income had just gone up.

Now that we were through with the health issues, the boss turned the conversation to LEMON's last report. He noted that there was information in the report that could probably be used for some business sales. He also noted that the corporation was working on developing some new technology that would significantly enhance its capabilities to anticipate the needs of its clients for both equipment and entire communications systems. "This project," he stated," was headed by Franklin, and after dinner, I want him to discuss it with you." At this point, Franklin nodded in LEMON's direction and received a nod and smile in response.

The boss then advised the Target that based upon his last report he had authorized me to provide a two thousand dollar bonus along with his July compensation. He added that he was impressed with the technical knowledge that LEMON was bringing to the corporation, and if this continued, he might soon be prepared to bring him on-board as an employee.

Just as the boss concluded these remarks, almost as if on cue, the room service personnel knocked on the suite door, and dinner arrived. It took a couple of minutes for Patrick to direct the room service attendants in placing the various courses on the sideboard and opening the wines. Once this was accomplished and the personnel tipped and sent on their way, the boss invited everyone to the table. Of course, he sat at the head, with LEMON to his right. I was at the other end, and Franklin sat facing the Target.

We had planned that conversation at dinner would focus on our continued effort to impress LEMON with the breath and scope of the boss' contacts and political influence, especially within the Soviet Bloc. Thus, after several minutes discussing the composition of the first course of chowder and clams, Winston moved into a story infused with humor regarding a supposed dinner he recently had with an unnamed East German official. He is quite a natural storyteller, which is an excellent skill for a CO to have.

The boss noted that the clams reminded him of a business dinner he had with a senior East German government official, whom he did not further identify, about a year ago. They were discussing the purchase from the corporation of a system of radio repeater digital signal equipment, which the East German Government wanted primarily for secure communications for its military and internal security forces. The system was to include certain technology developed and sold by a French subsidiary of an American company, and was in the category of technology that that was prohibited from export to any country in the Warsaw Pact. That, however, was not going to be a problem as several of the French subsidiary's senior officials were long-established "consultants" to the corporation. It would be arranged that false end-user certificates would be provided, which identified the destination of the components as a civilian telecommunications firm in North Africa. In reality, the components would be shipped to Cairo, and then repacked, listed as different components, and shipped onward to a corporation facility on the island of Corsica. There, they would be installed in the system and shipped to a minor port in Turkey, and then sent overland by truck, eventually ending up in East Germany.

The boss explained this was actually a rather standard method of defeating the "silly" regulations and restrictions that the U.S. and its NATO allies placed on modern technology. However, since the business arrangement involved the purchase of the system's components and the installation of the prohibited U.S. components, as well as the transportation of the various pieces of equipment to various locations, the corporation was going to see a significant profit from the deal. And, of course, the East German Official who was responsible for contracting for the system was

CHAPTER TWENTY-ONE: LEMON

also to receive a "consultant" fee since he had ensured that the boss got the contract.

So, the boss continued, this dinner was to discuss and settle any final details related to the deal. And, since the official was a great lover of food and drink, they were in a private room of a restaurant in Leipzig, well-known for its fresh seafood. The official, like many Germans, had a great affinity for beer and had drunk several liters of the local pilsner during the conversation before dinner. So, he was, perhaps, a bit less alert as the dinner progressed and he added glasses of white wine to his previous consumption. However, the wine only increased his appetite, and his favorite dish that evening turned out to be clams on the half shell, which he digested in a rather large quantity. However, possibly due to his alcohol consumption, by his third plate and fourth or fifth glass of wine, only about half the slippery clams actually made it into his mouth. Several ended up resting on his dress shirt's quite large paunch, which was no doubt the result of his love of food and drink.

Now, the boss explained, like most German officials, this individual was a man of importance, and certainly could not be embarrassed in public due to a food slippage mistake. His dignity would not allow it, and for the boss to even notice it, let alone mention it, would not have been good for their personal or professional relationship. So, the boss tried very hard not to watch as a procession of clams slid down the front of the official's shirt and began to settle into a pool on the crest of his stomach. As one can imagine, as the number of misdirected clams increased, it became more difficult not to look at them, let alone continue the social conversation required of the situation. I noticed that even Patrick, whose demeanor is always perfect and respectful, was coming close to cracking.

Luckily, the official stated that he must go to the men's room to empty out the beer, in order to make more room for the wine, he joked. When he arose from his chair, the pile of clams slid down his pants onto the floor. He apparently did not, or did not care to, notice, and in an only partially successful attempt at a dignified bearing, stumbled towards the private bathroom connected to the private dining salon. Patrick quickly summoned a waiter, who immediately cleared the uneaten clams from the floor. The boss then asked Patrick to have the main course, a baked North Sea fish stuffed with crab, brought to the table. Thus, it seemed that the meal could progress with no further issues ~~that~~ that might in any way disrupt the sociality of the dinner.

However, that simply was not to be. As the official returned to the table, it became quite apparent that he had forgotten to zip up his fly, and indeed had forgotten to even button the waistband of his pants. His large belly and underwear were quite visible. So, for the remainder of the meal, and the after-dinner coffee and cognac, both the boss and Patrick worked very hard to keep their eyes away from his protruding belly and not do anything that might affect his sense of dignity. It was a difficult challenge considering the situation. But, both managed. When the official had finished his second cognac, the boss explained that his private plane was going to take him to Italy that evening in preparation for some meetings the next morning. With this excuse, he had Patrick summon the official's driver, who carefully maneuvered him into his car and drove him home.

The boss concluded the story by stating that in subsequent meetings with the official, there had never been any mention of any problems at that dinner. Thus, he assumed that the official was so drunk that he did not know what had happened, and because of his position both in the government and the East German Communist Party, no one was going to bring it up.

Now, while an amusing story in itself, there were three aspects of it carefully considered to appeal to LEMON. The first was that Romanians tend not to like Germans, East or West. This is the result of traditional German arrogance regarding other Europeans, and especially Eastern Europeans. German actions in their country during World War II also didn't help their reputation. So, we figured that LEMON would particularly enjoy a story that made fun of the pride and sloppy behavior of an East German official. Secondly, Winston provided just enough details in describing the official without actually naming him that we were fairly confident the Target would recognize the official as Otto Pieckmann, the

CHAPTER TWENTY-ONE: LEMON

Deputy Minister of Trade, who was also very highly placed in the East German Communist Party based upon his marriage to a women related to two senior Communist Party officials. Informally, he was known as a fool and bore, but politically, he was untouchable. We thought LEMON would enjoy hearing a story about his drunkenness and slovenly behavior. Finally, the story reinforced the level of contacts the boss had in terms of access to individuals who were politically connected and thus able to make deals profitable, for all concerned, in the Warsaw Pact.

Upon completing the story, the boss shifted the conversation somewhat. He asked me how one of my business deals regarding the procurement of a new radar receiving system was progressing. I responded that actual purchase of the system was going to have to be done through a company I was creating in Canada, as its sale outside of NATO was not authorized. However, I had a law firm in Ottawa working on the establishment of a Limited Partnership that acted as a subsidiary of a Cayman Islands holding company. When this was set up, I would move the necessary funds to the Canadian company, and they would file a purchase order for the radar system, stating that it was for use in an about-to-be-constructed Canadian provincial airport. Once the equipment was at the company, I would arrange to have it transshipped to the real Middle East purchaser.

The boss expressed mild approval at my efforts, stating that the Middle East was becoming a lucrative market for certain types of electronic and information technology. He pondered out loud whether he needed to assign a senior corporate official to the region to ensure that personal relations were well tended among his contacts there. Then, he and I engaged in a short discussion of his contacts in the region, not by name but by their positions in several of the wealthier countries. Once again, our purpose was to demonstrate the scope of influence and contacts the corporation had throughout the world.

As we concluded dessert, the boss advised that he still had some work to do since it was the business day in the Far East. He rose from the table, and followed by Patrick, went into the bedroom portion of the suite. I then motioned LEMON and Franklin to move back to the sitting area, and provided all three of us with another glass of scotch as we made ourselves comfortable.

As he sipped his scotch, I told LEMON that his knowledge of communications systems, especially those used within the Warsaw Pact, did seem to have significant potential for corporate profits. That said, we had to position ourselves where we could anticipate what was needed and desired by the various governments rather than simply react to their equipment requests. Thus, Franklin was developing a project that should give us this capability, and this is why the boss wanted you and him to meet this evening. I then nodded to Franklin to explain further.

Franklin began by complementing LEMON on his expertise in the communication's field. He continued that he, too, was a specialist in that field, with a PhD in electrical engineering from the Massachusetts Institute of Technology in Boston. His particular field of interest was in laser technology, and he was involved in a cutting-edge research project for the corporation studying the use of laser technology to copy imprinted data and images without direct physical contact. He and a small team had been working on this problem for almost a year and a half, and were starting to obtain the first clear results that a digital copy of the physical data could be captured by a laser and projected onto a computer screen. Franklin noted that this was exciting work.

At this point, I broke into the conversation, noting the information LEMON had provided had been of value, but in the case of the communications system, it was already in place. The corporation might well be able to recommend updates to a government, but that would be about it. The ideal solution would be to have "real-time" information of what a government was communicating with its various offices. This would include the internal communications procedures and data linkage within the networks. With these details, the corporation could monitor the current status of the government's technologies, as well as what future upgrades were being considered. Thus, we could offer goods and services before the government was ready to ask for them. As a side benefit, we would also have advanced knowledge of other business deals under consideration by the Romanian

CHAPTER TWENTY-ONE: LEMON

Government. Such knowledge could be profitably used in numerous ways.

"At present," I said, "you are only able to give us bits and pieces of such information as it comes to your attention. And, this is understandable since you have to be careful in protecting your relationship with us." I then went on to explain that if LEMON could provide copies of all the communications traffic sent and received by the Consulate, our marketing people could analyze and identify the most profitable issues for the corporation to focus on. However, that is not a practical solution as the risk to LEMON would be too great. But, if Franklin's project was eventually successful, we may be able to read all the Consulate traffic without any need for LEMON monitoring it. Since copying the radio traffic which goes into and comes out of the Consulate is a simple matter, only requiring a collection site somewhat near the facility, this would be a cost-effective way to identify potentially profitable business opportunities.

As anticipated, my comments were quite a surprise to LEMON. While it took him a while to comment, his facial expression demonstrated he was both surprised and shocked at my statements. Yet, when he did speak, he did so calmly and carefully. He first stated," The idea of the corporation desiring all the communications from the Consulate never crossed my mind. However, I understand in principle that such access would open up a wide range of business opportunities. But, I also know there would be little actual commercial interest in the majority of the communications, so a great deal of filtering through useless data would be necessary." Franklin interrupted here, stating that LEMON was correct, but this had already been considered, and a word or phrase identification program could be used to filter the information digitally, and select only information of commercial value. I added that while LEMON had made a good point, we were a bit ahead of him in thinking through this project.

The target once again took a moment to think, and then responded, "You are probably correct, although I do not have enough knowledge and experience to know the present state of such types of programs. But, any attempt to bring such a device into the Consulate would be impossible." I agreed with him, as did Franklin, who noted it was apparent the system would be quite large and certainly could not be carried by one person. "Besides," I added, "what we were looking for is a way to get the Consulate's information in the most effective manner possible, while also protecting you remains a key priority."

This was where I attempted to calm the target down. I spoke up, and said that we were still early in this project and there was much work to be done to even ascertain if the desired results could be obtained. So, LEMON certainly didn't have to worry about being asked to take any additional risks for the corporation. Rather, the boss simply wanted him to be aware of one of the future approaches we were considering which might involve him.

I then moved into the reassurance portion of this scenario. I noted "Over the past weeks, the boss has developed trust and confidence in your efforts, and apparently is thinking about hiring you as a full employee, and with all the benefits that provides. However, in purely financial terms, he doubts if you can produce adequate useful information from simply monitoring Consulate communications. So, in addition, he wants to use your communications expertise in support of other corporate projects such as Franklin's. In this way, your contributions to the corporation will justify the compensation and benefits provided." Franklin agreed with me and added that, based on what he had seen of LEMON's technical background, he definitely could be of assistance with the project. Both of us continued in this vein for some time, repeating in different ways the main themes of the benefits of full employment for LEMON. I concluded by stating firmly that regardless of the tasking, the boss had ordered that LEMON's personal security must always be of primary concern. Therefore, we had to have a frank talk about any type of security concerns he had regarding our commercial relationship.

While our reassurances had some success in calming LEMON's concerns, he continued to make the point that while he was committed to working for the boss, his personal safety, and indeed that of his family and relatives back in Romania, was of great concern. We talked about this issue for several minutes. It was apparent the Target was concerned regarding what

CHAPTER TWENTY-ONE: LEMON

role he would be expected to play in future corporate tasks. So, as it was well after 11 p.m., I decided it was better to end the meeting. This would allow LEMON to think through his options, and for our joint operational team to do some planning and strategizing as well.

I told LEMON that it was getting late, and he had to work tomorrow. I said that I understood his concerns and we would have to talk more about this in the future. I suggested that we have dinner at the same restaurant where we last met in two days. I explained that I had several business appointments in the region during the next two days, but could be back in the city for an 8 p.m. dinner on July 17th. He agreed. I then paid him his July retainer and the bonus that the boss mentioned. This totaled three thousand five hundred dollars, which he did not count. He placed the manila envelope in his coat pocket and asked me to thank the boss for the bonus.

After once again reviewing the place and time of our next meeting, I went and got Patrick, who drove the Target back to the pickup point near his residence. It had been a three-hour-plus meeting and certainly not all to my liking. We had considered some resistance from LEMON when it became clear that we wanted all of the Consulate's communications, specifically from the perspective of the risks involved for him. But, we felt we could reassure him in this regard, and obviously we had not been able to do so. Thinking quickly about how to react to his concerns, I suggested the dinner meeting in a few days as another opportunity to convince LEMON that corporate employment was his best option. I thought that in a one-on-one meeting, I could help him "understand" that the benefits of employment with us were in his best interests and those of his family, and that the expertise and political power of the corporation could protect him as needed.

Even though it was late, when Patrick returned, the four of us sat down and discussed the meeting and LEMON's hesitation for another hour, with no final conclusions. I asked Larry to advise Ralph of the situation and ask him to come to the Station the following afternoon so we could talk out this problem and develop some plans to address it.

By this time, it was well after midnight, so it was decided that Winston would stay overnight in the suite, both as a practice matter to allow Patrick to get home quicker and also to provide support to the cover story that he was actually staying there. I finally got home after 2 a.m. for a few hours of restless sleep. I knew that I had to be in the office early to advise Headquarters of the results of the meeting and then start to develop a logical scenario that would convince the Target to continue to cooperate with the corporation.

Chapter Twenty-Two: Putting It Back Together

I first heard the term "putting it back together" in high school, when my soccer coach muttered it to an assistant coach just before the end of the first half of a game. I overheard the comment, but it did not mean much to me until I thought about it later. About halfway through the first half, our team just seemed to fall apart. We were outmaneuvered by the opposition, and our team discipline just fell apart. At halftime, after a few minutes to rest and get some water, the coach called us together. He did not yell, did not plead, nor did he try to give any emotionally charged pep talk to ignite our emotions. Rather, he carefully analyzed the errors we had made and proceeded to identify the weaknesses of the opposing players as demonstrated in the first half. He calmly instructed each of the players how to adjust to their opponent. He concluded by simply stating that we were the better team and all we had to do was go out there and play our normal game.

His approach worked. The team went back out on the field and won the game. Whenever a plan falls apart, I try to remember not only what the coach said, but also how he acted to "put it back together": calmly, identifying the problems, and then providing clear guidance regarding how to fix the problem. Seems like common sense, and it is, but that doesn't mean people always do it.

Well, we certainly did have a bit of a setback to our plans. LEMON was more apprehensive about our objective than we thought he would be. OK, so now we have to get the operation back on track so we can task him to provide samples of the coded tapes. I still had faith in the overall analysis we had built regarding the Target's motivation, but perhaps we could have been more sensitized to his risk aversion level. We had only a short time to adjust our approach. So, Winston, Stan, Edmund, Larry and I sat down in my office and began to focus on last night's meeting.

Stan and Edmund had some questions, as one would expect since they were not at the meeting, and Winston, Larry and I answered them as best we could. We discussed what each of us felt about Target's behavior and did some critical analysis of our joint conclusions. Then, we reviewed our approach regarding LEMON's risk-taking level and attempted to identify what particular issues would help him rationalize assuming a greater risk. We came to some conclusions: our opinions on the Target's personal motivations for working with the corporation were accurate, but there were still some additional confidence-building measures required to convince him that the corporation could, and would, protect him if necessary. After discussing this for a while, we broke for a quick lunch before the Field Office contingency arrived for the formal joint planning session.

Ralph, Matt, and Patrick arrived in the early afternoon. They, apparently, had held their own preparatory planning session based upon Patrick's perceptions of the meeting. So, we all knew what the problem was—we just needed to decide how best to solve it.

Matt began the discussion by stating that the basic motivations we had previously identified and manipulated seemed to have worked to a certain degree. But, even with the "carrots" in place, Briarpatch was now hesitant to follow instructions. He felt it was time to employ the "stick and force LEMON to cooperate. "The Target should," Matt continued," be made aware that should his past activities come to light, he would be in serious trouble." In other words, Matt opted for a threatening approach, emphasizing the danger to LEMON if he did not continue to cooperate with the corporation. Once again, this was a standard FBI and law enforcement approach to agent handling—use the threat of exposure

CHAPTER TWENTY-TWO: PUTTING IT BACK TOGETHER

with the assurance of protection if cooperative as the control mechanism.

I agreed with him that there needed to be a clearer discussion of benefits versus risks with the Target. And, I meant this. However, I suggested that we needed to include this in a "come to Jesus" type of personal discussion that I would have with LEMON. As we all agreed that our compensation package of retainer, bonuses, and health care for both the son and the Target was greatly valued by him, the real issue was how to boost his confidence that future tasks would be without too much risk. Also, we should be able to give him some assurances that in the worst case of his being exposed, we have a plan to protect him and his family. After some debate, this approach was agreed to.

As to the general outline for the restaurant meeting of the next night, Winston and I offered up the following: a "friendly" discussion of the benefits LEMON was enjoying, a "frank and candid" discussion of the risks he might take, a conversation on how the corporation's capabilities could reduce that risk and assist him in a worst-case scenario, and a reminder that the boss liked him personally and was considering making him a full employee. Assuming LEMON accepted our argument and agreed to continue his cooperation, I would schedule another hotel meeting for about two weeks hence, with LEMON meeting with me and Franklin. At that meeting, we would give him the task of bringing out the small portions of the coded tapes. In support of this tasking, Franklin would provide a complicated and scientific phrased explanation of how these tape portions would advance the laser project.

This concept seemed to suit everyone, with the possible exception of Matt, who was a bit less satisfied, but chose not to express any negative views. Before they left, I asked Ralph to provide full surveillance coverage on LEMON from the morning of the meeting through his arrival and departure from the restaurant meeting. I asked them to pay particular attention to any unusual activities within the Consulate and especially the behavior of the Romanian Government security personnel. I explained that if LEMON had made the decision to stop his association with the corporation, one possibility he might explore to protect himself from his past actions would be to tell his friend the Consulate General that he had been independently working to identify American intelligence personnel working against the Consulate and was now ready to expose them. And, he could use the restaurant meeting to allow Consulate security officials to monitor it and try to identify me. Therefore, I felt we needed to go into the full counterintelligence defensive mode for the meeting of July 17th.

Ralph immediately agreed with my concerns and promised his Field Office resources would be employed as desired.

After the SAs departed, I had a brief chat with Winston, and we both began to write up our reports on the hotel meeting of the 15th. We were comprehensive in our description of the meeting and especially so in describing how LEMON reacted to learning of our eventual objective of acquiring access to all Consulate communications. I also included a review of the Station's planning session with the Field Office for the meeting on the 17th. Our reports went out late that afternoon. The final operational task of the day was to stop on the way home at a pay telephone and make a reservation at the Italian restaurant for a table for two for dinner. Knowing the restaurant's layout, I requested a specific location once again under the guise of the need to discuss a complicated business deal during the meal.

The next morning was spent framing out the scenario I would use with LEMON. It was going to be pretty much along the lines of what a good used car salesman tries to do with a customer. However, there were a few tricks of the trade that I had used before, which I included. Upon completion of my outline, I called in Winston and Stan to review it with them for suggestions. Edmund was out conducting another development operation at the time. During this meeting, I also received a brief reply from Headquarters regarding our reporting on the meeting of the 15th. It was from the NSA Liaison unit, and simply advised that they were aware of the problem and understood we were working to solve it. This expression of confidence was encouraging and greatly appreciated.

As usual, prior to an operational meeting, I left the Station several hours before the scheduled meeting. I did a particularly careful countersurveillance run, and then settled into a movie at a local shopping mall's theater

CHAPTER TWENTY-TWO: PUTTING IT BACK TOGETHER

before taking a taxi to the restaurant. I planned my timing to arrive about fifteen minutes before LEMON should show up. Upon exiting the taxi at the restaurant, I took a brief moment to scan the area for any indications of surveillance. I did not see any.

Inside the establishment, I had to wait but a few minutes until I was shown to my table in the requested area, pretty much visually isolated from the main portion of the restaurant and not visible from outside. LEMON arrived on schedule, we shook hands, and he sat down. Per usual, we ordered some scotches and I opened the conversation by inquiring about his son's health. It is always good to keep one of the main motivating elements up front. He provided an update, indicating that the treatments seemed to be working, and Anton's energy level and mental prowess had seemed to improve. I next asked about his dental problems. He responded quite happily, stating that the antibiotics really seemed to have kicked in and he was really feeling much healthier and vigorous. However, he noted, he was still somewhat concerned about the pain involved as the dentist planned to basically redo this entire mouth.

By this time, we had finished our second scotch, and I suggested we order since I wanted to talk with him about his employment with the corporation. We rather quickly reviewed the menu and ordered.

I began my scenario by noting that our dinner this evening was "off the books." I had not advised the boss of his concerns over our corporate plans, and he was also not aware that you and I were meeting this evening. I said "You should consider this as a private session between two friends and colleagues, Just between us, the boss has taken a personal interest in you and your son's health issues. He is a soft-hearted guy, and incredibly loyal to his people. He appreciated the detail you put into your reporting, and even though it has, frankly, not been of great value to corporate profits, he sees it as demonstrating your technical expertise which he believes can be useful in other corporate projects." I concluded by noting "I know the boss is considering you for acceptance as a full employee, even while you continued your position with the Romanian Government."

LEMON reacted well to these comments and compliments, expressing his sincere appreciation for the funds and the health care benefits which the corporation had provided. He stated that he was very impressed with the boss in the sense of his obvious business skills, but even more in his sincere interest in him and his family. He went on to say that the boss was exactly the type of person he admired; one who cared about his people and could be counted on to take care of them. This type of person, he noted, was not all that common at the Ministry of Foreign Affairs or among his comrades in the Romanian Communist Party. He then continued his praise of our relationship, mentioning that since we had started to work together, he had felt that I was a loyal friend and colleague whom he could trust. That was why he felt comfortable expressing his concerns about what might be asked of him by the corporation to me, even though it was somewhat awkward with Franklin in the room.

I thanked him for his trust and confidence, and stated that what I wanted was to see him enjoy the benefits of full corporate employment and the comfort and security this would provide. And, in this regard I wanted to give him privately, on a person-to-person basis, some additional insights into the reach and scope of the boss' influence.

At this point, the antipasto arrived along with a bottle of the Chianti. As we ate, I explained, that a major attraction of employment by the boss, even if a non-public relationship was involved and, indeed, this was the case with a significant number of corporate employees who kept their official positions to support corporate objectives, was the high compensation level, which could be paid in a manner to render insignificant both public record exposure and tax liability. Also, the comprehensive health care and investment plans provided by the corporation were outstanding. I noted he was aware of the excellent health plan already, and that even as a current probationary employee, the corporation paid all costs of the program. I added that once he became a full employee, there were investment options he could choose, which would assure his financial future and shield his financial accounts from the view of any government. After about ten years, he would likely be in a position to live anywhere he wanted in the world with a comfortable retirement package that may even include the provision

CHAPTER TWENTY-TWO: PUTTING IT BACK TOGETHER

of a residence, car, etc., depending upon how he chose to take his annuity package. This course of conversation clearly interested LEMON, who asked a few questions about the investment options, but really gave away his interest with his facial expression and body language.

As we addressed our entrée, I became serious in both demeanor and tone. I stated, "To be quite frank and truthful with you, there are several risks involved with your activities for the corporation based upon your employment by the Romanian Government." I noted that I knew he was well aware of these risks, but that it was important for him to understand that we were also aware of them. I continued that while this dual employment situation was new to him, the corporation was very experienced in handling such situations. We had numerous employees involved in similar situations worldwide. "Obviously," I confided, "I cannot provide any specifics about these situations since the corporation prides itself on the confidentiality of its activities. That said„ I want to give you as full a picture as possible of how any risks you take for the corporation can be managed to protect you and your family."

I began by explaining,We have experts within the company who have analyzed security procedures at both private and government organizations worldwide. Thanks to other contacts developed over many years, our information base included information from governmental organizations as well as private security research firms. Thus, when you combine this degree of information with the knowledge of the individual already working within the installation, a very clear picture can be drawn of what procedures are in place and how to overcome them. Any time you would be asked to bring out or take in any material, it would only be after you, and our experts, were fully confident that it could be accomplished safely in light of the security practices in effect."

"However," I continued," regardless of the best planning, there is always going to be some risk. So, the corporation will have backup plans to assist you and your family should you accidentally be caught in an action. First, you will have a plausible story to explain why what you were doing was within the scope of how you saw your job. This story would be created by you and the corporation prior to you undertaking any such activity. While you might be punished for poor judgment, the story would blunt any indications that you were actually providing protected information to someone outside of the Consulate. In the past, there have been some instances where an employee has been detected by his other employers, and the "story" has worked, with the individual receiving only a reprimand or a reduction in pay. The basic human reaction to finding a friend or colleague doing something wrong is to believe that it was a mistake and not a deliberate act."

"But, assuming that the story did not stand up, and again this has never happened as yet, there will be other plans also in place. Considering the absolute worst situation, that you were caught and sent home with your family for punishment, specifically in your case, the corporation would have the capability to affect the way in which the Romanian Government handles your case. I certainly cannot go into details, but rest assured that any punishment you received would be light. And, that after an appropriate period of time, you and your family would be able to leave the country and settle elsewhere, while still employed by the corporation. This would be handled in a manner that also ensured your relatives remaining in Romania would not be affected at all." I added "You already have some idea of the scope and depth of the contacts that the boss had within the Warsaw Pact, so you can understand how such capabilities would be used to protect you."

LEMON appeared to think deeply about my statements, and the seriousness of his facial expression reflected this. Certainly, some of the stories told by the boss at our previous meetings had reflected these types of relationships. Was he going to buy it?

Now, in reality, just how much of a lie had I just told LEMON: probably not as much as non-professionals might think. We did know a great deal about security procedures within the Consulate, both as they were supposed to be practiced and as they really were. And, at the meeting where the Target would be asked to bring out the material, he would also be fully debriefed on how he perceived security measures were handled at the Consulate. So, his actions and his cover story would be based on accurate knowledge of the procedures he had to defeat to be successful. However, as to the support he could expect if sent back to Romania, here the situation becomes a bit messy. If caught by the local security service, we would have little effect on how he was judged and punished. However, we certainly would try to be supportive of his family, and look at any opportunity to trade a Warsaw Pact spy for him. So, much of what I told the target was substantially accurate, details notwithstanding.

LEMON remained quiet for several minutes as we finished our main course, and the waiter brought the dessert, coffee, and cognac, which I thought we both needed at this point. I broke the silence by noting, in my most sincere voice, that now the Target had all the facts I could provide to him. He was well aware of the benefits he would enjoy as an employee of the corporation, and he knew the risks he might have to take, as well as the precautions and support the corporation could provide to mitigate those risks. He responded slowly and carefully, looking deep into my eyes, and stated "I appreciate how frank you have been, especially your willingness to explain how the corporation could reduce the risk factors." "It is," he continued, "a matter of trust in my mind." He explained that the money and particularly the health care for his son were very important to him. Neither would be possible without the corporation. Should he become a full employee of the corporation, he and his family's future would certainly be assured. He and his wife could live very comfortably either in Romania or elsewhere, and their son could be assured of a good education and solid financial start in his own life. He concluded, "I am lucky just to have this opportunity."

"Yet," he continued, "I am not a fool and recognized the risk involved regardless of any precautions that might be made to reduce them. It is really a matter of trust. Who do I trust more, you and the corporation, or my government and the Romanian Communist Party? Where I put my trust, I put my family's future. "I nodded in agreement and took a heavy belt of my cognac. We were about to arrive at the moment of truth—had I put it back together or was the ultimate objective of the operation about to vanish? I say that because even if he refused to assist in obtaining the coded tapes, it was quite possible he would agree to continue meetings to discuss what he read on a daily basis and what was going on within the Consulate. That information would still have some intelligence value to both the Agency and the Field Office. But, frankly, very little when compared to what the Intelligence Community would gain from access to Romanian communications.

LEMON took a large gulp of his cognac, almost emptying the glass, put his hand on mine, and said, "While I am still afraid of the risk, I owe it to my family and myself to place my trust in the corporation." He then explained that having seen the way political influence and personal gain operate as the principal factors in promotions and financial success within his government and Party, he had to have more trust in the corporation. Perhaps more importantly, he trusted me and the boss because we had been loyal to him and provided things like health care that he never would have been able to do on his own. LEMON explained, "In my dealings with the boss, it is obvious that he is an extremely powerful man, and the few details he gave about his interaction with Communist officials described the system as I have come to know it." He said, "I want to continue as an employee of the corporation, and just hope that whatever tasks I am asked to perform are planned in such a manner as to protect me from exposure within the Consulate."

I calmly responded that I felt he had made the right decision, and that there was no real comparison between the expertise and capabilities of the corporation and that of the Consulate. I then signaled the waiter and order two more cognacs, and put on my most tranquil facial expression as I quietly took a couple of deep breaths. Now all I had to do was arrange another meeting and we were back on track. The adenine was flowing, but I couldn't show it.

We finished our drinks while I set up another meeting for early in the first week of August. As was now standard procedure, LEMON was to call my office on July 27th to get all the details. I mentioned that Franklin would also be at this meeting to further discuss details of his project and

CHAPTER TWENTY-TWO: PUTTING IT BACK TOGETHER

possibly ask LEMON's advice on certain parts of it. As we were about to leave the table, I put my hand on LEMON's shoulder and softly said, "Now remember, our dinner this evening was just a private one between you and me. Do not mention it ever to anyone else in the corporation. It is our little secret." LEMON responded with a slight nod and a firm handshake.

I walked with him out to the street and waited until he had departed in a taxi. I then took a short five-minute walk around the hotel area, and noted that pedestrian traffic was becoming light and most of the shops had closed. So, I hailed a taxi and took it to a second hotel a few miles away, which happened to have entrances on two parallel one-way streets. Entering one entrance, I slowly walked through the lobby to the other entrance, and grabbed a cab to the shopping mall and my car.

Driving home, I had an awful thought. What if I had not been persuasive, or if LEMON had already confessed his sins to his security folks? Had his behavior at the restaurant only been an act to sucker me in for a double agent operation? Funny how suddenly you can go from elation to despair so quickly. Regretfully, this is also a common trait in a CO's personality. However, the pragmatic side of my nature quickly recovered. If LEMON was playing with me, as opposed to the other way around, the Field Office should have picked up some indications of this either at the Consulate or during their surveillance of the target.

When I got home, I was still too excited to sleep. And, anyway, I had to get the important details of the meeting down on paper while they were still fresh in my mind. Early in the morning, I went to bed and slept pretty well, actually believing that we did have the operation back on track, and that my report to Headquarters in the morning would be an optimistic one.

Upon entering the Station mid-morning, the first thing I did was call in Winston, Stan and Edmund to brief them on the atmospherics of the dinner. After that, I finalized my report to Headquarters and was about to send it when I got a call from Larry. I had sort of forgotten about advising the Field Office of the successful meeting, but his call gave me the excuse to say that I was just about to call Ralph when he telephoned. I then briefly told him the result of the meeting and that he and I would both be at the next meeting in early August. I asked him to pass the good news about LEMON's continued cooperation along to Ralph and Matt, noting that I would send a copy of my report on the meeting as soon as I had it completed. As I was about to hang up, Larry advised that the reason he had called was to give me a report on the Field Office's monitoring of the Consulate and LEMON's activities. Once again, I had been so focused, or perhaps relieved is a better word, on advising Headquarters that the operation was back on track that I had forgotten my earlier counterintelligence concerns.

Larry had good news. The Field Office had arranged for real-time language support and monitored its audio and telephonic penetrations of the Consulate for the entire business day. They also surveilled all three of the known Romanian security officials assigned to the facility throughout the day and had similar coverage on LEMON from the time he left his residence yesterday morning until he arrived home after our dinner. None of their efforts picked up any indication that LEMON's meeting with me was known to the Consulate or that any surveillance activities took place at or from the restaurant.

After thanking Larry and requesting that he thank Ralph for all the labor intensive support the Field Office had put into this effort, I decided that I should add this information into my meeting report. That took me about half an hour so the report was not actually transmitted until a few minutes after noon.

We now had about nine days to decide where and when to hold the next meeting. And, several days after that to finalize our scenario for the actual tasking of LEMON to bring out the code tape portions. Plenty of time to look at the status of the operation objectively, and that was good because at the moment a subjective sense of accomplishment seemed to be guiding most of my thinking.

Late in the afternoon Ralph called and we spoke briefly about the meeting. We agreed that we would hold a strategy session the next week and he noted that Larry would be available at our convenience to assist in planning for the next meeting. I hoped that before that session we would have some

CHAPTER TWENTY-TWO: PUTTING IT BACK TOGETHER

response from Headquarters and agreement that we should go ahead with the coded tape portions' tasking.

Headquarters did respond Monday afternoon. Actually, we got two separate messages, one from the NSA/LU and one from the Deputy Chief of the SE Division. Paul's message was informal and typical of his personality. He said it was to be expected that LEMON would now start to get concerned about his personal security because he was starting to realize the actual objectives he was being paid to attain. He said this was normal and that we should manipulate the situation to our benefit, as after all, that is why the Agency pays us so well. He concluded by writing "Now get the fuck back on the job and get us those tapes."

The liaison unit's communications were much more professional. It said that while it did not handle the recruitment of human assets, it did realize that the recruitment cycle always had its ups and downs. They expressed confidence in how we were handling the operation and reminded us that if we did need any additional Headquarters support, they were prepared to provide it. They concluded their message by adding an additional requirement to obtaining the tape portions—they also wanted a small sample of the plastic wrap which encased the coded tapes. And, they offeed a suggestion that we could explain the desire for the plastic within the concept that the laser apparatus would have to read the tape's marking through the plastic wrap, so its composition and width were important elements to factor into the calibration of the laser reader.

I responded that same afternoon to both messages, expressing appreciation for the Section's continuing support, and telling Paul that the real reason the Agency paid me so much was that I was working in the field, not pushing a damn pencil in a Headquarters office. I also added that I was hard at work on getting the tapes, and he should busy himself in some meaningless bureaucratic issues and let the field guys handle things. I figured he would appreciate my feisty tone and wording. Now this is not normally the way one corresponds with a senior officer in any management structure, either private sector or government, but as fellow CO, we shared a common understanding of how human intelligence operations are run. And, within the CO community, alpha-type behavior is pretty acceptable, within limits. Also, I knew Paul well enough that he would take my response as I had taken his—as collegial banter.

Thursday morning, Ralph, Matt, and Larry arrived at the Station for our planning session. The objective of the next meeting, which we decided would be August 4th, was to task LEMON with providing the tape portions and a piece of the plastic wrapping of the tapes. The real planning was how to arrange a scenario for Larry to use in explaining the concept of the laser reader and why we needed the samples to assist in calibrating the apparatus. We ponder whether we needed to find an expert in laser technology to give Larry a quick tutorial on the technology involved. The Agency certainly could find such an individual, but the question was whether someone could be found and a meeting arranged before the early August meeting. Ralph noted that the Field Office might have some contacts at a nearby National Laboratory who could help, but that might also take too much time to arrange. So, we decided that Larry was going to have to do some independent study and then come up with an appropriately sounding technical explanation of how the laser reader was being developed to work, and how the tape and plastic wrapping bits fit into the development. Larry was alright with this approach, and it was agreed that he would spend the next week studying the technical subject and drafting a story that accomplished both purposes in convincing LEMON that his tasking was necessary to the project's completion.

I also explained that since the hotel meeting would not be as grand a stage as when Winston was present, I would pick up the Target and take him to the hotel, where Franklin would be waiting in the suite. Also, in my operational role, I would handle booking the room and acquiring the rental car. I thought this was a fair tradeoff since, from a Field Office perspective, we were going to be using a great deal of Larry's time in preparation for this meeting.

The next day, I booked the suite at a suburban five-star hotel and also reserved a new model town car at the airport. I then returned to the Station and prepared the message I wanted my Wilmington "office" to give

CHAPTER TWENTY-TWO: PUTTING IT BACK TOGETHER

to LEMON when he telephoned in on the 27th. It was a simple message: you will be picked up at 7:45 p.m. on August 4th at the corner of 23rd and Harcourt Street.

The morning of the 28th I received a priority message from Headquarters: the telephone office had given LEMON the message but he responded that he could not make a meeting on the 4th because his boss was holding an event at the office and everyone was expected to attend. Instead, he suggested that the meeting be held on the 5th. In a case like this there is a standard operating procedure in place—the "office" advises the caller to telephone back in two days' time for a new message. Crap! This was much more than just inconvenient. What if his excuse about a Consulate professional obligation was arranged so that somehow the Romanians could manipulate the meeting in a counterintelligence plot? All the old counterintelligence fears immediately came back into focus. In my world, when the target starts to manipulate the operational environment, it usually means trouble. I walked into Winston's office and gave him the news. We decided the first thing we should do is check with Ralph and determine if the Field office was aware of any special event at the Consulate, and if so when it had been planned and announced.

I called Ralph, but he was in a meeting and could not be disturbed. So, I asked to speak with Matt, who was available. I told him of LEMON's response to the message setting the date and time for the meeting, and asked if he knew anything about a special Consulate function on the evening of August 4th. He said he would check with his squad and get back to me as soon as possible. I thanked him and noted that I had to get the message of an alternate meeting time and date back to Headquarters quickly.

It was Ralph who called back about an hour later. He explained that since he had used his language capabilities to do "live" monitoring of the Consulate for several days during the recent meetings, he had then given them some comp time off. When they came back, there was a small backlog of translations to be completed, and then SAs had to review the transcripts for information of counterintelligence interest. All this took time, so he now had his people reviewing all the conversations at the Consulate from the 27th backward to the 17th. I told him that I needed to get a message to Headquarters no later than early the next morning to reset a time and date with LEMON for the next meeting. He replied that he would have his people work overtime as required.

I did not hear from the Field Office until just after the Station opened the next day. Matt phoned with some good news. On July 21st, a meeting was called by the Consul General, who advised that one of their key contacts in the local Romanian—American community was about to celebrate his 60th birthday. Since this individual was highly thought of by both Government and Party officials back in Bucharest, the Consul General had received instructions to hold a birthday celebration at the Consulate for the man. The evening of August 4 was to be the date, and the Consul General made it clear that all the Consulate employees and their spouses were expected to attend the event. Matt further confirmed that the American citizen whose birthday was to be celebrated was indeed considered an important contact by the Romanian Government, and so this honor made sense.

Based on this news, I wrote a message to the Telephone unit advising them that when LEMON called in that evening, he was to be told the meeting would be held on the 3rd, and the pickup location and time, the same as before, would again be given to him. I then decided to change the hotel and rental car reservations that afternoon, while I went out to get myself some lunch. The next morning, Headquarters advised LEMON had called in, got the message, and confirmed a meeting for the evening of the 3rd.

Now we only have a few days to finalize the operational scenario for the meeting. Most of the burden would fall on Larry explaining why we needed the tape and plastic wrapping bits. But I also had to use the meeting to continue building up LEMON's trust and confidence in the corporation. I had a pretty well-developed plan in this regard, and, to his credit, Larry had spent numerous hours studying the basics of laser technology and working the concept of the density and depth of the two materials into his scenario. So, all we had to do was coordinate our scenarios and then develop the chronology of the meeting. We also had time to run our final approach past Winston and do a dress rehearsal with him, Stan and Edmund in attendance.

Chapter Twenty-Three: The Laser Project

Larry drove out to the Station about midafternoon on the 3rd, and after a brief chat to review our planning, we drove in my car to the airport long-term parking area, and took the shuttle bus to the terminal. Then, after an in-terminal countersurveillance exercise, we went to the rental car office to pick up the town car. We drove to the hotel, checked in, and Larry and I prepared the room with the usual type of business clutter. We had a couple of hours to kill, so we organized the room service dinner and decided we would watch some TV. A decision which confirmed the popular view that afternoon TV programming is a wasteland.

I left the hotel garage about half an hour before the pickup time, and moved to a parking garage within five minutes of the pickup time in moderate traffic. With seven minutes to go, I left the garage and drove to the location. LEMON was waiting on the street corner and quickly jumped into the passenger seat. As we drove to the hotel, we had a bland conversation about the weather and downtown traffic. Upon arrival, I parked the car and we took the elevator to the suite. As we entered, Franklin greeted LEMON and shook his hand. I then suggested that after the stressful battle with local commuters, we all needed a drink. Off to the scotch bottle went Franklin, and soon we were sitting down and enjoying what I anticipated to be the first of many scotches that evening.

I opened the meeting by asking about the status of his son's health issues,

CHAPTER TWENTY-THREE: THE LASER PROJECT

noting the boss's personal interest in the subject. LEMON advised that all was going very well. The medicine continued to work, and his son's physical and mental activities continued to improve. I then inquired about his dental problems, again noting that it was a subject of personal interest to the boss. He responded that the gum disease was responding well to the medicine, and that the dentist had made several filling replacements during his last visit. But, at the next visit, it was planned to remove two teeth, which the dentist described as "rotten to the core and start treatment to replace them with implants. LEMON explained that overall, he felt better than he had in the last couple of years. But, he added, he was very anxious and dreaded the next visit. I attempted to set his mind at rest, explaining that modern dentistry techniques had greatly reduced the pain involved. Franklin added that perhaps he should ask the dentist to give him a mild tranquilizer before the treatment to help mitigate the anxiety and provide comfort during the treatment. LEMON thought that was a very good idea.

By now, we were into our second scotch, and it was time to get into the laser scenario. I introduced the subject by noting that Franklin wanted to explain the laser project to LEMON in some detail and determine if perhaps he had any thoughts on the development phase that might prove useful. Then, Franklin began his comprehensive, complex, technically worded, and purposely confusing description of the project. The basic point was that using a computer-guided laser as a reading device was based upon the depth of indentation in a material, and once established, images from that material could be "read" and subsequently printed out as accurate copies of those indentations. To accomplish this, the desired material would have to be rotated 360 degrees for a period of time for the laser to establish penetration and establish "read-in" points which would allow identification and copying of the indented images. Interestingly, LEMON warmed to the opportunity and asked some questions about the manner of timed rotation of the material and how the laser could penetrate without leaving any marks on the material itself. Franklin responded that this was actually the most difficult part of the research, and depended upon accurate measurement of both the material to be copied and any wrappings or covering materials protecting that material. In this vein, LEMON and Franklin discussed the project for about fifteen minutes, with Franklin explaining that initial tests had been mostly successful as long as all the materials to be penetrated were accurately measured.

We seemed to be moving nicely, but were interrupted by room service delivering the dinner. Our scenario called for Franklin to use the dinner to tell his story of joining the corporation and highlighting the professional and personal nature of his relationship with the corporation and the boss. I, in turn, would use a story to compare the corporation's benefits to those of a rival company, obviously with the corporation being the most generous and caring to its employees. So, we followed that script through dinner. After dessert, and yes, once again, LEMON had his torte, and I took this to be a good omen, we took our coffee back to the sitting area. Now Franklin made his pitch. He asked the Target how the tapes were packaged prior to use. LEMON responded that they were pressure sealed in a heavy plastic sleeve, and when opened, had to be done so in the presence of either the Consulate General or the Consulate's head of security. Then, upon cutting the sleeve open, he and the other official had to note the time and date of opening in a log. The tape was then placed back into the communications vault until it was used later that day. Once opened, he was authorized to remove it from the vault as needed to code or decode the communications traffic. If he were absent, his assistant would perform those duties, but with the Consulate General or the senior security officer present at all times.

Franklin then engaged LEMON in a discussion about his estimates of the thickness of the plastic sleeve and the tapes themselves. LEMON tried to make an estimate, but under specific questioning admitted that he did not have actual knowledge of their thicknesses. This led to a discussion of how to program the computer to have the laser accurately penetrate the plastic in order to read the tape. Franklin feigned frustration and then stated that, based upon what LEMON had said earlier, the only solution was to get actual samples of the plastic sleeve and the tapes so that their thicknesses could be accurately measured. LEMON rather reluctantly agreed that this was the logical approach.

Great, we had his agreement, but now had to discuss exactly how to do it. So, Franklin directly asked LEMON how the best way to obtain the samples could be accomplished. I added "You must factor into your answer the way which also made it safest for you to do so.," as if I really needed to mention it. LEMON gave this some thought for a few minutes. He finally responded that when a coded tape roll had been used up, and a new one had to be opened, he also had the responsibility of destroying the old tape and packaging, again with either the Consulate General or the senior security officer as the witness. However, usually both coded tapes did not get used up at the same time, and he often kept a used tape in the communications vault so he could destroy them both at the same time. He explained that destroying the tapes was done by placing the tape and packaging in an incinerator in the communications area and burning them to ashes.

He asked how big a section of the tapes and packaging was required, and Franklin responded that only a small portion was necessary to measure their width; however, the portions should be large enough to determine, particularly for the wrappings, if the width varied within the entire wrapping. So, about an inch should be sufficient. Somewhat surprisingly, LEMON felt the sample size suggested was too small.

Next, we discussed how to actually obtain the samples. And LEMON suggested that when the next coded tape was used up, he could cut off about an inch from its end and from its wrapping, and carry out those samples concealed on his person that evening. He would then hide the samples at his residence until the other tape ran out and repeat the process. Then, when he had all the samples desired, he would pass them to us. I noted, "That sounds like an excellent plan, and one that places you at very little risk." He agreed, noting that during the actual destruction of the used coded tapes, he was the only one who handled them, and the witness never inspected them before he placed them in the incinerator. The witness's only role was to note in the communication's log that the tapes had been destroyed securely. And, he added, this procedure had become pretty informal in reality.

I then queried when he felt he could provide the samples. He responded, "The current decoding tape is about two-thirds used, and the encoding tape about half used. I estimate the first tape will be finished in about two to three weeks, with the second tape one to two weeks later since there are several routine reports that have to be sent to Bucharest before the end of the month." I suggested that once he had all the portions of the samples in his possession, he call my office and leave a message that "his report was ready for delivery." My assistant would then give him a location, date, and time when he could expect Franklin or me to pick him up and get the samples. This plan gave him the option of when and how to get the samples without any deadline pressure, while still giving us control over the reception of the material.

LEMON agreed, and we had another scotch while we moved into the final phase of the meeting: the payment and security discussion. As we sipped our drinks, I opened my briefcase and brought out an envelope containing his one thousand five hundred dollar salary for August. He took the envelope with a polite "thank you" and, as usual, placed it in his suit coat inside pocket. I then raised the issue of his overall security, prefacing the topic on the fact that the corporation wanted him to understand and feel confident about his personal safety as he took some additional risks. This led to a half-hour-plus conversation covering how he spent or saved his "extra" funds, and what and how he let Consulate colleagues know about the treatment of health and dental issues. It turned out that LEMON was actually pretty disciplined in his handling of the funds and providing a cover story to explain his dental work. He apparently kept his son's medical treatments a private affair within the family. As expected, he had told his wife all about his association with the corporation, and she was supportive of his efforts, especially when the son's health was so well addressed by the medical benefits involved. When I complimented LEMON on his discretion, he responded that for anyone living in a Communist country, keeping personal matters private, particularly those

CHAPTER TWENTY-THREE: THE LASER PROJECT

involved in activities not openly sanctioned by the government, was a matter of practical survival.

This discussion ended the meeting, and I drove him back to the pickup site while Franklin remained in the suite. On the way back he seemed both pleased and relaxed. I felt great, of course, since we had gotten over a serious hurtle and the operation was back on track.

I returned to the hotel and rejoined Larry in the suite. We sat down and reviewed the meeting from each of our perspectives. We also wrote down some memory jogging notes that we could use to write our formal report the next day.

Just a little note here, since I just noted that my remembrance of all these meetings includes, what a civilian might think is a great deal of drinking. Well, that has to be taken in the context of the period and the target environment. During the period of the Cold War, our primary target was the Soviet Bloc, and within those countries, people drank a great deal. Thus, as early as basic CO training, we were taught to use alcoholic refreshments in our agent meetings. The unintended consequence, or perhaps it was intended, was that we became accustomed to operating in a disciplined and professional manner while consuming a decent amount of alcohol. Obviously, some people handled this better than others. The point is that one does build up a body tolerance with practice.

Anyway, Larry and I cleaned up the suite and I drove him back to his car, and then went home to type up my raw report. Once again I returned the car the following morning before going into the Station.

Upon arrival at the Station, I briefed Winston on the meeting and then spent the morning finalizing my report to Headquarters. I was briefly interrupted by a call from Ralph offering congratulations and advising that Larry's report on the meeting would be hand-carried by him to the Station. He did so a few days later, and I sent a copy of his report with some comments, complimenting his efforts in the operation, to Headquarters. SE Division complimented us on the progress being made, and the NSA/LU did likewise, and noted they looked forward to receiving the samples. Later in the week, we held a brief strategy meeting with the Field Office to organize resources for the next meeting, when LEMON would actually pass us the material samples. We agreed that the Agency's telephone office would be advised that when LEMON called in with the agreed-upon message, he would be told that three nights hence, at 8:10 p.m., he should be at the corner of Harcourt Ave. and Water Street to await pickup. When we received the word that LEMON had called and received the instructions, I would make arrangements to pick him up in a rented car. However, the Field Office would also have Matt and another SA stake out the pickup site and then follow me during the brief car meeting when I received the samples. Once I left LEMON off back at the site, they would continue to follow me back to the Station, where I would drop off the samples for safekeeping. That was about it. Now, we just wait.

Two weeks went by, and no call from LEMON. I checked with Ralph, who reported that everything seemed normal at the Consulate and at LEMON's residence. So, we waited.

Finally, five days before the end of the month, Headquarters advised that LEMON had called in the previous evening and given the message indicating he was ready to pass he samples. I went out and arranged to rent the car, and then briefly reviewed arrangements with Matt regarding their surveillance of the car pickup meeting. Everything was set to go.

I went through the usual procedures in picking up the car the afternoon of August 27th, and it was parked in a garage near the pickup location by 7:20 p.m. A bit early to be at that location in terms of usual tradecraft timing, but I was anxious. Matt and his partner were already in their vehicle, sitting on the pickup site. At 7:53 p.m. I left the parking garage and proceeded to the site, hitting it almost exactly on time after almost also hitting a pizza delivery vehicle, which aggressively pulled into the right lane on the one-way street to stop and deliver an order. City driving can be crazy, and particularly frustrating when trying to make very specific driving progress. LEMON quickly entered the passenger side, and we drove off. I drove a prearranged route taking us onto an interstate highway, still quite busy with rush hour traffic. While driving, I asked if LEMON had any problems or security concerns or any other problems. He responded

CHAPTER TWENTY-THREE: THE LASER PROJECT

negatively, and I asked him to give me the material. He explained that he had two envelopes for me, one with the tape portion from an encryption tape and wrapping, and a second with the decryption tape portion and wrapping. Each envelope was marked appropriately. I took the envelopes and placed them in my coat pocket.

As I exited the highway to a city street and proceeded back towards the pickup location, I asked him if he had any problems in obtaining the samples. He said that he did not, and that the senior security officer who witnessed the destruction of the two used tapes paid little attention to them as he placed them in the incinerator. For that matter, he added, the samples had been so small that the material taken from the tapes and wrappings was hardly noticeable unless closely examined. I complimented him, stated that the boss will be very pleased with his work, and told him to call my office in one week to receive instructions regarding our next meeting. By this time, I had returned to the site, and after a firm handshake, LEMON left the car and began walking in the direction of his residence. I drove slowly for a few blocks, allowing time to see that Matt was behind me, and then drove back to the Station. At this point, the SAs were providing security for me in case something went wrong and I was unable to get the samples to the Station. But, there were no problems and I placed the samples inside a safe in my office, reset the Station's security apparatus, bade a "goodnight" to the SAs, and drove home.

The next day after returning the rental car, I went into the Station and sent a message stating the samples had been received and requesting instructions as to how they were to be sent to Headquarters. That afternoon, a reply came from the NSA/LU advising that Betsey would fly to the Station the following day and hand carry the samples back to Washington. She did arrive and was in the Station just long enough to pass along her unit's appreciation for our hard work. She boarded a plane back to Washington within three hours of her arrival.

I submitted my brief report of the car meeting for the record, and then once again all we could do was wait. LEMON was schedule to call in the evening of September 3rd. But, until we got Headquarters' readout on the samples and what to do next, there was little we could do in the way of planning.

On September 1st, we received some guidance. Betsey had taken the samples out to NSA on the 30th of August, and they were in the process of verifying them. Also, her unit was studying the samples to determine if they had similar materials in their stockpile in preparation for any future tape copying operation. We were advised that both examination processes could take several weeks, so from the Headquarter's perspective, the next meeting with LEMON could be postponed as long as we thought appropriate. Since he was about to call for details of the next meeting within a few days, I consulted with Winston, and we decided that from a "handling" perspective, we did not want to wait too long. So, we decided that we needed a hotel meeting on September 18th, with the objective of reinforcing LEMON's loyalty to the corporation.

Depending on the results from the NSA, we could always add other objectives to this meeting. I telephoned Ralph to discuss our thinking, noting that we would want Larry to play a role at this meeting as well. We agreed that we would hold a more formal planning session prior to the meeting.

The next morning I sent a message to the telephone unit advising them to tell LEMON the next meeting would be on September 18th, and providing him with the necessary information about the time and location of the pickup point. Two days later we were advised he had called in, received the instructions, and verified that he would be at the pickup point as directed. Now we had about two weeks to do our preparations.

At this point, Larry was also informally acting as a liaison between the Field Office and the Station in terms of keeping us advised of any unusual activities that were taking place either at the Consulate or LEMON's residence. He normally had little to report, but in the first week of September he called to advise that his squad had been advised by the local police that the wife of the junior Consulate security officer had been detained by store security at a high end lady's apparel shop in the

CHAPTER TWENTY-THREE: THE LASER PROJECT

main business area of the city. She was not formally arrested, as she had diplomatic status from her husband, and the store did not wish to publicize the incident. However, the police had obtained a copy of the video of her interrogation by the store security officer. Matt wanted to use the video to threaten the wife, and more importantly, the husband, into cooperating with the Bureau. He was confident that if exposed publicly, the Consulate would be embarrassed, as would the Consul General, and the couple would be sent back to Romania and probably punished. Larry was calling, actually at Ralph's request, to get my opinion on whether attempting to recruit the junior security officer would have any impact on the Briarpatch case.

I recognized at once that this was going to be a difficult conversation. The value of this recruitment to the Field Office was obvious, and even if it failed, the action by itself would be seen in FBI circles as a successful counterintelligence move. Yet from my perspective, this was going to be a "cold pitch," without any reason to assume it would be successful except for the threat involved. I would have to give it a fifty—fifty chance of success because I had no other information on the wife or her husband. In reality, based upon the Agency's attempts at "cold pitches" against Soviet Bloc targets, the odds tended to be much lower in terms of success—more like a ninety percent failure rate. However my biggest concern was what a rejection by the husband would do to the counterintelligence environment inside the Consulate.

If the husband refused to cooperate, his next step would have to be to advise his superior, the senior security officer, of the attempt. This would then be reported to the Consulate General and to the security officials in Bucharest. Both officials at the Consulate would be embarrassed, and logically, the counterintelligence posture of the installation would be heightened immediately. This could certainly affect LEMON's capabilities to bring out the coded tapes, and would probably also affect his emotional state regarding this task. Therefore, from the perspective of the LEMON operation, this was a risk not worth taking. Yet, it was one the Field Office might see much differently and had every legal right to do as they saw fit.

By this time, I considered Larry to be part of the team, but certainly did not expect him to see things from an Agency perspective. So, I spoke with him on the secure line and talked out the pros and cons of the situation as I saw them, emphasizing the value of the ultimate objective of the operation—acquisition of total access to Romanian and hopefully some Warsaw Pact communications—in contrast to the degree of risk involved. He listened carefully and said that he agreed with me that the risk and potential gain for US counterintelligence of attempting a "cold pitch" was not worth threatening the Briarpatch case. However, it was Ralph's call, and he asked if I wanted to speak with him. I responded that I recognized this was Ralph's decision, and all I could ask was that he advise Ralph of my argument against the recruitment attempt. I thanked him and hung up.

Later that afternoon, the sky cleared once again. Ralph phoned to tell me that in discussion with the Field Office SAC and Matt, the decision had been made not to attempt a recruitment of the junior security officer for the time being. Instead, Matt's squad would increase surveillance of the wife and attempt to develop more evidence of her criminal behavior, and other squad members would start to put together a personality profile on the husband to see if there were any indications that he might be susceptible to cooperating with the FBI. No action would be taken until the Briarpatch case was fully exploited. This was a very well thought-out decision, and it actually made me wonder if I had been far too dismissive in my judgment of the strategic counterintelligence thinking of the Field Office.

About that time, I also received a brief message from the SE Division Chief, stating that their evaluation panel had met and decided that LEMON could now be considered a "valid commercial recruitment" and the Station could claim him as such in its correspondence. While this was good news bureaucratically, it had little practical effect on the operation. However, when I told Ralph, he was quite pleased and noted that Matt would be even happier. Apparently the official designations of LEMON as an "agent," or "asset" in FBI parlance, would benefit the SAs in their performance evaluations. I must admit this designation would also benefit Brenda, Stan, Edmund and Winston in their annual performance reviews. However, as this was a highly compartmentalized operation, their services would

CHAPTER TWENTY-THREE: THE LASER PROJECT

be noted in a separate memorandum not seen by the entire Performance Review Panel. Now, as to benefiting me, as Chief of Station, there were a great many other factors which came into play when Headquarters appraised my annual performance.

About a week before the scheduled meeting, we got confirmation from NSA that the tape samples were indeed from a recently expended set of coding tapes used by the Romanian Government. That meant our next meeting could be full of compliments and rewards for LEMON. We would structure it as a celebratory dinner party, with the boss presiding. The boss would also authorize a bonus of $2500 for the samples. The meeting would be short, but sweet, we hoped, in LEMON's eyes. Larry was also tasked with the usual health and dental updates. The last thing we wanted was to plan the party and have LEMON suddenly advise his son was not doing well, or that his dental treatments were creating problems. Happily, Larry was able to report good news in both health areas.

I also hoped we might hear from the NSA/LU before the meeting so we could start to mention what might be the next reporting requirements. But if not, the agent would just be advised to stay alert for any communications he saw that might have commercial value.

The usual cast of characters would be at the hotel meeting, and procedures would be the same as with the previous meeting where the boss was present. Ralph handled arrangements for the hotel suite and town car. Since there was no tasking per se, and the evening was to be focused on camaraderie among corporate personnel, we did not need much of a detailed scenario. Winston did, however, script out a couple of stories he would tell over dinner to further impress LEMON with his access and power.

The morning of the 17th, we heard back from the NSA/LU. We were advised that after a search of their paper stockpile, which they described as representative of paper stock available to most countries in the world, they had not found a match for the paper used in the samples. They advised that they were in the process of contacting individuals at the NSA to determine if anyone knew where the Romanian Government obtained this paper stock. Finally, and obviously, they noted that no plans could go forward to copy the tapes until an exact paper match could be made. Although I did not know it at the time, in this type of copy operation, while the actual tape is copied onto a similar tape, the tape that is returned to the agent is the copied one, not the original, which is retained by the unit for passage to NSA. The agent is never told this, of course. NSA/LU requested that we determine if LEMON had any information as to where his government procured the paper for the coded communications tape. I decided that the best way to bring up this subject was to have Larry handle it as the corporation's technical expert. So, we added that to our scenario.

Everything went as usual on the 18th, and by 7:43 p.m., Patrick had LEMON at the door of the suite. Winston, Larry, and I were already having drinks in the sitting area, and the agent was welcomed, invited to join us, and served a drink by Patrick. After a few minutes of meaningless social conversation, the boss inquired as to how the son's health was. And, LEMON was very pleased to report that the doctor's efforts were proving highly successful. His comments again echoed what the doctor had told Larry, and he made a point of noting how pleased and happy both he and his wife were with their son's progress. Now, as usual, he thanked the boss for his personal interest in the son's health. Winston responded that when he came to know and like a person, he always took a personal interest in that individual's family. He added that in addition to his physical well-being, LEMON and his wife should also be thinking about their son's future education, even though he was still too young for school. Winston concluded that education was the key to future success, and the corporation understood this and had various employee benefits in support of this.

The boss then inquired as to the agent's personal dental status. LEMON stated that both his wife and his son had recently had checkups with the dentist, and with the exception of one filling for his wife, both were judged to be in good dental health. As to himself, LEMON noted happily, his gum disease had been cured, and the dentist was in the process of several other dental procedures. While feeling much better, the bad part was that the dentist's work created some pain at each visit. But, he added, because his

CHAPTER TWENTY-THREE: THE LASER PROJECT

mouth felt so much better, he was enjoying eating more, and had even put on a few pounds over the past month. In response, the boss expressed satisfaction that the dental problems were being addressed.

Winston then moved on to the samples which LEMON had provided. He said that Franklin had told him how important it was to the development of the laser project that these samples be available for calibration of the test equipment. That the agent had been able to provide them so quickly was a significant value to the progress of what was a very difficult and expensive research project. "Based upon your actions, which I believe clearly demonstrated your commitment to the corporation's objectives," Winston said, "I have instructed Robert to provide you with a bonus of $2500." The boss continued, "Based upon your initiative in support of our business goals, I am considering making you a permanent employee of the corporation." LEMON responded with a smile and thanked the boss for his confidence.

When room service arrived, and Patrick had completed organizing the dinner service, we four sat down and proceeded to eat. This evening, the meal featured a French theme, with accompanying wines. Over dinner, Winston regaled us with a couple of stories of international business dealings involving paying off various governmental officials to obtain exclusive contracts and to allow the transshipment of equipment to countries in spite of international agreements prohibiting them. Winston ended one story by noting that a senior official in one of the major promoter countries of a ban on advanced computer technology was actually a junior stock owner in a corporation whose European country sold the equipment, knowing full well its actual destination. He concluded his remarks by stating that "For those in the know, business is business and petty political differences seldom stand in the way of business."

After dinner we returned to the sitting area and a bit more scotch, although Winston continued to drink the French Chateau St. Clair Burgundy, which, after the agent had departed, he explained he was developing a taste for. Then, I reminded him of the actual cost of the bottle and he quickly decided that California Burgundy probably was also to his taste.

Anyway, once we settled in, Franklin mentioned that his research folks were a bit surprised at the density of the tape samples. Apparently, the tapes they had been using as testing materials were less dense. So, Franklin wondered if these tapes were made from some special paper rather than from regular stock used by various countries for communications tapes. LEMON thought about the question for a moment, taking a long sip of his drink, and then said that his professional responsibilities were just to control and utilize the coded tapes, and that the tapes were provided by the Ministry of Foreign Affairs in Bucharest. He continued that while he was stationed at the Ministry, he had worked with individuals from the procurement branch of the Communications Bureau, but had never heard anything about how they obtained their paper stock.

Franklin attempted to dig a bit deeper and ask if LEMON had ever seen any procurement documents that might have identified where paper stocks were being purchased. The agent responded, "No, I have never seen such information. "Franklin's last question did produce a slightly more helpful answer: did the agent know if the Ministry or the Romanian Government produced their own paper stock for official use, perhaps including the communications' tapes? LEMON said that he was pretty sure that the paper material used for the tapes was purchased, and that it was not like the other paper stock used by the government for documents and normal writing and printing purposes.

This seemed to be about all the agent knew on the subject, so Franklin ended this course of questioning. I then moved the conversation back to a casual subject: world soccer. For a few minutes, we discuss the current state of play in Eastern Europe, with LEMON being quite knowledgeable on the players and standings of various Warsaw Pact national teams.

As it approached 10:30 p.m., Winston stood up and said, "Gentlemen, it has been a most enjoyable evening, but I fear I must excuse myself as I depart early in the morning for a meeting in Egypt. Patrick, please drive Mr. Bazna back to where you picked him up. Good night." He then walked into the suite's bedroom.

CHAPTER TWENTY-THREE: THE LASER PROJECT

Franklin and I stood, as did LEMON, and I gave him an envelope with his September retainer and the $2500 bonus. Once again, without looking inside the envelope, he placed it in his coat jacket pocket. I then told him that I had a busy schedule for the next several weeks. I suggested that he call my office on the evening of October 9th, and by that time, I should know when I would be back in the city. I also reminded him to always call from a pay telephone in an area away from both the Consulate and his residence, and to use one that seemed to have frequent use. With that, we all shook hands, and Patrick escorted him down to the car in the basement parking garage.

Upon hearing LEMON leave, Winston re-appeared and we three spend about an hour discussing our perceptions of the meeting and jotting down some notes for our official reports. We cleaned up the room, and when Patrick returned we all departed, following our usual security practices, because that is what professionals do.

When I arrived at the Station the next morning, with a fairly complete meeting report prepared before going to bed last evening, I found that Winston had decided to sleep-in. He came in a couple of hours later, explaining that perhaps red wine was a bit hard on his constitution. I commented that this would surely save him a great deal of money considering his expensive taste in wine last night.

Chapter Twenty-Four: Waiting

We had our reports completed by noon, and after a brief secure telephone conversation with Larry to make sure that his report was similar to ours' in details, they were sent to Headquarters. We had three weeks to set the date and develop an agenda for the next meeting. Now that we had a cooperating agent, we could start some planning for the removal of the tapes and their copying.

Yet, it was also clear that it was the NSA/LU that would decide when we did the deed. Until they were prepared to do the copying there was little point in removing the tapes. And, as we soon learned, their task was not as simple as one might think. At this point they did not even have the right type of paper to use to make copies.

The complexity of the unit's issues began to dawn on us near the end of the month. We received a message from them advising that contacts with their usual paper suppliers had proven useless—none had that particular paper stock. The one bright spot was that they had a lead from a European Liaison service that a company in Austria was a supplier of paper stock to the Ministry of Foreign Affairs in Romania. They advised that they were in the process of sending two of their officers to the city of Purkersdorf, near Vienna. If the company did make the stock, the officers would order several rolls. From there, it would be brought, in a clandestine manner, to the NSA and made into tape spools.

It was apparent that we were in for a several-month delay before we could remove the tapes from the Consulate. Still, we understood the work required to purchase and ship the paper once it was found. But, the FBI

CHAPTER TWENTY-FOUR: WAITING

does not always fully understand the difficulties and time involved in accomplishing such tasks in a secure manner. For example, if the Bureau wants to document a SA in an alias or use a commercial entity to purchase or transport goods, it is usually as an American citizen or entity, and they have extensive contacts within the US business community that permit them to quickly associate themselves in that role. The Agency, however, must use more discreet and often foreign guises in such activities.

So, I did have to do a little explaining to Ralph and Matt regarding why operational momentum with LEMON was going to be a bit slow, at least for the next couple meetings or so. Of course they understood once it was explained—we just work in a more difficult environment then they do for the most part.

By October 7th, we had decided that the next meeting with the agent would be a hotel meeting, with LEMON, Larry, and me. We planned a rather brief meeting, with drinks and snacks, where Larry would conduct a debriefing of the agent regarding security procedures for the coded tapes within the Communications room. We decided the date would be October 20th, and a message providing all the details for the car pickup was forwarded to Headquarters on October 8th. The morning of the 10th, we were advised that LEMON had received the message and confirmed his appearance.

There really wasn't much more to do until the meeting. Larry kept us advised of any unusual activities at the Consulate or LEMON's residence, as well as visiting both the doctor and the dentist to monitor any health issues. The son was doing fine, but the dentist noted he was working very hard not to have to remove all of the upper teeth and go to a full upper false plate. Larry also mentioned, just as an aside, that he had noticed a picture in the dentist's office of a sailboat, and soon, he noted, he expected to see a photo of a yacht on that wall.

We also received an update on the NSA/LU's progress regarding the paper stock at the Austrian company. Their officers were prepared to travel to Austria either in late October or early November. That was good news.

Everything went smoothly on the 20th. We were in the hotel suite by 7:45 p.m., with Franklin serving drinks. As usual, I first inquired if all was going well and if LEMON had any problems at work. He replied no to these questions, but noted that he had been busy since radio traffic from Bucharest and other Warsaw Pact countries had been heavy. He noted that the Soviets were instructing several countries to take a hard line in their dealing with so-called "reformist" elements who were involved in public protests in some of the Warsaw Pact nations. He added that the Consul General had been instructed to put word out in the local Romanian-American community that these reformist elements were actually being directed and financed by the US Government to provoke bloodshed in the streets. We discussed this for a short time, with LEMON's opinion being that those protests were probably nothing more than local attempts by troublemakers to get press coverage.

LEMON did mention one concern he had, as he had visited the dentist two days previously and gotten some bad news. The dentist advised he would not be able to save four teeth in his lower left jaw; they would have to be pulled and replaced with a full bridge. The dentist admitted that even with pain numbing injections this was going to hurt and there would be a period of several days when his left jaw would be quite swollen.

We both expressed our sympathy, but also noted that in the long run, his overall health would benefit from all his dental work. However, the agent continued, he was not just concerned with the pain. He said that several weeks ago, he had mentioned to his colleagues that he had identified a dentist who was working on his mouth. He told them that the dentist was an Indian national and that his prices were much lower than those of American dentists. However, the dentist's equipment was also old, and this often made for some painful sessions. LEMON believed that this story explained why he could afford at least some dental care, as he was concealing the extent of the work from his colleagues. Now, it seemed it would be obvious to his colleagues that he was having extensive dental work once he showed up at the Consulate with a swollen left jaw.

We talked about this concern for a while, finally agreeing that the best cover story would be to build on his previous comments regarding the poor equipment and technique of the "Indian dentist." LEMON would explain that the dentist had attempted to repair some teeth and in the process an infection had set-in, which had caused his jaw to swell. It was agreed this story should satisfy his colleagues, since few people really want to probe into an issue involving a painful dental injury.

As we worked into a second scotch, I reminded LEMON that the boss had mentioned that he was considering making him a full employee. I said that, privately speaking, the boss was very near doing so, and I suspected I might make his decision soon. The agent smiled and made some casual comments about continuing to try and do all he could to assist the corporation.

Franklin then moved the conversation to the coded tapes. He explained that the research project was moving along, but there were occasional problems with calibrations that had to be solved. Meanwhile, in order to fully understand how the procedures in the Communications room worked, he wanted the agent to answer some questions. First, he asked about the procedures for opening in the morning and closing down at night. Who did what and how it was done. Then, he got to the real objective—the reception, storage, use and destruction of the coded tapes. LEMON and Franklin spent almost an hour on these subjects, and we learned a great deal. The Romanian Ministry of Foreign Affairs sent the coded tapes by diplomatic pouch, accompanied by an official Ministry courier, whenever the Consulate notified it that they had just unsealed the last coded tape at the Consulate. Two coded tapes of each kind, decoding and encoding, were included in each shipment. LEMON repeated his earlier description of how the tapes were checked and witnessed by either the Consul General or the senior security officer when opened and when destroyed. However, he was responsible for utilizing the opened tapes and storing them, along with the unsealed tapes, in the Communications room vault. And, the vault did not have a timer that recorded when the vault was opened and closed.

Now having the information we wanted, I moved the conversation towards whether the agent had heard or seen anything at the Consulate that might have some commercial exploitation possibility for the corporation.

LEMON responded that the only thing he had seen recently was a notice from Moscow that it was about to sell the People's Republic of China several million rubles worth of police crowd control items, including various armored motor units. Since these items were Soviet internally produced, and to be shipped via the Trans-Siberian Railway to China, he was not sure there was any way the corporation might profit. I said that I tended to agree with him, but would advise the corporation and let it decide if this offered any commercial possibilities.

It was getting on past 10 p.m. as we had yet another drink, and I gave LEMON his monthly retainer for October of $1,500. I then explained that I had a lengthy business trip to the Far East planned for November, which might extend into December. However, he was to call my office on November 14th because by then, I would know when I would be back in the city.

My thinking here was that unless the NSA/LU reported some quick action in acquiring the proper tape paper, we would have little to do other than maintain our rapport with the agent. So, perhaps the best approach would be to have an early December meeting and then let him enjoy the holidays.

There were no problems dropping him off, and we were out of the hotel before midnight. I had Larry back at his car within twenty minutes. I drove home and, as is my habit, wrote up my meeting notes before going to bed. Truth is my mind was always working so fast that until I got my thoughts on paper, there was no way I could actually go to sleep.

We did our usual reporting, held a couple of meetings with Ralph and his guys, and hoped Headquarters would advise us of some breakthrough on finding the right paper. Actually, we had no operational agenda for the next meeting. And, by November 12th, we had no new information on the progress, or lack thereof, by the NSA/LU team. So, we decided to schedule the next meeting as a "friendly pre-holiday" dinner, with the objectives of keeping the agent happy and motivated. I advised our Headquarters Telephone Unit to tell LEMON to be at the car pickup point at 7:30 p.m. the evening of December 10th.

CHAPTER TWENTY-FOUR: WAITING

There is always a security risk involved in any personal meeting with an agent, yet at the same time, we are dealing with a human being who constantly needs "comforting" in his secret relationship with his CO. Therefore, scheduling a meeting without a specific operational objective is always a "risk versus gain" equation. My view, and that shared by Larry and Winston, was that we needed to keep LEMON well motivated and feeling "loved" by his business colleagues since pretty soon we would be asking him to actually bring out the tapes. So, we decided that Larry and I would host the agent to a holiday dinner, at which he would be given his November and December retainers, a small holiday bonus for his "business" expenses, and a personal gift from the boss. We would also set the next meeting for mid-January, as we hoped that Headquarters would be ready to move forward by that time.

However, security was still a key issue. I decided that we could pick up the agent and then drive to an "expense account" steak house located in the suburbs. The Field Office believed this was an area where it was unlikely anyone who knew LEMON might be present. But, just out of caution, I booked a small, private room for dinner.

On the 15th I was advised LEMON had gotten the meeting arrangements and confirmed his ability to be at the car pick up site.

There was little to do but worry occasionally about the operation in general. Yet, even in this period of relative calm, the Field Office remained watchful for any indications by the agent or others in the Consulate of anything unusual that might indicate a problem. Matt advised LEMON was committing to a great many social activities during the holiday season, in some cases representing the Consul General at lesser diplomatic events and local émigré functions. It was comforting to see that he was still in the good graces of his superior.

By late afternoon on December 10th, there had still been no news from Headquarters. On the health and dental front, all had gone well, with the small exception of the oral discomfort LEMON had suffered earlier in the month. Larry reported that by the time the dentist was done, the agent would have a completely redone mouth.

Larry came to the Station, and we took my car to the airport, where I went through the usual routine, switched into my alias persona, picked up the car, and then picked up Larry at the airport departure area. We drove into the city using a modified countersurveillance route and pulled into a parking garage near the pickup site with about twenty minutes to spare. At 7:23, I pulled out of the garage, and we hit the pick-up site just at 7:30 p.m. Larry was in the back seat, and LEMON quickly jumped into the passenger seat. After a brief initial welcome, Franklin engaged the agent in conversation while I did some countersurveillance driving, and we proceeded towards the suburbs. When I felt confident no one was following us, I explained that we were going to a special restaurant for dinner, and that I had several things the Boss wanted me to tell him. For the remainder of the trip, Franklin engaged him in conversation regarding how his duties at the Consulate were going and if everything was going well with his family.

Upon arrival at the restaurant we gave the keys to the valet and went directly to the private room, which was accessible without passing through the main dining area and the bar. Franklin brought with him a large shopping bag which contained the Boss' holiday gift for LEMON.

A bottle of expensive single malt scotch and three glasses were on the table as we sat down, and Franklin did the honors, giving each of us a healthy glass. I made an appropriate toast, "To a happy and joyful holiday season and a New Year filled with success. " This was going to be the evening's theme. Till the meal arrived, we spoke of general social topics, including, of course, LEMON's health and that of his family. Franklin and I also mentioned fictitious plans we had with our fictitious families for the holiday season. LEMON responded by describing his plans and noting that, as strange as it may sound for Communist countries, the Christmas to New Year period was always a period of partying. I also provided a description of the Christmas day dinner I had experienced at the boss's country estate in Northern England a few years ago. In retrospect, it may have sounded a bit too much like something out of a Dickens novel, but the agent seemed to enjoy hearing about it.

CHAPTER TWENTY-FOUR: WAITING

Dinner began to arrive after our second scotch. I had ordered a prime rib to be carved at the table, complete with all the traditional side dishes and a couple of bottles of a reserve French Rhone red. We ate well and jovially, and I had ample opportunity to mention how pleased the boss was with LEMON's work, and that he might expect a pleasant surprise regarding his employment status in the New Year. After a dessert of a rich Christmas pudding, we settled into our coffee and a glass of fine cognac.

As we sipped the coffee, I reached into my briefcase and brought out a thick manila envelope, which I placed on the table. I told LEMON that his retainers for November and December were in the envelope, along with another one thousand dollars, which the Boss instructed me to give him to cover any assorted expenses he may have during the holidays. I continued that these might be for various professional gifts he had to provide to colleagues or friends, as well as for entertainment expenses related to the holiday season. Because this time the funds were in various small denominational dollar bills, the packet was still bulky, but he was able to fit them into his coat pocket. As expected, he asked me to thank the boss, and noted that he particularly appreciated the additional one thousand since he would, indeed, have to give "gifts" to the Consulate General, some other senior Consulate and Ministry officials.

I then noted that the boss also asked us to give LEMON a personal holiday gift. Franklin then placed the shopping bag on the table and brought out a box containing several bottles of Royal Salute scotch. I said that the boss wanted LEMON to enjoy the season with a decent scotch. I mentioned that this was a personal gift from the Boss, and not from the corporation. The agent appeared quite touched by the gift and said he felt bad that he had not brought a presents for the boss. I commented that the boss did not expect a present, as it was his nature to reward his employees for their respect, loyalty, and hard work.

Shortly thereafter, Franklin left the room to pay the dinner check and have the valet deliver the car to the front of the restaurant. I took the opportunity to remind LEMON that he had to be careful in his spending of his personal and "business" funds to avoid any suspicion by his colleagues.

We discussed this for a few minutes, and I must admit the agent seemed to be exercising good personal discipline in his use of the funds we were providing. Specifically, he advised that since "gifts" to senior officials were expected at this time of the year, it was assumed that one would save funds to make these purchases. And, while the gifts, particularly to the Consulate General and a couple of officials back in Bucharest, would be costly, they would also be in a price range which would seem normal for an officer of his rank stationed abroad.

I then informed the agent that, due to the holiday season, even corporate business slowed down, so he should call my office on January 10th to get information on our next meeting. At that point, Franklin returned to advise that the car was ready, and we departed the restaurant. The drive back to the pickup point was uneventful. Prior to leaving the car, LEMON wished us both a very happy holiday season, and once again reminded us to tell the boss how grateful he was for the opportunity to work for him and how appreciative he was of the gift of the scotch.

Larry and I both felt the agent's expressed gratitude was genuine and sincere. Following the usual procedures, I dropped Larry off at his car, returned the rental car at the airport, went home, and wrote up some notes on the meeting. This was a rather relaxed meeting, so the adrenaline was more subdued than is normally the case with me.

Over the course of the next couple of days, I submitted my report along with a copy of Larry's report, conferred with Ralph and Matt, gave them a copy of my report, and we briefly outlined some general planning for the New Year. Then, the rash of holiday parties hit, and socialization, vice operational activities, took over. Even the Agency tends to slow down from just before Christmas until after New Year's. The Station had to have its party, with a heavy FBI presence, but also with members of other USG Intelligence Community officials in the city, as well as some local law enforcement senior officials who were helpful to us. We also had to attend parties at the Field office, and Winston and I had to make appearances at a couple of parties for senior USG officers.

However, the most important party was the one at my residence for my

CHAPTER TWENTY-FOUR: WAITING

Station personnel. While my wife, as usual in such social situations, did the actual planning and work, I greatly valued the opportunity to invite my folks into my home and demonstrate just how much I appreciated their hard work and efforts. I don't know how much this really meant to them, but it meant a great deal to me.

During the period from Christmas until after New Year's, the Station operated at a reduced level, with the staff taking periodic annual leave, and communications from Headquarters and elsewhere were sparse, with only the occasional operational action required. Nothing related to the LEMON operation happened. The Field Office subsequently reported that he had taken part in the usual Consulate holiday activities, and his colleagues had treated him in the normal manner. At his residence, his family life also seemed calm and normal. He had been generous in gifting to both his wife and their beloved son, but not to the extent that anyone outside the family would become suspicious.

Still, as I sat in my office just before New Year's I wonder how the NSA/LU had done in Austria, and wished I had a better sense of when we were going to get our hands on the encrypted communications' tapes. I felt pretty confident that we had LEMON in a mindset wherein we could convince him to bring out the tapes. But, this was the riskiest task yet, and we had to be very careful how we convinced him that it was a manageable risk.

Chapter Twenty-Five: The New Year

A few days after New Year's, business started to get back to normal. Headquarters finally gave us an update on NSA/LU's activities. Operating under the cover of representatives of a printing company, two NSA/LU officers had traveled to Austria and spent nearly two weeks visiting various paper manufacturers. By the conclusion of their trip, they had paper samples from two manufacturers that seemed to match the samples provided by LEMON. By the end of November, the newly acquired samples had been sent to both the NSA and one of the National Laboratories for comparison with Lemon's samples. Just prior to the week of Christmas, both organizations, acting independently, had identified one of the Austrian samples as the same as that used in the encrypted tapes.

Now, the NSA/LU officers would order several hundred pounds of the paper rolls and have them sent to the "business" in Latin America. Once at the "business" warehouse, it would be reshipped to a "client" on the East Coast and from there transported to NSA. The NSA would then reformat the documents into the specific tape format used by the Romanian Ministry of Foreign Affairs. This entire process would probably take at least several months; about two months for the shipping of the paper rolls by sea to Latin America, a couple of weeks in Latin America to process the onward shipping to the U.S. port, several weeks for the rolls to reach that port, and additional weeks for NSA to fabricate the tape rolls. Now we were looking at early spring as the target period for the first tape copying operation.

So, we had about a hundred days to play with until LEMON would, hopefully, bring out the encrypted tapes from the Consulate. While that might seem like plenty of time, we had a great deal to do just from the agent operation perspective, let alone the logistics and security required for the physical aspects of the tape copying. Within the LEMON operational scenario, we had to strengthen the cover story regarding the laser "reading" of the tapes to be sure the agent was convinced that they would not be opened. We felt this was a key element in satisfying his security concerns regarding the risks involved. We also had to provide him with a plan for physically removing the tapes from the Consulate and passing them to us in a manner with which he felt comfortable and secure.

We would have to line up the best day for the removal of the tapes with the NSA/LU's capability to setup their tape copy operation, which apparently involved a great deal of equipment and several of its personnel. This would require a secure location, isolated from both Station and the Field Office in order to keep the operation compartmented within both organizations.

With these details of NSA/LU's progress, I decided that the next meeting should be near the end of January. That would give us time to plan the cover story regarding the laser reader and enable Winston to make a motivational appearance to "promote" the agent into a corporate employee, with a slight monthly salary increase.

On January 5th, our Headquarters Telephone Unit was instructed to advise LEMON that he was to be at a car pickup site at 7:40 p.m. on the 29th. He was also told that the boss was looking forward to seeing him.

The next operational task was to get the details of the laser reader cover story worked out. For this, I requested Headquarters support in the form of a Directorate of Technology Engineering Graphic Artist. At Headquarters, NSA/LU did the legwork of talking with the appropriate Technology Directorate officials and identifying a suitably skilled officer for the project. He would have to be added to the bigot list for the LEMON operation, although in reality, his knowledge would only be of the machine he was supposedly documenting by drawings and operating instructions. He would, in theory at least, not know even the location of the operation or the nationality of the target tapes, let alone anything about the human agent involved.

My plan was to send Larry back to Washington to meet with the engineer and NSA/LU representatives in a safehouse in suburban Maryland, and over the course of a day or so, communicate what we wanted the laser reading apparatus to supposedly do. He would not advise his FBI status, nor would he state where he was stationed. Based upon their conversation, the artist would create a series of technical drawings of the machine and how its laser would penetrate the package wrappings. He would also prepare a convincing but fictitious description of how the machine operated.

Ralph agreed with my thinking, and Larry flew back to Washington in mid-January for a few days. I wanted him back in plenty of time to prepare for the meeting on the 29th. While we were not yet ready to explain the functioning of the laser reader to LEMON, I did want Larry to be able to say a few words indicating that development of the machine was moving along smoothly. When Ralph, Matt, Winston, Larry, and I met upon his return to the city, he seemed quite satisfied with his time with the artist. He felt the technical drawings would convince LEMON that the required information could be collected without opening the sealed tapes. At this point, it looked like we were ready to provide the cover story, which we hoped would satisfy LEMON's concerns over the risk involved.

While in Washington, it had also been arranged that NSA/LU would treat Larry to a little local sightseeing and other social activities. This was both in the way of a "thank you" for his efforts to date, and also some institutional rapport building since when the NSA/LU copy team came to the city it would be the Field Office, with its official law enforcement credentials, that would provide security for the physical copy location and the actual encrypted tapes once we got them from the agent.

Our planning for the meeting on January 29th took its usual pattern, we provided the basic outline of the characters to be present, their roles and interactions, and the general objectives of the meeting. In discussions with Ralph and Matt, final specifics were added. Larry provided updates on health and dental issues. In regard to LEMON's mouth, the dentist was close to the down payment on the yacht. The good news was that with his final work soon to be completed, the agent's general health had greatly

CHAPTER TWENTY-FIVE: THE NEW YEAR

improved.

The dentist turned out to be right, and in retrospect, in terms of the operation's eventual progress, he was well worth the money. Especially since it was FBI funds and not from the Station's budget. LEMON did go through some serious discomfort in treatment, but by the time the dentist was completely finished, the agent told us he had never felt better in his life. This tells me two things: never get your dental work done in a Soviet Bloc country and if you give a man a new set of teeth, he will eat with you forever—or something like that. Our commitment to his well-being and that of his son proved to be one of the key motivations for the agent's cooperation in this operation.

As the date of the meeting approached, Ralph got the hotel suite, Patrick rented the town car, and Winston, Larry, Patrick, and I did a couple of rehearsals of how the meeting should go. Winston pushed hard for bottles of Chateau St. Clair Burgundy for the meal, and since we had to have something suitable anyway, what the Hell. As it turned out, the hotel's wine cellar did have a few bottles left. The meal was going to be rather British in its orientation: roast beef, carrots, pudding, etc. We brought a couple of bottles of a single malt scotch, one we had not tried before but was appropriately expensive, for the pre-dinner drinks with the plan that the boss would state that he had just discovered this brand and brought a couple of bottles with him so that he could get LEMON's opinion: a little ego building here to fit in with the larger theme of enhancing the agent's loyalty and rapport with the boss and the corporation.

The afternoon of the meeting we went through our usual tradecraft tactics, with no indications that anyone was observing us. Just as a precaution, Ralph also used his special surveillance unit to stakeout the hotel prior to and during the meeting to see if any suspicious activities were noticed—none were.

Patrick made the car pickup within the acceptable operation time window and delivered the agent to the suite between 8 p.m. After the greetings, Patrick poured the scotch for us, being careful to ensure that the agent saw the label of the bottle. After taking a sip of his drink, Winston moved into the scenario regarding the single malt scotch. He said that he had tried this scotch at a friend's New Year's party in London and was somewhat taken with it. But, he knew that LEMON was a scotch expert, and decided that he wanted the agent's opinion on the whiskey. LEMON played right into the ploy, smelling and sipping the scotch a couple of times, he said that this was the first time he had drunk this specific whiskey. He noted its deep flavor and smoothness on the tip and back of the tongue, and stated that to his taste it was one of the best single malts he had drunk. Winston said he agreed, and Franklin and I sagely nodded our heads.

That bit of ego enhancement accomplished, the boss made a few comments about the holiday season in general, and then described some of the supposed traditions of the Christmas season at his estate in England. Winston's recalling of the Christmas day shooting party, and to this day, I still do not know if he had actually experienced such an event or just read about it, was especially humorous and vivid. Whether a wounded pheasant could actually fall onto a tea table setup for the ladies in the party behind the firing line seemed questionable to me. But, LEMON seemed to like the story. For anyone who has read stories of the British upper class during the late nineteenth or early twentieth century, Winston's descriptions of his estate and country squire existence would seem familiar. Indeed, in a neutral environment, such a story might seem to be the fiction it actually was. Yet, in the setting we had created, and the character that Winston was able to play physically, it rang true.

When Winston had finished, he asked the agent about his holiday. LEMON provided a description of his family's Christmas and the joy he and his wife experienced as their now healthy and mentally alert son opened his presents. He also noted that thanks to his relationship with the corporation, he had been able to purchase a lovely necklace for his wife. And, as a gift for the family, he bought a color television with a VCR included. He then took this opportunity to thank the boss for the bottles of scotch. He noted that he had used one of them as a gift to his friend, the Consulate General, but had kept the others for his own use.

LEMON also mentioned that as a representative of the Consulate, he had

CHAPTER TWENTY-FIVE: THE NEW YEAR

attended several holiday parties within the local diplomatic community. So, he concluded, it had actually been both an enjoyable and often tiring holiday period. To which Winston responded that he also would be happy to get back into the routine pattern of his business activities, as being 'lord of the manor" entailed a great deal of social and civic responsibilities which all too soon became a burden for him.

At this point, I entered the conversation, excusing myself for bringing up a business issue, but asking the agent some questions regarding these holiday purchases. I noted that from what he had said, the presents for the wife and family, I was concerned that these items might cause some suspicion among his Consulate colleagues. When I finished my comments, the Boss gave LEMON an authoritative stare and dryly said, "I am sure our friend has been very careful in his spending habits Robert, but your points are valid, and it would be useful to hear how he has explained these expenditures." LEMON actually looked quite confident as he made his reply. He said that he was, indeed, very careful in his expenditures and had most of his monthly retainers and bonuses hidden away in his residence. He continued that the necklace for his wife was going to be kept only within the family, and she would not wear it outside the house until they had returned to Romania, where it could be explained as purchased through savings from his posting abroad. As to the television, it was normal for those posted overseas to save and buy modern electronic items which could then be taken back to Romania. As to the gifts for the son, once again, these were items for use inside the residence and could be simply part of the toys and items that loving parents gave to their child.

I should also note that we did have additional confirmation that LEMON was not displaying too much in the way of his additional income in public. Brenda, who had slowly disengaged her association with the couple but still remained in sporadic contact, reported that she had run into them at a holiday diplomatic charity function. LEMON was there representing the Consulate, as apparently the Consul General did not care much for charity events. In that role, he donated a case of Romanian wines to the charity auction, which subsequently did not go for very much as they are pretty bad wines. Brenda said she even bid on them so LEMON would not be embarrassed by the lack of interest in the audience. Luckily, a local businessman placed a second bid and they were sold. As to the LEMONS, Brenda had a brief conversation with them and was able to report that both seemed to look healthy, LEMON especially so since she had last seen him several months ago. Both seemed happy. Most importantly, she noted that both were dressed in nice, but not very expensive, clothes; the wife in a fashionable but moderately priced black cocktail dress, and LEMON had a new suit, also of moderate price. I passed this information along to both Ralph and our Headquarters.

LEMON also noted that with the knowledge of, and sometimes in partnership with, the Consulate General, he had engaged in assisting local businessmen in the Romanian émigré community, and this usually resulted in a "commission" which also could explain his ability to make the television purchase. He concluded that he had taken my instructions very much to heart and saw it as a necessary part of keeping his relationship with us secret from his colleagues. He noted that he had also made a point of giving the Consulate senior security officer a nice holiday present as well, to ensure they remained "friends."

As LEMON finished, Winston looked at me and said, "Well, Robert, I suspect that he has answered your questions." I responded that he had indeed, and that I was most pleased that he had taken my instructions to heart. I added that in our business, we have to be very disciplined and careful. The agent nodded in agreement, and the boss said, "I think it is time to give our colleague the good news. Based upon your service, and your loyalty, which I personally value highly, I have decided to make you a salaried employee of the corporation, effective the first of January of this year." LEMON smiled broadly, and Franklin and I quickly added our congratulations to Winston's pronouncement. The boss continued, "Your monthly salary will now be $2000, which of course may be augmented with bonuses for actions of particular value to corporate business. Your health benefits, both for you and your family, will continue, and at a later time, perhaps after dinner, Robert will discuss with you various corporate investment opportunities which might be of assistance in your retirement planning."

As we raised our glasses of scotch to drink to LEMON's new status, room service arrived with the dinner. The Boss engaged us with light social conversation while Patrick supervised the setup of the dining table and the food. He then announced that dinner was served. We were seated, and Patrick poured the wine, and with great gusto Winston swirled the glass, sniffed the aroma, and took a healthy sip. He smiled and assured the table that we would enjoy the vintage. It was obvious that he would as well.

During dinner, we focused the conversation on happy memories of our past holiday seasons to keep the mood light and pleasant. However, LEMON provided some very interesting information in the course of explaining how his colleagues celebrated the season. He stated that the tradition at the Consulate was to have a holiday party, which meant heavy drinking from noon well into the evening, for the staff only—no dependents. Of course, a few of the wives, usually the younger ones without children, worked at the Consulate and therefore attended the party. A second, larger party, usually held on Christmas Day, was jointly sponsored by the Consulate and wealthy Romanian-Americans from the local community. In reality, it was the local businessmen who footed the bill for the food, drinks, and entertainment, but the function served as an "outreach" to the city's Romanian émigré population and encouraged communication and mutual support between this group and the Consulate. This party included all family members, and the children were treated to gifts in addition to the refreshments and entertainment provided to all.

LEMON noted the larger party was a nice social event, but it was a very dull affair in comparison to the staff party at the Consulate. He then described some of the drunken antics at the Consulate's party, which were definitely of interest to the FBI. He noted that during the party, the younger wife of the junior security officer, who was employed as a secretary to that office, was caught by her husband having sex with his boss, the senior security officer, in the secure reading room, on the reading table.

All three were quite drunk at the time, and the incident quickly moved out into the conference room where most of the party participants were treated to a half-naked woman and two officers, one without his pants, involved in a halfhearted attempt to beat each other up. The Deputy Consul General finally intervened, not very successfully, and the incident ended with all four entangled on the floor. Tempers soon cooled as the Consul General negotiated a settlement, and insisted all those involve have a drink together—and this was done formally, still with the wife naked to the waist and the senior security without his pants.

Larry asked whether the incident had indeed been settled and if any hard feelings existed between the two security officers. LEMON responded that rumors within the Consulate were that the wife had been involved with her husband's boss for several months, but that now that it had become public, there was no way the junior officer could avoid the shame and embarrassment of the situation. Since the party, relations between the man and his boss have been less than professional, and the Consul General may soon have to decide whom to send home to keep discipline within the office. The agent also noted that the senior security officer had a well-deserved reputation for chasing the younger wives employed at the Consulate, and a couple of other officers were not friendly with him because of this. However, he explained, the senior security officer was a ranking Communist Party official within the Consulate and held a great deal of political power. The Consul General had been very careful to include him in some money-making ex-official business deals in order to cultivate his friendship. Therefore, LEMON assumed that it would be the junior officer who would be sent home, accompanied by a performance evaluation placing all the blame for the party incident on a drunken amorous wife and her drunken husband.

In one other interesting comment, LEMON told the group that during the early evening, when everyone was well into the liquor, the Consul General boasted to him that early in the new year he had arranged with a local businessman to obtain six new model air conditioners at one fourth of their retail price and he planned to ship them as a diplomatic pouch

CHAPTER TWENTY-FIVE: THE NEW YEAR

back to Bucharest. He explained that he got such a good price because his local contact had probably stolen them. The Consul General said that he was going to give five of them to senior Ministry and Communist Party friends, and have the sixth placed in storage for his use when he returned to the capital. He boasted to LEMON that these "gifts" would ensure his extension here for another three years, by which time he would have made enough extra income to pay off his house outside Bucharest and retired into a comfortable official job with decent pay and few actual responsibilities.

As the dinner wound down and Patrick served coffee, I gave him a prearranged signal. This was to indicate that in about five minutes' time, he was to go over to Winston and whisper into his ear. This would prompt the boss to take a final sip of his coffee, rise from the table, and say, "I am reminded that I have a business call to make to Jakarta. Please excuse me. Robert, I believe you and Franklin have some additional issues to talk about with our new employee. Good night." And, with that, he and Patrick would disappear into the separate master bedroom area.

As we had all stood when Winston left the table, I motioned for us to move back to the sitting room, where Franklin offered us another glass of the scotch. Once we were comfortable, I suggested to Franklin that he provide LEMON with an update on the progress in the laser reader project. Thus, Franklin went into his carefully scripted technical explanation of how much progress had been made in computer-adjusting the focus of the reader through various densities of packaging material as a test package was rotated 360 degrees within a pressurized field, which adjusted pressure intensity based upon the various weight angles of the package. LEMON seemed fascinated by the explanation and asked several questions about the project. Franklin concluded by noting that at the next meeting, he would bring along the most recent status report on the testing as well as some engineering drawings of the equipment. The agent appeared quite pleased to be accepted as part of the team working on the research program.

Now it was my turn to handle the financial aspects. First, I once again congratulated LEMON on his new status as a corporate employee and gave him an envelope containing two thousand dollars, his new monthly salary. I then said, "As an employee, you now have access to a corporate unique savings plan to build up funds for your retirement." I noted that in his case, where it served his best interests not to let anyone outside the corporation know that he had additional monthly compensation, this plan would permit him to invest part of his monthly salary while also enjoying periodic corporate contributions to the plan.

I explained that the corporation, under a different legal entity but actually controlled by the boss and senior corporate officers, managed a set of investment opportunities, held in overseas accounts in areas where local banking laws protected the identities of the account holders. At some point, I advised that LEMON might want to consider involvement in these investment opportunities. In response to his questions regarding these investments, I provided some vague details and made it clear that, like all of the boss's business activities, these investments tended to make profits well above normal expectancy.

I added that most employees, including myself, had found that by maximizing my monthly contributions and earning such a high rate of return, my retirement savings were growing at an impressive rate. And, at this rate, should I choose to do so, I could retire in quite a lavish lifestyle whenever I choose to. I also re-emphasized that the agent was in the favorable position of being able to actually invest most of his corporate income while at the same time shielding his additional funds from public view. LEMON immediately saw the value of these joint objectives. He asked, "How much of my monthly salary should I invest?" I responded that from what he had said previously, he already had a couple of thousand dollars hidden at his residence. So, perhaps he should start today by investing his entire January salary, and continue to do so each month until he has used up all the funds at home.

The agent pondered this suggestion as he took a couple more sips of his drink. He then looked up and stated "I agree this is a wise approach." Obviously this "investment plan" was a sham, which we created both to

CHAPTER TWENTY-FIVE: THE NEW YEAR

increase LEMON's commitment to the "corporation" and to convince him not to have on hand extra funds he could not explain.

With the financial issues handled, I suggested that we call it a night. As to the next meeting, I advised LEMON to call my office on February 12th for specific instructions. Franklin then proposed a final toast to LEMON as our fellow corporate colleague.

I then summoned Patrick, who escorted the agent to the hotel basement and drove him back to the drop-off point. Once they had left, Winston joined us and decided to finish up the last open bottle of the wine. We were all in good spirits. LEMON seemed happy and content with his new status, his new salary, his new retirement investment plan, and was actively interested in the development of the laser reader. And, of course, he had provided potentially valuable information on the junior Consulate security officer, which certainly would be of great interest to the Field Office.

When Patrick returned about twenty minutes later, we got his views of the evening as well. While a great deal had been accomplished in terms of operational control, we all recognized that the information about the junior security officer's wife and his superior was the prize of the evening.

The next week was spent submitting our reports and passing copies of them between the Station and the Field Office. I also sent a request to the NSA/LU asking for the status of their activities regarding the paper stock from the Austrian company.

Later in the week, I scheduled a meeting with the Field Office to discuss how to exploit the information on the junior security officer. It was obvious that neither Larry nor Patrick had heard this information before, but it was possible that the Field Office may have learned of it in some other manner. But, Ralph told me that this was brand new information. So, without LEMON's reporting, the Field Office might never have learned of the fight between the junior security officer and his superior.

By the start of the second week in February, Headquarters responded, providing their comments on the operational potential of the information concerning the junior security officer. The Agency, led by the Counterintelligence Center, wanted our comments on an attempt to recruit the junior officer based on his personal issues with his superior. We were urged at the next meeting with LEMON to develop additional personality and professional information on the officer. It was also suggested that we ask the Field Office for any additional information they had on this potential target.

Well, I seriously doubted if that plan was going to work. I could well understand that recruiting a young Romanian security officer on his first tour abroad might produce an agent able to grow into a long-term asset of significant counterintelligence value. The CI folks were looking for a "seeding" operation wherein a recruited young individual could be assisted in developing his career into increasingly more senior levels of responsibility within his organization. This might even include providing him with information, and perhaps even "sources," which would enhance his career development. However, from our perspective, while we had knowledge of his deep dislike for his boss, we knew little about his personality, his personal life, and his profession, let alone his loyalty to his government and the Romanian Communist Party. Sure, we could try to develop an operation for assessment purposes, and certainly could gather more information about him from LEMON. But, this would take time, and from what LEMON had said, the junior officer's time at the Consulate may well be quite short. So, from the Station's perspective, starting an operation against this guy did not seem worthwhile.

Of course there were also two more important reasons that I was going to shoot down Headquarters suggestion: the LEMON operation was too far developed to risk any suspicion within the Consulate that US intelligence was active against it and you could be damn sure that FBI Headquarters was going to claim primacy of the junior security officer as their own target. But, before I responded to Headquarters, I needed to confirm with the Field Office that my instincts were correct. With this confirmation, I could phrase my rejection of the Counterintelligence Center's desire in a more acceptable manner than simply rejecting it.

Ralph and Matt, accompanied by Larry and Patrick, came out to the Station a few days later to discuss the junior security officer. Ralph

CHAPTER TWENTY-FIVE: THE NEW YEAR

telephoned the day before, explaining that he had received compliments on the Briarpatch meeting and also guidance on how to utilize the information on the brawl at the Consulate's holiday party. He stated that FBI Headquarters had instructed him to start an investigation into the life and activities, both personal and professional, of the junior officer with the objective of recruiting him as an informant inside the Consulate. I replied that I understood why the FBI would want to take this action, and that my Headquarters had made a similar recommendation. So, we did need to discuss how best to accomplish this.

Winston and I met with the four SAs in my office. Ralph opened with complimentary comments on how well the Briarpatch case was going, and Matt added how pleased the FBI was with the major role Larry was playing in it. I countered by praising both Larry and Patrick for the performances to date—and really meant it. Ralph then got down to the point: FBI Headquarters believed that any effort to recruit the junior security officer was the legal responsibility of the FBI as the primary counterintelligence agency in the US. Thus, the Field Office, specifically Matt's Squad, had been ordered to begin developing an investigation of the individual. Matt then explained that he planned to use LEMON to get additional personality data and perhaps orchestrate an introduction to an undercover SA. When I heard this, I looked at Ralph and caught just the slightest roll of his eyes. Larry and Patrick also appeared somewhat nervous. Apparently, all three expected me to react to Matt's comments.

Now it was my turn. I responded, "I can understand the FBI's position, since we all recognized your primacy role regarding counterintelligence in the US. I also know, somewhat, but certainly not in full detail, of your efforts against the Consulate and its personnel. My Headquarters also wants us to develop an operation against this target." At that statement, Matt seemed to stiffen somewhat. However, I noted," I am confident that Headquarters will also understand the FBI is primary on this case, and I intend to add the Station's support for that position." Matt relaxed noticeably, and Ralph allowed a small smile to cross his face.

I continued, "Our joint operation has been successful because we have closely cooperated in sharing information and resources, and in order for this to continue, it is vital that both organizations feel their authorities and responsibilities are respected." I noted "I hope we will be kept informed of your progress against the junior officer, and will be happy to discuss using any capabilities we have to further your efforts. Obviously, LEMON might have some additional information on this individual of value to Matt's Squad, and as long as we can obtain such information without arousing any suspicion on the agent's part we will do so." Larry, I suggested, would be the best person to act as a liaison between the Station and Matt's activities against the junior security officer. But, I quickly added, it would be unwise to have Larry directly exposed in any way to their target or their investigative actions since he was involved as a major role player with LEMON. I concluded, "It was quite possible that your investigation might turn up some useful information for our joint operation."

All this seemed to go down pretty well with Matt, who really was the audience for my remarks. Ralph then asked Matt to share a few insights into how his Squad planned to proceed. Matt said that his SAs were reviewing the USG trace information on the target, as well as the biography and other information that the Field Office had put together. Once Matt finished, Winston said that Matt's plan was indeed comprehensive and well thought out. I added my agreement, and Matt seemed quite pleased.

The SAs departed the Station confident that they could report back to their Headquarters that they indeed had primacy in this case and, hopefully, that the Station had once again demonstrated the type of cooperation that was now known as "best practice" within the USG.

I now had to write back to the Counterintelligence Center and advise that the Field Office had taken primacy, which was their legal authority, but had agreed to keep us information of the investigation so that none of their activities represented any threat to the LEMON operation. I did so later that afternoon, and it took me until the early evening before I got just the right tone of sad reluctance but acceptance that the FBI exercised its primacy in this matter.

A response to my message was forthcoming in the next day's afternoon cable traffic. It was from the office of the Chief of the Counterintelligence Center and stated that while Headquarters would have preferred taking a shot at the junior security officer, Station's actions in recognizing and accepting FBI primacy in the case were correct. Legally, the FBI had the authority. I noted that the Chief of the NSA/LU, the Chief of SE, and the Deputy Director for Counterintelligence had all coordinated on the cable. Issue settled, as long as I could be confident that Matt's Squad did not do anything that might adversely affect our operation. With Larry acting as liaison, I actually felt somewhat comfortable.

As we started planning for the agent's call-in on February 12th, I received a reply from the NSA/LU regarding the status of the paper. Four large rolls were being transshipped to a Latin American port and then would be transshipped to an East Coast port. It was estimated that the actual paper tapes would not be ready for copying until late in April. So, we would be using our meetings with LEMON in February and March to continue to prepare him for the task of bringing out the encrypted tapes sometime in late April or May.

We were advised the morning of the 13th that LEMON had accepted the instructions for a car pickup in the evening of February 26th. Larry and I would pick him up and drive to a hotel for a meeting with only two objectives: continue to make him a "partner" in our planning to get the encrypted tapes and keep his confidence in his corporate relationship at a high level. This meeting, and the one in March, were going to give us time to convince LEMON that our planning, with his input, for the removal and "reading" of the tapes was so thorough that his actions represented minimal risk. Then, in April, we anticipated all the pieces would be in place and we could plan a specific scenario and date for the first tape copying operation.

Since we were operating in the "business" mode, we had to blend our meeting sites to support that cover story. Luckily, we could explain rationally to LEMON why we preferred car pickups to simply having him meet us at a location. Yet, it was poor tradecraft to constantly use the same pickup site, even if it was the most convenient one for the agent. So, when we passed the meeting instructions to the Headquarters telephone unit, we included a reason which we hoped explained why the location where we would pick him up was different than the previous time. In this case, the reason given was that I was coming from an appointment with a client in a nearby community and thus coming off a major highway, which made the pickup point easier for me to drive to on my way back to my hotel room. Whether LEMON accepted this reason, or for that matter, even cared why we suggested various pickup points, never came up.

So, with about two weeks before the next meeting, I requested that the technical description of the laser reader and its related drawings be sent to the Station no later than February 22nd, so that Larry and I would have adequate time to incorporate it into our scenario of explaining how the reader could copy the tapes without actually opening the packaging. We assumed LEMON was well aware that each tape package contained various seals and other trappings of which close examination would reveal if the package had been opened. These devices were the reason that the Consul General and the senior Consulate security office were to be present when the tapes were first opened and then put into use. Needless to say, since the NSA/LU team would not only open the packages but actually give back to LEMON duplicated tapes and their wrappings, another key portion of the tape copying operations was the "flaps and seals" reproduction of these markings. Each marking had to be duplicated exactly as on the originals, just in case either Consulate official actually checked them. NSA/LU advised us that they could accomplish this to the point that no difference could be noted between the original and duplicate packaging, but depending upon the complexity and number of seals and trappings used, the time required could be significant. This was one of the many factors we had to consider when deciding when LEMON was to bring out the encrypted tapes.

We also went through the usual procedures of having Larry check with the doctor and dentist to ensure all health issues were going well—and they were. He also continued to monitor his Squad's investigative efforts against the Consulate junior security officer. So far, he noted, their efforts had not identified any individuals in close contact with him or his wife who might be able to provide some personality assessment.

Several days before the scheduled meeting, Larry, Winston and I sat down to finalize the outline of the scenario. It was rather simple compared to some of the previous meetings. The technical description and drawing had not yet arrived from Headquarters, but we planned how and where they would fit in—Larry would handle the briefing of the Agent and it would be done during pre-meal drinks so LEMON would have the entire meeting to ask any questions or express any concerns that we might need to address. Once we finalized the outline, Larry took it back to Ralph, and the next morning, he telephoned to give his concurrence. I then sent it to Headquarters for their information.

All we now required was the technical information, and true to form, Headquarters sent it to us on the morning of the 23rd. After scanning the information, I called Larry, and he spent that afternoon reviewing the supposed operation of the laser reader and understanding what the technical drawings were demonstrating. Both the information and the drawing were impressive, at least to us non-technical types. So, with three days to spare, we were all prepared and ready to go.

Or so we thought. Late on the 24th, Murphy's Law intervened. Ralph called as I was about to leave for home to advise me that he had just learned that the Consulate's senior security officer had told the Consul General that he was concerned that his junior officer may have been compromised by the American security services. The senior security officer said that his sources in the local Romanian community had reported that the FBI was asking questions about the junior officer in a manner that demonstrated more than a casual interest was involved. Ralph suggested we should consider whether this information had any effect on our planning for the Briarpatch case.

I drove directly to the Field Office and went to Ralph's office, where Matt and Larry were waiting. Ralph once again reviewed the information he had just learned. Matt, in what seemed to be a somewhat defensive manner, stated that this was probably just the senior security officer's way of getting back at the junior officer over the holiday party incident. Matt continued that his Squad had been careful and discreet in their inquiries. Trying to be supportive, which seemed like the smart move for many reasons, I added that this could well have been the case. Ralph pondered this for a moment, and commented that we really had no idea what the Senior Security Officer was up to." Perhaps," he said, "LEMON can give us some additional insight?" I responded that we certainly could casually rise what he had already said about the incident and ask if the Consul General had taken any action as yet. All agreed this was the approach we would take.

The final issue to discuss was whether this information had any effect on how we planned to conduct our meeting with the agent on the 26th. I stated that there did not appear to be any related issues here, other than whether or not the senior security officer had subsequently suggested to the Consul General that an increased level of security should be implemented at the Consulate. And, even if this were the case, there were no indications of any suspicion regarding the behavior or actions of LEMON. So, notwithstanding the early evening emergency meeting at the Field Office, we were still set to go on February 26th.

However, Matt's Squad's investigation of the junior security officer now seemed to be in trouble. So, the next morning, I wrote a quick message to Headquarters advising of the meeting between the Consulate officials reported by Ralph and my meeting at the Field Office the previous day. I reported the facts of the meeting with no commentary regarding whether or not the FBI had drawn suspicion by how they conducted their investigation. On a professional level, this was no time to pile on since all operations involve risk versus gain and we all do the best we can. Also, on a local political level, I figured I had gotten some goodwill out of supporting Matt at the meeting.

We followed our usual procedures of my renting of the hotel suite and town car, and the pickup of LEMON took place on time with no suspicious incidents. Due to the troubling conversation between the senior security officer and the Consul General, Ralph offered to provide

CHAPTER TWENTY-FIVE: THE NEW YEAR

countersurveillance cover of both the pick-up site and the hotel. I readily agreed, not because I had any concerns, but because it never hurts to test your operational security, especially when you have been using the same technique—car pick-ups and hotel meetings—for an extended period of time. The Field Office surveillance unit subsequently reported no indications that either the pick-up site or the meeting site had drawn any unusual interest.

After we settled into the suite, Franklin poured the single malt scotch, and we exchanged some social chatter about the usual general topics. I then asked the usual questions about his son's health and his dental issues, noting the boss's personal interest in these subjects. LEMON responded that his son was doing excellently, and his dental treatment was just about completed. He then noted how well he had gotten along with the dentist and what a skilled practitioner he was. I nodded and mentioned that the boss would be very pleased.

Now it was Franklin's turn to open his briefcase and bring out the stack of technical drawings of the laser reader. He began by explaining that the testing phase of the development program was now complete and only some minor computer gauging adjustments were necessary before the reader was fully operational. He then provided a lengthy description, heavily infused with technical terminology, of the testing procedures. LEMON listened intently and asked some questions about how the testing phases had been conducted, but seemed quite content that the laser reader was just about ready for use. What really sealed the deal, in my opinion, were the technical drawings that Franklin used to explain the reader's functionality to the agent. These showed the target package being rotated within a pressure field while numerous laser beams continually penetrated the package and sent their finding back to a computer program, which slowly reconstructed the depth of the various portions of material within the package. The "reader" did this layer by layer, ascertaining and registering the density of each component. One of the drawings depicted the computer's printouts in phased layers, which then resulted in a combined two-dimensional final copy of the tape with the perforations accurately included.

By the time Franklin had completed his presentation, I was almost convinced the laser reader worked, and it seemed apparent that LEMON certainly did.

Shortly thereafter room service delivered dinner, and we moved to the next part of the script—some elicitation regarding the conflict between the junior and senior security officers. As we ate and drank a decent Italian red wine, Franklin noted that he remembered LEMON's story of the brawl that broke out during the Consulate's holiday party. He said that every time he pictured the four people lying on the floor, he broke out laughing. We all smiled, and I added that I actually felt sorry for the junior officer. After all, he was the one whose personal life had been made a joke, and after his actions with a senior officer, I doubt if his professional career was going to do well. I noted that in most organizations, a senior official, rightly or wrongly, holds considerable sway over the career prospects of their staff. LEMON said that this was certainly true at the Ministry of Foreign Affairs, and that the senior security officer was very well connected to important and powerful individuals in the Ministry and the Romanian Communist Party.

I then asked if anything further had developed regarding the incident. I mentioned that previously he had felt the young officer might be punished by the Consul General by sending him home. LEMON responded, "The Consul General told me privately that the senior security officer was very upset with the indignity involved in the brawl, and was pressuring him to send the young officer home with a recommendation that he was not fit for overseas assignments." The Consul General knew how well connected the senior officer was and did not want to make an enemy of him. As they were having a few drinks in the Consul General's office alone, after work a day ago, LEMON was told that earlier that day, the senior security officer had informed the Consul General that his sources in the local Romanian community had reported that the FBI was expressing interest in the younger officer. The Consul General said that he didn't necessarily believe this to be true, and suspected that this was simply an attempt to force the junior officer's transfer back to Bucharest. However, since the senior security officer was planning to report that information, along with his own assessment of the situation, to the Ministry's Security Office, true or false, he had to act on it. So, the junior officer would be sent home in disgrace, and probably never have another opportunity to serve abroad. Of course, the wife would also leave, so to a small degree, the senior officer would also be losing something, although as the Consul General noted, there were other women in the Consulate he could have. In fact, he said, there were a couple women who would probably be quite happy to accommodate him if they thought it would benefit their husbands' careers and their lifestyle.

Franklin commented that this senior security officer sounded like a mean and dangerous colleague, and LEMON agreed. He said that he made it a point to stay on the good side of the officer. He added that for the past holidays, he had given the senior security officer a nice gift.

With dinner completed, we moved back to the sitting area

I then took out of my briefcase a ledger sheet, supposedly that of LEMON's salary history. I pointed out to LEMON that the starting balance of two thousand dollars, which I noted we had back dated to 1 January per the boss' instructions, was listed under employee contributions. The next column was entitled corporation contributions and a figure of two hundred. I explained that this 10 percent represented the corporation's contribution to his retirement fund.

At this point, as I reached into my briefcase and brought out the envelope containing his February salary, I asked how he wanted to handle his two thousand dollars for the month. He responded that he really didn't need any more cash at the moment and was still carefully and slowly spending his current funds from the corporation. "Fine," I said, "we'll keep this payment in your account and record it as forthcoming when you decide how you wish to use it." LEMON nodded in agreement.

With the financial issues settled, we went through our operational agenda. However, we still engaged the agent in another fifteen minutes or so of social chatter before advising him to call my office on March 10th for details of the next meeting. We then all departed the suite, went to the car, and returned the agent to the pick-up site. Larry and I then returned to the hotel, cleaned up the suite, and headed back to the airport. On the way, we agreed that he would report the information LEMON provided on the fate of the junior security officer, since its main impact was on a Field Office case, and I would only refer to it in passing, referencing Larry's report for details.

The next morning I sent my report to Headquarters after briefing Winston and obtaining his input on my draft. I made a point of thanking the graphic artist for his fine work as well as the finance folks for their spreadsheets: both made our explanations to LEMON easier for us and more convincing to him. The following day Larry sent me a copy of his report to FBI Headquarters, and I sent that to Headquarters as well.

Later in the week, I spoke with Ralph and learned the Consulate junior security officer had been ordered back to Bucharest by the Consul General, according to their technical penetration of the installation. This ended the Field Office's recruitment case, and I acted appropriately empathetic.

So, with several days before advising the agent of the date of the next meeting, we had to figure out what we wanted to accomplish, the venue we would use, and develop the scenario to accomplish our objectives. Since we were actually just killing time until we could move to schedule a tape copy operation, I thought maybe we could try to use the meeting to get some additional gossip about activities and personalities at the Consulate. Certainly, the Field Office would like this; we could bring up the subject in terms of our interest in protecting LEMON from suspicion by better understanding his relationships with people in his office. Ralph and Matt readily agreed, so our objectives for the meeting, which we decided would be on March 28th, were basically two: info on personalities inside the Consulate and continued rapport and trust building of the agent.

LEMON called in on March 10th, and when advised of a meeting on the 28th, stated that he had an official function to attend that evening and asked if the meeting could be held the next evening. Since our plan always had a backup date, the Headquarters Telephone Unit office stated that the

CHAPTER TWENTY-FIVE: THE NEW YEAR

27th would be an acceptable date. LEMON readily agreed and took down the car pick-up location. I should note the obvious necessity of having alternate dates for meetings when the communications plan is structured in a manner where the CO is not directly in contact with the agent. In our plan for this operation, we had three options: the day before, the day after, and seven days after our primary date. As we always want to keep some measure of control over meetings, when LEMON suggested the 29th, the Headquarters office immediately responded with the 27th.

When advised of the change in dates and the reason given by the agent, I telephoned Ralph to see if he could confirm that the excuse given by LEMON was valid. Sound operational security demands that any excuse he gives should be checked out. A few days later, Larry advised that Consulate transcripts verified that the Consul General had asked LEMON to attend a reception at the Polish Consulate the evening of March 28th. It was being held in honor of a high-ranking Trade Delegation from Warsaw visiting the city as part of a tour of the US.

We had also received Headquarters agreement to our plans for the March meeting. Most importantly, however, in mid-March we got a message from NSA/LU advising that NSA was making good progress in shaping the paper into tape rolls exactly like those encrypted tapes used by the Consulate. They anticipated that by the first week in April the duplicated tapes would be ready and we could start addressing a date for the first copying operation.

Everything seemed to be going right throughout March as we prepared for another hotel meeting and dinner. As usual, Larry checked on the health issues, as well as insuring that the Field Office's monitoring of the Consulate had not indicated any problems for the operation.

Larry and I did a last rehearsal in my office early afternoon on the 26th, with Winston and Matt sitting in as advisors.

Early evening of March 27th, the car pick-up went smoothly, and we were in the hotel suite by a few minutes before 8 p.m. Once Franklin served the drinks, he told LEMON that the laser reader tests had gone very well, and he now anticipated the reader would be operational by late April or early May. The agent responded with a few questions—the basic point behind them was can the reader accurately duplicate the tapes without breaking the seals on the wrappings? Franklin responded that this was the whole point behind the project: to be able to read characters without disturbing their external packaging. Moving to the larger commercial picture, I joined in the conversation by advising that a great deal of the corporation's commercial success was based upon our ability to know what was needed by a government or enterprise before it was public knowledge, or even recognized within the organization. This usually required "insider knowledge" either from organizational leadership friendly to the corporation or individuals working for us within the organization's structure. The laser reader was yet another tool to accomplish this. This, of course, was the often-repeated theme we wanted LEMON to accept as a truth.

Since we planned this to be a shorter meeting than usual, room service arrived with dinner at 8:45. Since the boss was not present, the wine with the meal was slightly less expensive—but well within the price range that would be expected of a charge account business dinner. Over the many months I have been involved with LEMON, I have never found him to be anything less than an avid eater, even during the time he had serious dental issues. Often, with an agent, you create a scenario at a meeting where a potentially risky task is mentioned before a meal, and then you watch to see how the agent acts during the meal. LEMON never seemed to fit into this model—he always seemed to enjoy the drinks and the food regardless of what had been said prior to the meal. Winston once opined that he had seen this same character in other Eastern European agents he had handled overseas—he attributed it to the fact that even this long after the war, most Warsaw Pact countries still had scarce food distribution capabilities compared to the West.

We had planned that dinner conversation would be where we brought up the need to know more about the other individuals at the Consulate. Franklin opened by noting "I have been thinking about your comments about the senior security officer and particularly about his responsibilities

CHAPTER TWENTY-FIVE: THE NEW YEAR

regarding the encrypted tapes. Also, the incident of the holiday party brawl demonstrated the senior security officer is a dangerous person."

Now it was my turn to add, "The boss is always concerned with the safety of his employees, so I wanted to be confident that I could reassure him that I know of no risks to your personal security." I then firmly said, "To enable us to best protect you if ever necessary, you better tell us all you know about the Consulate's senior security officer." The question did not seem to faze LEMON in the least, and in between bites of his Rack of Lamb, he proceeded to provide us with a comprehensive picture of Nicolea Petran.

The agent explained that Petran was the second most powerful individual in the Consulate, after the Consul General. He was a career Securitate officer and had family ties to senior leaders in his organization. Franklin, feigning ignorance of what the Securitate was, asked LEMON to explain its functions and role at the Consulate.

LEMON explained, "The Securitate is the secret police of my country, whose mission is to protect and ensure that the ruling Communist Party leadership stays in power. Its authority in the country is unquestioned, and its methods are often ruthless, particularly against "enemies of the state" involved in any political activities. Petran is an experienced officer who has held middle-level management positions back at the Securitate Headquarters as well as at least three other overseas assignments." (Note: According to both the Bureau's and our files, he had served abroad at least four times, and had made several brief trips into the West using alias identity documents.) The agent continued, "While serving as the senior security officer for the Consulate, most of his actual responsibilities involved running contacts within the local Romanian community and ensuring that no one in that community made any inappropriate comments regarding Romania or its Government. Also, he has, on occasion, mentioned that he worked with the secret service representatives from the other Warsaw Pact official installations in the city to handle security issues. Once, after some drinks in the Consul General's Office several months ago, he let slip that he was running several secret operations for the benefit of not only Romania but also the Soviet Union."

LEMON said that based upon various communications which had come through the Consulate, he knew that the intelligence services of the USSR, Poland, and Hungary were sending Petran information and tasking. Franklin, acting confused, asked why the Romanian Consulate would be the communications point for other countries. The agent smiled and explained, "The Consulate was an official diplomatic institution in the city, while the Russians, Poles, and Hungarians only had commercial or 'cultural' offices here. Therefore, they do not have secure communications capabilities as their offices are not protected by diplomatic agreement."

LEMON continued to describe Petran's personality "He was a loud talking man, who liked to show that he had power in the Consulate. His ego was always evident in his interactions with others, and he was particularly harsh and demanding with employees he considered below his rank."

"Luckily," the agent advised, "as I am the senior Communications Officer, Petran is usually polite to me, probably because he needs me to handle special traffic related to his security and intelligence activities," LEMON added that since he was also a close personal friend of the Consul General, this fact also probably motivated Petran to be nice to him.

By this time, the agent was really warming up to the subject. And, it was obvious that he did not hold Petran in high regard. He continued "Petran saw himself as a great "ladies' man," and was forever chasing the younger wives who were childless and worked at the Consulate. Over the past two years, he had two or three brief affairs with the wives of junior officers before the incident involving the wife of his assistant. All these were known within the office, but with the exception of the junior security officer, none of the other husbands had dared to complain. Often he provided the women with gifts which apparently satisfied both them and their husbands." LEMON continued "As the security and intelligence officer for the Consulate, Petran has sole access to a "special fund" used to finance investigations and activities conducted by his office. Even the Consul General does not have access to these funds."

The agent said that while he had no personal knowledge of how these funds were spent, with a few exceptions where he had seen communica-

CHAPTER TWENTY-FIVE: THE NEW YEAR

tions ordering Petran to pay someone or pass funds to another Warsaw Pact officer, it seemed obvious that the Security Officer was spending more than his official salary could justify. Of course, he was also heavily involved in commercial dealings with the local Eastern European community and, no doubt, making some decent money using his diplomatic position to facilitate them. Also, there were rumors in the Consulate, and he had even heard these from the Consul General, that Petran periodically would use his "secret" funds to purchase electronic items which were subsequently sent back to Romania, specifically addressed to senior Ministers and senior members of his service, as diplomatic pouch baggage.

With that, the agent said that was about all he knew of the senior security officer's activities. As he had stated, he felt his relationship with Petran was good and that Petran posed no threat to him. He added that Petran was lazy and not very attentive to his responsibilities regarding the unsealing and logging of the encrypted communications' tapes.

I responded that we were glad he felt he had no issues with the security officer, but that now that we know a bit about him, I suspect the boss will want regular updates on his actions, especially those which affect his relationship with you or his responsibilities in the Communications Office. Franklin seconded my comments. And, I was thinking that I bet Larry wished we had been taping this meeting because this information on Petran was exactly what Matt wanted.

I then asked LEMON about his junior Communications Officer, since he worked in the same room with the agent on a daily basis and thus would be the most likely to detect any unusual behavior on the agent's part. LEMON noted, "The junior officer, Andrei Gabor, is relatively inexperienced in the Ministry and on his first assignment overseas. He came from a labor class of gypsies and his social status made him unique as a Ministry of Foreign Affairs employee. However, his father had been a loyal Communist after the war and, according to rumors in the Ministry, had been an informer on gypsy political organizing as the Soviet supported government was establishing itself. Also, in technical school, he apparently had demonstrated superior skills in radio maintenance and repair. So, he was taken in by the Ministry and had spent nearly six years there, gradually moving up the ladder of technical expertise. His skills were such that he was selected to work overseas. Privately, I have been told Gabor is to work under me for two or three years in the United States. If he behaves and proves trustworthy, he will next be posted to Africa, where he will serve as the technical officer for all the Romanian installations in East Africa. So far, Gabor has done well. He has been respectful of others at the Consulate, done exactly as told, and kept all the radio communications equipment in excellent condition. During the upgrade last year, he quickly absorbed all the information provided in the new manuals." The agent felt that Gabor had a good future in the Ministry, even though he was a gypsy.

As to Gabor's relationship with LEMON, the junior officer understood that LEMON was his mentor and protector in Consulate politics, which was way above his level of experience. He treated the agent with great respect and never questioned anything LEMON did. And, as the junior Communications Officer, he was not allowed to unseal the encrypted tapes and only permitted to load them into the communications system if LEMON was absent, and then only in the presence of the senior security officer. The agent concluded that his junior officer posed no threat to him.

By this point, we were working on dessert, so to change the focus of the conversation, I asked about his plans for his son if he stayed in the United States for a few more years. Yes, he said, this was a question he and his wife had been pondering recently. LEMON explained that Anton was nearly five years old and soon should be starting his education. The Consulate, and for that matter, none of the Warsaw Pact organizations in the city, had a school which he could attend. So it was a matter of attending an American public school or attending a private school, perhaps one like the local French School, which followed a European model of education. His wife has spoken with other wives in the community and found that most Warsaw Pact children went to American public schools until about fifth grade, when they were sent home for schooling, even if it meant separation from parents posted abroad. "Of course, as you well know," he continued, "we could afford a private school and our objective is to give Anton the best

CHAPTER TWENTY-FIVE: THE NEW YEAR

possible education. But, explaining how I could afford a private school would undoubtedly cause suspicion in the Consulate."

Franklin and I both expressed our understanding of the dilemma. I suggested that the agent might be able to accomplish both of his objectives—developing a good education for his son and not showcasing his additional income—by allowing Anton to go to an American public kindergarten, but then hiring a private tutor to coach his son in whatever skills he needed help with. In a worst-case situation, should Consulate colleagues learn of the tutor, LEMON could explain that since his child's education was of such great importance to the family, he was using some of his savings from his overseas allowances to pay the tutor. LEMON considered my suggestion and said he would talk it over with his wife. The decision would have to be made by this summer, as public school registration is in August.

We left the dining area and moved to the sitting area for the traditional "one for the road" scotch. And, I took this opportunity to reach into my briefcase and pull out the envelope with his March salary. Placing it on the coffee table, I asked him how he wanted to be paid. He responded that he still had sufficient cash at his residence and did not need all the money. He suggested that he would take two hundred in cash and that I deposit the remaining eighteen hundred dollars in his account. I responded that this would be no problem and handed him two hundred dollars in cash from the envelope.

Since we had touched on the theme of personal security in his spending habits while discussing Anton's education, there seemed little need to bring it up again. I am quite sure that just as all COs are conflicted on bringing up this subject so often with their agents, the agents are equally tired of being told the same thing every time they are paid. Unfortunately, human nature being what it is, repetition of warnings regarding operational security is a necessary evil. But, these admonitions must be balanced against maintaining personal rapport with the agent. And, the bottom line is simply that many agents never follow this advice anyway.

The final order of business was to instruct LEMON to call my office the evening of April 11th to get his instructions for the next meeting. After finishing our drinks, LEMON and I left the hotel, and I drove him back to the pickup point. Larry remained in the suite, under the guise of having an international business call to make. In reality, he stayed there in order to have a chance to write up extensive notes on the information that the agent had provided on Petran and the junior communications officer. All this information would be pure gold for the Field Office.

Upon returning to the suite, Larry and I went over our notes. With regard to the information on both Consulate officers, we agreed that his report would be the comprehensive narrative of LEMON's information. In my report to Headquarters, I would mention the issue but reference his report as the primary document. However, as I would later discuss with Ralph, the Agency would probably want a more active role in any operation against Petran because, should he ever be recruited, his greatest value to US intelligence would come from a posting outside the U.S. or back in the Ministry. And, handling him there would be an Agency job, not that of the FBI.

After departing the hotel, we went through the usual security procedures, and I got home a bit before midnight. Since Larry was doing the bulk of the reporting on the two Consulate officers, I wrote up my notes and was in bed a little after 1 a.m. Things were going so well that I had no problem going to sleep.

The next morning I briefed Winston on the meeting, wrote up my report and sent it in to Headquarters. The following day Larry brought over his report. After reading it, I forwarded it to Headquarters. I also gave him a copy of my report, and mentioned that I probably would need to speak with Ralph and Matt about how the Field Office planned to exploit the information on Petran. He said he would talk with them about when a meeting could be arranged.

Chapter Twenty-Six: The Tapes

Now we were close. We had spent months and months developing the agent, and had near certainty that he would undertake bringing out the encrypted communications tapes. This was a significant accomplishment, but not the end in itself. Even experienced COs sometimes forget that the agent is only a tool to be used to produce intelligence. So, this is a time when there are conflicting thoughts about how to proceed. The objective was to obtain and copy the tapes. But, because of the commercial cover story used to develop and recruit the agent, we had to keep our planning scenario in that mode. Not to do so might well cause the agent to suddenly feel he has been tricked, which of course he had been. But, as we are about to task him to take the greatest risk of our relationship, we needed him to have complete confidence in his relationship with us–and that means us: the boss, the corporation, me, and Franklin. I was pretty confident that LEMON believed that the laser reader was capable of doing its job without disturbing the outer packaging. Hell, between the technical drawings provided by Headquarters and the detailed briefing by Larry, I just about believe it.

So, for the late April meeting, we would use all the leverage we had. It would be a hotel meeting with Winston, who would provide the "father figure" in tasking and expressing confidence that it could be done safely from the agent's perspective. If necessary, due to any hesitation on LEMON's part, Winston was prepared to promise a five-thousand-dollar bonus for bringing out the tapes. Larry and I would work out a plan for bringing out the tapes based heavily on what LEMON felt was the most secure way of doing it. All of this would be wrapped up in our complete confidence in the newly developed laser technology.

It was agreed that the meeting would be on April 22nd. LEMON would be given that date as the primary date for a car pickup by Patrick and he would be advised that the boss will be hosting him to dinner that evening. Ralph would have his surveillance personnel cover the pickup location and the hotel to check for any suspicious activities.

Since we had about a week before the agent was to call in, we also needed to address the operational issue of the potential targeting of Petran, the Consulate senior security officer. Thanks to the solid relationship we now enjoy with the Field Office, the issues of who and how such an operation would be conducted were settled quickly and easily. The Field Office, Matt's Squad, would handle initial information gathering, using their established capabilities of reporting assets and electronic and physical surveillance. Matt already had a basic file on Petran. In fact, Matt, as the FBI SA responsible for protecting the diplomatic status of the Consulate, had already met Petran once. He would seek a way to get another meeting with him.

When Petran first arrived in the city, the FBI requested Agency traces on him and was provided with a basic package containing what facts were available from his previous postings abroad. With the new interest in him, Headquarters reviewed its files and provided Matt with a more comprehensive analysis of his career, personal interests, and related material. While posted abroad, he had only limited contact with any Agency COs, but he did have professional and social relationships with several security officials in those countries. And, many of these officials or individuals did report information about his personality, professional responsibilities, and interests to their Station contacts.

Also, since LEMON's information tied him to espionage activities in the city, the Field Office was able to obtain legal authority for additional monitoring of his activities. But this would take some time.

Station's role would be supporting, with Larry as the liaison officer, the Field Office in its activities. As their operation matured, and if they

CHAPTER TWENTY-SIX: THE TAPES

were able to get someone in regular contact with him, our role might become more active. Meanwhile, Matt decided on the name "TOPDOG" for Petran and the operation against him. Following our own logic, Headquarters decided that it also needed a cover name and chose "Elevator." Now, while it seems somewhat silly that two different cover names are used for the same USG intelligence target/operation, there is a logic that transcends just internal organizational structure. That logic is compartmentalization. Different cover names make it much more difficult for a foreign intelligence or security organization to identify USG agents. If, for example, an FBI SA becomes an agent of a foreign intelligence service, and this can and has happened, that service may also have some access to Agency material. If the cover name is the same, it is easier for their asset to just look for Agency material under that name. If, for example, the FBI actually obtains cooperation of an individual while in the United States and then returns to his or her own country, or another country, where the Agency takes control of the operation, a different code name ensures there is no direct link between the FBI and the Agency file. Thus, while knowing the individual had assisted the FBI during a specific time, the Foreign Service can only guess whether the individual had been employed while on other foreign tours or back in their own country. In counterintelligence investigations, looking to answer questions like this takes extensive time and resources. And, one of the key principles of a defensive counterintelligence program is to make it as difficult and costly as possible for any foreign service to identify and understand who the agent is, the access s/he had, and just when exactly s/he began working for US intelligence.

With the TOPDOG/ELEVATOR issue settled to everyone's satisfaction, with the possible exception of the Agency's Counterintelligence Center which still felt it should play a more active role, we were ready to focus on the meeting of April 22nd. LEMON accepted the date at his April 11th call-in, and seemed quite pleased that the boss would be at this meeting.

We all knew what we needed to accomplish over drinks and dinner, so the only remaining issue was to ensure the NSA/LU was prepared to travel to the city and set up its copying equipment within a specific time frame between mid to late May. Larry and I, in our Robert and Franklin roles, would handle the reception of the tapes and their transportation to the copy site. However, once we had the tapes SAs from Matt's squad would provide additional authority and security just in case something went wrong—like a traffic accident or some other surprise event. However, as we learned once the NSA/LU advised that the period 12 to 23 May would be when they were available, the copying operation was quite a logistical undertaking.

The morning of 15 April, NSA/LU advised not only of their availability but also of their requirements. They would drive their equipment to the city in two nondescript trucks with two officers per vehicle. The remaining seven officers would arrive several days before by air and rail. All would be in alias and book their own hotel rooms as commercial travelers. Our job was to find a suitable location for their copy setup and transportation for them between their hotels and that site. They needed a large space at least 30 feet long and 25 feet wide to accommodate their copying lines, as well as a separate area where their experts could remove, copy, and replace the security seals placed on the encrypted tape packages. The easy part was the local transportation. Matt volunteered that members of his Squad would act as drivers for the NSA/LU personnel, using unmarked Field Office cars to transport them as necessary, 24 hours a day during the copy operation. The logistics for the copying room were somewhat more complicated, as the actual purpose of the exercise had to be kept strictly compartmentalized.

Ralph and I considered where the location should be and the type of security required over the course of several days in both telephonic and personal conversations. Both the Station and the Field Office were ruled out because the sheer size of the activity would raise questions and cause gossip within the offices. We agreed our criteria had to include a location with 24/7 security, an underground parking and unloading area, and a space which could be closed off for between five and ten days without drawing too much attention. We also wanted a space reasonably close to

CHAPTER TWENTY-SIX: THE TAPES

the location where LEMON would pass us the tapes, just in case there was a need to get the tapes back to him quickly for some unanticipated reason. Murphy's Law had to be considered.

I finally came up with the idea of using space in another USG organization, one with a large office in a downtown federal building. This agency had been very helpful in some of the Station's other operations, and on a personal level, I had developed a solid relationship with both the senior officer in charge and the deputy in charge of investigation. I recalled that as a regional office, in addition to their regular office space they also had a separate conference room—training room which was large enough to suit our purposes. Being housed in a federal building, they also had General Services Office armed security guards on duty twenty-four hours a day, seven days a week. Their parking area was under the building, and freight elevators were available from the basement to every floor.

Once I explained all this to Ralph, he agreed that we should contact the agency chief and ask for her cooperation. He noted that while he did not know the agency's personnel as well as I apparently did, he had met her and their working relations had been smooth during his time at the Field Office.

With no time to waste, that afternoon I arranged an appointment with the senior officer for the following day. Both Ralph and I met with her and the senior investigative officer. Without going into too much detail, but enough to permit these officers to understand the importance and sensitivity of our request, we explained we needed access and control of their conference—training room for about a ten day period in mid-May. Checking her training and conference schedule, the officer advised that no regional or office training had been scheduled, but there was a one-day conference planned in that period for in-house review of some administrative personnel procedures. She said that she could reschedule that conference if necessary. Ralph and I both expressed our appreciation for her cooperation, mentioning that if everything worked out as planned, we would arrange for her Washington Headquarters to be made aware of the assistance she had provided.

So, we moved on to discuss the cover story required to explain the closure of the training room for several days, and the supposed activities occurring inside it during that period. We agreed on the story that the room was to be examined, and then tested from a counter electronic surveillance perspective so that it could retain its certification as a Top Secret level conference and training location for local and regional events. Thus, technicians from Washington, along with their equipment, would be arriving to undertake the testing and evaluation. This would explain the trucks and equipment movement and the activities within the room. During this period, the room would be closed to all except the technicians since their work was of a sensitive nature. This story would provide an acceptable and seemingly logical reason for the room being closed.

Now, all we needed to do was provide the actual dates we needed the room, preferably a week or ten days in advance. I have to say that the level of cooperation we received from this particular agency was excellent. Eventually, CIA Headquarters presented awards to both officers.

With the copying site obtained we completed the remaining logistical tasks for the April 22nd meeting, and Winston, Larry, Patrick and I worked out our scripts. Meanwhile, Matt worked out the details of the countersurveillance coverage.

Patrick made the car pickup securely and had LEMON in the hotel suite a bit before 7:30 p.m. Scotches were poured, and the boss went through a few minutes of pontification on recent corporate business developments. He then discussed his satisfaction with the way the laser reader development program had succeeded. He praised Franklin for his technical leadership and program management, and noted that this technical breakthrough would greatly benefit the corporation's bottom line profits. He then announced that, based upon this success, he was promoting Franklin to the Deputy Chief of Research and Development, with an appropriate increase in salary and a special bonus for completing the project. We all applauded Franklin's success and drank to his accomplishments. With the scene now set to task LEMON, the boss moved into that conversation.

The boss looked directly at LEMON and said, "Now, we are set to

CHAPTER TWENTY-SIX: THE TAPES

capitalize on your access to the communications tapes. Once we have them scanned, we can all sit back and let our technicians monitor the radio traffic for commercial value. This information, when compared to our ongoing commercial activities and contacts, will significantly enhance our capabilities to provide timely offers of equipment to your government and its allies. Also, I suspect we will learn of other governmental needs of which we were unaware, yet have the capability to address through existing corporate capabilities. While your government will not know it, we will be in a position to assist them more effectively, both in terms of time and expense, than ever before. And, based upon this new technology, we will be able to do so at a greater profit to the corporation."

He then looked in my direction and instructed me to discuss with the agent how best to get the tapes from the Consulate. With this cue, I asked LEMON how he thought we should accomplish this. I added that, according to our technicians, they would need between ten and fifteen hours to properly align the laser reader and scan the wrapped tapes. I noted that, as this was the first time the tapes were examined and scanned, the time required was longer than would be the case in subsequent laser reading sessions. LEMON remained silent for several seconds and took a deep breath. A serious expression quickly flashed across his face.

Then, in a very business-like manner, he asked whether we wanted to start with the open tapes without the packaging or the packaged tapes. I responded that we wanted to start with whatever unopened tape packages he held. I explained that the reader was calibrated for the packaging, so it was best to use those tapes.

In reality, we wanted the unopened tapes for another reason—it gave us better control and less risk in the operation. Whenever a physical item, even documents, is removed from a facility to copy, one of the main fears is that some event outside your control can suddenly demand that the item is required for use at the facility. In those circumstances, you have to get the item back inside immediately, and this is very dangerous because you cannot control everything that is going on. Specifically with communications tapes, there is always the chance that an immediate message might come into the Consulate and needs to be decrypted at once. If we had an open tape, we would have to get it back to the agent, and he would have to get it back into the Communications Office, all within the supposed time period it would take him to go directly from his residence to the Consulate to handle the message. And, in cases of immediate messages after normal working hours, usually other senior officials were also called in. So, significantly less risk was involved going with the unopened tapes, since in theory they would remain in the communications safe out of view of anyone if we did not have adequate time to permit LEMON to actually return them to the Consulate.

I asked LEMON how many unopened tapes he had. He responded that normal procedure was to have one each of the encryption and decryption tapes open for use, and two each in their packages as reserves. He explained that when the open packages were about half used, he would send a message to the Ministry and request shipment of a new tape. So, on occasion, he might actually have three packaged tapes in his safe, along with one opened tape just about used up and another tape partially used. He repeated what he had told us previously about the security procedures related to the opening of each new tape package, noting that often these procedures were not exactly followed.

Considering the size of the tapes, I asked him how he thought he could get them out of the Consulate without arousing suspicion. He said, and this is what we had hoped for and would have moved him towards, that for months he had been carrying a briefcase with him to and from work. He usually had his lunch, reading materials, and other personal paperwork he wanted to do while at work . Never had he been asked about it, let alone asked to open it for inspection as he entered or departed the building. LEMON said that luckily, two tapes would fit nicely into his briefcase, and this would be the easiest way of transporting the tapes. Franklin and I agreed, and the boss gave a nod of approval.

At this point it was Franklin's turn to start discussion of the best times to remove the tapes. He began by asking how often the Consulate received an immediate message after normal business hours that required the agent to

CHAPTER TWENTY-SIX: THE TAPES

go to the Communications Room and decode the message. He also asked if others were called in at the same time, or whether it was left up to LEMON to decide who needed to read the message once he decoded it.

LEMONS advised that very seldom, in fact only a couple of times since he had arrived at the Consulate, had he been called in after normal working hours to process and decode a communication. He said the usual procedure would be for the Ministry's Communications Center to telephone him at his residence and advise that a radio message was in process. He would then go to the Consulate, process the radio traffic, and notify the appropriate official of the need to come in and read the message. However, he noted, when he had been the junior officer at a post in Africa, on one occasion, the senior security officer had been called at his home and told to go to the Embassy to read an immediate message. In this case, the security officer had then notified the senior Communications Officer and met him at the Embassy, where together they processed the incoming message. But, he added, this did not seem to be the procedure at the Consulate. Yet, he added that if the immediate message was from the security service, they might notify their officer first.

The next question I asked was, "Assuming you and another officer, perhaps the senior security officer or the Consulate General, were called in at the same time, would the other officer be able to view the contents of the communications safe as you took out the decoding tape? Or, would that be your job only, and the other officer would wait in a different part of the room?" LEMON responded that the communication's safe was in a corner of the room next to his desk, while the radio equipment was in the main area of the room, with a pillar creating about a ninety-degree angle blocking his desk area from view. The junior Communications Officer's smaller desk was almost opposite the radio equipment, and that is where LEMON assumed the other officer would sit and wait.

Franklin then rejoined the conversation, asking when the agent felt the best time would be to remove the tapes, and how long he thought they could be outside the Consulate. LEMON thought for about thirty seconds, while Franklin and I tried not to appear anxious. He then said that a Friday night removal would be best, as that would provide the corporate technical team almost forty-eight hours to handle their tasks. Also, on most Fridays, the staff departed the building early in the afternoon, and he was usually the last to leave in order to get all the Consulate's reporting out before the weekend. Once in a while, if the outgoing backlog was light, he allowed his junior officer to leave a bit early as well, while he finished up the message transmission and locked up the room.

He added that only one security guard was on duty at the desk by the main entrance to the Consulate, and he never bothered to check LEMON, or for that matter, anyone else, as they left the building. He then noted that the security guard, of whom there were two assigned to the Consulate with one always on duty, were not very alert: since they worked shifts of twelve hours on and twelve hours off, they usually seemed tired and dazed. The senior security officer had complained of their lax attitude a couple of times, but to no avail, and had just accepted the situation.

At this point, the boss commented that he expected us to accept LEMON's opinion of when best to remove the tapes, since he had the best sense of when doing so would present the least amount of risk. As the weekend was the period we had anticipated, I responded that we would handle our planning based on a weekend. I then asked the agent how his encrypted tape inventory would be in late May. He answered that he anticipated having about sixty-five percent of his encryption tape, just recently put in use, still unused, and a slightly larger amount of his opened decryption tape unused. So, he assumed he would have one package of unopened encryption and decryption tapes available for scanning. Quickly checking my pocket notebook calendar, I suggested that the weekend starting on Friday, 22 May, through Monday morning of 25 May might be a good target date. I asked the agent if this period worked for him.

LEMON checked his pocket diary and said that those dates seemed fine. He added that no diplomatic weekend events or official visits had been scheduled. However, he noted, there was always the possibility that something could come up in the couple of weeks prior to that date. I responded that we would have to develop a plan to handle such

CHAPTER TWENTY-SIX: THE TAPES

contingencies, since the most important aspect of the planning was to have him undertake the least risk while bringing out the tapes.

Room service arrived with the meal at this point, and we moved into more general conversation while Patrick organized the table and food. During the meal, Winston took the lead in providing entertaining stories of his supposed experiences while in boarding school, and during his first business forays in Southeast Asia after World War II. He was a remarkable story teller, and all of us were enthralled by his tales—even though I was well aware they were variations on themes of British writers such as Graham Greene and Somerset Maugham, with a bit of Hemingway added for color. The boss concluded his dinner performance with some reaffirmations of how the corporation rewarded loyalty just to keep LEMON thinking in the right direction.

After dessert and coffee we returned to the sitting area, and the boss remained with us, as I discussed with LEMON how we would coordinate the date and time of the tape removal and "scanning." I noted that during dinner I had been considering how we could handle this and had come up with a plan we could discuss and modify as LEMON thought necessary. "We will tentatively set the dates for May 22 to 25, with the idea being that you would provide the tapes to Franklin and me after work on the 22th, and they would be returned to you early evening of the 24th, for placement back in the Communications Room safe the morning of the 25th. " I continued that "You should call my office on May 5th, and at that time you will be advised where to meet either me or Franklin to discuss the final details of how we will exchange the tapes on Friday evening and Sunday." "This meeting," I noted," would take place at least a week before the planned tape removal, and should be adequate time to ensure that we all felt comfortable with all the arrangements involved." I concluded that "if at any time right up until the 22nd anything should come up at the Consulate that affected removing the tapes, you should call my office at once, and we will adjust our planning as necessary."

LEMON agreed that the plan seemed to cover everything. The boss interjected that the plan seemed well considered, but then directly asked the agent if he was fully comfortable with it. LEMON responded that he was, and the boss then stated, "Fine, then we will go with it."

At that point, we engaged the agent in conversation about how his wife and son were doing, and continued along these lines of inquiry through a couple of glasses of scotch. At about 10:30 p.m., the boss excused himself to make some business call from his bedroom area, and I transitioned the conversation into his April salary of two thousand dollars, which as usual was presented to him in an envelope—a relatively hefty envelope. I asked if he wanted the entire amount, and he advised that he would take three hundred dollars in cash but wanted the remainder placed in his account. I agreed, gave him the three hundred, and placed the remaining funds back in my briefcase. Now was the time to mention the bonus he could expect for providing the tapes. So, turning back to him, I said, "While I am not officially authorized to tell you this, the boss has previously told both Franklin and me that he is considering a large bonus for you after the tapes are copied." I continued: "He did not give us a figure, but I think it will be in the range of several thousand dollars." I concluded: "I wanted to mention this to you privately because I think it represents the faith and confidence that the boss has in you, and certainly bodes well for your future with the corporation." Franklin added his supporting comments, and LEMON smiled slightly, and responded that he was very pleased to be part of the corporation and very happy to enjoy the confidence of the boss.

As Franklin poured our traditional "one for the road" drink, I once again confirmed that the agent was comfortable with the dates and planning we had discussed and agreed to for the tape removal. He stated "Yes," and did indeed appear confident and unworried. As we finished our drink, Franklin summoned Patrick from the bedroom, and LEMON was escorted to the car and subsequently taken back to the pickup point. All had gone well. The following day, the Field Office surveillance personnel reported that no suspicious activities had been observed during the pickup, hotel meeting, or during the drop-off.

When Patrick returned to the suite, we cleaned up the area and departed the hotel, Patrick and Winston in the car, and Larry and I separately, with

CHAPTER TWENTY-SIX: THE TAPES

no problems.

The next afternoon, before our reporting was sent to Headquarters. I sent an immediate operational cable advising NSA/LU that the dates for the copying of the tapes had been set and a location identified for the copying site. The following day, Winston and I met with Ralph, Matt, and Larry and agreed upon a plan for the exchange of the tapes using a department store in a large commercial center between the Consulate and the agent's route to his residence. LEMON would be briefed on this plan, and actually driven through the entire route as a visual re-enforcement of the briefing during a mid-May car pick up triggered by his May 5th call to "office."

It was agreed that the Field Office's surveillance unit would monitor LEMON from the time he left the Consulate on May 22nd until he settled into his residence that evening. They would do the same starting at his residence on May 23rd, throughout the night, until he returned the tapes to the Consulate on the morning of May 24th. The details of these plans were sent, separately, to each of our Headquarters.

A few days later, we received notification from NSA/LU that they would start arriving on May 18th, with the team leader wanting to view the copying site early on the 19th. The two trucks would arrive early on May 20th, and start that evening to move the equipment into the site and set up the copying work line. The message included the arrival times of the other team members, and we made arrangements for Field Office personnel to pick them up at the airport and train stations and take them to their hotel rooms. Ralph and I planned to pick up the team leader, get her to her hotel room and settled, and then take her the next morning to look at the copying site.

With the dates set, I visited the head of the organization allowing us to use their space and explained the timing and actions we would be taking regarding use of their room. Once this was accomplished, I returned to the Station and sent a cable to NSA/LU confirming that all was ready.

Our next task was to confirm the car pickup when LEMON called in on May 5th. We advised the Telephone Unit to inform the agent of the location and time on May 10th when he would be picked up by Franklin. Actually, while Franklin would be driving, I would be in the backseat with the agent explaining the plan as Franklin drove the actual route from the Consulate to the commercial center and then by LEMON's residence twice to confirm he fully understood the plan.

On the morning of May 6th we were advised the agent had received the instructions, and confirmed that he understood them. The car pickup for May 10th was set. Everything seemed to be in place.

Chapter Twenty-Seven: Doing the Deed

We had been thinking about the logistics and planning for the reception and subsequent return of the tapes since the mid-April period, once NSA/LU had confirmed its availability. Winston, Larry, and I had spent several hours working to ensure our plan fully conformed to LEMON's routine activities. Once we had the broad outline, we sat down with Ralph, Matt, and Patrick and began to refine the operation step by step. The SAs had only a few constructive suggestions to add, which we did. The Field Office was also generous in its allocation of its resources to monitor and protect the transfers of the tapes. So, after advising our Headquarters of the details, and receiving quick approval with no additional suggestions, we had the plan in place to brief the agent during the May 10th car pick-up meeting.

Our plan for the reception of the tapes involved Field Office surveillance of LEMON with his departure from the Consulate Friday evening until he reached his residence. Its principal task was to ascertain if the agent was being followed. If this were the case, and it was certainly the worst scenario, it probably meant that either the agent was under suspicion or the tapes were actually part of a deception plan by the Romanian Government. In either event, we had backup plans to protect LEMON and his family if there was suspicion and another plan if our verification of the tapes indicated they were not legitimate.

Our primary plan was for LEMON to place the two unopened tapes in his briefcase and depart the Consulate, taking his usual bus route home. We already had several copies of the same briefcase he had, since we knew it would be used to carry out items, and that switching the briefcases would probably be necessary at some point. This was standard operating procedure, although it was not mentioned to the asset at that time. When we briefed him on the exchange operation, we would simply tell him we had obtained an exact copy of his briefcase, without further details.

Notes from previous meetings reminded us that often LEMON would stop on his way home at a local department store, on his bus route, to pick up various items. At least once a month he went there to purchase a toy for his son. We cased the store, learning that the toy department was on the third floor, and could be reached from the ground floor of the commercial center in which it was located by two sets of escalators; one from the ground floor to the second and another one, inside the department store, from the second to the third floor. So, this became the site for the clandestine briefcase exchange—the toy section just off the escalator on the third floor of the center.

Having both escalators as "channeling lanes" to identify any surveillance of the agent was a key part of the final determination regarding whether the agent had been followed. It is standard procedure to plan a route with such features.

The scenario was carefully timed, as all such clandestine actions must be, and involved Field Office surveillance advising me, via a pager buzz, when LEMON had entered the store and was on the escalator moving towards the third floor. As I was already in the toy department, based on earlier notification that the agent was on the bus, I would move over to a counter ninety degrees to the right of the exit point of the escalator. As LEMON reached the third floor, he would turn right and immediately place his briefcase at my feet by the display counter, while I gave him the duplicate briefcase. Without breaking stride, he would proceed to the stuffed animal area of the department and spend a few minutes selecting a stuffed toy which he would then purchase for his son. Having given him the duplicate briefcase, I would use my foot to push his briefcase next to the counter, where my legs shielded it from public view. To further obscure the exchange, two SAs from Matt's Squad, one male and one female, were

CHAPTER TWENTY-SEVEN: DOING THE DEED

positioned to move towards the escalator just as LEMON made his right turn, physically blocking anyone immediately following him who might observe the switch of briefcases.

After LEMON had spent a few minutes making his purchase, he would take the escalator back down to the street and wait for another bus to take him to his residence. Giving the agent about twenty seconds to get away from me, I would pick up the briefcase containing the tapes and walk to the third-floor elevator, taking it to the parking garage below the building. Another of Matt's SAs would discreetly follow me as a security measure. Upon reaching the garage, I would enter a Field Office unmarked car driven by Larry, and we would proceed to the Federal Building where the copy line had been set up.

Once the NSA/LU copy team had the tapes, we would be done until they notified us that they had validated the authenticity of the tapes and completed their copying of them. Of course, we would also check with the Field Office surveillance teams regarding their identification of any surveillance on the agent, and that he had arrived home safely.

Once the copying was completed, the duplicate tapes and the original tapes were to be kept at the copying site, with FBI guard, until early evening on Sunday, when Larry and I would pick them up for passage back to LEMON.

Matt's folks would be monitoring all actions at the Consulate over the weekend. But, we anticipated that it would be closed as normal for a weekend.

Our operational plan to pass the tapes back on Sunday to LEMON was much simpler. The agent was to depart his residence a half hour after dark, for a stroll after dinner, which was his custom, a couple of times during the week. However, he would also be on an errand for his wife to pick up some feminine hygiene products for her. This would be the reason he brought his briefcase along. His explanation, if ever questioned, would be that he was embarrassed to be seen carrying those items, so he used his briefcase to carry them from the store to his home. He would, of course, be surveilled by the Field Office.

After purchasing the items from a neighborhood store, he would return home by way of a nearby tree-covered park. Then, at a prearranged dark portion of the park, he and I would exchange briefcases as we passed each other at a brisk walking pace. In case others were present in the park walkways, it was also arranged that when Larry, from his car parked near the area of the exchange, saw LEMON and I approaching, he would radio another FBI unmarked car to hit its lights and siren and skid around the corner of the park opposite where the exchange was being made. Our view was that this activity would immediately draw the attention of anyone who might otherwise have casually seen the briefcase exchange.

The evening of May 10th, with Larry driving a rented town car and me in the back seat, we picked up LEMON. As he joined me in the car, I explained that the purpose of tonight's meeting was to go over with him how we would exchange the tapes. I noted "The boss is a very careful planner, and had instructed me to ensure that you fully understood the procedures we will follow and that you are comfortable with them." I continued, "We have developed a plan based upon careful evaluation of what would be normal for you to do. So, if anyone accidentally observes you, you can explain your actions as just part of your everyday activities." The agent appeared to accept this, and I began briefing him on the scenario for passing me the tapes. This included diagrams of the interior of the commercial center, the department store, and the toy department.

As I went through his movements from leaving the Consulate until he arrived home that Friday evening, Larry drove a pre-arranged route into the suburbs and then back into the city. This gave me almost an hour to go through the initial exchange and the return of the tapes to him on Sunday evening. As we returned to the area near the Consulate, I went through the scenario again, and this time Larry drove the bus route LEMON takes home so I could specifically point out the department store, even though he already knew it from previous visits. Once past the store, I repeated the instructions for his actions inside the store. Larry next drove by LEMON's resident building, and then took the streets the agent would walk to get to the store to purchase the female hygiene product, and subsequently walk back through the park. We briefly stopped at the park so I could show him the exact portion of the walk where I would exchange briefcases with him. Then, we repeated the same routes and again described the actions to be taken.

From there, Larry drove to a suburban cocktail lounge, while I continued to review the plan with LEMON, especially his actions within the store during the actual exchange of the briefcases—this split second encounter was the most difficult of the plan and probably the most stressful for the agent. Once at the cocktail lounge, we went to a dark booth in the rear, where we once again discussed the plan, reviewed the diagrams, and double-checked that the agent both understood them and was comfortable with them.

Over scotches, noticeably inferior to what we would drink at our other meetings, LEMON stated his approval of the scenarios and his understanding of his role in both exchanges. While on our second drink, I pulled out a sheet of paper which sketched out the third floor of the department store, showing how he was to make the ninety-degree right turn off the escalator. We reviewed how he was to do this for a few minutes. I also suggested that the next evening, on his way home from work, he practice the scenario by stopping at the store, taking the escalators, and making the right-hand turn while proceeding to look at the available toys. However, he was not to purchase a toy, only look at them, as buying two toys in a short period of time was not part of his normal activities. He agreed this practice run would be a good idea.

We finished our drinks, returned to the car, and as Larry drove back to the pick-up point I yet once again went over the plan in detail with the agent. Just as we arrived at the drop off point, I told him to call my Delaware office the afternoon of May 22nd if for any reason he could not pass the tapes that night. I also noted that, assuming the tape exchange went as anticipated, he was to call my office on May 30th for instructions for the next meeting. He had not asked about his May salary, so I quickly mentioned that I would handle that at the next meeting. Finally, with the most sincere and confident look I could muster, I firmly took his hand and said, "I have complete confidence that we can do this with no problems whatsoever, and I have told the boss exactly that. I will see you on Friday night." Larry also said goodbye, and we drove off into the night.

It was my opinion, as well as that of Larry's, or at least so he said, that LEMON was comfortable with the plan and confident he could do it. During our repeated discussion of the plan, he asked several questions, especially regarding specifics on how to handle the physical exchanges of the briefcases. By tradecraft standards used in foreign areas where internal security services control the environment, this was a very simple plan. And, added features of which the agent was unaware provided additional operational security protection without affecting LEMON's role.

The next day, our reporting went into our respective Headquarters, and with less than two weeks to go, we began assigning roles to all the moving parts. We had a week before the NSA/LU team arrived, so our first actions were to reconfirm preparations, including cover stories to explain the equipment unloading and setup at the federal office building. This actually went much easier than anticipated. The office chief issued a memo to her staff that the conference-training room was being inspected and modified, and would be out of use for about two weeks. Since the modifications included sensitive counter audio measures, it would be considered a restricted area until the work was complete. She also had her deputy provide a similar cover story to the GSA security guards, along with requests for their assistance in the parking and unloading of the trucks bringing the testing equipment and technical personnel. Since inspection, updating, and reconfiguration of federal office space used for classified discussions is a pretty routine activity in government, no questions arose at the building.

Considering the number of Field Office personnel involved, from both the surveillance element and Matt's Squad, it was obvious that the number of people knowledgeable of LEMON's association with the USG was about to increase significantly. While these FBI folks would not necessarily have to know exactly what the agent was doing, they certainly could guess that he was passing some type of information. So, I left it up to Ralph's

CHAPTER TWENTY-SEVEN: DOING THE DEED

discretion as to how much to tell his people regarding how their actions fit into the larger picture.

There is no question that I felt uncomfortable with this, not because I distrusted them, but because within Agency culture, compartmentalization is a religion. In reality, I could have requested Agency personnel to handle the surveillance duties and the other activities related to the operation. While it would have meant bringing a couple of dozen people into the city, there is little doubt that Headquarters would have approved the request. But, this would also have meant more people knowledgeable of the operation anyway—just folks from the Agency rather than the Bureau. And, of course, this would have been perceived as an insult to the Field Office, which, professionally, it would have been. So, the only choice I had was to use Field Office personnel and work closely with Ralph and Matt in the briefing and practice sessions of their people.

As noted, the Field Office's role was to provide surveillance of LEMON from the time he departed the Consulate, through the briefcase exchange, until he entered his residence on the 22nd. They would perform the same function on the 24th to cover the return of the tapes to him. In between these times, three surveillance teams and other Field Office resources would have to be on duty and ready to respond to any unusual events at the Consulate that might affect the copy operation. Other members of Matt's Squad would be "live" monitoring the Consulate as well as all the Consulate employees. The most probable issue we could think of would be a call to the Consul General, or LEMON, from the Ministry in Bucharest advising that an immediate communication was being sent and should be read at once by the appropriate official at the Consulate. We thought we could handle this. If we did not have adequate time to get the tapes back to the agent, and this probably would be the case since he would have to go directly to the Consulate, we felt that the chances of anyone else looking into the communications safe were unlikely.

However, if the Consul General or the senior Security Officer was called in without the agent, then we had to take some action. We knew from previous discussions with LEMON that the Consul General, as Head of

Mission, did have the combination to the safe, but the agent did not think the senior Security Officer did. However, he could not be positive that the Consul General may have provided a copy to the senior Security Officer for use in an emergency. Also, based upon the technical expertise required to open up the communication link, the junior Communications Officer would have to be involved. So, this exclusion of LEMON would be a pretty solid confirmation that he was no longer trusted. In that case, our response would be to ensure the Consul General and the senior Security Officer were unable to get to the Consulate until we had the agent and family at a safe site. Minor traffic accidents are often useful in such situations. Once the asset was secure, we could have him react as the situation developed, and we had a better feel for the degree to which his activities were suspect.

Larry's and Patrick's roles were: Larry would drive me to and from the copy site to the exchange sites, and Patrick and another SA would be in a following car to provide security or authority should any issue arise on route. Also, the male and female SA team who provided the distraction during the department store briefcase exchange would also be the two SAs in the FBI car that would be involved in the distraction when the tapes were returned to the agent. Finally, Field Office SAs would be at the copy site throughout the operation to provide security and authority as required.

So, during the actual operation, the Station's role was only for me at the briefcase exchanges and retrieval of the tapes from the NSA/LU team at the copy site.

Ralph and Matt, ably assisted by Larry and Patrick, did excellent work briefing their people. Winston and I sat in on the final review session and could only add some notes of praise for their assistance when asked to comment.

Our next task began on the 18th when the NSA/LU team leader arrived. I briefed Betsey at the Station after having had Winston pick her up at the airport. Later that day, and the next, other team members made their way to the Station and were brought up to date on our plans. When the trucks arrived with the copying equipment mid-afternoon of the 20th,

CHAPTER TWENTY-SEVEN: DOING THE DEED

Betsey's entire group assisted in the unloading and worked well into the next morning, setting up and testing the equipment. First, they set up a complex double line of various technical equipment used to duplicate the tapes. Then, a separate area was screened off where the packing experts would remove the actual tapes from their packaging and also prepare the packaging for the duplicate tapes to be returned to the agent. Finally, in another screened-off area near the entrance, they placed a table and chairs for the use of the Field Office SAs who would stand security watch until the operation was completed. They were then taken to their hotel rooms to rest up and prepare for the actual copying. The morning of the 22nd, they returned to the room and tested all the equipment in final preparation for the copying to start that evening.

The final "go" signal was no telephone call from the agent the afternoon of the 22nd. And, while we did not suspect any problems, and the Field Office's monitoring of the Consulate and its personnel did not indicate any issues, Winston and I were still nervous as the hours past. The adrenaline was running high.

That evening at six o'clock, we moved into action. We had about an hour plus before the department store exchange was to occur, but wanted to be in position well before that. Ralph and Matt reported that all seemed normal at the Consulate during the day, and that most of the employees had already departed the building. They subsequently reported that the junior Communications Officer had departed the building at about 6:30 p.m. Then, a few minutes after 7 p.m., we were advised that LEMON had departed the building and was awaiting a bus. Ten minutes later, he was reported as on the bus and with FBI surveillance personnel following.

I proceeded to the department store. A pager message informed me that the bus had stopped at a traffic light a block away, and I moved to my position by the counter next to the escalator. After what seemed like way too long a time, but actually was only a few minutes, LEMON came up the escalator, turned right, and we exchanged the briefcases. With my foot, I quickly moved the briefcase containing the tapes next to the counter, as the agent casually walked towards the stuffed animals holding the now paper-stuffed briefcase. I gave him to the count of thirty in my mind, and then picked up the briefcase and went to the elevator and the parking area.

Once in the car we had radio communication with the rest of the Field Office personnel involved, and as we pulled out into the street Larry reported that LEMON had left the store, with a stuffed lion in a shopping bag, and was waiting at the bus stop. The unmarked FBI security car moved in behind us, and we drove quickly to the copying site.

There was a light rain falling, and the only sour note of the evening was that one of the surveillance teams following the agent on his bus ride home was involved in a fender bender with an over-aggressive office worker on her way home. The Field Office team stayed with their cover as commuters, and while a small traffic jam developed, it did not affect the operation or the agent. Another team surveillance car simply took the primary "eye" on the target and confirmed he was safely home.

A little after eight pm, we pulled into the underground parking at the federal building and gave Betsey the briefcase. She advised that she would be in touch if any problems arose. Now the operation was in her hands. We had successfully obtained the tapes, and while the smoothness of the execution of the scenario was satisfying, the real value of the entire operation now hung on whether the tapes could be authenticated, copied, and then replaced without anyone at the Consulate being the wiser. The value to the U.S. Government of countless hours over a couple of many, many months all came down to the technical expertise of the NSA/LU team. Once again, espionage is a team sport, regardless of what we, Case Officers, like to believe.

Chapter Twenty-Eight: Success

I guess I should say the weekend passed quickly, but it did not. I felt each hour passing uncomfortably slowly. I was constantly alert for any telephone calls, and even spent some time speaking with Ralph, who was equally anxious about how the copying was going. I had agreed with Betsey that contacting her would only be in the event of something happening that required immediate repackaging and return of the tapes. I would have loved to call her periodically just to ask how the copying was going. But, that would hardly have been professional. Certainly, everybody at the Station and Field Office involved would have liked at least a couple of status updates on the team's progress, but that would only interrupt what I knew was going to be very difficult and painstakingly careful work.

Betsey finally called in the early hours of Sunday, advising that the copying had been completed and her folks were working on resealing the duplicate tapes. She suggested we pick up the tape packages at about noon. As previously agreed, Larry and I would pick up the actual tapes and the duplicates and take them to the Station. There, the original tapes would be prepared for secure shipment to Headquarters. The duplicate tapes would stay at the Station until late Sunday afternoon, when Larry and I would start to set up for the return exchange with LEMON.

We collected the tapes on time, and I noticed that Betsey and her team looked exhausted. When I made a polite point of asking if all had gone as expected, she wearily replied that the job had been completed. She added that they did experience a minor breakdown in the duplicate tape processing equipment, but her folks had been able to repair it. She noted that the repair had cost them almost two additional hours of downtime while the equipment was fixed.

After leaving the tapes at the Station, both of us went home to catch another couple hours of rest if not exactly relaxation, with our nerves slightly calmer. All we had to do now was return the tapes to the agent and then all he had to do was carrying them back into the Consulate and put them in the communication's safe unobserved. That was all.

We had timed the exchange for a bit after eight pm, since it was dark but not too late for someone working the following day. Winston, Larry, and I met at the Station about 4 p.m. and reviewed our plans. A lengthy secure telephone call with Ralph and Matt about 5 p.m. confirmed that all was quiet at the Consulate and none of the staff had exhibited any unusual behavior over the weekend. Ralph also confirmed his Field Office personnel were briefed and ready to go. A bit after 6 p.m., I got the duplicate tapes out of the Station vault, and with Larry driving and an unmarked FBI car following, we proceeded to a parking lot downtown, about fifteen minutes from the park. We got there quite early, and had about an hour before we drove to the point near the park where I would be let out to start my approach. Once again, signals from a pocket pager would advise me of LEMON's progress towards the exchange site.

At 7:55 p.m., Larry deposited me at the drop-off point, and I slowly started my walk towards the park. He then proceeded to park in a position to observe the exchange site and the opposite approaches from which the agent and I would be walking. At 7:58 p.m. I entered the park and, about ninety seconds later, saw LEMON approaching from the other side of the park. Some thirty seconds later, we passed each other and made the exchange, just as the FBI car sped around the corner from where the agent had entered the park, lights flashing and siren at full blast. Just as that occurred, LEMON turned around and with a look of concern on his face glanced in that direction briefly before continuing on his way out of the park towards his residence.

Note to myself, maybe we should have planned some other less dramatic type of diversion since the agent might well have panicked and done

CHAPTER TWENTY-EIGHT: SUCCESS

something which might have affected the operation. Luckily, LEMON had the discipline to just carry out our plan regardless of the extra drama involved.

I continued through the park and Larry picked me up about a block away. And, as he drove me back to the Station we received radio confirmation that LEMON was safely back in his home. Now all we had to worry about was his return of the tapes to the Consulate Monday morning.

Winston and I were at the Station by eight Monday morning, awaiting a confirmation call from Ralph that LEMON had arrived at the Consulate, and that nothing unusual was taking place as it opened for business at 9 a.m. Shortly after 8:30 a.m we got the first confirmation, and about forty-five minutes later, Ralph called to advise that surveillance of the location, both human and technical, had not indicated anything unusual. Relieved, I thanked Ralph for all of his support, and we agreed that later in the week, we would meet to exchange our reporting and do a post-operation review to assist planning for the next tape exchange. Putting down the telephone, I immediately sent a message to Headquarters advising the operation had been a success, with details to follow, as did Ralph to FBI Headquarters.

I spend much of the day preparing my detailed report, including descriptions of how the Field Office and the NSA/LU personnel had performed. I took time out to drive Betsey and another team member to the airport, where we met an SA from Matt's squad who was present to ensure our officers had no problems getting aboard the flight. The remainder of the NSA/LU broke down the copying equipment, packed it back into their trucks, and by Wednesday, were on their way back to Headquarters. They left the room looking exactly as they found it, and even sent an official-looking notice to the office chief advising the room still required formal Washington certification before it could be used for discussions up to the Top Secret level.

The rest of the week was dull, certainly compared to the weekend's activities. We got some nice messages from Headquarters, confirmation that the tapes had been delivered to NSA for exploitation, and our meeting with Ralph and Matt went smoothly. We did identify some changes we would make for the next tape exchange, including a different approach to a diversion when the duplicate tapes were given back to the agent. All in all, we felt quite satisfied with ourselves.

LEMON called in and was instructed to be at a car pickup point at 7:30 p.m. on June 12th. He agreed, and in response to a question we had asked the Telephone Unit to ask him, he responded that everything at work was normal. At the end of the week, I decided to host a TGIF party for the Station in our conference room—opting for snacks and beer which did become a bit messy, but what the Hell, life is short. The COs involved in the LEMON operation, along with the Station's Communications Officers and Administrative Officer, knew what the party was about, but the other COs probably just thought it was a nice gesture of appreciation for their efforts.

In our business, you spent dozens and dozens of "time on target" hours trying to validate a Target's access and then develop a relationship that allows you to offer something you believe they want in exchange for something they are willing to do. It doesn't always, or for the matter, usually, work out. A failure rate well over fifty percent is normal. But, you still have to spend the time and effort even to get to the point where you know it is not going to work out.

The next week, we started our scenario planning for the June 12th hotel meeting, to include an appearance by the boss. Later in the week we got a detailed Headquarters respond to our operational reporting—all positive of course. And, an "eyes only" message from NSA/LU stating that NSA had confirmed the tapes were authentic. NSA could now read both "point to point" communications from the Consulate to Bucharest and Bucharest to the Consulate, and "circular" communications which Bucharest sent to all its official installations worldwide, and the Consulate sent to other official installations. NSA also confirmed that Romanian intelligence and security services used this encryption for their reporting on both their activities and the activities they conducted in support of the Soviet Union and other Warsaw Pact nations.

This was great news, and that the Romanian intelligence organizations used these communications meant that the Field Office would be getting significant insights into Warsaw Pact spying and influence activities in the area. All their investment in resources had been amply rewarded. We could now anticipate strong support at the Field Office for almost any future operation.

There was also a down side to this type of operation—I and the Station would never know how extensive and valuable the tapes would be. We would only be advised by the NSA of any information that affected our operations in the city or the LEMON operation. All information coming from the use of these tapes would be handled in restricted channels and provided on a "need to know" basis within the USG. Within the FBI, the information of a counterintelligence nature would probably have a larger distribution based on the manner in which they operate. But, it would still be very closely held.

Our objectives for the June 12th meeting were to reinforce LEMON's allegiance to the corporation, determine if there were any indications he was under any type of suspicion, and in general, ensure he was a cooperating "partner" in the best sense of the word. Now that he had provided the tapes, his commitment had been fully tested. He could not go back and confess some lapse of judgment or involvement through trickery that had resulted in providing the tapes. He had committed treason in the eyes of this country. His and his family's future depended upon working with us to ensure he was not caught. So, all we had to do was keep him happy and well rewarded. Oh, and of course, safe!

There was a minor debate, mostly between me, Ralph, and Matt, about the degree to which we should engage the agent in reporting on other activities and personalities within the Consulate. For obvious reasons, Matt wanted LEMON to do so aggressively. My position, fully supported by Ralph and indeed the correct one for obvious reasons, was that at all costs, LEMON should avoid any suspicious activities at the Consulate. The primary focus of his collection efforts should be the periodic provisions of the encrypted tapes. Agency Headquarters and FBI Headquarters also stated this position when, more for the record than debate, Ralph noted

Matt's suggestion in his reporting. Matt's Squad had more than adequate insights into any counterintelligence threats from the Consulate. However, in the spirit of cooperation, I advised Matt that as a regular part of all future meetings, we would be discussing the agent's situation at the Consulate, and his interactions with others there. And, should any information on Consulate personalities or activities be of interest from Matt's perspective, we would find a way to get more information on it from LEMON. That seemed to satisfy Matt—at least somewhat.

The June 12th hotel meeting came off as planned. No surveillance was observed when Patrick picked up the agent. In the hotel suite, Winston was in perfect character, congratulating LEMON on providing the tapes and praising his efforts as a valued member of the corporation. The boss gave him a ten-thousand-dollar bonus for his efforts, and he was particularly amusing during a relaxed drinks and dinner phase of the meeting. At this time, I also complimented LEMON on the poise he exhibited during the exchanges of the tapes and then subtly inquired if he had noticed any unusual behavior towards him by other Consulate officials. He responded in the negative, even noting that his relationship with the Consulate General was as strong as ever—apparently LEMON had recently given the Consulate General a couple of bottles of good scotch as a gift on the anniversary of his appointment as head of the Consulate. Franklin then added his compliments to the agent and noted that the laser equipment had worked quite well, but that it would still take some time to actually utilize the encryption tapes in understanding the communications.

LEMON then asked a question which, in retrospect was a clear indication that he was now a partner with us. He asked "How are you planning to record the encrypted radio signals coming into the Consulate so you can use the tapes to read them?"

Since we hadn't specifically planned for this question, Franklin took a moment to frame his response and said, "Well, my team is not quite there yet. We have been focusing on the laser technology, and now have to think through this part of the process. Just off hand, I suspect that since the radio waves travel in specific band spectrums, we can set up an antenna

CHAPTER TWENTY-EIGHT: SUCCESS

in a suburban site under the guise of some commercial entity, and collect them there for later manipulation against the encryption tapes." LEMON agreed this was a good plan and then mentioned the bandwidths used by the Consulate.

At this point the boss interrupted and complimented LEMON on his comments. He added that the corporation had already determined the wave length used by the Ministry of Foreign Affairs in Bucharest, but appreciated the agent confirming those details.

Dinner was its usual hearty fare, with good wine and Winston once again in excellent form, telling stories of international business connections as well as humorous anecdotes of his role as Lord of the Manor in his English village. At a later date, I asked Winston where he got all his material for these stories, and if, indeed, his parents had been in such positions. Well, his parents were of the merchant class, wealthy enough that he did attend a British public school, but never at the level of Manor society spoken of in his stories. Turns out he based his international business stories on American television programs like "Mission Impossible" and "I Spy," and his village stories on various dramas on American Public Television. You have to love the initiative and skills of a good CO!

After dinner, as the boss retired to his bedroom to make some international business calls, I discussed compensation issues with the agent. With his ten-thousand-dollar bonus and his monthly salary for May and now June, he had a great deal of money due him. LEMON stated that he wanted five hundred dollars in cash and wanted the remaining amount placed in his employee account. He explained that he wanted to get some swimming lessons for his son, and this would cost a couple of hundred dollars for an eight-week program. He also mentioned that he was using his regular Consulate salary to partially pay for other summer activities for the child, and had casually mentioned this to others at the Consulate. So, his colleagues knew that he was using much of his salary on family expenses, while saving as much as possible for big household purchases when he was posted back to Romania. I complimented him on his common-sense approach to keeping people "advised" of his financial situation.

After a "one for the road" final scotch, Patrick took LEMON back to the drop off point and we cleaned up the hotel suite and departed in our usual manner. Winston got to take home a half bottle of his favorite wine, and Larry took home a third of a bottle of scotch. I should note that if the bottles had been unopened, they would have been returned to Station stock for use in other operations. Government regulations are quite strict in this regard.

Chapter Twenty-Nine: The Aftermath

Over the next year or so, we continued to hold meetings with the agent about every six weeks. Often enough to reinforce and gauge his relationship with the corporation, yet not so often as to create operational security problems. Usually, Larry and I handled the meetings, but about three times a year, we brought out Winston to play the paternal boss role. While the operation was focused on planning for the tape exchanges, we always discussed activities in the Consulate and whether the agent noticed any unusual behavior towards him. And, as I promised Matt, when LEMON noted anything about Consulate activities or personnel, we did get additional details to pass along to the Field Office. During this time, we did tape exchanges about every six to eight months.

With LEMON as an active partner in planning the exchanges and with experience in developing and orchestrating the exchange scenarios, things ran pretty smoothly. We still did extensive coordination with the Field Office and NSA/LU, as well as careful and specific scenario planning, but we got into a good routine—not over confident just comfortable. Oh, we had our share of Murphy's Law incidents and minor concerns, as personnel issues in the Consulate sometimes involved the agent. But, nothing too serious—just enough to keep us aware that planning, coordination and operational discipline always had to be thorough and tight.

Two specific incidents come to mind regarding unanticipated events during the operation. The first involved a meeting for rapport reinforcement with the boss in attendance. Our scenario was pretty standard by then, but the trouble arose when Larry went into the bathroom in order to actually write down some of the information LEMON had provided as Consulate gossip. The information concerned the senior Security Officer, who was an ongoing target of the Field Office. After jotting down some notes, Larry decided to wash his hands to give the appearance that he had used the toilet. However, when he went to turn off the faucet, it snapped, and a stream of water began gushing out all over the bathroom. Obviously, we needed a plumber and some cleanup immediately. But, exposing LEMON and us together to anybody we did not know was an operational security problem. So, the agent, Winston, and I had to hide in the suite's bedroom, quietly, for well over an hour while two hotel employees replaced the faucet and several others cleaned up the water and dried the floor.

The second incident was of much more concern than just inconvenience. And it was the result of a breakdown in equipment in the copying operation. Nobodies' fault certainly, but because I was not advised why the copying had been terminated before all the tapes had been duplicated, I ended up pounding on Betsey's hotel room door very early on a Sunday morning, demanding to know what had happened. Communication could have been better, but her team had been trying for several hours to repair the equipment, and when they finally gave up, they had gone to bed simply telling their FBI guards that they had not been able to copy all the tapes. When Ralph advised me of this, I was, I think, understandably upset, and wanted to know what the problem was and how it impacted the overall operation. Once she explained the issue, we knew we had to plan for another tape exchange as early as the following weekend so that NSA would have current encryption tapes in their inventory. Every time LEMON removed the tapes from the Consulate, there was a risk that something could go wrong, so we were not pleased. But the NSA/LU team spent the week repairing and testing their equipment, and the next weekend, all the tapes were copied. And, while we had to change a few details of the exchange scenarios, in the end, all went well.

As I noted, we did not have access to all the communications traffic from and to the Consulate, except that which directly impacted on our operations. And, eventually we received word that LEMON's posting

CHAPTER TWENTY-NINE: THE AFTERMATH

to the Consulate was going to end in a few months. It was clear that he was being posted back to Bucharest to the Communications Office in the Ministry of Foreign Affairs. LEMON also provided us with this information at the next meeting, a couple of weeks later.

Now we faced several decisions. What would be his access back in Bucharest, and could it be exploited in-country for USG advantage? Did we feel that his cooperation with us had been well enough protected that he could go back safely? If we could run him inside Romania, would we have to tell him that it was US intelligence rather than the international corporation that was actually directing him? How would he feel about cooperating inside his country? And, many more such issues. Finally, from a professional perspective, did we have the capabilities to run him in Romania?

In the three and a half months we had before his departure, I communicated with Headquarters units involved in Eastern Bloc operations, the NSA/LU, and various counterintelligence offices as we made certain decisions and explored what our options were. I kept Ralph fully informed, and while the responsibility for handling LEMON in Romania was solely the Agency's, I tried to ensure that the Field Office continued to feel a true partner in our planning. As our plans became more focused, I returned to Headquarters for a week of meetings with various offices and managers. Unfortunately, but certainly not usual in any government personnel action, the agent did not know specifically what his responsibilities would be at the Ministry. He felt he might be told just before his transfer, but it was also possible he would not know until he actually returned to Budapest.

Our planning decision was in the best practices of a bureaucracy and, honesty, a logic conclusion: we would wait until he was established back in Bucharest and knew the job responsibilities he would hold. We provided him with a city address and name, which ostensibly was that of a Romanian emigre he had become friendly with during his posting at the Consulate. In reality, it was a "mail drop" at a residence in the neighborhood populated by Eastern European emigres, supported and serviced by the Field Office. Once back in the country and at work, LEMON was to send a postcard simply advising "greetings and that the family was settling-in and happy to be back home." This postcard would be the "sign of life" notice that he was back, at work, and that all seemed well. If the postcard expressed greeting and that the family was settling-in, without referencing "happy," this was to indicate LEMON felt he might be under suspicion. In this case, Headquarters and Bucharest Station would start to try and ascertain if he was under suspicion and if it would become necessary to develop a plan to evacuate him and his family from the country.

Assuming the agent did feel safe and comfortable, he was also given a contact plan for Athens, Greece. Headquarters had advised that trusted members of the Romanian Communist Party were often permitted to take a vacation in Greece. Thus, when he was allowed to take his family on a vacation to Greece, and we estimated it might take about six months back in country before he could do so, he was to send a post card to the city residence stating "just wanted to say family is doing well, and hope all is well with your family." This would indicate that we could expect him to call an agency-controlled telephone number in Greece once he arrived in Athens. When he called, he would be told that two days hence, he was to be at a street location where I would meet him. He was to be there at 10:47 a.m., and if we did not make contact, he was to return to the location at 8:19 p.m. that evening. Should we still not make contact, he was to repeat the meeting site and times two days later.

From our end, once the telephone call was received, I would immediately leave for Greece, traveling under an alias as an academic tourist interested in early Greek trade routes, and settle into a hotel, and recon routes to and from the point of contact given to the agent. Once we met up, I would briefly explain that I was going to introduce him to another colleague who would talk with him about his future, and then walk him on a pre-arranged countersurveillance route to a small café, where I would introduced him to a CO from Bucharest Station—his "inside" handling CO.

Time passed, the "sign of life" postcard arrived, and Bucharest Station advised that LEMON was working at the Ministry, but doing exactly what they did not yet know. A bit over seven months later, the second postcard

CHAPTER TWENTY-NINE: THE AFTERMATH

arrived, and the Athens trip was set up. Shortly after arriving in Athens, and trying my best to adjust to the terrible pollution, which apparently was a constant problem in the city, I met with the Bucharest CO and we planned our turnover of the agent. The real issue was what to tell LEMON about the affiliation of the new CO. Working with him in Romania would involve disciplined "internal handling" tradecraft, and it might be impossible to keep up the commercial cover story.

The new CO had read the file on LEMON, but wanted a personal view of his personality and motives for cooperation. While I certainly knew the agent personally, I was unsure how he would react if he were told that he was working for the US Government. Now, I did believe he was fully committed to working for the corporation and to continuing to get his monthly salary and, at some point, claim the thousands of dollars in his employee retirement account. But, would it be too great a shock to learn it was the US Government running the show? We decided that advising him of the US Government role was a necessity, based upon how he would have to behave if he were to be handled in Bucharest. However, the new CO would have to decide how to advise him of this, and when the right moment would be to do so.

All went as planned. Nobody in Athens seemed particularly interested in me or LEMON. When we arrived at the café, I pretended that the Bucharest CO was an old and trusted friend, and quickly went over the compensation plan currently in place for LEMON while he settled back in Bucharest. This is an important administrative task at all turnover meetings to ensure the agent agrees with the current set of financial arrangements and that the new CO clearly understands the obligations involved. LEMON had been on a monthly salary of $1800 per month since he arrived back in Romania. I noted that his new colleague, alias Gregor, could give him some funds from his employee account if he so desired. Then, after a few more minutes of social conversation, I excused myself, stating that he and Gregor were the team, and the boss expected them to work efficiently and well together. As I departed, I hugged the agent briefly and said I would probably see him in the near futurea lie. Then, I left the café.

I was now out of the operation. Whatever came next was the responsibility of the Bucharest CO and Station. After several years of working with, and certainly spending endless hours worrying about, the operation it ceased to exist for me in my professional capacity. I had passed it along and no longer had any "need to know" about it.

Returning to my hotel, without anyone seeming to be particularly interested, I had dinner and went to bed. I spent the next two days in museums and at ruins related to my cover academic interest. I departed for Rome, and then onward to the US.

Several months after the trip to Athens, I rotated back to a Headquarters' managerial assignment and became involved in its duties. I kept in contact with Ralph, who eventually was transferred to FBI Headquarters as part of his grooming for higher management positions. I found my new assignment to be very interesting, and the LEMON operation faded into my memory—he was someone else's responsibility now.

Chapter Thirty: Postscript

Almost a year later, I was notified that the LEMON operation had been selected for a new award in the Intelligence Community—the HUMINT Operation of the Year.

On a bright and breezy day in the fall, in the Agency auditorium, known as the "bubble" due to its design, the other COs and I were presented with the award. Ralph, Matt, Larry, and Patrick were present. Since then, like all awards, its criteria for qualifying have been lessened, and it is now given out to numerous operations several times a year. But at that time, there was one award, once a year.

Operations such as LEMON are compartmentalized very tightly within the Agency and the US Intelligence Community. After I left the café in Athens, I no longer had a "need to know" about the operation, and if, in other management responsibilities, I had to know something from that operation, it would be provided in a form which protected the source of the information.

Many years later, in a casual conversation with a colleague, I did learn that LEMON had worked for the Agency both in Bucharest and in another field assignment he had for the Romanian Ministry of Foreign Affairs. I learned no details of tradecraft used, product provided, or even the location of the foreign assignment. I did learn that he recently retired from his government position, and with the demise of the Soviet Union and the Warsaw Pact, he and his family had migrated to a Western country, where he had settled comfortably with the funds he had earned over the years. This was an informal conversation among friends because my colleague knew I had led the start of the operation.

That may not be a particularly satisfying closure, but par for the course in the CO business. What we did had worked, we squeezed the LEMON slowly and got the "juice" we needed. Could it have been done differently? Sure. All I know is that our way worked.

A Note from the Author

Squeezing the Lemon Slowly is about as close as the public gets to reading the internal case notes of an operation. The essential points of the acquisition of the asset are the mentality and motivation of the Target, and the tradecraft used to ensure security and operational progress. Read along as the plan moves forward, from initial targeting, validation of access, development, manipulation and, hopefully, towards a solid, productive recruitment.

About the Author

Kenneth A. Daigler is a former CIA operations officer who served for nearly 25 years in the clandestine service, including multiple overseas assignments and senior positions at CIA headquarters. After retiring from the CIA, he turned his attention to writing and historical research, with a particular focus on intelligence operations during the American Revolution.

He is the author of *Spies, Patriots, and Traitors: American Intelligence in the Revolutionary War* (2014, Georgetown University Press) and, as P.K. Rose, he authored *Founding Fathers of Intelligence* and *Black Dispatches: Black American Contributions to Union Intelligence During the Civil War* (CIA.gov).

AUTHOR WEBSITE:
  https://allthingsliberty.com/author/ken-daigler

Also by Kenneth A. Daigler

Spies, Patriots, and Traitors: American Intelligence in the Revolutionary War

Founding Fathers of Intelligence

Black Dispatches: Black American Contributions to Union Intelligence During the Civil War

www.ingramcontent.com/pod-product-compliance
Lightning Source LLC
Chambersburg PA
CBHW030540080526
44585CB00012B/208